¡Así se dice!

Glencoe Spanish 1

More than just a textbook !

QuickPass

Use your chapter-specific Web code for quick and easy navigation. Access the Online Student Edition, extra practice, and self-check quizzes with QuickPass at glencoe.com.

Download the entire audio program to your MP3 player.

Not online? No problem! Access your Student Edition, Audio Program, and Workbook with StudentWorks™ Plus CD-ROM.

VIDEO

Enrich your Spanish skills with videos tailored to your learning needs: vocabulary, grammar, dialogue, and culture.

¡Así se dice!

Glencoe Spanish **1**

Conrad J. Schmitt

Glencoe

Information on featured companies, organizations, and their products and services is included for educational purposes only and does not present or imply endorsement of the ¡Así se dice! program. Permission to use all business logos has been granted by the businesses represented in this text.

The *McGraw-Hill* Companies

 Glencoe

Send all inquiries to:
Glencoe/McGraw-Hill
8787 Orion Place
Columbus, OH 43240-4027

ISBN: 978-0-07-877400-3
MHID: 0-07-877400-4

Printed in the United States of America.

1 2 3 4 5 6 7 8 9 10   071/055   14 13 12 11 10 09 08 07

About the Author

Conrad J. Schmitt

Conrad J. Schmitt received his B.A. degree magna cum laude from Montclair State University, Upper Montclair, New Jersey. He received his M.A. from Middlebury College, Middlebury, Vermont, and did additional graduate work at New York University. He also studied at the Far Eastern Institute at Seton Hall University, Newark, New Jersey.

Mr. Schmitt has taught Spanish and French at all academic levels—from elementary school to graduate courses. He served as Coordinator of Foreign Languages for the Hackensack, New Jersey, public schools. He also taught courses in Foreign Language Education as a visiting professor at the Graduate School of Education at Rutgers University, New Brunswick, New Jersey.

Mr. Schmitt has authored or co-authored more than one hundred books, all published by The McGraw-Hill Companies. He was also editor-in-chief of foreign languages, ESL, and bilingual education for The McGraw-Hill Companies.

Mr. Schmitt has traveled extensively throughout Spain and all of Latin America. He has addressed teacher groups in all fifty states and has given seminars in many countries including Japan, the People's Republic of China, Taiwan, Egypt, Germany, Spain, Portugal, Mexico, Panama, Colombia, Brazil, Jamaica, and Haiti.

Contributing Writers

Louise M. Belnay
Teacher of World Languages
Adams County School District 50
Westminster, Colorado

Reina Martínez
Coordinator/Teacher of Foreign Languages
North Rockland Central School District
Thiells, New York

Contenido

Student Handbook

Student Handbook

GeoVistas
Explorando el mundo hispanohablante... SH42

Lecciones preliminares

Objetivos

In these preliminary lessons you will:

- greet people
- say good-bye to people
- express yourself politely
- count to 100

- identify the days of the week
- identify the months of the year
- find out and give the date
- ask and tell the time
- discuss the seasons and weather

Capítulo 1 ¿Cómo somos?

Objetivos

You will:
- identify and describe people and things
- tell where someone is from
- tell what subjects you take and express opinions about them
- talk about Spanish speakers in the United States

You will use:
- nouns, adjectives, and articles
- the verb **ser**
- **tú** and **usted**

Capítulo 2 La familia y la casa

Objetivos

You will:
- talk about families and pets
- describe a house or apartment
- describe rooms and some furnishings
- discuss a family from Ecuador

You will use:
- the verb **tener**
- possessive adjectives

Capítulo 3 En clase y después

Objetivos

You will:
- talk about what you do in school
- identify some school clothes and school supplies
- talk about what you and your friends do after school
- compare school and after-school activities in Spanish-speaking countries and the United States

You will use:
- present tense of **-ar** verbs
- the verbs **ir, dar,** and **estar**
- the contractions **al** and **del**

Capítulo 4 ¿Qué comemos y dónde?

Objetivos

You will:
- identify foods and discuss meals
- talk about places where you eat
- order food or a beverage at a café
- compare eating habits in Spain, Latin America, and the United States

You will use:
- present tense of regular **-er** and **-ir** verbs
- expressions with the infinitive— **ir a, tener que, acabar de**

Capítulo 5 Deportes

Objetivos

You will:
- talk about sports
- describe a soccer uniform
- identify colors
- compare team sports in the United States and Spanish-speaking countries

You will use:
- present tense of stem-changing verbs
- verbs such as **interesar, aburrir,** and **gustar**

CONTENIDO

Capítulo 6 El bienestar

Objetivos

You will:
- describe people's personality, conditions, and emotions
- explain minor illnesses
- talk about a doctor's appointment
- learn about a literary genre—the picaresque novel

You will use:
- **ser** and **estar**
- indirect object pronouns

Capítulo 7 De vacaciones

Objetivos

You will:
- talk about summer and winter weather and activities
- discuss summer and winter resorts in Spanish-speaking countries

You will use:
- preterite tense of regular **-ar** verbs
- preterite of **ir** and **ser**
- direct object pronouns

Capítulo 8 En tu tiempo libre

Objetivos

You will:
- talk about a birthday party
- discuss concerts, movies, and museums
- discuss Hispanic art and music

You will use:
- preterite of **-er** and **-ir** verbs
- the verbs **oír, leer**
- affirmative and negative words

Capítulo ❾ ¡Vamos de compras!

Objetivos

You will:
- talk about buying clothes
- talk about buying food
- compare shopping in Spanish-speaking countries with shopping in the United States

You will use:
- more numbers
- the present tense of **saber** and **conocer**
- comparatives and superlatives
- demonstrative adjectives and pronouns

CONTENIDO

Capítulo 10 En avión

Objetivos

You will:
- talk about packing for a trip and getting to the airport
- tell what you do at the airport
- talk about being on an airplane
- discuss air travel in South America

You will use:
- verbs that have **g** in the **yo** form of the present tense
- the present progressive tense

Capítulo 11 ¡Una rutina diferente!

Objetivos

You will:
- identify more parts of the body
- talk about your daily routine
- talk about backpacking and camping

You will use:
- reflexive verbs
- commands with **favor de**

 Literary Reader

Student Resources

Guide to Symbols

Throughout **¡Así se dice!** you will see these symbols, or icons. They will tell you how to best use the particular part of the chapter or activity they accompany. Following is a key to help you understand these symbols.

 Audio link This icon indicates material in the chapter that is recorded on compact disk.

 Recycling This icon indicates sections that review previously introduced material.

 Paired activity This icon indicates activities that you can practice orally with a partner.

 Group activity This icon indicates activities that you can practice together in groups.

 Critical thinking This icon indicates activities that require critical thinking.

 InfoGap This icon refers to additional paired activities at the end of the book.

 ¡Bravo! This icon indicates the end of new material in each chapter. All remaining material is recombination and review.

 Literary Reader This icon lets you know that you are prepared to read the indicated literature selection.

Why Learn Spanish?

¡Viva el español!

Spanish is currently the fourth-most-spoken language in the world. Studying Spanish will help you explore other cultures, communicate with Spanish speakers, and increase your career possibilities.

It's fascinating!

Culture Hispanic culture is full of diverse expressions of music, art, and literature. From dancing the tango or salsa to admiring a modern painting by Salvador Dalí, your studies will introduce you to an array of what the culture has to offer. You'll learn about the various customs, traditions, and values in Latin America and Spain. From food and family to school and sports, you'll learn all about life in the Hispanic world.

▲ **Dancers of the tango on the streets of Argentina**

It's all around us!

Communication The United States is home to more than forty-four million Hispanics or Latinos. Whether on the radio, in your community or school, or in your own home, the Spanish language is probably part of your life in some way. Understanding Spanish allows you to sing along with Latin music on the radio or chat with Spanish speakers in your school, community, or family. No matter who you are, Spanish can enrich your life in some way.

If you plan to travel outside the United States, remember that Spanish is the official language of twenty-one countries. Experiencing another country is more fun and meaningful when you can understand restaurant menus, read newspapers, follow street signs, watch TV, and better yet converse with the locals.

◀ **Singer Shakira performs.**

DENTISTA
Dra. Juana Ramos
741 – 8887

▲ **A Spanish-speaking dentist**

It's a lifelong skill!

Career Do you know what career you plan to pursue? Medicine, business, social work, teaching? What will you do if you have a Spanish-speaking patient, client, or student? Speak Spanish, of course! Whatever your career, you will be able to reach more people if you are able to converse in Spanish. After all, it's spoken by 13 percent of the U.S. population. You will also be open to many more career opportunities if you know Spanish. Businesses, government agencies, and educational institutions are always looking for people with the ability to speak and read more than one language.

It's an adventure!

Challenge When you study a language, you not only learn about the language and its speakers but also about yourself. Studying a language requires that you challenge yourself and more fully develop your skills. When you know about the customs and values of another culture, you are better able to reflect upon your own. Language is a means of self-discovery. Enjoy!

▼ **Fans of Enrique Iglesias**

Reading in a New Language

Following are skills and strategies that can help you understand what you read in a language you have just begun to learn. *Reading and Succeeding* will help you build skills and strategies that will make it easier to understand what you are reading in your exciting new language.

The strategies you use frequently depend on the purpose of your reading. You do not read a textbook or standardized testing questions the same way you read a novel or a magazine article. You read a textbook for information. You read a novel or magazine article for fun.

In the early stages of second-language learning, your vocabulary is, of course, very limited in comparison to the vast number of words you already know in English. The material presented to you to read in the early stages must accommodate this reality. Your limited knowledge of the language does not have to deter you from enjoying what you are reading. Most of what you read, however, will come from your textbook, since original novels and magazine articles are not written for people who have limited exposure to the language.

As you develop your reading ability in Spanish, you will encounter basically two types of readings.

Intensive Readings

These readings are short. They are very controlled, using only language you have already learned. You should find these readings easy and enjoyable. If you find them difficult, it means you have not sufficiently learned the material presented in the chapter of the textbook. The vast majority of these informative readings will introduce you to the fascinating cultures of the Spanish-speaking world.

A very important aspect of reading in Spanish is to give you things to "talk about" in the language. The more you read, speak, and use the language, the more proficient you will become. Whenever you finish reading one of the intensive reading selections, you should be able to talk about it; that is, you should be able to retell it in your own words.

Extensive Readings

Since it is unrealistic to assume that you will never encounter new words as you branch out and read material in Spanish, you will also be presented with extensive readings. The goal of these extensive readings is to help you develop the tools and skills you need in order to read at some future date an original novel or magazine article. They do indeed contain some words and structures that are unfamiliar to you. In this *Reading and Succeeding* section, you will learn to develop many skills that will enable you to read such material with relative ease.

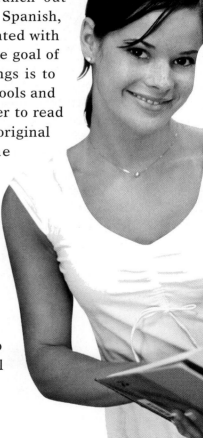

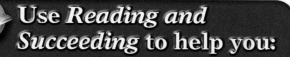
Identifying New Words and Building Vocabulary

What do you do when you come across a word you do not know as you read? Do you skip the word and keep reading? You might if you are reading for fun. If it hinders your ability to understand, however, you might miss something important. When you come to a word you don't know, try the following strategies to figure out what the word means.

Reading Aloud

In the early stages of learning a second language, a good strategy is to sit by yourself and read the selection aloud. This can help you understand the reading because you once again hear words that you have already practiced orally in class. Hearing them as you read them can help reinforce meaning.

Identifying Cognates

As you read you will come across many cognates. Cognates are words that look alike in both English and Spanish. Not only do they look alike but they mean the same thing. Recognizing cognates is a great reading strategy. Examples of cognates are:

cómico	nacionalidad	entra
popular	secundaria	clase
cubano	matemática	prepara
video	blusa	televisión

Identifying Roots and Base Words

The main part of a word is called its root. From a root, many new words can be formed. When you see a new word, identify its root. It can help you pronounce the word and figure out its meaning.

For example, if you know the word **importante**, there is no problem determining the meaning of **importancia**. The verb **importar** becomes a bit more problematic, but with some intelligent guessing you can get its meaning. You know it has something to do with importance so it means *it is important,* and by extension it can even carry the meaning *it matters.*

Identifying Prefixes

A prefix is a word part added to the beginning of a root or base word. Spanish as well as English has prefixes. Prefixes can change, or even reverse, the meaning of a word. For example, the prefixes **in-, im-,** and **des-** mean *not.*

estable/inestable   posible/imposible
honesto/deshonesto

Using Syntax

Like all languages, Spanish has rules for the way words are arranged in sentences. The way a sentence is organized is called its syntax. Spanish syntax, however, is a bit more flexible than English. In a simple English sentence someone or something (its subject) does something (the predicate or verb) to or with another person or thing (the object). This word order can vary in Spanish and does not always follow the subject/verb/object order.

Because Spanish and English syntax vary, you should think in Spanish and not try to translate what you are reading into English. Reading in Spanish will then have a natural flow and follow exactly the way you learned it. Trying to translate it into English confuses the matter and serves no purpose.

Example

English always states: *John speaks to me.*
Spanish can state: *John to me speaks.* or
To me speaks John.

The latter leaves the subject to the end of the sentence and emphasizes that it is John who speaks to me.

Using Context Clues

This is a very important reading strategy in a second language. You can often figure out the meaning of an unfamiliar word by looking at it in context (the words and sentences that surround it). Let's look at the example below.

Example

The glump ate it all up and flew away.

You have no idea what a *glump* is. Right? But from the rest of the sentence you can figure out that it's a bird. Why? Because it flew away and you know that birds fly. In this way you guessed at the meaning of an unknown word using context. Although you know it is a bird, you cannot determine the specific meaning such as a robin, a wren, or a sparrow. In many cases it does not matter because that degree of specificity is not necessary for comprehension.

Let's look at another example:
The glump ate it all up and phlumped.

In this case you do not know the meaning of two key words in the same sentence—*glump* and *phlumped.* This makes it impossible to guess the meaning and this is what can happen when you try to read something in a second language that is beyond your proficiency level. This makes reading a frustrating experience. For this reason all the readings in your textbook control the language to keep it within your reach. Remember, if you have studied the vocabulary in your book, this will not happen.

Understanding What You Read

Try using some of the following strategies before, during, and after reading to understand and remember what you read.

Previewing

When you preview a piece of writing, you are looking for a general idea of what to expect from it. Before you read, try the following.

- Look at the title and any illustrations that are included.
- Read the headings, subheadings, and anything in bold letters.
- Skim over the passage to see how it is organized. Is it divided into many parts? Is it a long poem or short story?
- Look at the graphics—pictures, maps, or diagrams.
- Set a purpose for your reading. Are you reading to learn something new? Are you reading to find specific information?

Using What You Know

Believe it or not, you already know quite a bit about what you are going to read. Your own knowledge and personal experience can help you create meaning in what you read. There is, however, a big difference in reading the information in your Spanish textbook. You already have some knowledge about what you are reading from a United States oriented base. What you will be reading about takes place in a Spanish-speaking environment and thus you will be adding an exciting new dimension to what you already know. Comparing and contrasting are important critical skills to put to use when reading material about a culture other than your own. This skill will be discussed later.

Visualizing

Creating pictures in your mind about what you are reading—called visualizing—will help you understand and remember what you read. With the assistance of the many accompanying photos, try to visualize the people, streets, cities, homes, etc., you are reading about.

Identifying Sequence

When you discover the logical order of events or ideas, you are identifying sequence. Look for clues and signal words that will help you find how information is organized. Some signal words are **primero, al principio, antes, después, luego, entonces, más tarde, por fin, finalmente.**

Determining the Main Idea

When you look for the main idea of a selection, you look for the most important idea. The examples, reasons, and details that further explain the main idea are called supporting details.

Reviewing

When you review in school, you go over what you learned the day before so that the information is clear in your mind. Reviewing when you read does the same thing. Take time now and then to pause and review what you have read. Think about the main ideas and organize them for yourself so you can recall them later. Filling in study aids such as graphic organizers can help you review.

Monitoring Your Comprehension

As you read, check your understanding by summarizing. Pause from time to time and state the main ideas of what you have just read. Answer the questions: **¿Quién?** (Who?) **¿Qué?** (What?) **¿Dónde?** (Where?) **¿Cuándo?** (When?) **¿Cómo?** (How?) **¿Por qué?** (Why?). Summarizing tests your comprehension because you state key points in your own words. Remember something you read earlier: reading in Spanish empowers your ability to speak by developing strategies that enable you to retell orally what you have read.

Thinking About Your Reading

Sometimes it is important to think more deeply about what you read so you can get the most out of what the author says. These critical thinking skills will help you go beyond what the words say and understand the meaning of your reading.

Compare and Contrast

To compare and contrast shows the similarities and differences among people, things, and ideas. Your reading experience in Spanish will show you many things that are similar and many others that are different depending upon the culture groups and social mores.

As you go over these culturally oriented readings, try to visualize what you are reading. Then think about the information. Think about what you know about the topic and then determine if the information you are reading is similar, somewhat different, or very different from what you know.

Continue to think about it. In this case you may have to think about it in English. Determine if you find the similarities or the differences interesting. Would you like to experience what you are reading about? Analyzing the information in this way will most certainly help you remember what you have read.

- Signal words and phrases that indicate similarity are **similar, semejante, parecido, igual.**
- Signal words and phrases that indicate differences are **diferente, distinto, al contrario, contrariamente, sin embargo.**

Cause and Effect

Just about everything that happens in life is the cause or the effect of some other event or action. Writers use cause-and-effect structure to explore the reasons for something happening and to examine the results of previous events. This structure helps answer the question that everybody is always asking: Why? Cause-and-effect structure is about explaining things.

- Signal words and phrases are **así, porque, por consiguiente, resulta que.**

Using Reference Materials

In the early stages of second-language learning, you will not be able to use certain types of reference materials that are helpful to you in English. For example, you could not look up a word in a Spanish dictionary as you would not be able to understand many of the words used in the definition.

You can, however, make use of the glossary that appears at the end of your textbook. A glossary includes only words that are included in the textbook. Rather than give you a Spanish definition, the glossary gives you the English equivalent of the word. If you have to use the glossary very frequently, it indicates to you that you have not studied the vocabulary sufficiently in each chapter. A strategy to use before beginning a reading selection in any given chapter is to quickly skim the vocabulary in the **Vocabulario 1** and **Vocabulario 2** sections of the chapter.

Expand your view of the Spanish-speaking world.

¡Así se dice! will show you the many places where you will be able to use your Spanish.

Cultural and geographic information is at your fingertips with **GeoVistas**, your virtual field trip to the Spanish-speaking countries.

Start your journey into language and culture.

Opening photo provides a cultural backdrop for the chapter.

Aquí y Allí introduces you to the chapter theme and invites you to make connections between your culture and the cultures of Spanish-speaking countries.

Objectives let you know what you will be able to do by the end of the chapter.

Access your eBook with QuickPass at <u>glencoe.com</u>.

Get acquainted with the chapter theme.

Explore each chapter's theme with vivid cultural photos and informative captions.

Introducción al tema
¿Qué comemos y dónde?

Los platos de muchos países latinoamericanos llevan pimientos que tienen nombres diferentes como chiles, ajíes, chipotles y morrones. ▶

Look at these photographs to acquaint yourself with the theme of this chapter—what we eat and where. You will notice here and throughout the chapter that in the Spanish-speaking world there is a great variety of interesting and delicious foods. What people eat in one area is different from what people eat in another area, just as in the United States. Do you recognize any of the foods you see here? Of all the foods, which would be your favorite?

Puerto Rico La señora prepara unas frituras de Puerto Rico en un puesto de comida en Piñones cerca de San Juan.

▲ **México** En su carrito en el famoso Parque de Chapultepec en la Ciudad de México, la señora prepara y vende bocadillos o sándwiches. En México son tortas.

El chocolate es un producto de las Américas. La palabra «chocolate» es de la palabra «xocoatl» en náhuatl, una lengua de los indígenas de México. Aquí vemos unos bombones de chocolate y una planta de cacao que produce el chocolate. ▶

▲ **Perú** La muchacha tiene un puesto en Huanchaco, Perú, donde prepara y vende raspadillas—un refresco de hielo granizado y el jugo de una fruta tropical.

MESÓN EL PANAL

◀ **España** Un mesón es un tipo de café adonde va la gente a comer tapas. Aquí vemos un jamón famoso de España—el jamón serrano—y un queso famoso—el queso manchego.

La Estancia

Argentina El delicioso bife argentino es famoso en el mundo entero. El señor prepara bife y pollo a la parrilla en un restaurante de Buenos Aires. ▶

126

See how the theme relates to different countries in the Spanish-speaking world.

Talk about the chapter theme with your new vocabulary.

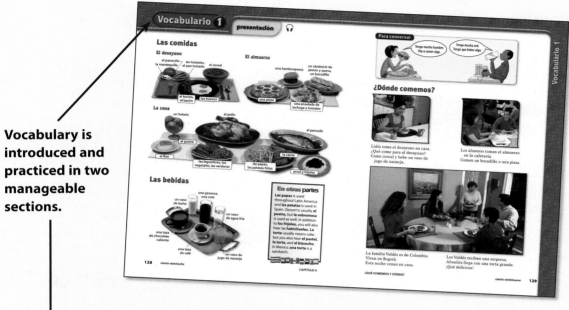

Vocabulary is introduced and practiced in two manageable sections.

Recorded presentation ensures proper pronunciation.

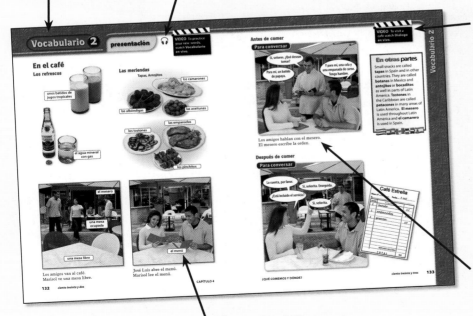

Watch video clips to experience the diversity of the Spanish-speaking world while reinforcing the language you have learned and improving your listening and viewing skills.

New words are used in a meaningful context.

Photos and illustrations aid comprehension and vocabulary acquisition.

Practice and master new vocabulary.

Practice authentic communication with InfoGap activities.

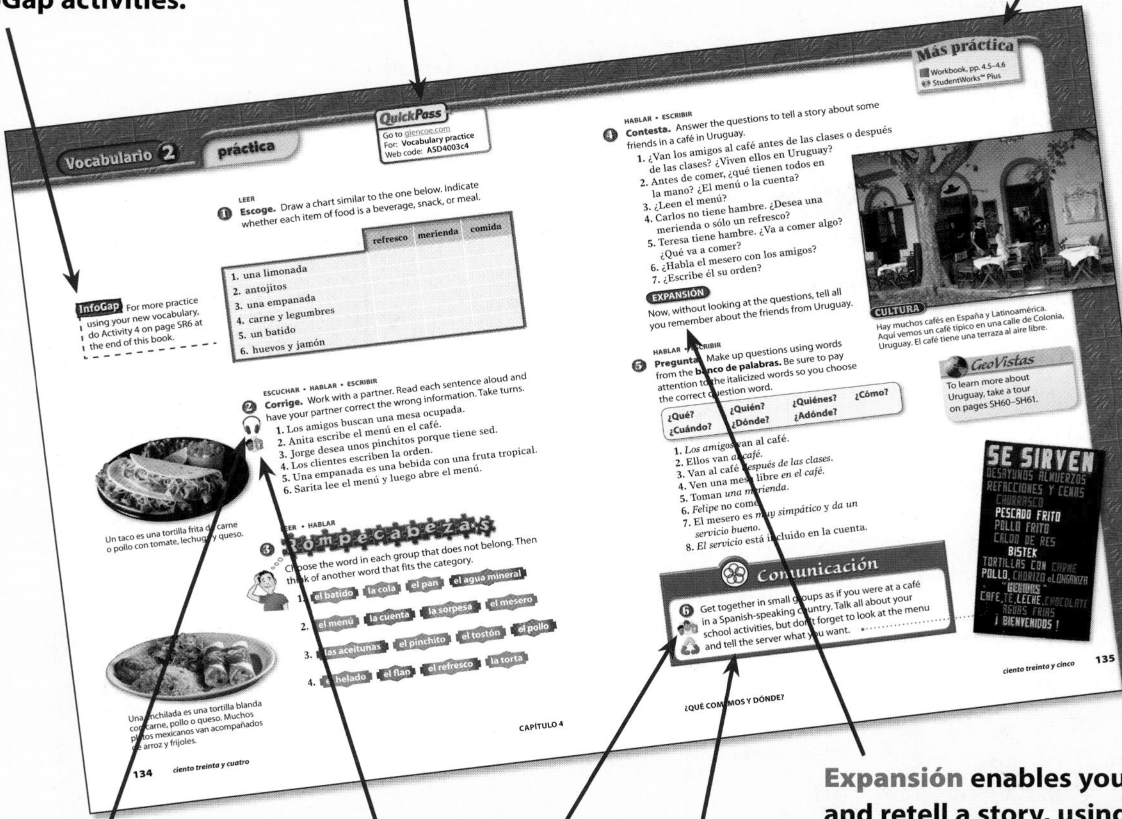

Use QuickPass to easily access additional vocabulary practice at glencoe.com.

Practice and master your new vocabulary with your Workbook and StudentWorks™ Plus.

QuickPass
Go to glencoe.com
For: Vocabulary practice
Web code: ASD4003c4

Vocabulario 2 **práctica**

Más práctica
- Workbook, pp. 4.5–4.6
- StudentWorks™ Plus

LEER
① **Escoge.** Draw a chart similar to the one below. Indicate whether each item of food is a beverage, snack, or meal.

	refresco	merienda	comida
1. una limonada			
2. antojitos			
3. una empanada			
4. carne y legumbres			
5. un batido			
6. huevos y jamón			

ESCUCHAR • HABLAR • ESCRIBIR
② **Corrige.** Work with a partner. Read each sentence aloud and have your partner correct the wrong information. Take turns.
1. Los amigos buscan una mesa ocupada.
2. Anita escribe el menú en el café.
3. Jorge desea unos pinchitos porque tiene sed.
4. Los clientes escriben la orden.
5. Una empanada es una bebida con una fruta tropical.
6. Sarita lee el menú y luego abre el menú.

Un taco es una tortilla frita de carne o pollo con tomate, lechuga y queso.

LEER • HABLAR
③ **Rompecabezas**
Choose the word in each group that does not belong. Then think of another word that fits the category.
1. el batido / la cola / el pan / el agua mineral
2. el menú / la cuenta / la sorpesa / el mesero
3. las aceitunas / el pinchito / el tostón / el pollo
4. el helado / el flan / el refresco / la torta

Una enchilada es una tortilla blanda con carne, pollo o queso. Muchos platos mexicanos van acompañados de arroz y frijoles.

134 ciento treinta y cuatro CAPÍTULO 4

HABLAR • ESCRIBIR
④ **Contesta.** Answer the questions to tell a story about some friends in a café in Uruguay.
1. ¿Van los amigos al café antes de las clases o después de las clases? ¿Viven ellos en Uruguay?
2. Antes de comer, ¿qué tienen todos en la mano? ¿El menú o la cuenta?
3. ¿Leen el menú?
4. Carlos no tiene hambre. ¿Desea una merienda o sólo un refresco?
5. Teresa tiene hambre. ¿Va a comer algo? ¿Qué va a comer?
6. ¿Habla el mesero con los amigos?
7. ¿Escribe él su orden?

EXPANSIÓN
Now, without looking at the questions, tell all you remember about the friends from Uruguay.

HABLAR • ESCRIBIR
⑤ **Pregunta.** Make up questions using words from the banco de palabras. Be sure to pay attention to the italicized words so you choose the correct question word.

¿Qué?	¿Quién?	¿Quiénes?	¿Cómo?
¿Cuándo?	¿Dónde?	¿Adónde?	

1. Los amigos van al café.
2. Ellos van al café.
3. Van al café después de las clases.
4. Ven una mesa libre en el café.
5. Toman una merienda.
6. Felipe no come nada.
7. El mesero es muy simpático y da un servicio bueno.
8. El servicio está incluido en la cuenta.

Comunicación
⑥ Get together in small groups as if you were at a café in a Spanish-speaking country. Talk all about your school activities, but don't forget to look at the menu and tell the server what you want.

CULTURA
Hay muchos cafés en España y Latinoamérica. Aquí vemos un café típico en una calle de Colonia, Uruguay. El café tiene una terraza al aire libre.

GeoVistas
To learn more about Uruguay, take a tour on pages SH60–SH61.

SE SIRVEN
DESAYUNOS ALMUERZOS
REFACCIONES Y CENAS
CHURRASCO
PESCADO FRITO
POLLO FRITO
CALDO DE RES
BISTEK
TORTILLAS CON CARNE
POLLO, CHORIZO oLONGANIZA
BEBIDAS
CAFE, TE, LECHE, CHOCOLATE
AGUAS FRIAS
¡ BIENVENIDOS !

¿QUÉ COMEMOS Y DÓNDE? 135 ciento treinta y cinco

InfoGap For more practice using your new vocabulary, do Activity 4 on page SR6 at the end of this book.

Expansión enables you to tell and retell a story, using your new words.

Communicative activities give you real-life experience speaking in Spanish.

Reinforce pronunciation and aural comprehension with audio activities.

Paired and small-group activities allow you to communicate about the chapter theme.

Learn grammar within the context of the chapter theme.

Learn colloquial phrases to make conversation easy.

Use QuickPass to access additional grammar practice at glencoe.com.

Useful tips help you avoid language pitfalls.

Graphic organizers make practice clear and easy.

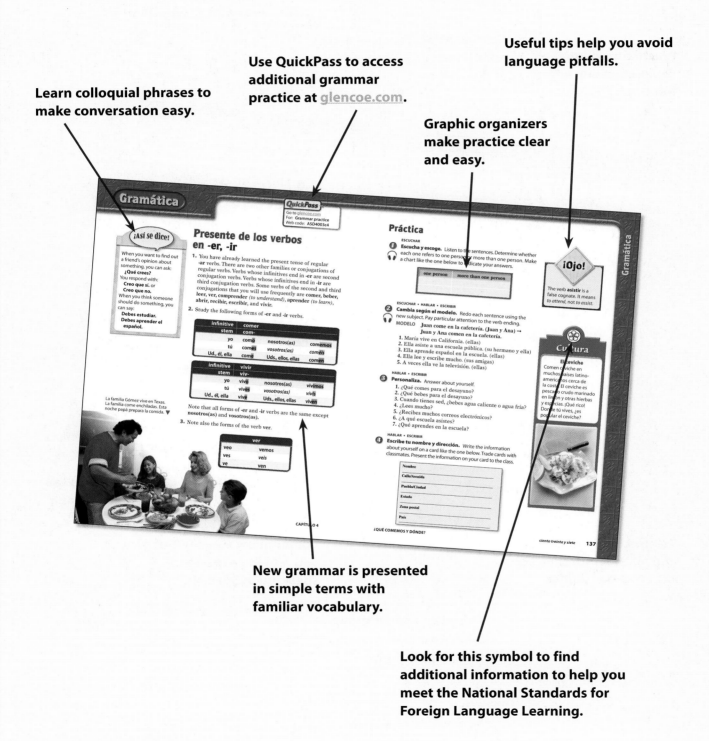

New grammar is presented in simple terms with familiar vocabulary.

Look for this symbol to find additional information to help you meet the National Standards for Foreign Language Learning.

Build on what you already know and improve pronunciation.

Use your new vocabulary as you practice the new grammar points.

Have fun using your Spanish to figure out the meaning of Spanish proverbs.

Listen to speakers from diverse areas of the Spanish-speaking world to improve pronunciation.

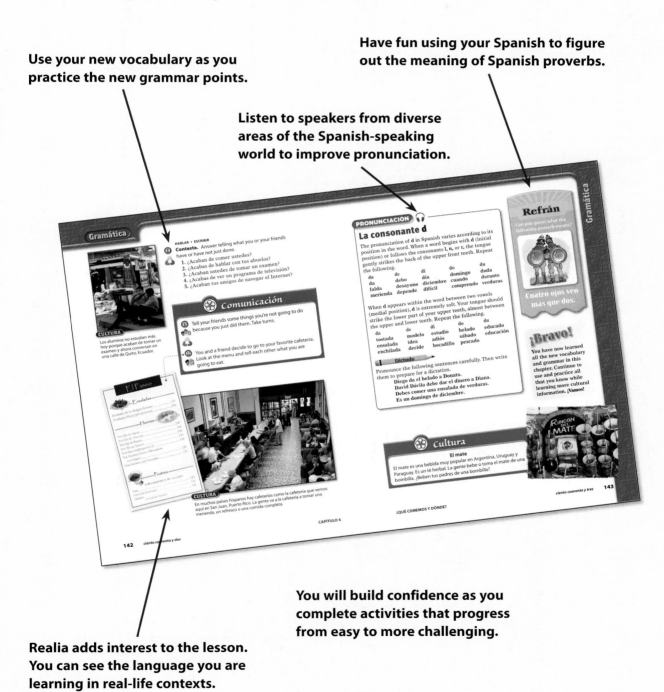

You will build confidence as you complete activities that progress from easy to more challenging.

Realia adds interest to the lesson. You can see the language you are learning in real-life contexts.

Engage classmates in real conversation.

Use QuickPass to access the Conversation online at glencoe.com.

You will have a sense of accomplishment when you are able to comprehend the conversation.

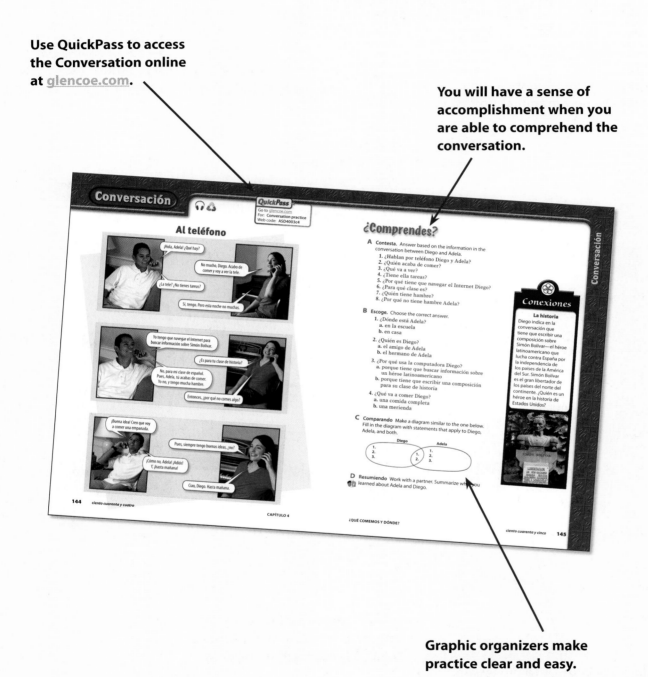

Graphic organizers make practice clear and easy.

Heighten your cultural awareness.

Step-by-step reading strategies help to develop your reading skills.

Cultural reading uses learned language to reinforce chapter theme.

Recorded reading online and on CD provides options for addressing various skills and learning styles.

Verify your comprehension throughout the selection with Reading Checks.

Un poco más reading reinforces the chapter theme and expands your understanding of the Spanish-speaking world.

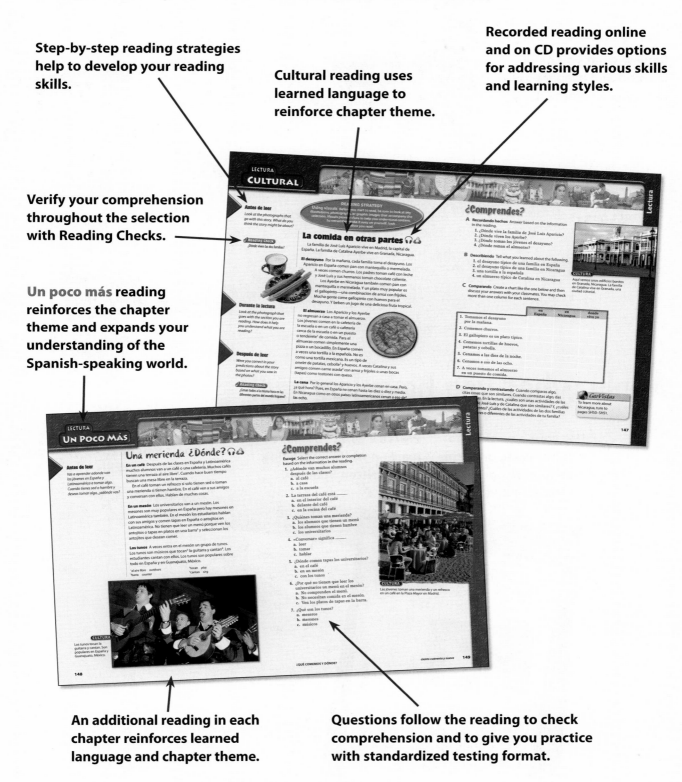

An additional reading in each chapter reinforces learned language and chapter theme.

Questions follow the reading to check comprehension and to give you practice with standardized testing format.

TOUR OF THE STUDENT EDITION

SH15

Show what you know!

Review what you have learned and prepare for your chapter test.

Reference notes direct you to the correct pages for review.

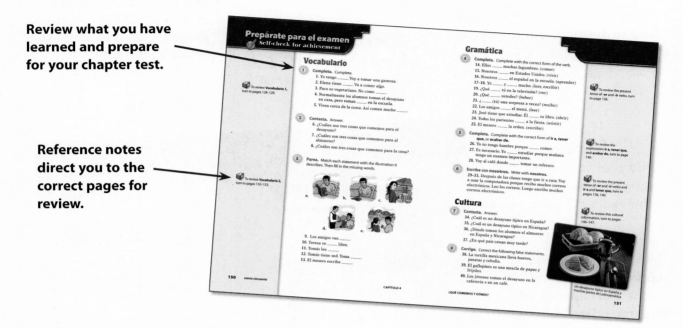

Apply what you have learned!

Use your new skills to communicate orally in meaningful, open-ended activities.

Practice what you have learned while improving your written Spanish.

Writing Strategy gives you the tools you need to develop better writing skills.

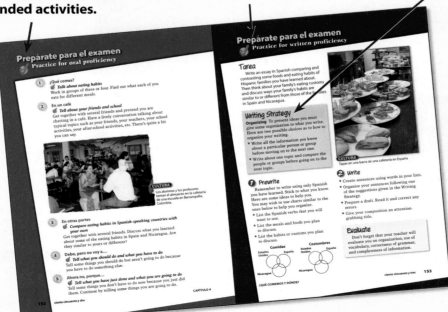

Review grammar and vocabulary at a glance.

Succinct grammar notes help you efficiently review chapter material.

Use this vocabulary list to review the vocabulary you have learned in this chapter.

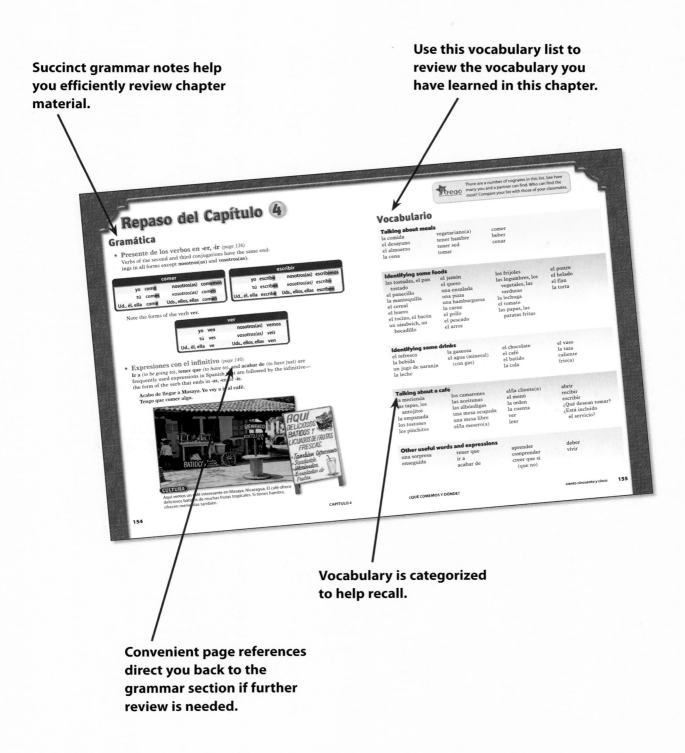

Repaso del Capítulo 4

Gramática

- **Presente de los verbos en -er, -ir** *(page 136)*
  Verbs of the second and third conjugations have the same endings in all forms except **nosotros(as)** and **vosotros(as)**.

comer			
yo	como	nosotros(as)	comemos
tú	comes	vosotros(as)	coméis
Ud., él, ella	come	Uds., ellos, ellas	comen

escribir			
yo	escribo	nosotros(as)	escribimos
tú	escribes	vosotros(as)	escribís
Ud., él, ella	escribe	Uds., ellos, ellas	escriben

Note the forms of the verb **ver**.

ver			
yo	veo	nosotros(as)	vemos
tú	ves	vosotros(as)	veis
Ud., él, ella	ve	Uds., ellos, ellas	ven

- **Expresiones con el infinitivo** *(page 140)*
  Ir a *(to be going to)*, **tener que** *(to have to)*, and **acabar de** *(to have just)* are frequently used expressions in Spanish that are followed by the infinitive—the form of the verb that ends in **-ar, -er** or **-ir**.

  Acabo de llegar a Masaya. Yo voy a ir al café.
  Tengo que comer algo.

CULTURA
Aquí vemos un café interesante en Masaya, Nicaragua. El café ofrece deliciosos batidos de muchas frutas tropicales. Si tienes hambre, ofrecen meriendas también.

154   CAPÍTULO 4

Vocabulario

¡Trego There are a number of cognates in this list. See how many you and a partner can find. Who can find the most? Compare your list with those of your classmates.

Talking about meals
la comida	vegetariano(a)	comer
el desayuno	tener hambre	beber
el almuerzo	tener sed	cenar
la cena	tomar	

Identifying some foods
las tostadas, el pan tostado	el jamón	los frijoles	el postre
el panecillo	el queso	las legumbres, los vegetales, las verduras	el helado
la mantequilla	una ensalada	la lechuga	el flan
el cereal	una pizza	el tomate	la torta
el huevo	una hamburguesa	las papas, las patatas fritas	
el tocino, el bacón	la carne		
un sándwich, un bocadillo	el pollo		
	el pescado		
	el arroz		

Identifying some drinks
el refresco	la gaseosa	el chocolate	el vaso
la bebida	el agua (mineral) (con gas)	el café	la taza
un jugo de naranja		el batido	caliente
la leche		la cola	frío(a)

Talking about a café
la merienda	los camarones	el/la cliente(a)	abrir
las tapas, los antojitos	las aceitunas	el menú	recibir
la empanada	las albóndigas	la orden	escribir
los tostones	una mesa ocupada	la cuenta	¿Qué desean tomar?
los pinchitos	una mesa libre	ver	¿Está incluido el servicio?
	el/la mesero(a)	leer	

Other useful words and expressions
una sorpresa	tener que	aprender
enseguida	ir a	comprender
	acabar de	creer que sí (que no)
		deber
		vivir

¿QUÉ COMEMOS Y DÓNDE?   *ciento cincuenta y cinco* **155**

Vocabulary is categorized to help recall.

Convenient page references direct you back to the grammar section if further review is needed.

Practice what you have learned so far in Spanish.

Cumulative activities allow you to practice what you have learned so far in Spanish class.

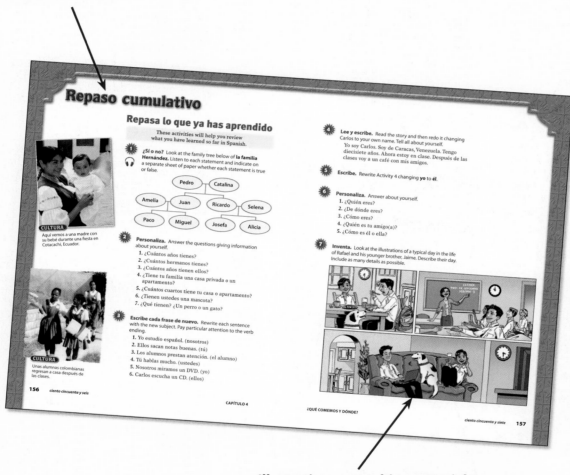

Illustrations recombine material to remind you what you have already learned in Spanish. Use the illustration as a prompt to demonstrate how much you can say or write.

Enhance your appreciation of literature and culture.

Literary Reader gives you another opportunity to apply your reading skills in Spanish.

Literary selections present another view of Hispanic culture.

Literary Reader

Contenido

The Literary selections in the pages that follow will introduce you to Hispanic literature while helping you to develop reading skills and a better understanding of Hispanic culture. These selections have been carefully adapted to match your developing language skills. As you draw on your knowledge of Spanish grammar and vocabulary and apply the reading strategies you have learned, you will discover that you are able to comprehend and enjoy the selections. ¡A leer!

◄ La biblioteca de El Escorial, un palacio y monasterio cerca de Madrid, construido en el siglo dieciséis

396

397

Level-appropriate literature selections make reading fun.

Foldables

Dear Student,

Foldables are interactive study organizers that you can make yourself. They are a wonderful resource to help you organize and retain information. Foldables have many purposes. You can use them to remember vocabulary words or to organize more in-depth information on any given topic, such as keeping track of what you know about a particular country.

You can write general information, such as titles, vocabulary words, concepts, questions, main ideas, and dates, on the front tabs of your Foldables. You view this general information every time you look at a Foldable. This helps you focus on and remember key points without the distraction of additional text. You can write specific information—supporting ideas, thoughts, answers to questions, research information, empirical data, class notes, observations, and definitions—under the tabs. Think of different ways in which Foldables can be used. Soon you will find that you can make your own Foldables for study guides and projects. Foldables with flaps or tabs create study guides that you can use to check what you know about the general information on the front of tabs. Use Foldables without tabs for projects that require information to be presented for others to view quickly. The more you make and use graphic organizers, the faster you will become able to produce them.

To store your Foldables, turn one-gallon freezer bags into student portfolios which can be collected and stored in the classroom. You can also carry your portfolios in your notebooks if you place strips of two-inch clear tape along one side and punch three holes through the taped edge. Write your name along the top of the plastic portfolio with a permanent marker and cover the writing with two-inch clear tape to keep it from wearing off. Cut the bottom corners off the bag so it won't hold air and will stack and store easily. The following figures illustrate the basic folds that are referred to throughout this book.

Good luck!

Dinah Zike

Dinah Zike
www.dinah.com

Category Book

Los números Use this *category book* organizer as you learn dates and numbers.

Step 1 **Fold** a sheet of paper (8½" x 11") in half like a *hot dog*.

Step 2 On one side, **cut** every third line. This usually results in ten tabs. Do this with three sheets of paper to make three books.

Step 3 **Write** one Arabic number on the outside of each of the tabs. On the inside write out the respective number. As you learn more numbers, use *category books* to categorize numbers in this way.

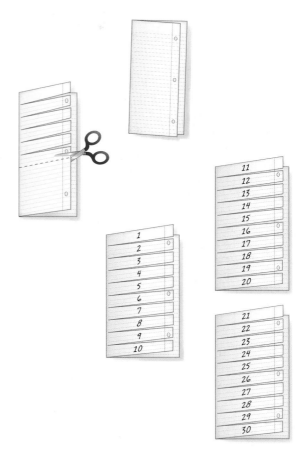

Other Suggestions for a *Category Book* Foldable

You may wish to use *category book* foldables to help remember numbers. As you learn numbers, make two *category book* foldables. One will have the numerals on the outside and the numbers written out on the inside. The other will have the numbers written out on the outside and the numerals on the inside. This is a good way for you to practice your numbers on your own. You may also wish to make one foldable containing even numbers and one containing odd numbers.

A *category book* foldable may be used to help you remember the names of school subjects. Use pictures, numbers, or a few Spanish words you already know to describe the subject on the outside of the foldable. You will write the name of the subject in Spanish on the inside. Then show your descriptions to a partner and have the partner come up with the name of the subject in Spanish. You may also use this foldable to group school subjects by discipline.

Forward-Backward Book

Las estaciones Use this *forward-backward book* to compare and contrast two seasons of your choice.

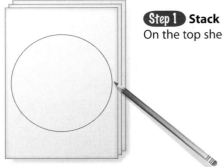

Step 1 **Stack** three sheets of paper. On the top sheet, trace a large circle.

Step 2 With the papers still stacked, **cut out** the circles.

Step 3 **Staple** the paper circles together along the left-hand side to create a circular booklet.

Step 4 **Write** the name of a season on the cover. On the page that opens to the right list the months of the year in that particular season. On the following page draw a picture to illustrate the season.

front

inside

El invierno

Step 5 **Turn the book upside down** and write the name of a season on the cover. On the page that opens to the right list the months of the year in that particular season. On the following page draw a picture to illustrate the season.

back

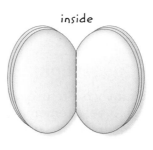

inside

El verano

Other Suggestions for a *Forward-Backward Book* Foldable

You may wish to use a *forward-backward book* foldable to organize summer and winter activities. You may use titles such as *the beach* and *skiing* in Spanish. On the inside, list activities that go with each on the right-hand page and illustrate a scene on the opposite page. To give information for the second category, turn the book upside down.

It may be helpful to use a *forward-backward book* foldable to organize the food groups. You could use the name of a food group in the target language (meat, vegetable, fruit, etc.) as the title. On the inside, list as many foods in this food group as you can on the right-hand page and illustrate these foods on the opposite page. Give the same information for a second food group by reversing the book.

Pocket Book

La geografía Use this *pocket book* organizer in your ongoing study of all the countries in the Spanish-speaking world.

Step 1 **Fold** a sheet of paper (8½" x 11") in half like a *hamburger*.

Step 2 **Open** the folded paper and fold one of the long sides up two inches to form a pocket. Refold the *hamburger* fold so that the newly formed pockets are on the inside.

Step 3 **Glue** the outer edges of the two-inch fold with a small amount of glue.

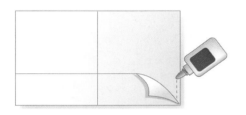

Step 4 **Make a multipaged booklet** by gluing six pockets side-by-side. Glue a cover around the multipaged *pocket book*.

Step 5 **Label** five pockets with the following geographical areas: **Europa, la América del Norte, la América del Sur, la América Central,** and **Islas del Caribe.** Use index cards inside the pockets to record information each time you learn something new about a specific country. Be sure to include the name of the country (in Spanish, of course) and its capital.

Other Suggestions for a *Pocket Book* Foldable

You may wish to use a *pocket book* foldable to organize masculine and feminine nouns or singular and plural forms. You can make an index card to put in the correct pocket each time you learn a new word.

A *pocket book* foldable may be used to organize information about several subjects. For example, to organize information about airplane travel, label pockets with topics such as *preparing for a trip, getting to the airport, at the airport,* and *on the airplane* in Spanish.

Make cards for all the words and phrases you know that go with each topic.

If you wish to organize what you are learning about important people, works of art, festivals, and other cultural information in countries that speak Spanish, a *pocket book* foldable may be helpful. You can make a card for each person, work of art, or event that you study, and you can add cards and even add categories as you continue to learn about cultures that speak Spanish.

Vocabulary Book

Sinónimos y antónimos Use this *vocabulary book* to practice your vocabulary through the use of synonyms and antonyms.

Step 1 **Fold** a sheet of notebook paper in half like a *hot dog*.

Step 2 On one side, **cut** every third line. This usually results in ten tabs. Do this with two sheets of paper to make two books.

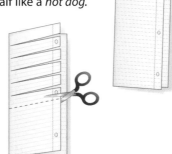

Step 3 **Label** the tops of the *vocabulary books* with the word **Sinónimos** on one and **Antónimos** on the other. As you learn new vocabulary in each unit, try to categorize words in this manner. Remember also to think of words you have previously learned to fill in your books.

Other Suggestions for a *Vocabulary Book* Foldable

You may wish to use a *vocabulary book* foldable to help you remember words related to minor illnesses and going to the doctor. Come up with categories to write on the outside such as *a cold, at the doctor's office,* or *at the pharmacy.* On the inside, write as many terms and phrases as you can think of that relate to that category.

You can use a *vocabulary book* foldable to help remember any verb conjugation in Spanish. Write the infinitive at the top. If you know several tenses of a verb, you should also write what tense or tenses are being practiced. On the outside of the foldable, write the pronouns, and on the inside, write the corresponding verb form. You can use this as a quick study and review tool for any verb. At a more advanced level, you may wish to write many verbs down the outside and entire conjugations on the inside.

You may wish to use a *vocabulary book* foldable to help organize different kinds of clothing. Come up with categories in Spanish to list on the outside, such as *school, casual, men's, women's, summer, winter,* etc. On the inside, list as many articles of clothing fitting the category as you can in Spanish.

You can use *vocabulary book* foldables to practice adjective forms. Create two *vocabulary book* foldables, one for singular forms and the other for plural forms. On the singular book, write either masculine or feminine singular adjective forms on the outside and the other forms on the inside. To make this more challenging, write a mix of masculine and feminine forms on the outside, with the corresponding form on the inside. Repeat this process on the second book for the plural forms.

Tab Book

Preguntas Use this *tab book* to practice asking and answering questions.

Step 1 **Fold** a sheet of paper (8½" x 11") like a *hot dog* but fold it so that one side is one inch longer than the other.

Step 2 On the shorter side only, **cut** five equal tabs. On the front of each tab, **write** a question word you have learned. For example, you may wish to write the following.

Step 3 On the bottom edge, **write** any sentence you would like.

Elena es una alumna en un colegio en Puerto Rico.

Step 4 Under each tab, **write** the word from your sentence that answers the question on the front of the tab.

Other Suggestions for a *Tab Book* Foldable

You may also use a *tab book* foldable to practice verb conjugations. You would need to make six tabs instead of five. Write a verb and a tense on the bottom edge and write the pronouns on the front of each tab. Under each tab, write the corresponding verb form.

You may wish to use a *tab book* foldable to practice new vocabulary words. Leave extra space on the bottom edge. Choose five or six vocabulary words and write each one on a tab.

You may also make multiple *tab book* foldables to practice more words. Under each tab, write a definition or translation of the word. If you can, write an original definition in Spanish. At a more beginning level, you may wish to illustrate the word or write the word in English. Use the bottom edge to write one or more original sentences using all of the words on the tabs.

Miniature Matchbook

Descripciones Use this *miniature matchbook* to help communicate in an interesting and more descriptive way.

Step 1 **Fold** a sheet of paper (8½" x 11") in half like a *hot dog*.

Step 2 **Cut** the sheet in half along the fold line.

Step 3 **Fold** the two long strips in half like *hot dogs,* leaving one side ½" shorter than the other side.

Step 4 **Fold** the ½" tab over the shorter side on each strip.

Step 5 **Cut** each of the two strips in half forming four halves. Then cut each half into thirds, making twelve *miniature matchbooks.*

Step 6 **Glue** the twelve small *matchbooks* inside a *hamburger* fold (three rows of four each).

Step 7 On the front of each *matchbook,* **write** a subject you are going to tell or write about, for example, **la escuela.** Open up the tab and list any words you think you could use to make your discussion more interesting. You can add topics and words as you continue with your study of Spanish. If you glue several sections together, this foldable will "grow."

Other Suggestions for a *Miniature Matchbook* Foldable

You may use a *miniature matchbook* foldable to test each other on your knowledge of the vocabulary. Work in pairs with each partner making a blank *miniature matchbook* foldable. Each partner writes a topic related to the subjects you have just studied on the front of each *matchbook.* You may use categories of vocabulary, verbs you have recently learned to conjugate, or the subject of a reading. Your partner then writes as much as he or she can about that topic under the flap. This can alert you if you need to go back and review a topic.

A *miniature matchbook* foldable may help you organize and remember information you have read. After doing a cultural or literary reading, write down a concept presented in the reading on the front of each *matchbook.* Open up each tab and write down supporting details that support the idea.

Single Picture Frame

Dibujar y escribir Use this *single picture frame* to help you illustrate the stories you write.

Step 1 **Fold** a sheet of paper (8½" x 11") in half like a *hamburger*.

Step 2 **Open** the *hamburger* and gently roll one side of the *hamburger* toward the valley. Try not to crease the roll.

Step 3 **Cut** a rectangle out of the middle of the rolled side of paper, leaving a ½" border and forming a frame.

Step 4 **Fold** another sheet of paper (8½" x 11") in half like a *hamburger*.

Step 5 **Apply** glue to the picture frame and place it inside the *hamburger* fold.

Variation:
• Place a picture behind the frame and glue the edges of the frame to the other side of the *hamburger* fold. This locks the picture in place.
• Cut out only three sides of the rolled rectangle. This forms a window with a cover that opens and closes.

Other Suggestions for a *Single Picture Frame* Foldable

You may wish to write about a shopping trip using a *single picture frame* foldable. Before you begin, organize what you will say by drawing your path through the shops at the market, through the supermarket, or through the mall. You can then write about the shopping trip using your drawings as a guide.

Work in small groups. Each student should create a *single picture frame* foldable with a picture glued into it. You may either cut out a magazine picture or draw your own, although it should be fairly complex. Then give your foldable to another member of the group who will write sentences about what is in the picture and what people in the picture are doing. That student will pass it on to a third student who will write sentences about what is not in the picture and what people in the picture are not doing. The foldables can be passed to additional students to see if they can add more sentences.

Minibook

Mi autobiografía Use this *minibook* organizer to write and illustrate your autobiography. Before you begin to write, think about the many things concerning yourself that you have the ability to write about in Spanish. On the left pages, draw the events of your life in chronological order. On the right, write about your drawings.

Step 1 **Fold** a sheet of paper (8½" x 11") in half like a *hot dog*.

Step 2 **Fold** it in half again like a *hamburger*.

Step 3 Then **fold** in half again, forming eight sections.

Step 4 **Open** the fold and **cut** the eight sections apart.

Step 5 **Place** all eight sections in a stack and fold in half like a *hamburger*.

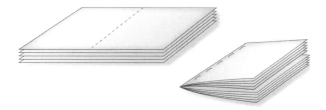

Step 6 **Staple** along the center fold line. **Glue** the front and back sheets into a construction paper cover.

Other Suggestions for a *Minibook* Foldable

Work in pairs to practice new verbs and verb forms using a *minibook* foldable. Illustrate different verbs on the left pages. If it is not clear what pronoun is required, you should write the pronoun under the drawing, for instance to differentiate between *we* and *they*. Then trade *minibooks* and write sentences to go with each picture on the right pages, using the new verb and the pronoun illustrated or indicated.

A *minibook* foldable can be used to help practice vocabulary about the family and house as well as possessive adjectives and the verb *to have* in Spanish. Draw your family members and the rooms of your house on the left pages. If you have several brothers or sisters, several cousins, and several aunts or uncles, you should draw each group on one page. On the right page, write sentences about the drawings, telling how many brothers you have, for example. Add additional sentences describing the family members and rooms using possessive adjectives.

Paper File Folder

Las emociones Use this *paper file folder* organizer to keep track of happenings or events that cause you to feel a certain way.

Step 1 **Fold** four sheets of paper (8½" x 11") in half like a *hamburger*. Leave one side one inch longer than the other side.

Step 2 On each sheet, **fold** the one-inch tab over the short side, forming an envelope-like fold.

Step 3 **Place** the four sheets side-by-side, then move each fold so that the tabs are exposed.

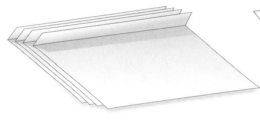

Step 4 Moving left to right, **cut** staggered tabs in each fold, 2⅛" wide. Fold the tabs upward.

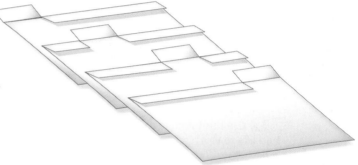

Step 5 **Glue** the ends of the folders together. On each tab, write an emotion you sometimes feel. Pay attention to when it is that you feel happy, sad, nervous, etc. Describe the situation in Spanish and file it in the correct pocket.

Other Suggestions for a *Paper File Folder* Foldable

You may use a *paper file folder* organizer to keep track of verbs and verb forms. You should make a folder for each type of regular verb and for each type of irregular verb. Write the conjugations for some important verbs in each category and file them in the *paper file folder* organizer. Add new tenses to the existing cards and new verbs as you learn them.

A *paper file folder* organizer can be useful for keeping notes on the cultural information that you will learn. You may wish to make categories for different types of cultural information and add index cards to them as you learn new facts and concepts about the target cultures.

Envelope Fold

Un viaje especial Use this *envelope fold* to make a hidden picture or to write secret clues about a city in the Spanish-speaking world you would like to visit.

Step 1 **Fold** a sheet of paper into a *taco* to form a square. Cut off the leftover piece.

Step 2 **Open** the folded *taco* and refold it the opposite way, forming another *taco* and an X-fold pattern.

Step 3 **Open** the *taco fold* and fold the corners toward the center point of the X, forming a small square.

Step 4 **Trace** this square onto another sheet of paper. Cut and glue it to the inside of the envelope. Pictures can be drawn under the tabs.

Step 5 Use this foldable to **draw** a picture of the city you would like to visit. Or if you prefer, **write** clues about the city and have your classmates raise one tab at a time until they can guess what city the picture represents. Number the tabs in the order in which they are to be opened.

Other Suggestions for an *Envelope Fold* Foldable

An *envelope fold* can be useful for practicing vocabulary related to school, sports, vacations, airports, or shopping. Draw a scene that depicts many of the vocabulary words. Then write on each of the four flaps the new words that are represented under that flap. You could also give the picture to a partner and have the partner fill in the words.

You may want to use an *envelope fold* to review a selection you have read. Depict a scene from the selection on the paper covered by the tabs. Number the tabs in the order they are to be opened and have a partner open the tabs one at a time to guess what scene is illustrated. The partner should then write a description of the scenes.

Large Sentence Strips

El presente y el pasado Use these *large sentence strips* to help you compare and contrast activities in the past and in the present.

Step 1 Take two sheets of paper (8½" x 11") and **fold** into *hamburgers*. Cut along the fold lines, making four half sheets. (Use as many half sheets as necessary for additional pages to your book.)

Step 2 **Fold** each half sheet in half like a *hot dog*.

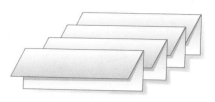

Step 3 Place the folds side-by-side and **staple** them together on the left side.

Step 4 About one inch from the stapled edge, **cut** the front page of each folded section up to the top. These cuts form flaps that can be raised and lowered.

Step 5 To make a half-cover, use a sheet of construction paper one inch longer than the book. **Glue** the back of the last sheet to the construction paper strip, leaving one inch on the left side to fold over and cover the original staples. Staple this half-cover in place.

Step 6 With a friend, **write** sentences on the front of the flap, either in the present tense or in the past tense. Then switch your books of sentence strips and write the opposite tense inside under the flaps.

Other Suggestions for a *Large Sentence Strips* Foldable

You may work in pairs to use *large sentence strips* to practice using direct and/or indirect object pronouns. On the front of each flap, write full sentences that have direct or indirect objects or both. Then trade sentence strips. You and your partner will each write sentences under the flaps replacing the direct or indirect objects with object pronouns.

Large sentence strips can help you contrast summer and winter activities. On the front of each flap, write sentences about activities that you do in either summer or winter. Under each

flap, you should write that in the other season you do not do that activity, and you should tell what you do instead. This may be done as an individual or a partner activity.

You may use *large sentence strips* to practice using verbs that can be used reflexively and nonreflexively. Write a sentence using a reflexive verb on the outside of each flap. Under the flap, write a sentence using the same verb nonreflexively.

Project Board With Tabs

Diversiones favoritas Use this *project board with tabs* to display a visual about your favorite movie or event. Be sure to make it as attractive as possible to help convince others to see it.

Step 1 **Draw** a large illustration, a series of small illustrations, or write on the front of a sheet of paper.

Step 2 **Pinch** and slightly fold the sheet of paper at the point where a tab is desired on the illustrated piece of paper. Cut into the paper on the fold. Cut straight in, then cut up to form an L. When the paper is unfolded, it will form a tab with the illustration on the front.

Step 3 After all tabs have been cut, **glue** this front sheet onto a second sheet of paper. Place glue around all four edges and in the middle, away from tabs.

Step 4 **Write** or draw under the tabs. If the project is made as a bulletin board using butcher paper, tape or glue smaller sheets of paper under the tabs.

Think of favorite scenes from a movie or cultural event that you enjoyed and draw them on the front of the tabs. Underneath the tabs write a description of the scene or tell why you liked it. It might be fun to not put a title on the project board and just hang it up and let classmates guess the name of the movie or event you are describing.

Other Suggestions for a *Project Board With Tabs* Foldable

You may wish to use a *project board with tabs* to illustrate different shopping venues. Draw a type of place to shop on the outside of each tab. Under each tab make a list of some of the things you might buy at that particular kind of place. Use your drawings and lists to create conversations with a partner or small group.

You may also use a *project board with tabs* to illustrate a party, museum, sport, or concert. Draw one aspect of it on the outside of the tab and write a description of your drawing under the tab.

You may work in pairs to practice the comparative and superlative. Each of you will make a *project board with tabs.* On the outside of each tab, draw a different comparison or superlative. Then trade with your partner and under each tab write a sentence describing the other's illustrations.

You may also wish to use a *project board with tabs* to practice the use of object pronouns. Draw a series of scenes involving two or more people on the outside of the tabs. Write sentences using object pronouns describing the people's conversations.

Sentence Strip Holder

Para practicar más Use this *sentence strip holder* to practice your vocabulary, your verbs, or anything else you might feel you need extra help with.

Step 1 **Fold** a sheet of paper (8½" x 11") in half like a *hamburger*.

Step 2 **Open** the *hamburger* and fold the two outer edges toward the valley. This forms a shutter fold.

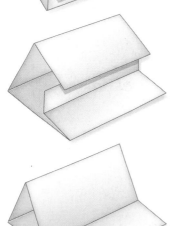

Step 3 **Fold** one of the inside edges of the shutter back to the outside fold. This fold forms a floppy L.

Step 4 **Glue** the floppy L tab down to the base so that it forms a strong straight L tab.

Step 5 **Glue** the other shutter side to the front of this L tab. This forms a tent that is the backboard for the flashcards or student work to be displayed.

Step 6 **Fold** the edge of the L up ¼" to ½" to form a lip that will keep the sentence strips from slipping off the holder.

Vocabulary and verbs can be stored inside the "tent" formed by this fold.

Other Suggestions for a *Sentence Strip Holder* Foldable

You may wish to practice new or irregular verbs using a *sentence strip holder*. Work in pairs. Make flash cards showing the infinitives of the verbs to practice in Spanish. You should each take half of the cards and take turns setting one verb on the *sentence strip holder*. One partner will then say as many sentences as possible using different forms of that verb, and the other will write down the subject and conjugated verb form (or just the verb form) for each sentence. Partners should check to make sure each verb form is spelled correctly. You can repeat this activity for each verb.

You may practice food vocabulary working in small groups and using a *sentence strip holder*. Groups may make flash cards containing the names of local restaurants that everyone will be familiar with, making sure to include different types of restaurants. Put the cards up on the *sentence strip holder* one at a time. Students will spend several minutes writing about what they like to eat at that restaurant. After writing about each restaurant on the list, share your favorite foods with the group.

El alfabeto español

a *a*vión

b *b*ebé

c *c*esta

d *d*edo

e *e*lefante

f *f*oto

g *g*emelos

h *h*amaca

i *i*glesia

j *j*abón

k *k*ilo

l *l*ago

m *m*ono

n *n*ariz

ñ *ñ*ame

o *o*so

p *p*elo

q *q*ueso

r *r*ana

s *s*ala

t *t*é

u *u*va

v *v*aca

w *W*ashington, D.C.

x e*x*amen

y *y*eso

z *z*apato

ch	chicle	
ll	lluvia	
rr	guitarra	

Ch, ll, and **rr** are not letters of the Spanish alphabet. However, it is important for you to learn the sounds they represent.

Spanish is the language of almost 400 million people around the world. Spanish had its origin in Spain. It is sometimes fondly called the "language of Cervantes," the author of the famous novel and character, *Don Quijote*. The Spanish **conquistadores** and **exploradores** brought their language to the Americas in the fifteenth and sixteenth centuries. Spanish is the official language of almost all the countries of Central and South America. It is the official language of Mexico and several of the larger islands in the Caribbean. Spanish is also the heritage language of more than forty-four million people in the United States.

▼ México

Perú ▶

▲ Puerto Rico

▲ España

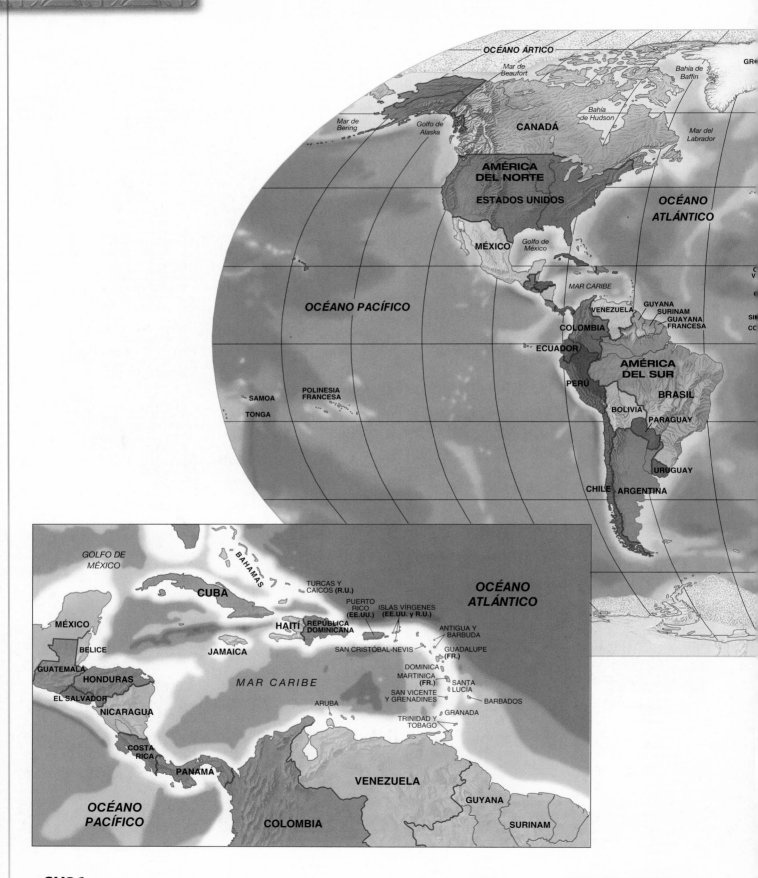

OCÉANO ÁRTICO

GR

Mar de Beaufort

Bahía de Baffin

Mar de Bering

Golfo de Alaska

Bahía de Hudson

CANADÁ

Mar del Labrador

AMÉRICA DEL NORTE

ESTADOS UNIDOS

OCÉANO ATLÁNTICO

MÉXICO

Golfo de México

C V

MAR CARIBE

OCÉANO PACÍFICO

VENEZUELA

GUYANA
SURINAM
GUAYANA FRANCESA

COLOMBIA

SI
CC

ECUADOR

AMÉRICA DEL SUR

PERÚ

BRASIL

SAMOA

POLINESIA FRANCESA

BOLIVIA

PARAGUAY

TONGA

URUGUAY

CHILE   ARGENTINA

GOLFO DE MÉXICO

BAHAMAS

TURCAS Y CAICOS (R.U.)

OCÉANO ATLÁNTICO

CUBA

PUERTO RICO (EE.UU.)

ISLAS VÍRGENES (EE.UU. y R.U.)

MÉXICO

HAITÍ

REPÚBLICA DOMINICANA

ANTIGUA Y BARBUDA

BELICE

SAN CRISTÓBAL-NEVIS

GUADALUPE (FR.)

JAMAICA

GUATEMALA

DOMINICA

HONDURAS

MAR CARIBE

MARTINICA (FR.)

SANTA LUCÍA

EL SALVADOR

ARUBA

SAN VICENTE Y GRENADINES

BARBADOS

NICARAGUA

GRANADA

TRINIDAD Y TOBAGO

COSTA RICA

PANAMÁ

VENEZUELA

GUYANA

OCÉANO PACÍFICO

COLOMBIA

SURINAM

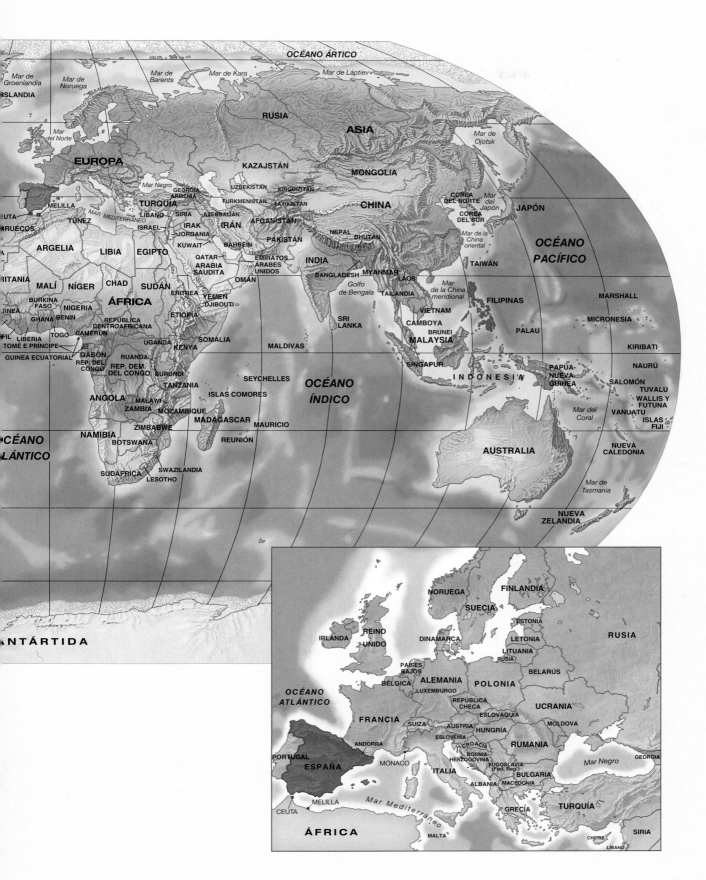

OCÉANO ÁRTICO

Mar de Groenlandia
Mar de Noruega
Mar de Barents
Mar de Kara
Mar de Láptiev

ISLANDIA

Mar del Norte

RUSIA

ASIA

Mar de Ojotsk

EUROPA

KAZAJSTÁN

MONGOLIA

Mar Negro
GEORGIA
ARMENIA
UZBEKISTÁN
KIRGUIZITÁN
TURQUÍA
TURKMENISTÁN
TAYIKISTÁN

CHINA

COREA DEL NORTE
Mar del Japón
JAPÓN
COREA DEL SUR

MELILLA

CEUTA

MARRUECOS

LÍBANO
SIRIA
AZERBAIJÁN
ISRAEL
IRAK
JORDANIA
IRÁN
AFGANISTÁN

Mar MEDITERRÁNEO

TÚNEZ

KUWAIT
BAHREIN
PAKISTÁN
NEPAL
BHUTÁN
Mar de la China oriental

TAIWÁN

OCÉANO PACÍFICO

ARGELIA

LIBIA

EGIPTO

QATAR
ARABIA SAUDITA
EMIRATOS ÁRABES UNIDOS
OMÁN

INDIA

MAURITANIA

MALÍ

NÍGER

CHAD

SUDÁN

ERITREA
YEMEN
DJIBOUTI

BANGLADESH
MYANMAR
LAOS

Golfo de Bengala

Mar de la China meridional

MARSHALL

BURKINA FASO
GUINEA
NIGERIA

ÁFRICA

ETIOPÍA

TAILANDIA

FILIPINAS

MICRONESIA

GHANA
BENIN
REPÚBLICA CENTROAFRICANA

SRI LANKA

VIETNAM
CAMBOYA

PALAU

FIL
LIBERIA
TOGO
TOMÉ E PRÍNCIPE
CAMERÚN
UGANDA
SOMALIA
KENYA
MALDIVAS
BRUNEI
MALAYSIA

KIRIBATI

GUINEA ECUATORIAL
GABÓN
REP. DEL CONGO
RUANDA
REP. DEM. DEL CONGO
BURUNDI
TANZANIA

SEYCHELLES

OCÉANO ÍNDICO

SINGAPUR
INDONESIA

PAPÚA-NUEVA GUINEA

NAURÚ

SALOMÓN

TUVALU

ANGOLA
MALAWI
ZAMBIA
MOZAMBIQUE

ISLAS COMORES

WALLIS Y FUTUNA
VANUATU

MADAGASCAR
MAURICIO

Mar del Coral

ISLAS FIJI

NAMIBIA
ZIMBABWE
BOTSWANA
REUNIÓN

OCÉANO ATLÁNTICO

SUDÁFRICA
SWAZILANDIA
LESOTHO

AUSTRALIA

NUEVA CALEDONIA

Mar de Tasmania

ANTÁRTIDA

NUEVA ZELANDIA

NORUEGA
FINLANDIA
SUECIA

IRLANDA
REINO UNIDO
DINAMARCA
ESTONIA
LETONIA
LITUANIA
RUSIA

RUSIA

PAÍSES BAJOS
BELARÚS

OCÉANO ATLÁNTICO

BÉLGICA
ALEMANIA
LUXEMBURGO
POLONIA

UCRANIA

REPÚBLICA CHECA
ESLOVAQUIA

FRANCIA
SUIZA
AUSTRIA
HUNGRÍA
MOLDOVA

ANDORRA
ESLOVENIA
CROACIA
RUMANIA

PORTUGAL
MÓNACO
BOSNIA-HERZOGOVINA
YUGOSLAVIA (Fed. Rep.)
GEORGIA

ESPAÑA
ITALIA
BULGARIA
MACEDONIA
Mar Negro

MELILLA
ALBANIA
TURQUÍA

CEUTA
Mar Mediterráneo
GRECIA
SIRIA

ÁFRICA
MALTA
CHIPRE
LÍBANO

España

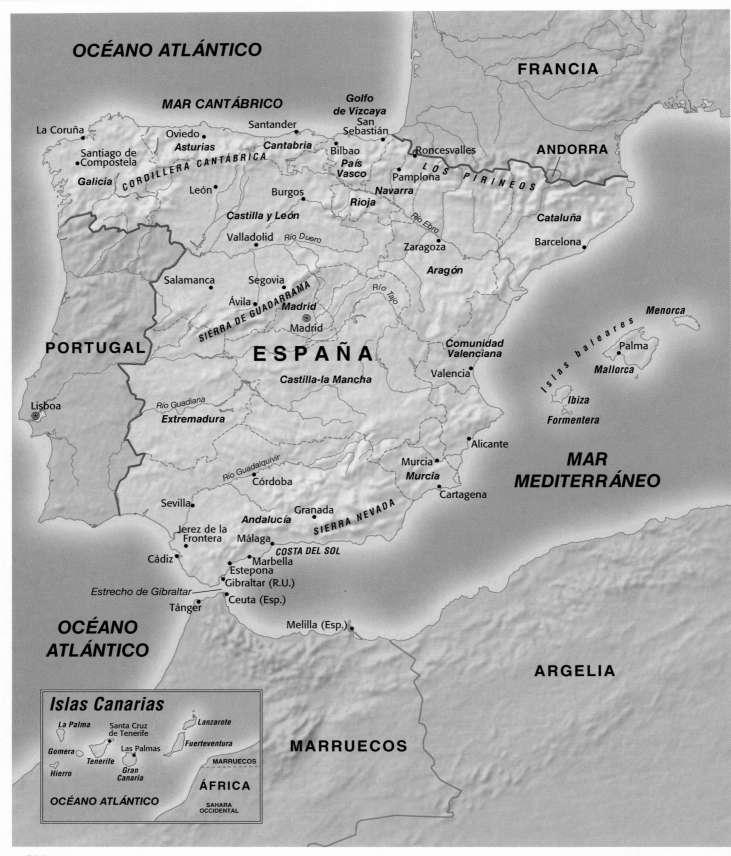

OCÉANO ATLÁNTICO

MAR CANTÁBRICO

FRANCIA

Golfo de Vizcaya

La Coruña

Santiago de Compostela

Galicia

Oviedo

Asturias

Santander

Cantabria

San Sebastián

Bilbao

País Vasco

Roncesvalles

ANDORRA

LOS PIRINEOS

León

Burgos

Pamplona

Navarra

Rioja

Río Ebro

Cataluña

CORDILLERA CANTÁBRICA

Castilla y León

Valladolid

Río Duero

Zaragoza

Barcelona

Aragón

Salamanca

Segovia

Ávila

SIERRA DE GUADARRAMA

Madrid

Madrid

Río Tajo

PORTUGAL

ESPAÑA

Comunidad Valenciana

Valencia

Menorca

Palma

Islas Baleares

Mallorca

Castilla-la Mancha

Ibiza

Formentera

Lisboa

Río Guadiana

Extremadura

Alicante

MAR MEDITERRÁNEO

Río Guadalquivir

Córdoba

Murcia

Murcia

Cartagena

Sevilla

Granada

SIERRA NEVADA

Jerez de la Frontera

Andalucía

Málaga

Cádiz

COSTA DEL SOL

Marbella

Estepona

Gibraltar (R.U.)

Estrecho de Gibraltar

Ceuta (Esp.)

Tánger

Melilla (Esp.)

OCÉANO ATLÁNTICO

ARGELIA

Islas Canarias

La Palma

Santa Cruz de Tenerife

Lanzarote

Gomera

Las Palmas

Fuerteventura

Tenerife

Hierro

Gran Canaria

MARRUECOS

ÁFRICA

MARRUECOS

OCÉANO ATLÁNTICO

SAHARA OCCIDENTAL

MAR CARIBE

OCÉANO ATLÁNTICO

Barranquilla
Maracaibo
Caracas
Cartagena
Lago de Maracaibo
Río Orinoco
VENEZUELA
GUYANA
Medellín
SURINAM
Santafé de Bogotá
GUAYANA FRANCESA
Cali
Río Magdalena
COLOMBIA

Ecuador
Otavalo
Quito
Río Amazonas
ECUADOR
Islas Galápagos (Ecuador)
Guayaquil
Cuenca

BRASIL

PERÚ

El Callao
Lima
Cuzco
Lago Titicaca
BOLIVIA
La Paz
Cochabamba
Brasília
Santa Cruz
Sucre

Trópico de Capricornio

CORDILLERA DE LOS ANDES
PARAGUAY
Asunción

CHILE

Vicuña
Córdoba
Río Paraná

OCÉANO PACÍFICO
Valparaíso
Rosario
URUGUAY
Santiago
Buenos Aires
Montevideo
La Plata
Río de la Plata
ARGENTINA
Mar del Plata

OCÉANO ATLÁNTICO

Puerto Montt

PATAGONIA

Estrecho de Magallanes
Islas Malvinas (R.U.)
Tierra del Fuego
Punta Arenas
Cabo de Hornos

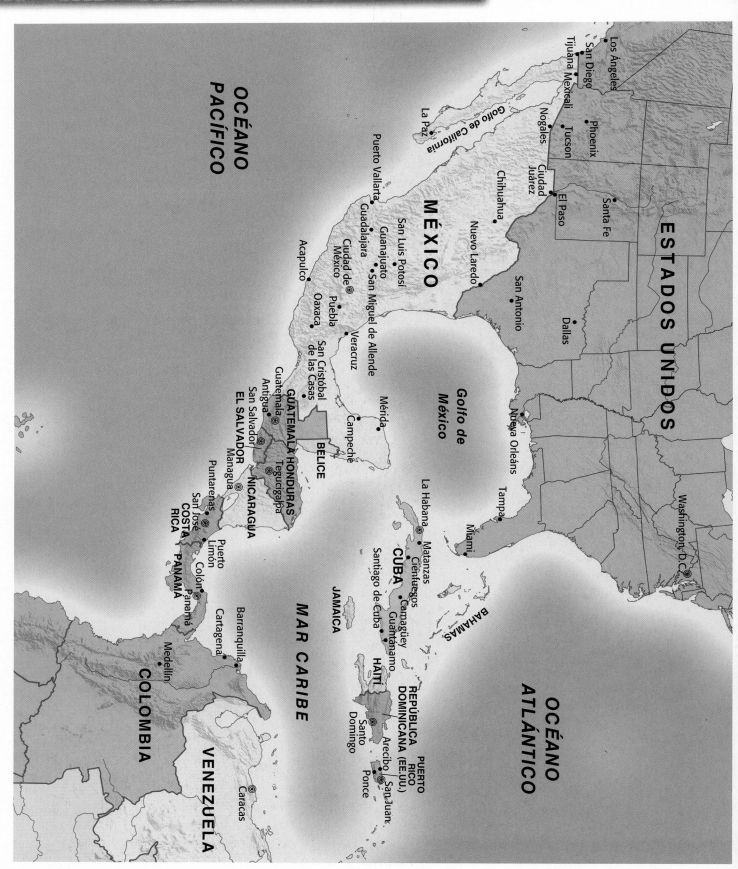

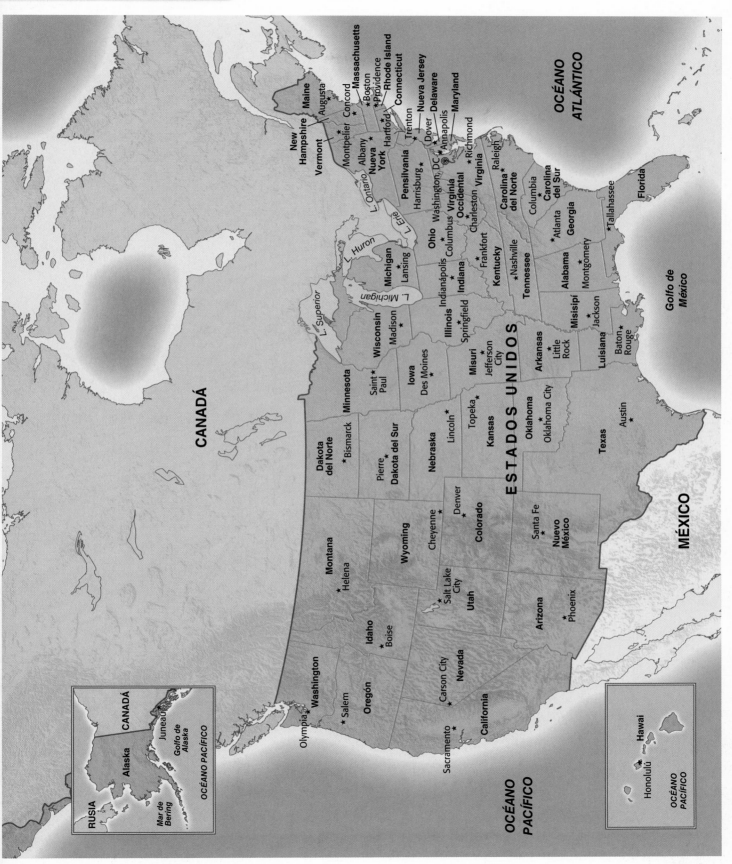

CANADÁ

OCÉANO ATLÁNTICO

Maine
★ Augusta
New Hampshire
Vermont
★ Montpelier
Concord
Massachusetts
★ Boston
★ Providence
Rhode Island
Hartford ★ Connecticut
Albany
Nueva York
L. Ontario
L. Erie
Pensilvania
Harrisburg ★
Trenton
Nueva Jersey
Dover
Delaware
Annapolis
Maryland
Washington, D.C. ★
Richmond
Virginia
Occidental
Charleston ★ Virginia
Columbus
Ohio
Raleigh
Carolina del Norte
Columbia
Carolina del Sur
Atlanta
Georgia
Tallahassee
Florida

L. Superior
L. Huron
L. Michigan
Michigan
Lansing
Wisconsin
Madison
Illinois
Springfield
Indianápolis
Indiana
Frankfort
Kentucky
★ Nashville
Tennessee
Alabama
★ Montgomery
Misisipi
Jackson

Golfo de México

Minnesota
Saint Paul ★
Iowa
Des Moines
Misuri
Jefferson City
Arkansas
Little Rock
Luisiana
Baton Rouge

Dakota del Norte
Bismarck ★
Dakota del Sur
Pierre ★
Nebraska
Lincoln ★
Topeka ★
Kansas
Oklahoma
Oklahoma City
Austin ★
Texas

ESTADOS UNIDOS

Cheyenne
Wyoming
Denver ★
Colorado
Santa Fe ★
Nuevo México

Montana
Helena ★
Salt Lake City ★
Utah
Arizona
Phoenix ★

Idaho
Boise ★
Nevada
Carson City ★

Washington
Olympia ★
Salem ★
Oregón
Sacramento ★
California

OCÉANO PACÍFICO

MÉXICO

RUSIA
Mar de Bering
Alaska
CANADÁ
Juneau ★
Golfo de Alaska
OCÉANO PACÍFICO

Hawai
Honolulú ★
OCÉANO PACÍFICO

GeoVistas

Lake Titicaca on the border of Peru and Bolivia

Explorando el mundo hispanohablante

GeoVista

Post office or Palacio de Comunicaciones in Madrid, the capital of Spain ▶

▲ Beautiful Moorish architecture in the Mezquita de Córdoba

Casares, a typical town of Andalucía in southern Spain ▼

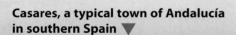

▲ A picturesque bay on the Atlantic coast of Galicia

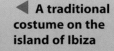

◀ A traditional costume on the island of Ibiza

▲ Windmills in La Mancha on the plains of central Spain

A scene from the famous novel *El Quijote* ▼

La del alba seria cuando
Don Quijote salio de l'venta,
tan contento, tan gallardo, tan
alboro zado por verse ya ar-
mado caballero que el gozo
le reventaba por las cinchas
del caballo.

(Don Quijote de la Mancha cap. IV)

▲ Delicious oranges from Valencia

◄ Two youngsters in a garden in Galicia in the northwest of Spain

An Iberian lynx found in Iberia, the name of the peninsula Spain shares with Portugal ▼

Golfo de Vizcaya

FRANCIA

Mar Cantábrico

La Coruña

San
Sebastián

Bilbao

Santiago
de Compostela

Pamplona

LOS PIRINEOS

Río Ebro

Río Duero

Zaragoza

Barcelona

Salamanca   Segovia

SIERRA DE GUADARRAMA   ★ Madrid

Río Tajo

ESPAÑA

Islas Baleares

Valencia

PORTUGAL   Mérida

Córdoba

Mar Mediterráneo

Río Guadiana

Río Guadalquivir

SIERRA NEVADA

Sevilla

Granada

Islas Canarias

Cádiz

Marbella

Estepona

Estrecho de   Gibraltar

Ceuta

Melilla

SH45

MARRUECOS

GeoVista

México

Monarch butterflies during the winter migration to the states of Mexico and Michoacán ▶

▲ A view of Lake Chapala near Guadalajara

The modern resort of Cancún on the Yucatan Peninsula on Mexico's Caribbean coast ▶

Outdoor cafés in the city of Puebla ▶

A typical skeletal mask for the Day of the Dead—el Día de los Muertos ▼

▲ Beautiful modern buildings in Mexico's capital

A fruit stand in Cabo San Lucas in Baja California

ESTADOS UNIDOS

Tijuana
Mexicali
Ciudad Juárez
DESIERTO DE SONORA
DESIERTO DE CHIHUAHUA
Chihuahua
Río Grande
Río Bravo
Nuevo Laredo
Golfo de California
SIERRA MADRE OCCIDENTAL
SIERRA MADRE ORIENTAL
Monterrey
Matamoros
Golfo de México
La Paz
MÉXICO
San Luis Potosí
Río Grande de Santiago
Guanajuato
San Miguel de Allende
Cancún
Puerto Vallarta
Guadalajara
Río Lerma
Campeche
Lago Chapala
México, D.F. ☆
Veracruz
Puebla
Volcán Pico de Orizaba
OCÉANO PACÍFICO
BELICE
Mar Caribe
Oaxaca
SIERRA MADRE DEL SUR
Acapulco
GUATEMALA

Colorful Mexican textiles in the state of Guerrero

Independence Monument on the famous Paseo de la Reforma in Mexico City, the capital of Mexico ▶

Famous ruins of the Toltec and Olmec indigenous civilizations in Monte Albán in the state of Oaxaca in southern Mexico ▶

GeoVista

▲ **Honduras** An ancient ballpark and stela in the Mayan ruins of Copán

▲ **Guatemala** A modern skyscraper in Guatemala City, the capital of Guatemala

Guatemala A view of the colonial city of Antigua, the former capital of Guatemala ▶

Honduras An iguana on the island of Roatán ▼

▲ **Guatemala** Lake Atitlán and the San Pedro Volcano

MÉXICO

Mar Caribe

BELICE

Tikal
Flores

Islas del Cisne

Golfo de Honduras

Islas de la Bahía

GUATEMALA

SIERRA DE LOS CUCHUMATANES
Cobán

Río Dulce
Puerto Barrios
Puerto Cortés

San Pedro Sula
La Ceiba

El Progreso

Huehuetenango
Lago de Izabal

Volcán Tajumulco

SIERRA DE MERENDÓN

Río Ulúa
Río Motagua

Río Patuca

SIERRA DE AGALTA

Puerto Lempira

Río Coco

altenango
Lago Atitlán

peque zatenango

Guatemala
Lago de Yojoa

HONDURAS

Copán
CORDILLERA DE OPALACA

Cerro Las Minas

Juticalpa

Escuintla

Puerto Quetzal

Tegucigalpa

Danlí

EL SALVADOR

Choluteca

Golfo de Fonseca

NICARAGUA

Guatemala
A quetzal—the national bird of Guatemala ▶

Guatemala Friday market in the town of San Francisco El Alto ▼

Guatemala Young girls in typical Mayan costumes ▼

▲ **Honduras** Vegetable vendors outside the church on a square in Tegucigalpa, the capital of Honduras

GeoVista

Nicaragua A modern high-rise and the colonial cathedral in Managua ▶

▲ **Nicaragua** View of the colonial city of Granada

▲ **Nicaragua** A modern theater in Managua, the capital of Nicaragua

El Salvador A spider monkey, one of those still inhabiting a few areas of El Salvador ▼

El Salvador Chaparrastique Volcano ▼

▲ **Nicaragua** A bay in San Juan del Sur on the Pacific coast

▲ **El Salvador**
Church of Santa Lucía in Suchitoto

Nicaragua
A group of students in a park in Matagalpa ▶

Nicaragua Cattle on a rural road in Viejo León ▼

GUATEMALA

HONDURAS

Río Coco

CORDILLERA DE TILARAN

Lago Güija
Cerro El Pital

Santa Ana
Volcán Santa Ana
Embalse Cerrón Grande
El Mozote
Sensuntepeque
San Salvador
Lago Ilopango
Acajulta
La Libertad
Puerto El Triunfo
Volcán de San Miguel
San Miguel

EL SALVADOR
Río Grande de San Miguel
Golfo de Fonseca

Pico Mogotón

Puerto Cabezas

CORDILLERA ISABELLA

Estelí
Matagalpa
Río Grande de Matagalpa

Chinandega
León
Lago Managua

NICARAGUA

Río Escondido

Islas del Maíz

Corinto

Managua
Granada

Bluefields

Rivas
Lago Nicaragua
Isla de Ometepe

Mar Caribe

OCÉANO PACÍFICO

San Carlos

Río San Juan

COSTA RICA

SH51

GeoVista

◀ **Costa Rica** Tourists in the Inbioparque Center in San José, the capital of Costa Rica

▼ **Costa Rica**
A Costa Rican toucan

▲ **Panama** A view of the modern capital of Panama, Panama City

▼ **Panama** The Panama Canal

▲ **Panama**
A view of the colonial section of Panama City

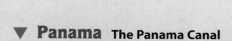

NICARAGUA

Lago Nicaragua

Mar Caribe

CORDILLERA DE GUANACASTE

Liberia

Río San Juan

COSTA RICA

Lago Arenal

Nicoya

CORDILLERA CENTRAL

Alajuela

Puerto Limón

Puntarenas

Caldera

San José

Volcán de Irazú

CORDILLERA DE TALAMANCA

Puerto Quepos

San Isidro

Bocas del Toro

Volcán Barú

Golfito

CORDILLERA CENTRAL

David

Canal de Panamá

Río Chagres

El Porvenir

Colón

Archipiélago de San Blas

SERRANÍA DE SAN BLAS

Lago Gatún

Ciudad de Panamá

Balboa

Río Chepo

Vacamonte

Lago Bayano

SERRANÍA DEL DARIÉN

La Palma

PANAMÁ

Penonomé

Isla del Rey

Río Tuira

Yaviza

Santiago

Archipiélago de las Perlas

Río San Pablo

Golfo de Panamá

COLOMBIA

Isla de Coiba

O C É A N O   P A C Í F I C O

▲ **Panama** Emberá girls in the tropical forest near Panama City

Panama A statue of Vasco Núñez de Balboa, the discoverer of the Pacific Ocean ▼

Costa Rica The Tortuguero Canal along the Caribbean coast of Costa Rica ▼

GeoVista

Colombia ■ Venezuela

▲ **Colombia** Young women marching in Cartagena

▲ **Venezuela** The famous Angel Falls

Colombia, Venezuela
A bear indigenous to many Andean areas ▼

◄ **Colombia** An ancient gold pendant in the form of a human from the area of Tolima

Isla de Providencia

Isla de San Andrés

Mar Caribe

Archipiélago Los Roques

Isla de Margarita

Santa Marta
Pico Cristóbal
Colón
▲
Barranquilla
Puerto Bolívar
Cartagena
SIERRA NEVADA DE SANTA MARTA
Río Magdalena

Golfo de Venezuela
Maracaibo
Lago Maracaibo

Coro
Valencia
Caracas
Lago Valencia
Maracay

PANAMÁ

Cúcuta
San Cristóbal
Mérida
Pico Bolívar ▲
Río Apure
San Fernando de Apure

Río Orinoco
Ciudad Bolívar
Ciudad Guayana

VENEZUELA

Bucaramanga

Canaima
Puerto Ayacucho

GUY

Medellín

Río Meta

Bogotá
Ibagué
Buenaventura
Cali

COLOMBIA
Río Guaviare

Pasto

Río Caquetá

LOS ANDES

Río Patumayo

Río Amazonas

BRASIL

ECUADOR

PERÚ

OCÉA ÁTL

▲ **Venezuela** A view of the modern city of Caracas, the capital of Venezuela

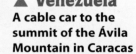

▲ **Venezuela** A cable car to the summit of the Ávila Mountain in Caracas

▲ **Venezuela** Oil rigs on Lake Maracaibo

▲ **Colombia** A church built over the Guaitara River in the south of Colombia

Colombia The beautiful colonial city of Cartagena on the Caribbean coast of Colombia ▼

GeoVista

Ecuador Perú Bolivia

Peru The ruins of Machu Picchu, an imperial city of the Incas ▶

Peru A view of the main square in Cuzco ▼

Peru Sisters in traditional dress in the Urubamba Valley ▼

Ecuador A beach in the port city of Manta ▼

◄ Ecuador
The cathedral in Cuenca, a beautiful city in southern Ecuador

Bolivia
A young man playing the zampoña during a festival in Potosí ▶

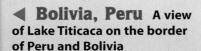

◄ Bolivia, Peru A view of Lake Titicaca on the border of Peru and Bolivia

▲ Bolivia A view of the city of Copacabana

◄ Ecuador La Rotonda in Guayaquil, the place that commemorates a famous meeting between San Martín and Simón Bolívar

GeoVista

Argentina Dancing the Argentine tango in the San Telmo section of Buenos Aires, the capital of Argentina ▶

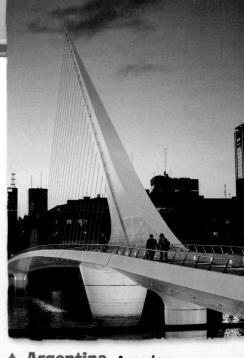

▲ **Argentina** A modern bridge over the Río de la Plata in the port area of Buenos Aires

▲ **Argentina** La Casa Rosada, *Pink House*, in Buenos Aires

Chile
A young man in the important fishing industry in Puerto Montt ▶

◀ **Chile** A view of the old and the new in Santiago, the capital of Chile

Chile Horses in the Torres del Paine National Park ▶

Chile A view of the beautiful Elqui Valley in northern Chile

Argentina Colorful houses in the picturesque area of La Boca in Buenos Aires ▶

PERÚ

BRASIL

BOLIVIA

Arica

PARAGUAY

Iquique

Antofagasta

Salta

San Miguel de Tucumán

Puerto Iguazú

Corrientes

Posadas

Nevado Ojos del Salado

La Serena
Coquimbo

Laguna Mar Chiquita

Río Paraná

←*Isla de Pascua*

CHILE

Córdoba

Santa Fe

URUGUAY

San Juan

Rosario

Viña del Mar
Valparaíso

Cerro Aconcagua

Buenos Aires
La Plata

Santiago

Río Maipo

Río de la Plata

Archipiélago de Juan Fernández

ARGENTINA

Concepción

Mar del Plata

Río Colorado

Temuco
Valdivia

Bahía Blanca

San Carlos de Bariloche

Puerto Montt

Lago General Carrera

Lago Viedma

Lago Argentino

Islas Malvinas

Río Gallegos

Estrecho de Magallanes

OCÉANO ATLÁNTICO

Tierra del Fuego

Ushuaia

Canal de Beagle

Cabo de Hornos

Torres del Paine

G. Perito Moreno

Ushuaia

Cueva del Milodón

Argentina Sea lions in the Patagonian area of Argentina ▼

GeoVista

Paraguay   **Uruguay**

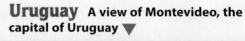

▲ Paraguay A young man of Guaraní background in Asunción, the capital of Paraguay

▲ Paraguay A species of pineapple native to Paraguay and Brazil

Uruguay A view of Montevideo, the capital of Uruguay ▼

◄ Uruguay
A hotel on the outskirts of the famous resort of Punta del Este in Uruguay

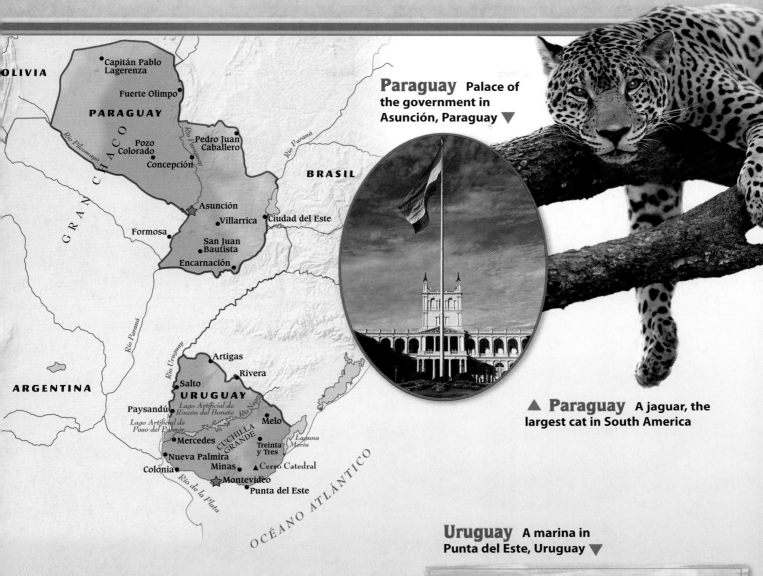

Paraguay Palace of the government in Asunción, Paraguay ▼

▲ **Paraguay** A jaguar, the largest cat in South America

Uruguay A marina in Punta del Este, Uruguay ▼

◄ **Paraguay** Iguazú Falls on the border of Paraguay, Argentina, and Brazil

GeoVista

◀ **Cuba** Scuba diving off the coast of Cuba

▲ **Dominican Republic** A square in Puerto Plata, a famous resort

▲ **Cuba** The town of Trinidad

Puerto Rico A group of students in their school uniform in Fajardo ▶

Cuba A view of the Vedado section of Havana, the capital of Cuba ▼

Golfo de México

BAHAMAS

OCÉANO ATLÁNTICO

La Habana

Río Sagua la Grande

SIERRA DE LOS ÓRGANOS

CUBA

SIERRA DE TRINIDAD

Camagüey

Isla de la Juventud

Río Cauto

Manzanillo

SIERRA MAESTRA

Guantánamo

REPÚBLICA DOMINICANA

PUERTO RICO

Islas Caimán

Pico Turquino

Santiago de Cuba

Santiago

La Vega

HAITÍ

San Pedro de Macorís

Bayamón

Arecibo

San Juan

Rincón

Santo Domingo

La Española

Mayagüez

Ponce

Carolina

Mar Caribe

▲ **Puerto Rico** Asopao, a typical dish of Puerto Rico

▲ **Dominican Republic** A view of tranquil Bayahibe Beach

Puerto Rico
El Yunque rain forest ▼

Puerto Rico
The coquí—a beloved creature of Puerto Rico that gets its name from the sound it makes ▼

GeoVista

Estados Unidos

◀ **New York**
The Puerto Rican Day
Parade in New York City

New York A Mexican restaurant in
Greenwich Village in New York City ▶

◀ **Washington** Latino
newscasters in Seattle

Florida The fort of San
Marcos in Saint Augustine ▼

▲ **Texas** The famous
River Walk in San Antonio

STUDENT HANDBOOK

▲ Arizona César Chávez, the Mexican American labor leader who fought for the rights of all workers

Florida A street sign in Ybor City, a section of Tampa ▼

RUSIA

Alaska

CANADÁ

Mar de Bering

Golfo de Alaska

CANADÁ

Washington

Oregón

Idaho

Montana

Dakota del Norte

Minnesota

Nevada

Utah

Wyoming

Dakota del Sur

Wisconsin

Michigan

New Hampshire

Vermont

Maine

Nueva York

Massachusetts

Rhode Island

Connecticut

Nueva Jersey

Pensilvania

Nebraska

Iowa

Illinois

Indiana

Ohio

Washington, D.C.

Delaware

Maryland

California

Colorado

Kansas

Misuri

Kentucky

Virginia Occidental

Virginia

ESTADOS UNIDOS

Arizona

Nuevo México

Oklahoma

Arkansas

Tennessee

Carolina del Norte

Carolina del Sur

OCÉANO PACÍFICO

Misisipi

Alabama

Georgia

OCÉANO ATLÁNTICO

Texas

Luisiana

Florida

Hawai

OCÉANO PACÍFICO

MÉXICO

Golfo de México

California The Spanish Mission in Santa Barbara ▼

▲ Florida Celebrating the Calle Ocho Carnaval in Miami's Little Havana section

◀ California A music store in San Francisco

ROCK EN ESPAÑOL

Lecciones preliminares

Objetivos

In these preliminary lessons you will:

- greet people
- say good-bye to people
- express yourself politely
- count to 100
- identify the days of the week
- identify the months of the year
- find out and give the date
- ask and tell the time
- discuss the seasons and weather

◀ Unos amigos de Puerto Rico

Greeting people 🎧

To get off to a good start in Spanish, it is important to learn how to greet people. Look at the photographs and take note of some of the gestures people use when greeting each other in Spanish-speaking countries.

¡Hola!

¡Hola! ¿Qué tal?

Hola, Juan.

Bien, gracias. ¿Y tú?

Hola, Pedro. ¿Qué tal?

Muy bien.

① **¡Hola!** Get up from your desk and walk around the classroom. Greet each classmate you meet.

② **¿Qué tal?** Work in pairs. Greet each other and find out how things are going.

③ **Muchachos** Look at these boys' names that are popular in the Spanish-speaking world. How many do you recognize? Which ones have English equivalents? Give Spanish names to the boys in this photo.

Cultura

Nombres de muchachos

Alejandro, Álvaro, Andrés, Ángel, Antonio, Carlos, Daniel, David, Eduardo, Emilio, Enrique, Felipe, Fernando, Francisco, Gabriel, Gerardo, Gustavo, Ignacio, Jaime, Javier, José, Juan, Lucas, Luis, Manuel, Mario, Mateo, Miguel, Moisés, Pablo, Pedro, Rafael, Raúl, Ricardo, Roberto, Stefano, Tomás, Vicente

④ Muchachas Look at these girls' names that are popular in the Spanish-speaking world. How many do you recognize? Which ones have English equivalents? Give Spanish names to the girls in this photo.

Cultura

• **Nombres de muchachas**
Adela, Alejandra, Alicia, Ana, Andrea, Beatriz, Catalina, Clara, Claudia, Cristina, Débora, Elena, Elisa, Esperanza, Éster, Eva, Gabriela, Guadalupe, Isabel, Josefina, Juana, Julia, Karina, Leonor, Luisa, Luz, Maïte, Mar, María, Marisa, Marisol, Marta, Patricia, Paz, Pilar, Rosa, Sandra, Teresa

⑤ ¡Hola, Mario! Greet these Spanish-speaking friends.

1. Mario
2. Alejandra
3. Julia
4. Felipe
5. Vicente
6. Andrea

Some Spanish greetings are more formal than **¡Hola!** When you greet someone, for example, you might say:

Buenos días, señora.
Buenas tardes, señorita.
Buenas noches, señor.

When speaking Spanish, the titles **señor, señora,** and **señorita** are most often used without the name of the person.

⑥ ¡Buenos días! Greet the following people appropriately.

1. Señora Álvarez in the morning
2. Señor Salas in the afternoon
3. Señorita Ramos at night

⑦ Saludos Look at these photographs of people in Mexico and Puerto Rico. Do they greet each other differently than we do? Explain how.

Saying good-bye 🎧

In this lesson you will learn how to say good-bye to people. You will notice that there are many different expressions you can use when taking leave of a person.

Adiós, Marta.

Adiós, Diego.

1. The usual expression to use when saying good-bye to someone is **¡Adiós!**

2. If you plan to see the person again soon, you can say **¡Hasta pronto!** or **¡Hasta luego!** If you plan to see the person the next day, you can say **¡Hasta mañana!**

3. You will frequently hear the informal expression **¡Chao!**, especially in Spain as well as in some countries of Latin America.

1 **¡Chao!** Go over to a classmate and say good-bye to him or her.

2 **¡Hasta luego!** Work with a classmate. Say **¡Chao!** to each other and let each other know that you will be getting together again soon.

3 **¡Adiós!** Say good-bye to your Spanish teacher. Then say good-bye to a friend. Use a different expression with each person.

Para conversar 🎧

¡Hola, Julio!

¡Hola, Mara! ¿Qué tal?

Muy bien. ¿Y tú?

Muy bien, gracias.

Chao, Julio.

Chao, Mara. ¡Hasta luego!

4 **¡Hola! ¡Adiós!** Listen to some Hispanic friends. Indicate on a chart like the one below whether they are greeting each other or saying good-bye.

greeting	saying good-bye

✿ Comunicación

5 **¡Hola, amigo(a)!** Work with a friend. Speak Spanish together. Have fun saying as much as you can to each other.

6 **Rompecabezas**

Join two pieces to form a word. When you have finished, you should have nine words. Do not use any piece more than once.

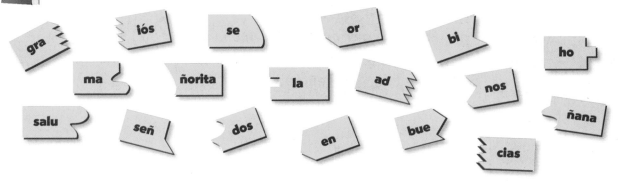

gra   iós   se   or   bi   ho

ma   ñorita   la   ad   nos

salu   señ   dos   en   bue   ñana

cias

Speaking politely

In this lesson you will learn how to request some foods and drinks in a polite way.

1. Whenever you ask for something, remember to be polite and say **por favor.** Whenever someone gives you something or does something for you, say **gracias.**

2. There are several ways to express *You're welcome* in Spanish.

   De nada.
   Por nada.
   No hay de qué.

1 **La cortesía, por favor.** Complete the following conversation.
—Una limonada, ___1___.
—Sí, señora.
(Server brings the lemonade.)
—___2___, señor.
—___3___, señora.

2 **Una cola, por favor.** You are at a café in La Palma, Canary Islands. Order the following things in a polite way. A classmate will be the server.

1. un sándwich
2. un café
3. una limonada
4. una ensalada
5. una pizza
6. una hamburguesa

3 **Por favor.** Order the following foods at a Mexican restaurant. Do you recognize them all? Be polite when you order.

1. un taco
2. una enchilada
3. una tostada
4. un burrito

CULTURA

Restaurante La Placeta en La Palma, islas Canarias

CULTURA

Amigos en un café en Guanajuato, México

Counting in Spanish 🎧

In this lesson you will learn to count to one hundred. You will also learn how to find out the price of something.

1	uno	11	once	21	veintiuno	31	treinta y uno	50	cincuenta
2	dos	12	doce	22	veintidós	32	treinta y dos	60	sesenta
3	tres	13	trece	23	veintitrés	33	treinta y tres	70	setenta
4	cuatro	14	catorce	24	veinticuatro	34	treinta y cuatro	80	ochenta
5	cinco	15	quince	25	veinticinco	35	treinta y cinco	90	noventa
6	seis	16	dieciséis	26	veintiséis	36	treinta y seis	100	ciento (cien)
7	siete	17	diecisiete	27	veintisiete	37	treinta y siete		
8	ocho	18	dieciocho	28	veintiocho	38	treinta y ocho		
9	nueve	19	diecinueve	29	veintinueve	39	treinta y nueve		
10	diez	20	veinte	30	treinta	40	cuarenta		

1 **De diez a cien** Count from 10 to 100 by tens. Then do it backwards!

2 **¿Qué número es?** Say the following numbers in Spanish.
   1. 32   3. 51   5. 77   7. 96
   2. 46   4. 67   6. 84   8. 23

Nota

Note that before a noun **ciento** shortens to **cien.**

   cien pesos
   cien euros

but

   ciento cincuenta pesos
   ciento cuarenta euros

3 **El número, por favor.** Say the following numbers.
   1. your area code
   2. the number you dial for an emergency
   3. your zip code
   4. the number of your house or apartment

4 **Juego** Create a math pattern similar to the one below. Your partner will try to figure out the missing number before you count to ten in Spanish. Take turns.

   tres   seis   nueve   _____   quince

Finding out the price 🎧

To find out or give the price of something, you say:

¿Cuánto es, por favor?

Diez pesos.

 5 **¿Cuánto es?** Work with a partner. Make believe you are buying
 something. Hold it up and get the price in pesos.

MODELO 20 →
—¿Cuánto es, por favor?
—Veinte pesos.

1. 30	**4.** 60	**7.** 78
2. 22	**5.** 15	**8.** 50
3. 45	**6.** 90	**9.** 84

euros

pesos

bolívares

✿ Cultura

Monetary systems When you travel, you will use
different currencies.

- Spain uses the **euro,** the currency of all countries of the
European Union.
- In many Latin American countries, such as Mexico, the
currency is the **peso.**
- Venezuela uses the **bolívar,** named in honor of the Latin
American hero Simón Bolívar.
- In Guatemala, the currency is named after the beautiful
national bird—**el quetzal.**
- In some countries, such as Panama and Ecuador, the
monetary unit is the U.S. dollar.

quetzales

6 **Las matemáticas** Count the money below. Give the total
amount.

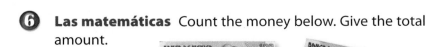

Identifying days of the week and months of the year 🎧

In this lesson you will learn the days of the week, months of the year, and how to give the date.

Look at the calendar to identify the days of the week.

lunes	martes	miércoles	jueves	viernes	sábado	domingo
					1	2
3	4	5	6	7	8	9
10	11	12	13	14	15	16

To find out and give the day of the week, you say:

Para conversar

¿Qué día es hoy?

Hoy es lunes.

Cultura

In Spanish-speaking countries, the week begins with Monday and ends on Sunday. Saturday and Sunday are truly **el fin de semana.**

In Spanish-speaking countries, the date is often abbreviated as day/month/year, instead of month/day/year as we do in the United States. For example, September 23, 2012, would be abbreviated as 23/9/12.

Nota

The days of the week and the months are not capitalized in Spanish.

1 ¿Qué día es? Work with a partner. Have a conversation.
  1. ¿Qué día es hoy?
  2. ¿Qué día es mañana?
  3. ¿Cuáles son los días de la semana?

Look at the calendars to identify the months of the year.

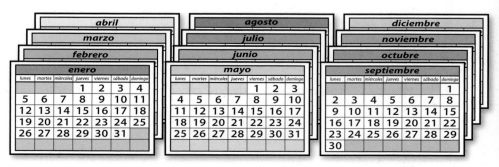

Finding out and giving the date 🎧

Para conversar

¿Cuál es la fecha de hoy?

Hoy es el diez de septiembre.

2 **Mi cumpleaños** Each of you will stand up and give the date of your birthday in Spanish. Listen and keep a record of how many of you were born in the same month.

3 **La fecha, por favor.** Look at these calendars and give the dates.

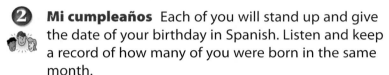

mayo						
			1	2	3	
4	5	6	7	8	9	10
11	12	13	14	15	16	17
18	19	20	21	22	23	24
25	26	27	28	29	30	31

febrero						
						1
2	3	4	5	6	7	8
9	10	11	12	13	14	15
16	17	18	19	20	21	22
23	24	25	26	27	28	

octubre						
		1	2	3	4	
5	6	7	8	9	10	11
12	13	14	15	16	17	18
19	20	21	22	23	24	25
26	27	28	29	30	31	

4 **Fechas importantes** Give the Spanish for the following important dates.

   1. January 1   2. July 4   3. February 14

5 **Un día favorito** Work with a partner. Tell the date of your favorite day of the year in Spanish. Your partner will try to guess the importance of that day. Take turns.

> **Nota**
>
> For the first day of the month you say:
>
> **Es el primero de octubre.**

✿ Conexiones

La música The following are the words for a song that is sung in Spain for a fiesta that takes place on July 7. Sing the song with your classmates.

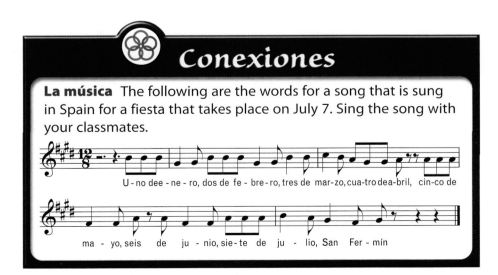

U - no dee - ne - ro, dos de fe - bre - ro, tres de mar-zo, cua-tro dea-bril, cin-co de

ma - yo, seis de ju - nio, sie-te de ju - lio, San Fer - mín

Telling time

In this lesson you will learn how to tell time in Spanish. You will also learn to tell at what time certain events take place.

To find out the time you ask:
¿Qué hora es?

Es la una.

Son las dos.

Son las tres.

Son las cuatro.

Son las cinco.

Son las seis.

Son las siete.

Son las ocho.

Son las nueve.

Son las diez.

Son las once.

Son las doce.

Cultura

In most Spanish-speaking countries it is not considered rude to arrive a bit late for an appointment. If you have a 10 A.M. appointment, it would not be unusual to arrive a bit later.

Son las siete...

y cinco.

y cuarto.

cuarenta.

y diez.

y media.

cuarenta y cinco.

1 **¿Qué hora es?** Give the following times.

1.

2.

3.

4.

5.

6.

2 **¡La hora, por favor!** Walk up to a classmate and ask for the time. Your classmate will answer you.

To find out and tell at what time something takes place you say:

¿A qué hora es la clase de español?

Es a la una.

3 **¿A qué hora es?** Work with a partner. Ask your partner at what time he or she has the following classes.

1. matemáticas
2. historia
3. educación física
4. ciencias
5. español
6. inglés

Cultura

Twenty-four-hour clock

In Spain and in many areas of Latin America, it is common to use the twenty-four-hour clock for formal activities such as reservations and train and airplane departures. Read the time below and figure out the time in the United States.

A las dieciocho horas
A las veinte cuarenta

¡Ojo!

Note that the words in Activity 3 are cognates. Cognates look alike in Spanish and English, but be careful. They are pronounced differently!

Talking about the seasons

In this lesson you will learn to identify the seasons and describe the weather.

Las cuatro estaciones son:

el invierno

la primavera

el verano

el otoño

1 **¿Qué estación es?** Name the season.
1. los meses de junio, julio y agosto
2. los meses de marzo, abril y mayo
3. los meses de diciembre, enero y febrero
4. los meses de septiembre, octubre y noviembre

2 **¿En qué estación?** Name the season for these events.
1. Thanksgiving
2. April Fool's Day
3. Valentine's Day
4. U.S. Independence Day

3 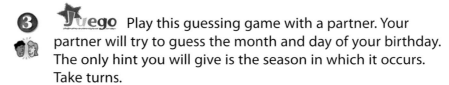 **Juego** Play this guessing game with a partner. Your partner will try to guess the month and day of your birthday. The only hint you will give is the season in which it occurs. Take turns.

Describing the weather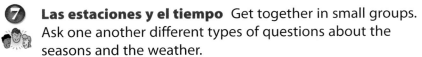

¿Qué tiempo hace?

Hace buen tiempo.
Hace (mucho) calor.
Hace (Hay) sol.

Hace mal tiempo.
Llueve.

Hace frío.
Nieva.

Hace fresco.
Hace viento.

4 **¿Qué tiempo hace hoy?** Tell what the weather is like today.

5 **El tiempo** Describe the weather.
1. ¿Qué tiempo hace en el verano?
2. ¿Qué tiempo hace en el invierno?
3. ¿Qué tiempo hace en la primavera?
4. ¿Qué tiempo hace en el otoño?

6 **La estación** Identify the season according to its weather.
1. ¿En qué estación hace fresco?
2. ¿En qué estación hace mucho calor?
3. ¿En qué estación llueve mucho? ¿En qué mes?
4. ¿En qué estación nieva?

7 **Las estaciones y el tiempo** Get together in small groups. Ask one another different types of questions about the seasons and the weather.

InfoGap For more practice with what you've learned so far, do Activity LP on page SR2 at the end of this book.

Repaso

Review what you have already learned. See all that you can do in Spanish.

1 Respond to each of the following.

1. ¡Hola!
2. ¿Qué tal?
3. ¿Qué día es hoy?
4. ¿Cuál es la fecha?
5. ¿Qué tiempo hace?
6. ¿A qué hora es la clase de español?
7. ¿Qué hora es?
8. ¡Adiós!

2 See how much you can already read in Spanish.

Es el mes de julio en Argentina. Hace mucho frío. ¿Hace frío en julio? En Argentina, sí. El mes de julio no es el verano en Argentina. Es el invierno. Cuando es el verano—los meses de junio, julio y agosto—en el hemisferio norte, es el invierno en el hemisferio sur. Las estaciones son contrarias en el hemisferio norte y en el hemisferio sur.

3 Answer the questions about the reading.

1. ¿Qué mes es en Argentina?
2. ¿Qué tiempo hace?
3. ¿Qué estación es en Argentina?
4. ¿Cuáles son los meses de invierno en Estados Unidos?
5. ¿Cuáles son los meses de invierno en Argentina?

CULTURA
Isla de Vieques, Puerto Rico

CULTURA
Bariloche, Argentina

Vocabulario

 There are a number of cognates in this list. See how many you and a partner can find. Who can find the most? Compare your list with those of your classmates.

Greeting people
saludos	Buenos días.	Buenas noches.	Bien, gracias.
¡Hola!	Buenas tardes.	¿Qué tal?	Muy bien.

Identifying titles
señor	señora	señorita

Saying good-bye
¡Adiós!	¡Hasta luego!	¡Hasta mañana!
¡Chao!	¡Hasta pronto!	

Being courteous
la cortesía	Por favor.	De (Por) nada.
	Gracias.	No hay de qué.

Identifying the days of the week
¿Qué día es hoy?	martes	viernes	hoy
la semana	miércoles	sábado	mañana
lunes	jueves	domingo	

Identifying the months of the year
¿Cuál es la fecha de hoy?	abril	septiembre	el mes
	mayo	octubre	el año
enero	junio	noviembre	el primero (de enero)
febrero	julio	diciembre	el dos (de enero)
marzo	agosto		

Telling time
¿Qué hora es?	Son las dos (tres, cuatro...).	y cuarto	¿A qué hora es?
Es la una.		y media	Es a la una (a las dos, a las tres...).

Identifying the seasons
¿Qué estación es?	el invierno	el verano
	la primavera	el otoño

Describing the weather
¿Qué tiempo hace?	Hace (mucho) calor.	Llueve.	Hace fresco.
Hace buen tiempo.	Hace (Hay) sol.	Hace frío.	Hace viento.
	Hace mal tiempo.	Nieva.	

Other useful words and expressions
¿Cuánto es?	cumpleaños

¿Cómo somos?

Aquí y Allí

Vamos a comparar Have you ever thought about what types of friends you might have if you lived in another country? The theme of friendship is universal, but the qualities that people like in a friend differ. In this chapter, you will learn how to describe friends—both their looks and their personality. Think about your own friends. What qualities do you look for in a good friend?

◄ Los jóvenes puertorriqueños son amigos muy buenos.

Objetivos

You will:

- identify and describe people and things
- tell where someone is from
- tell what subjects you take and express opinions about them
- talk about Spanish speakers in the United States

You will use:

- nouns, adjectives, and articles
- the verb **ser**
- **tú** and **usted**

Go to glencoe.com
For: **Online book**
Web code: **ASD4003c1**

Introducción al tema
¿Cómo somos?

Look at these photographs to acquaint yourself with the theme of this chapter. You will learn to describe yourself and many new friends from all over the Spanish-speaking world as well as some Latino students in the United States. What similarities and differences do you see in the teens in these photos? How do they compare with your friends and the students in your school?

◀ **República Dominicana**
Un grupo de amigos en Santo Domingo, la capital de la República Dominicana

Perú ¡Hola, amigos! Somos todos amigos de Lima, la capital de Perú. Y ustedes, ¿de dónde son? ▼

▲ **Colombia** Los muchachos son de Barranquilla, una ciudad y puerto en el norte de Colombia.

▲ **Puerto Rico** Unos amigos en la plaza principal de Isabela, Puerto Rico

▲ **Venezuela** Un grupo de amigos con motos en Mérida, Venezuela

Bolivia Dos amigas bolivianas en un paseo principal de la capital, La Paz ▶

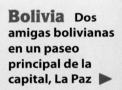

◀ **España** Un grupo de amigos en bici en Órgiva, España, un pueblo pequeño en el sur de España

¿Cómo es?

guapa, bonita

fea

baja

alto

pelirroja

morena

moreno

rubia

cómica, graciosa

seria

antipático

simpático

Para conversar

¿Quién es el amigo de Julia?

Roberto.

¿Cómo es él?

Es alto y gracioso.

Roberto es un amigo de Julia.
Roberto es un amigo bueno.
Julia es una amiga de Roberto.
Julia es una amiga buena.

Para conversar

¿De dónde es la muchacha?

Es de Ecuador.

¿De qué nacionalidad es?

Es ecuatoriana.

La muchacha joven es de Ecuador.
Ella es ecuatoriana.

En otras partes

In addition to **el muchacho,** you will also hear **el chico.** In Mexico you will hear **el chamaco.**

ESCUCHAR

❶ **Escucha y escoge.** Match each statement you hear with the picture it describes.

CULTURA

Elena es de Santiago, la capital de Chile. Es una muchacha simpática, ¿no?

LEER • HABLAR • ESCRIBIR

❷ **Parea.** Look at the words below and match the opposites or antonyms.

guapo   **simpático**   **antipático**

malo   **cómico**   **bajo**   **alto**

bueno   **feo**   **serio**

ESCUCHAR • HABLAR • ESCRIBIR

❸ **Contesta.** Look at the photo of Elena and answer the questions about her.

1. ¿Quién es la muchacha? ¿Es Elena o Cecilia?
2. ¿Cómo es la muchacha? ¿Es pelirroja o morena?
3. ¿Cómo es la muchacha? ¿Es fea o guapa?
4. ¿Cómo es la muchacha? ¿Es graciosa o seria?
5. ¿Cómo es la muchacha? ¿Es simpática o antipática?

HABLAR • ESCRIBIR

❹ **Describe a Eduardo.** Look at the photo of Eduardo. Describe him. You may wish to choose the appropriate words from the **banco de palabras** to use in your description.

CULTURA

Eduardo es de Antigua, Guatemala. Es un muchacho guapo, ¿no?

guapo	**feo**	**bajo**
moreno	**serio**	**guatemalteco**
gracioso	**alto**	**pelirrojo**

Comunicación

5 Habla de un(a) amigo(a). In Activity 4, you learned about Eduardo. Present to the class some similar information about one of your own friends.

Mi amigo(a) es...

HABLAR

6 **¡Manos a la obra!** Work in groups. Draw several faces. Exaggerate a feature on each one so members of your group can guess the adjective you have in mind.

HABLAR • ESCRIBIR

7 **Contesta.** Answer. Pay particular attention to the word that introduces each question.

1. ¿Quién es la muchacha? ¿Es Antonia?
2. ¿Cómo es Antonia?
3. ¿De dónde es Antonia?
4. ¿De qué nacionalidad es?

CULTURA

Antonia es una joven de Cuzco, Perú.

ESCUCHAR • HABLAR • ESCRIBIR

8 **Forma preguntas.** Form questions according to the model. Pay attention to the words in italics. They will help you figure out which question word to use.

MODELO   Rafael es *muy gracioso.* →
¿Cómo es Rafael?

1. *Elena* es de Chile.
2. Paco es *muy serio.*
3. Felipe es *de México.*
4. La amiga de Felipe es *Sofía.*
5. Bárbara es *norteamericana.*
6. Carlos es *guapo y gracioso.*
7. Fernando es *puertorriqueño.*
8. *El muchacho* es de México.

HABLAR

9 **Juego** Work with a group of friends. Each person secretly chooses a student in the class and gives as many adjectives as possible to describe that person. The others try to guess who it is. Keep score.

CULTURA

Es una vista de Punta Arenas, una ciudad en la Patagonia chilena. Aquí hace mucho frío.

¿Quiénes son?

los alumnos

la escuela

las alumnas

Para conversar

¿Quiénes son amigos?

Los alumnos.

Los alumnos son mexicanos.
Son alumnos en una escuela secundaria.
Son alumnos en la misma escuela.
Ellos son amigos también.

¡Así se dice!

When you want to get someone's attention you can say **¡Oye!**
    ¡Oye! ¿Quién es?

Mucho gusto, Ricardo.

Ricardo es un alumno nuevo.

ambiciosos

perezosos

VIDEO To meet some new friends in Argentina, watch **Diálogo en vivo.**

una clase grande

el profesor

Es la clase de español.
Los alumnos son inteligentes.
Son muy buenos. No son malos.
Son ambiciosos. No son perezosos.

¡Ojo!

A cognate is a word that looks similar and means the same in two or more languages. But be careful. Although cognates look alike, they are pronounced differently. Guess the meaning of the following school subjects.

el español
el inglés
el francés
la ciencia
los estudios sociales
la historia
las matemáticas
la música
el arte
la educación física

la profesora

una clase pequeña

Es una clase interesante. No es aburrida.
El curso es bastante difícil (duro).
No es fácil.

QuickPass

Go to glencoe.com
For: **Vocabulary practice**
Web code: **ASD4003c1**

ESCUCHAR

1 **Escucha y escoge.** Listen to each statement and indicate which photograph it refers to.

a.

b.

c.

d.

 For more practice using your new vocabulary, do Activity 1 on page SR3 at the end of this book.

ESCUCHAR • HABLAR • ESCRIBIR

2 **Contesta.** Look at the photo and make up answers about Rosa and Gabriela, two good friends from Colombia.

1. ¿Quiénes son las dos muchachas?
2. ¿Son amigas?
3. ¿Son ellas colombianas?
4. ¿Son alumnas en una escuela en Barranquilla?
5. ¿Son muy inteligentes?
6. ¿Son alumnas buenas o malas?

ESCRIBIR

3 **Categoriza.** You have already learned a number of adjectives. Some describe physical appearance and others describe personality. Make a chart like the one below and put the adjectives you know into the appropriate category.

CULTURA

Las muchachas son de Barranquilla, una ciudad bonita en el norte de Colombia.

apariencia física	características de personalidad

ESCUCHAR • HABLAR • ESCRIBIR

4 Personaliza. Answer the questions about your own Spanish class.

1. ¿Es grande o pequeña la clase de español?
2. ¿Quién es el/la profesor(a) de español?
3. ¿Es interesante el curso de español?
4. ¿Es fácil o difícil?
5. ¿Son inteligentes los alumnos?

Comunicación

5 Work with a partner. Using words you have already learned, describe your courses to each other. Then share your results with the class. See how many of you agree.

ESCRIBIR

6 Rompecabezas

Join two pieces to form a word. When you have finished, you should have eight words. Do not use any piece more than once.

reno cil nos pe

cia go

cur cien so

nue mo

alum vo

queña ami difí

7 Completa. Complete the story with the correct words. **¡Cuidado!** You will now use different types of words, including nouns, adjectives, and verbs.

¿____1____ son los muchachos? El muchacho ____2____ Diego y la muchacha ____3____ Marta. Marta es una ____4____ de Diego y Diego es un ____5____ de Marta. Son alumnos en la misma ____6____. Son alumnos ____7____. ¿Cómo son? Diego es ____8____ y Marta es ____9____. ¿De ____10____ nacionalidad son? Son ____11____.

FOLDABLES® Study Organizer

Antónimos   Sinónimos

VOCABULARY BOOK

See page SH24 for help with making this foldable. Use this study organizer to help remember synonyms and antonyms. Compare your list with a partner to see who came up with more pairs.

Conexiones

La biología

La biología es una ciencia. La biología es el estudio de los animales y las plantas. El/La biólogo(a) es el científico. El microscopio es un instrumento muy importante para el/la biólogo(a).

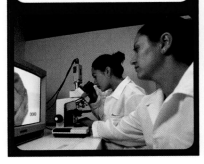

QuickPass

Go to glencoe.com
For: **Grammar practice**
Web code: **ASD4003c1**

Artículos y sustantivos

1. The name of a person, place, or thing is a noun. In Spanish, every noun has a gender, either masculine or feminine. Almost all nouns that end in **-o** are masculine and almost all nouns that end in **-a** are feminine.

2. *The* in English is called a definite article. In Spanish, the definite article is either **el** or **la.** You use **el** with masculine nouns and **la** with feminine nouns.

el muchacho	**la muchacha**
el amigo	**la amiga**
el curso	**la escuela**

Note that in the plural (more than one) **el** becomes **los** and **la** becomes **las.**

los muchachos	**las muchachas**
los amigos	**las amigas**
los cursos	**las escuelas**

3. *A, an,* and *some* are called indefinite articles. Note the following forms of the indefinite articles in Spanish.

un muchacho	**una muchacha**
un amigo	**una amiga**
unos muchachos	**unas muchachas**
unos amigos	**unas amigas**

4. Note that when a noun ends in **-e,** you have to learn whether it is masculine or feminine.

el continente	**los continentes**
la clase	**las clases**

Comparaciones

In the United States we use the word "friend" a great deal. Spanish speakers use the word **amigo** a great deal, too, but **un amigo** is used only for a person they know well. If they don't know the person well, they say **un conocido.** Spanish speakers tend to use the word **conocido** more than we use the word "acquaintance."

CULTURA

Los muchachos son unos amigos muy buenos.

Práctica

ESCUCHAR • HABLAR • ESCRIBIR

 ① Completa. Complete with **el, la, los,** or **las.**

1. _____ amigo
2. _____ muchacha
3. _____ escuela
4. _____ alumnos
5. _____ amigas
6. _____ muchachos
7. _____ cursos
8. _____ alumno

EXPANSIÓN

Now repeat the words in the activity. Change
el, la, los, and **las** to **un, una, unos,** and **unas.**

ESCUCHAR • HABLAR • ESCRIBIR

② Contesta. Answer with *yes.* Pedro and María are
friends from the United States. Answer the questions
about them.

1. ¿Es norteamericano el muchacho?
2. ¿Y la muchacha? ¿Es ella norteamericana?
3. ¿Son norteamericanos los amigos?
4. ¿Son los muchachos alumnos buenos?
5. ¿Es Pedro un amigo de María?
6. ¿Es María una amiga de Pedro?

CULTURA

Las jóvenes son alumnas en la misma
escuela en Antigua, Guatemala.

CULTURA

Pedro y María son alumnos
en una escuela pública en la
ciudad de El Paso en Texas.

VIDEO Want help with the agreement of nouns and adjectives? Watch **Gramática en vivo.**

Adjetivos

1. An adjective is a word that describes or modifies a noun. In Spanish, unlike English, the adjective must agree with the noun in gender (masculine or feminine) and number (singular or plural). Study the following examples.

ADJECTIVES ENDING IN -O

el muchacho argentino	los muchachos argentinos
la muchacha argentina	las muchachas argentinas

ADJECTIVES ENDING IN -E

el curso interesante	los cursos interesantes
la clase interesante	las clases interesantes

ADJECTIVES ENDING IN A CONSONANT

el curso fácil	los cursos fáciles

2. Note that you use the masculine form when a group consists of both boys and girls.

Juan y José son alumnos buenos.
María y Teresa son alumnas buenas.
José y Teresa son alumnos buenos.

Colegio Hispánico
Miguel de Unamuno
Calle Rúa Antigua, 5
Teléfono (923) 21 20 55
Fax (923) 27 14 18
37008 SALAMANCA (España)

CULTURA
Marisol es de Puerto Vallarta, México. Ella es una alumna muy buena.

Práctica

ESCUCHAR

3 **Escucha.** Listen to each statement and determine if it is about one person or thing or more than one. Make a chart like the one below to indicate your answers.

singular	plural

ESCUCHAR • HABLAR • ESCRIBIR

4 **Contesta.** Answer the questions. Pay attention to the form of the adjective.

1. ¿Es gracioso el muchacho guatemalteco?
2. ¿Es graciosa la muchacha guatemalteca?
3. ¿Son graciosos los muchachos guatemaltecos?
4. ¿Son graciosas las muchachas guatemaltecas?

CULTURA

Las amigas guatemaltecas son alumnas en la misma escuela.

LEER • ESCRIBIR

5 **Cambia Carlos a María.** Change Carlos to María. Be careful to make all the necessary changes.

Carlos es colombiano. Él es moreno. No es rubio.
Carlos es muy inteligente y es bastante gracioso.
Carlos es un amigo bueno.

LEER • ESCRIBIR

6 **Completa.** Complete with the correct form of the adjective.

1. La escuela no es _____. (pequeño)
2. La escuela es _____. (grande)
3. Las clases no son _____. (pequeño)
4. Las clases son _____. (grande)
5. Un curso es _____. (difícil)
6. Y otro curso no es _____; es _____. (difícil, fácil)
7. Unos cursos son _____. (fácil)
8. Y otros cursos son _____. (difícil)

CULTURA

Una escuela primaria en Saquisilí, un pueblo en los Andes de Ecuador

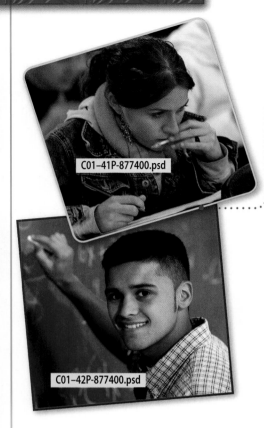

C01–41P-877400.psd

C01–42P-877400.psd

Comunicación

7 Look at these photographs of a girl from Mexico and a boy from Chile. Give them each a name and say as much as you can about them. Use the diagram below to tell what they have in common.

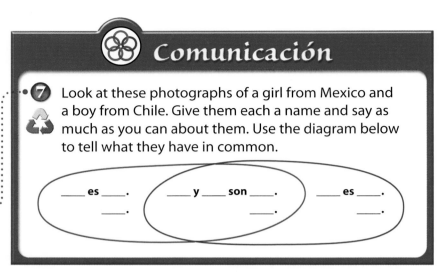

____ es ____.
____.

____ y ____ son ____.
____.

____ es ____.
____.

El verbo ser

1. Study the following forms of the verb **ser**.

ser			
yo	soy	nosotros(as)	somos
tú	eres	*vosotros(as)*	*sois*
Ud., él, ella	es	Uds., ellos, ellas	son

2. Note that the form of the verb changes with each subject. Since the verb changes, the subject pronouns **yo, tú, usted, él, ella, nosotros(as), ustedes, ellos,** and **ellas** are often omitted in Spanish.

(Yo) soy Juana.

(Nosotros) somos alumnos.

You use **yo** to talk about yourself.

You use **nosotros(as)** to talk about yourself and someone else.

(Él) es rubio y (ella) es rubia también.

You use **él** or **ella** to talk about someone.

You use **ellos** or **ellas** to talk about two or more people.
Note that **ellos** also refers to a group of males and females.

3. Unlike in English, there are several ways to express *you* in Spanish.

You use **tú** when speaking to a friend or person the same age.
> **José, (tú) eres de México, ¿no?**

You use **usted** when speaking to an adult or someone you do not know well. **Usted,** often abbreviated **Ud.,** shows respect.
> **Señor López, usted es de México, ¿no?**

Ustedes is a plural form. In the plural there is no distinction. You use **ustedes (Uds.)** when addressing two or more friends or adults.
> **¿Son ustedes de México?**

However, **vosotros(as)** is used in Spain as the plural of **tú** when addressing two or more friends.
> **Sois de España, ¿no?**

Práctica

ESCUCHAR • LEER • HABLAR

8 **Practica la conversación.** Practice the conversation with a classmate. Take turns playing each role. Pay close attention to the verb form you use when speaking about yourself as opposed to talking to a friend.

Susana	¡Hola!
Andrés	¡Hola! ¿Quién eres?
Susana	¿Quién? ¿Yo?
Andrés	Sí, tú.
Susana	Pues, soy Susana, Susana Gómez. Y tú, ¿quién eres?
Andrés	Soy Andrés. Andrés Álvarez.
Susana	Mucho gusto, Andrés. ¿Eres norteamericano?
Andrés	No. Soy de México.
Susana	¿De México? ¡Increíble! Yo también soy mexicana.

CULTURA

Monumento de la Independencia, Ciudad de México

¿CÓMO SOMOS?

treinta y cinco **35**

ESCRIBIR • HABLAR

9 Completa. Complete the chart based on the information in the conversation. Then summarize the conversation using complete sentences.

	¿quién es?	¿de dónde es?	¿de qué nacionalidad es?
la muchacha			
el muchacho			

HABLAR • ESCRIBIR

10 Personaliza. Answer about yourself. Think about which verb form you use when you talk about yourself.
1. ¿Quién eres?
2. ¿Eres norteamericano(a)?
3. ¿De qué nacionalidad eres?
4. ¿De dónde eres?
5. ¿Eres gracioso(a) o serio(a)?

LEER • HABLAR • ESCRIBIR

11 Completa la conversación. Complete the conversation with the correct form of **ser.**

Catalina	Hola, Ricardo. ¿ __1__ de Puerto Rico?
Ricardo	Sí, Catalina. __2__ puertorriqueño.
Catalina	¿ __3__ de San Juan?
Ricardo	Sí, __4__ de la capital.
Catalina	¿ __5__ alumno en una escuela privada en San Juan?
Ricardo	No, __6__ alumno en una escuela pública.
Catalina	¿ __7__ un alumno bueno o malo?
Ricardo	¡Oye, Catalina! Yo __8__ un alumno bueno.

EXPANSIÓN

Now, without looking at the conversation, tell all you remember about Ricardo and Catalina. Your partner will add anything you forgot.

Una vista de San Juan, Puerto Rico

HABLAR • ESCRIBIR

12 Personaliza. Answer each question about yourself and a friend. Remember to use the **nosotros(as)** form of the verb.
1. ¿De qué nacionalidad son ustedes?
2. ¿Son ustedes alumnos(as)?
3. ¿En qué escuela son alumnos(as)?
4. ¿Son ustedes amigos(as) buenos(as)?
5. ¿Son ustedes alumnos(as) en la misma clase de español?

Comunicación

 13 Work in small groups. Interview one another to find out as much as possible about yourselves and your friends. Take turns. Share what you have learned about one another with your classmates.

ESCUCHAR • HABLAR • ESCRIBIR

 14 **Forma preguntas con De dónde.** Ask where the people are from. Use **tú, usted,** or **ustedes** as appropriate.

1. Adelita

2. Linda y Marta

3. Señor Nadal

4. Señor y Señora Gómez

5. Antonio

HABLAR

15 🌟**Juego** Work in teams. One person begins by giving **el, la, los,** or **las.** Each member will then add a new word until a complete sentence is formed.

Comunidades

The Latino demographics in the United States are changing. Until recently, most Latinos were of Mexican, Cuban, or Puerto Rican background. Today there are people from many other Latin American countries. For example, sections of New York City that were predominantly Puerto Rican now have more Dominican residents than Puerto Rican. Are there any Latinos in your community? What areas are they from?

HABLAR • ESCRIBIR

16 **Completa.** Complete with **ser.** You will now have to use all forms of this verb.

¡Hola! Yo __1__ un amigo de Marcos. Marcos y yo __2__ muy buenos amigos. Marcos __3__ de Puerto Rico y yo __4__ de la República Dominicana. Puerto Rico y la República Dominicana __5__ dos islas en el mar Caribe. __6__ dos islas tropicales.

Ahora nosotros __7__ alumnos en una escuela secundaria en Nueva York. Nosotros __8__ alumnos muy buenos. Marcos __9__ un alumno muy bueno en matemáticas y yo __10__ un alumno bueno en historia. Y nosotros dos __11__ alumnos muy buenos en español.

Y ustedes, ¿de dónde __12__? ¿Y quiénes __13__? ¿__14__ ustedes alumnos buenos en español también?

CULTURA

Una plaza colonial en Santo Domingo, la capital de la República Dominicana

ESCRIBIR

17 **Forma frases.** Choose words from each column to make sentences. Be sure to make the adjectives agree with the words they describe.

yo	somos	dominicano
usted	es	norteamericano
tú	eres	puertorriqueño
Julia y Roberto	son	chileno
nosotros	soy	venezolano
la amiga de José		

18 **Completa.** Complete the following activity. **¡Cuidado!**
You will have to use nouns, articles, adjectives, verbs, etc.

Carlos __1__ Teresa __2__ alumnos en __3__ escuela __4__ en Lima, __5__ capital de Perú. Ellos son __6__ muy buenos. __7__ clase de español __8__ muy interesante y __9__ profesora __10__ español es simpática. Carlos y Teresa __11__ alumnos y amigos.

PRONUNCIACIÓN

Las vocales a, e, i, o, u

When you speak Spanish, it is important to pronounce the vowels carefully. The vowel sounds in Spanish are short, clear, and concise. The vowels in English have several different pronunciations, but in Spanish they have only one sound. Note that the pronunciation of **a** is similar to the *a* in *father*. The pronunciation of **e** is similar to the *a* in *mate.* The pronunciation of **i** is similar to the *ee* in *bee.* The **o** is similar to the *o* in *most,* and **u** is similar to the *u* in *flu.* Repeat the following.

a	e	i	o	u
Ana	Elena	Isabel	o	uno
baja	peso	Inés	no	mucha
amiga	Felipe	italiano	Paco	mucho
alumna	feo	simpático	amigo	muchacho

 Dictado

Pronounce the following sentences carefully. Then write them to prepare for a dictation.

> Ana es alumna.
> Adán es alumno.
> Ana es una amiga de Adán.
> Elena es una amiga de Felipe.
> Inés es simpática.
> Sí, Isabel es italiana.

Refrán

Can you guess what the following proverb means?

Un amigo sincero es un tesoro divino.

You have now learned all the new vocabulary and grammar in this chapter. Continue to use and practice all that you know while learning more cultural information. ¡Vamos!

QuickPass

Go to glencoe.com
For: **Conversation practice**
Web code: **ASD4003c1**

UN ALUMNO NUEVO

¿Comprendes?

A **Contesta.** Answer based on the information in the conversation between Sandra, Anita, and José.

1. ¿Es alto o bajo José Cárdenas?
2. ¿Son amigos José y Sandra?
3. ¿Es José un alumno nuevo en la escuela?
4. ¿Es guapo?
5. ¿De dónde es?
6. Y, ¿de dónde es Anita?
7. ¿Son colombianos los dos?

GeoVistas

To learn more about Colombia, take a tour on pages SH54–SH55.

B **¿Sí o no?** Correct any wrong information.

1. José es alto.
2. Sandra y José son amigos.
3. José es norteamericano.
4. José es colombiano y Sandra es colombiana también.

C **Resumiendo** Work with a partner. Summarize what Sandra, Anita, and José talked about.

D **Dando opiniones** Do you think Anita and José will be friends? Why or why not?

CULTURA

Una vista de la parte moderna de Cartagena, Colombia

LECTURA CULTURAL

Antes de leer

Read the title of the reading. Based on the title, what do you think this reading is about?

READING STRATEGY

Using titles and subtitles What is the first thing you see when you look at any reading? The title, right? Titles provide important information about the content of a reading. As you read, remember to also focus on any subtitles. Understanding titles and subtitles will clarify content and help you understand and enjoy what you read.

✓ Reading Check

¿Es el español una lengua extranjera para Francisco y Guadalupe?

Durante la lectura

Look at the subtitle of each section. How does it help you understand what you are reading?

✓ Reading Check

Ramón y Marisa son de ascendencia cubana. Pero no son de Cuba. ¿De dónde son?

Amigos latinos en Estados Unidos 🎧 ♻

Mexicanoamericanos ¡Hola, amigos! Somos Francisco Chávez y Guadalupe Garza. Somos alumnos en una escuela secundaria en Norteamérica. Somos alumnos en una escuela secundaria norteamericana pero para nosotros el español no es una lengua extranjera[1]. ¿Por qué? Porque nosotros somos de ascendencia[2] mexicana. Somos mexicanoamericanos. Somos el grupo número uno—el grupo mayoritario—de hispanohablantes[3] en Estados Unidos.

Cubanoamericanos Somos Ramón Ugarte y Marisa Dávila. Somos de Miami en la Florida. Como muchas personas en Miami, somos de ascendencia cubana. Somos cubanoamericanos.

El español es una lengua importante en todas partes de Estados Unidos. En Estados Unidos hay[4] más de cuarenta y cuatro millones de hispanohablantes.

[1]extranjera *foreign*
[2]ascendencia *background*
[3]hispanohablantes *Spanish speakers*
[4]hay *there are*

Después de leer

Did the reading discuss what you predicted? Explain.

Marisa y Ramón

Guadalupe y Francisco

¿Comprendes?

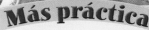

Más práctica

■ Workbook, pp. 1.14–1.15
● StudentWorks™ Plus

A **Recordando hechos** Answer the questions to see how much information you remember from the story.

1. ¿Dónde son alumnos Francisco y Guadalupe?
2. ¿De qué ascendencia son?
3. ¿Es el español una lengua extranjera para Francisco y Guadalupe?
4. ¿De dónde son Ramón y Marisa?
5. ¿De qué ascendencia son Ramón y Marisa?

B **Buscando información** Find the following information in the reading.

1. estado con muchos residentes o habitantes de ascendencia cubana
2. el grupo mayoritario de latinos en Estados Unidos
3. la población (el número de habitantes) latina en Estados Unidos

Comunidades

Hay muchos latinos en todas partes de Estados Unidos. ¿Hay latinos en la escuela donde tú eres alumno(a)? ¿De dónde son ellos? ¿De qué países o naciones hispanohablantes son?

GeoVistas

To learn more about the United States, take a tour on pages SH64–SH65.

CULTURA
Influencia mexicana en Santa Cruz, California

C **Describiendo** Write as much information as you can about the following people.

Francisco Chávez y Guadalupe Garza	Ramón Ugarte	Marisa Dávila

Antes de leer

You are going to read about two main characters in a famous Spanish novel. Have you ever heard of Don Quijote and Sancho Panza in other courses?

Dos personajes importantes 🎧 ♻️

Una descripción Una novela famosa de la literatura española es *El Quijote.* El autor es Miguel de Cervantes Saavedra.

El Quijote es la historia del famoso caballero andante¹ don Quijote de la Mancha. La Mancha es una región de España.

CULTURA

Don Quijote montado a caballo y Sancho Panza montado en un asno

Conexiones

La literatura
The novel *El Quijote* is the second most widely read book in the world. The first is *La Biblia. El Quijote* has also been translated into more languages than any other literary work.

Don Quijote es alto y flaco². Sancho Panza es el compañero de don Quijote. Pero don Quijote y Sancho Panza son dos personajes muy diferentes. Sancho, ¿es alto y flaco como don Quijote? No, de ninguna manera. Él es bajo y gordo³. Sancho Panza es una persona graciosa. Él es cómico pero don Quijote, no. Él es muy serio y es una persona honesta y generosa. Pero según⁴ Sancho Panza, don Quijote es tonto⁵. Y según don Quijote, Sancho es perezoso.

¹caballero andante   *knight errant*
²flaco   *thin*
³gordo   *fat*

⁴según   *according to*
⁵tonto   *foolish, crazy*

¿Comprendes?

A Escoge. Choose the correct answer or completion.

1. El título de la novela es _____.
a. *España*
b. *Un caballero andante*
c. *El Quijote*
d. *Don Quijote y Sancho Panza*

2. Cervantes es _____.
a. un personaje en la novela
b. un famoso caballero andante
c. una región de España
d. el autor de la novela

3. ¿Cómo es don Quijote?
a. Es perezoso.
b. Es serio.
c. Es bajo.
d. Es gracioso.

4. _____ es un defecto.
a. Ser cómico
b. Ser serio
c. Ser perezoso
d. Ser un caballero andante

5. _____ es un atributo positivo.
a. Ser tonto
b. Ser perezoso
c. Ser honesto
d. Ser alto

B Categoriza. Make a chart similar to the one below. Place a check under the character each adjective describes. Then use the adjectives and the verb **ser** to compare Don Quijote and Sancho Panza.

característica	don Quijote	Sancho Panza
alto		
bajo		
gordo		
flaco		
gracioso		
serio		
generoso		
honesto		
tonto		
perezoso		

CULTURA

Unos molinos de viento en La Mancha

Vocabulario

1 **Parea.** Match each description with the girl it describes.

To review **Vocabulario 1** and **Vocabulario 2,** turn to pages 22–23 and 26–27.

1. una muchacha rubia   **3.** una muchacha graciosa

2. una muchacha alta   **4.** una muchacha inteligente

2 **Completa.** Complete.

5. El joven es _____. No es alto.

6. Ella no es muy seria. Es bastante _____.

7. Carlos es un _____ muy bueno en matemáticas.

8. La clase de español no es pequeña. Es _____.

9. Rosa no es antipática. Es _____.

10. La señora Ortiz es una _____ de español.

3 **Escoge.** Choose the correct answer.

11. ¿Quién es?

   a. Carlos   **b.** la clase   **c.** grande

12. ¿Cómo es él?

   a. mexicano   **b.** José   **c.** alto

13. ¿De dónde es?

   a. Puerto Rico   **b.** la escuela   **c.** sincero

14. ¿Quiénes son?

   a. los cursos   **b.** José   **c.** José y Tomás

Gramática

 To review **artículos y sustantivos,** turn to page 30.

4 **Escoge.** Choose.

15. _____ muchacho es de Guatemala.

   a. El   **b.** Los   **c.** La

16. Carlos es _____ amigo sincero.

   a. una   **b.** un   **c.** unos

17. _____ escuelas son grandes.

   a. Unas   **b.** Una   **c.** La

18. _____ cursos son fáciles.

   a. El   **b.** Las   **c.** Los

5 **Completa.** Complete with the correct form of the adjective.

19. La amiga de Enrique es _____. (rubio)

20. Los cursos son _____. (difícil)

21. La clase es _____. (aburrido)

22–23. Los alumnos son _____ y _____. (inteligente, bueno)

24. Paco y Anita son _____. (ambicioso)

25. Las profesoras son muy _____. (simpático)

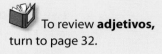 To review **adjetivos,** turn to page 32.

6 **Completa con ser.** Complete with the correct form of **ser.**

26. ¡Hola! Yo _____ Teresa.

27. ¿De qué nacionalidad _____ tú?

28. Nosotros _____ amigos.

29. ¿_____ ustedes alumnos en la misma escuela?

30. Él _____ un alumno muy bueno.

31. Los cursos _____ interesantes.

32. ¿_____ usted argentino?

33. Las escuelas _____ grandes.

34. Ella _____ una alumna nueva.

To review **ser,** turn to pages 34–35.

To review **tú** vs. **usted** (Activity 7), turn to page 35.

To review this cultural information (Activity 8), turn to pages 42–43.

7 **Forma una pregunta.** Make up a question asking each person where he or she is from.

35. Carlos   **36.** Señora Álvarez

Cultura

8 **¿Sí o no?**

37. Hay muchos cubanoamericanos en Miami, en la Florida.

38. Los cubanoamericanos son el grupo número uno de hispanohablantes en Estados Unidos.

39. Para los mexicanoamericanos en Estados Unidos, el español es una lengua extranjera.

40. El español es una lengua importante en Estados Unidos.

CULTURA

La calle Ocho es una calle importante en la Pequeña Habana en Miami.

Prepárate para el examen
Practice for oral proficiency

1 Un amigo nuevo
Describe a friend

Work with a partner. Look at this photograph of your new friend, Sergio Díaz, who is from Puerto Rico. Tell as much as you can about Sergio. Then ask each other questions about him.

2 La escuela y los cursos
Talk about school and subjects you take

Work with a partner. One of you will be Isabel Cortés, a student from Guatemala. She does not know much about schools in the United States and she has questions about your classes and teachers. Answer her questions.

3 Un alumno nuevo
Talk about yourself and get information about someone else

It's difficult to be a new student in a new school—even more difficult when you are in a new country. Take turns with a partner. Practice "breaking the ice." One of you will be Miguel Ramos, a new student from Nicaragua. Tell him about yourself and ask him things you want to know about him.

4 Personas interesantes
Describe people

Bring in a photograph of several people. It can be a family photograph or a picture from a magazine. Give each person in the photograph a name. Say as much as you can about the people in the photograph.

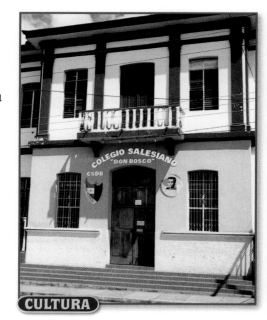

CULTURA

Un colegio, o una escuela secundaria, en Masaya, Nicaragua

Prepárate para el examen
Practice for written proficiency

Tarea

Picture two of your best friends—a boy and a girl. Write a description of each of them. Include some things about them that are the same and other things that are different.

Writing Strategy

Describing Grab any popular novel and you will find colorful, detailed descriptions. Why? A good description brings a simple noun to life. Would you prefer to meet **una persona** or **una persona interesante?** The more adjectives you use to describe a person, the more interesting the portrait of that person is.

❶ Prewrite

There may be things you want to say about your friends, but you can't because you have not yet learned how to say them. When writing in Spanish, stick to what you know. Here is a suggestion to help you do that.

- Make a chart similar to the one below. Think of all the adjectives you have learned and put them in the appropriate categories in your chart.

	physical appearance	personality	background
boy			
girl			

❷ Write

- Describe each friend in a separate paragraph. From your chart, pick out the adjectives you need for that person.

- Begin each paragraph with a good introductory sentence. Be sure your introductory sentence identifies the person you are going to describe. A good example might be, **Anita es una amiga muy buena.**

- Be sure each paragraph has a logical order. Ask yourself if the paragraph describes the physical characteristics of your friend first and then his or her personality traits.

- Proofread your work and correct any errors. Check the endings of words you used to describe each person.

- Give your composition a title.

- You may wish to share your work with a classmate to have him or her edit your composition.

Evaluate

Don't forget that your teacher will evaluate you on your ability to bring your friends to life through vivid description, correctness of grammar, sentence structure, and the completeness of your message.

Repaso del Capítulo 1

Gramática

- ### Artículos y sustantivos *(page 30)*
  Nouns in Spanish are either masculine or feminine. The definite and indefinite articles that modify a noun must agree with the noun in gender and in number.

el amigo	**los amigos**
un amigo	**unos amigos**
la clase	**las clases**
una clase	**unas clases**

- ### Adjetivos *(page 32)*
  An adjective must also agree with the noun it describes or modifies.

El amigo es simpático.	**Los amigos son simpáticos.**
La muchacha es seria.	**Las muchachas son serias.**
La escuela es grande.	**Las escuelas son grandes.**
El curso es difícil.	**Los cursos son difíciles.**

- ### Ser *(pages 34–35)*
  Review the forms of the verb **ser** *(to be)*.

singular		plural	
yo	**soy**	**nosotros(as)**	**somos**
tú	**eres**	*vosotros(as)*	*sois*
Ud., él, ella	**es**	**Uds., ellos, ellas**	**son**

- ### Tú vs. usted *(page 35)*
  Remember that there is more than one way to express *you* in Spanish.

  Tomás, (tú) eres un amigo bueno.
  Señora Cortés, (usted) es una profesora buena.

CULTURA

Es una escuela o instituto secundario en Punta Arenas en el sur de Chile.

Vocabulario

Identifying a person or thing

el muchacho	el amigo	la escuela	el profesor
la muchacha	la amiga	la clase	la profesora
el joven	el alumno	el curso	
la joven	la alumna		

Describing a person

guapo(a)	pelirrojo(a)	cómico(a)	simpático(a)
bonito(a)	alto(a)	gracioso(a)	antipático(a)
feo(a)	bajo(a)	serio(a)	inteligente
moreno(a)	bueno(a)	ambicioso(a)	joven
rubio(a)	malo(a)	perezoso(a)	

Finding out information

¿quién?	¿cómo?	¿de qué
¿quiénes?	¿de dónde?	nacionalidad?

Identifying nationalities

argentino(a)	cubano(a)	guatemalteco(a)	peruano(a)
chileno(a)	dominicano(a)	mexicano(a)	puertorriqueño(a)
colombiano(a)	ecuatoriano(a)	norteamericano(a)	venezolano(a)

Describing classes and courses

grande	interesante	difícil, duro(a)
pequeño(a)	aburrido(a)	fácil

Identifying school subjects

el español	la ciencia	las matemáticas	la educación física
el francés	los estudios sociales	la música	
el inglés	la historia	el arte	

Other useful words and expressions

secundario(a)	también	pero
nuevo(a)	bastante	¡Mucho gusto!
mismo(a)	muy	¡Oye!

Repaso cumulativo

Repasa lo que ya has aprendido

These activities will help you review
what you have learned so far in Spanish.

Unos amigos puertorriqueños

 Escucha y escoge. Listen to each expression. On a
separate sheet of paper, indicate whether you use the
expression when you greet someone **(saludos)** or when
you take leave of someone **(despedidas).**

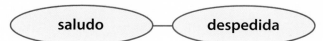

saludo — despedida

 Completa. Make a calendar like the one below. Fill it in
with the current month. Include numbers and days of the
week. Remember which day is the first day of the week on
a Spanish calendar.

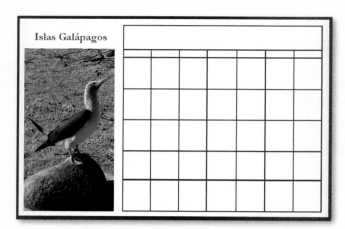

Islas Galápagos

 ¿Qué hora es? Tell what time it is on each clock.

1.

2.

3.

4.

5.

6.

4 Personaliza. Answer giving information about your school day.

    1. ¿A qué hora es la clase de español?

    2. ¿A qué hora es la clase de matemáticas?

    3. ¿A qué hora es la primera clase?

 5 Contesta. Answer.

    1. ¿Qué tiempo hace hoy?

    2. ¿Qué estación es?

 6 Contesta. Answer.

Give the expressions you know in Spanish to be polite.

7 Personaliza. Answer about yourself.

¿Quién eres?

¿De dónde eres?

¿De qué nacionalidad eres?

¿Cómo eres?

¿En qué escuela eres alumno(a)?

¿Qué tipo de alumno(a) eres?

 8 Rompecabezas

 ¿Quién es el/la culpable? Look at the following people. Read the clues to find out who is to blame for stealing the pie.

Es pelirroja. Es baja. Es seria. ¿Quién es?

Rosa   Eugenio   Roberto   Reina

La familia y la casa

Aquí y Allí

Vamos a comparar In both Spain and Latin America, families were often quite large. However, family size is decreasing. Do you think families are also becoming smaller in the United States? The extended family, including aunts, uncles, cousins, second cousins, etc., is very important in the Spanish-speaking world. Do you think the same is true in the United States?

Objetivos

You will:

- talk about families and pets
- describe a house or apartment
- describe rooms and some furnishings
- discuss a family from Ecuador

You will use:

- the verb **tener**
- possessive adjectives

◀ **Una familia de Santo Domingo, la capital de la República Dominicana**

Go to glencoe.com
For: **Online book**
Web code: **ASD4003c2**

Introducción al tema
La familia y la casa

Look at these photographs to acquaint yourself with the theme of the chapter. You will learn to describe your family and home, as well as families and homes in Spanish-speaking countries. What do you notice about the families and homes seen here? Do any look like your own? How are they similar? How are they different?

▲ **España** Las casas típicas de Guipúzcoa en el norte tienen balcones. En cada balcón hay flores bonitas.

República Dominicana ▶
Una familia dominicana durante una fiesta familiar—abuelos, tíos, padres, primos y nietos

◀ **Argentina** Una casa en una zona residencial de Buenos Aires, Argentina

Costa Rica Es una casa en San José, Costa Rica. Como muchas casas en Latinoamérica tiene un patio bonito en el centro. ▶

◀ **Panamá** Son casas típicas de los indígenas en las zonas tropicales de muchos países latinoamericanos. Son casas sobre pilotes con techos de paja.

México Una familia mexicana en la sala de su casa en Guadalajara, México ▼

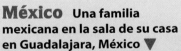

▲ **México** Una casa lujosa en una zona residencial de la Ciudad de México

La familia

¡Hola! Soy Daniela López. Yo tengo una mascota cariñosa. Su nombre es Rayas. Tengo muchos parientes.

mi gatito Rayas

mis abuelos

mi abuelo Juan López

mi abuela Ana López

mis padres

mi padre Pedro

mi madre Alicia

mis tíos

mi tía Laura

mi tío Alberto

mis hermanos

mi hermano David

mi hermano Julio

nuestro perro Duque

mi primo Emilio

No tengo hermanos. Soy hijo único.

¡Ojo!

Pariente is a false cognate. It looks like *parent* but it means *relative*. We call a false cognate **un amigo falso.**

Mi tía Laura es la hermana de mi padre. Su hijo Emilio es mi primo y yo soy la sobrina de mi tía.

¡Hola! Soy Emilio Martínez. Mis abuelos son Juan y Ana López. Yo soy su nieto.

Para conversar

¿Cuántos años tienen tus hermanos?

Los dos tienen diez años. Son gemelos.

Nota

You may have a stepparent or stepbrother or sister. You can say:

mi padrastro el marido (el esposo) de mi madre

mi madrastra la mujer (la esposa) de mi padre

mi hermanastro el hijo del esposo de mi madre o de la esposa de mi padre

mi hermanastra la hija del esposo de mi madre o de la esposa de mi padre

el pelo castaño

el pelo rubio

el pelo negro

los ojos azules

los ojos verdes

los ojos castaños

LA FAMILIA Y LA CASA

cincuenta y nueve **59**

QuickPass

Go to glencoe.com
For: **Vocabulary practice**
Web code: **ASD4003c2**

ESCUCHAR

1 **Escucha y escoge.** Listen to the statements. Decide if each statement is correct or not. Make a chart like the one below to indicate your answers.

correcto	incorrecto

How many did you get right?

8/8	¡Estupendo!
7/8	¡Excelente!
6/8	¡Muy bien!
5/8	¡Bien!
0–4/8	No muy bien. ☹

CULTURA

Una familia latina en Estados Unidos

Nota

The suffix **-ito** as in **gatito** can convey the meaning *small*. It can also express affection. Children often address their grandparents as **abuelito** and **abuelita.** Parents often say **mi hijito(a)** when speaking to their children.

LEER • ESCRIBIR

2 **Personaliza.** Answer about yourself. Pay attention to the gender.

1. ¿Eres el hijo o la hija de tu madre?
   Soy _____ de mi madre.
2. ¿Eres el sobrino o la sobrina de tu tía?
   Soy _____ de mi tía.
3. ¿Eres el nieto o la nieta de tus abuelos?
   Soy _____ de mis abuelos.
4. ¿Eres el primo o la prima de los hijos de tu tío?
   Soy _____ de los hijos de mi tío.

LEER

3 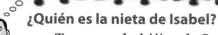 **Rompecabezas**

¿Quién es la nieta de Isabel?

Teresa es la hijita de Isabel.
Juana es la hermana de Teresa.
Sofía es la hermana de Paco.
Teresa es la madre de Paco.

Pista (*Hint*) Draw a diagram of the relationships to help discover the answer.

ESCUCHAR • HABLAR • ESCRIBIR

4 **Contesta.** Answer the questions to tell a story about Felipe and Emilia using the information given.

1. ¿Es Felipe un hijo único? (no)
2. ¿Qué tiene Felipe? (una hermana, Emilia)
3. ¿Son hermanos Felipe y Emilia? (sí)
4. ¿Cuántos años tiene Felipe? (catorce)
5. ¿Cuántos años tiene Emilia? (dieciséis)
6. ¿Quién es menor? (Felipe)
7. ¿Quién es mayor? (Emilia)
8. ¿Tienen Felipe y Emilia una mascota cariñosa? (sí)
9. ¿Qué tienen? ¿Un perro o un gato? (un perro)
10. ¿Cuál es su nombre? (Roco)

InfoGap For more practice using your new vocabulary, do Activity 2 on page SR4 at the end of this book.

EXPANSIÓN

Now, without looking at the questions, tell your partner all you remember about Felipe and Emilia. Then your partner will add any information you forgot.

 Comunicación

 5 Work in small groups and tell who in your Spanish class has the following.

ojos azules	**ojos castaños**	**ojos verdes**
el pelo negro	**el pelo castaño**	**el pelo rubio**
el pelo rojo		

LEER • ESCRIBIR

6 **Personaliza.** Complete to tell all about yourself.

¡Hola! Yo soy __1__. Tengo __2__ años. Soy bastante __3__. No soy muy __4__. Tengo el pelo __5__ y tengo ojos __6__.

HABLAR

7 **¡Manos a la obra!** Using pictures from a magazine, pick who you want your ideal family to be. Make a collage of your family and introduce the members to your classmates, indicating what relationship each of these people is to you.

CULTURA

La familia Suárez es de Arica, Chile. Los señores tienen dos hijos.

La casa

un árbol

un carro

el jardín

una flor

La familia Benavides tiene una casa privada
en las afueras (los suburbios).
Hay un jardín delante de su casa.
Los Benavides tienen un carro nuevo. No es viejo.
Hay una bicicleta detrás del carro.

¡Ojo!

Note that the word **cada** does not change.
cada casa
cada apartamento

un edificio alto

una casa de apartamentos

un apartamento

un piso

La familia Solís tiene un apartamento en la ciudad.
Los Solís tienen un apartamento en un edificio alto.
Cada piso del edificio tiene seis apartamentos.

Los cuartos y los muebles

la cocina

el comedor

una mesa   una silla

la sala

una lámpara

un sofá

una mesita

el cuarto de baño

el cuarto de dormir, la recámara

la cama

¡Así se dice!

- The expression **hay** means *there is* or *there are*.
  Hay un garaje al lado de (*next to*) **la casa.**
  Hay árboles alrededor de (*around*) **la casa.**
- Whenever **de** is followed by **el**, it becomes one word, **del.**
  delante del árbol
  detrás del sofá

En otras partes

- The word **el carro** is used in almost all areas of Latin America. In Spain, **el coche** is used.
- The word **piso** means *floor.* In Spain, **el piso** can also mean *apartment.* Other common terms for *apartment* are **un departamento** and **un apartamiento.**
- **La recámara** is used in Mexico as well as in some other countries of Central and South America. Other commonly used terms in many areas are **el dormitorio, la alcoba, la habitación,** and **la pieza.** Ask Spanish speakers in your class what words they use to express these items.

QuickPass

Go to glencoe.com
For: **Vocabulary practice**
Web code: **ASD4003c2**

ESCUCHAR

1 **Indica.** Decide if the statements you hear are true or false. Make a chart like the one below to indicate your answers.

verdad	falso

HABLAR • ESCRIBIR

2 **Identifica.** Identify each item. Use **el** or **la.**

1.

2.

3.

4.

5.

6.

ESCRIBIR

3 Rompecabezas

Change one letter in each word to form a new word.

cama   el   madre

un   su

Más práctica

📙 Workbook, pp. 2.5–2.6
💿 StudentWorks™ Plus

HABLAR • ESCRIBIR

4 **Contesta.** Based on the layout, answer the questions about the Perez family's apartment. •••••••••••

1. ¿Tienen los Pérez un apartamento?
2. ¿Tiene un balcón su apartamento?
3. ¿Es grande o pequeño el apartamento?
4. ¿Cuántos cuartos tiene?
5. ¿Qué cuartos tiene?

EXPANSIÓN

Now, without looking at the questions, tell all you remember about the home of the Perez family. Your partner will fill in any information you forgot.

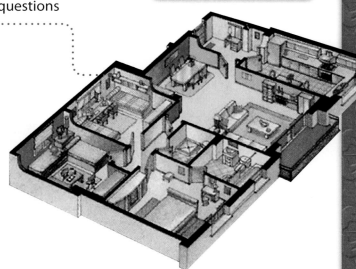

LEER • ESCRIBIR

5 **Completa según el dibujo.** •••••••••••
Complete according to the illustration.

1. Hay _____ delante de la casa.
2. Hay _____ detrás de la casa.
3. Hay _____ al lado de la casa.
4. Hay _____ al lado del árbol.
5. Hay _____ detrás del carro.
6. Hay _____ al lado del sofá.

HABLAR

6 **uego** Draw any part of a house, inside or outside, with a tiny cat for your partner to find. When your partner discovers the cat's hiding place, he or she exclaims, for example, **¡Hay un gato detrás del sofá en la sala!** Then reverse roles.

Comunicación

7 Think of a family you know. Tell as much as you can about them—members of the family, what they look like, their house or apartment, and their pets if they have any. Answer any questions your partner may have.

QuickPass

Go to glencoe.com
For: **Grammar practice**
Web code: **ASD4003c2**

El verbo tener

1. You will use the verb **tener** *(to have)* a great deal as you speak Spanish. Study the forms of this verb.

tener			
yo	tengo	nosotros(as)	tenemos
tú	tienes	*vosotros(as)*	*tenéis*
Ud., él, ella	tiene	Uds., ellos, ellas	tienen

2. You use the verb **tener** to express age (**la edad**).

¿Cuántos años tienes?
Yo tengo catorce años.
Mi hermana menor tiene once años.

Práctica

HABLAR • ESCRIBIR

1 **Contesta.** Use the photos to tell what Antonio has and what the Ayerbes have.

Antonio

los Ayerbe

ESCUCHAR • HABLAR

2 **Conversa. Practica la conversación.** Practice the conversation with a classmate. Take turns playing each role. Pay attention to the changes in the forms of **tener.**

—Pepe, ¿**tienes** hermanos?
—Sí, **tengo** dos—un hermano y una hermana.
—¿Cuántos años **tiene** tu hermana?
—Mi hermana **tiene** diez años y mi hermano **tiene** dieciséis.
—Y tú, ¿cuántos años **tienes?**
—**Tengo** dieciséis años también. Mi hermano y yo somos gemelos.

EXPANSIÓN

Now, without looking at the conversation, tell all you remember about Pepe. Your partner will add anything you forgot.

HABLAR • ESCRIBIR

3 **Personaliza.** Answer about yourself.
1. ¿Tienes una familia grande o pequeña?
2. ¿Eres hijo(a) único(a) o tienes hermanos?
3. ¿Cuántos hermanos tienes?
4. Y tú, ¿cuántos años tienes?
5. ¿Tienes ojos azules, verdes o castaños?
6. ¿Tienes una mascota?
7. ¿Tienes un perro adorable?
8. ¿Tienes un gato cariñoso?

CULTURA

Son las mascotas de una familia en Guadalajara, México. Los perros son grandes, ¿no?

4 **Rompecabezas**

Complete the sentences with the correct form of **tener** and then solve the puzzle. **¿Cuántos años tiene Alberto?**

Yo ___1___ una familia grande. Yo ___2___ dieciséis años. Mi hermana Reina ___3___ veintidós años. Los gemelos ___4___ catorce años. Susana ___5___ diez años y mi hermano Roberto ___6___ siete años. Si el total de los años de todos los hijos es ciento, ¿cuántos años tiene mi hermano Alberto?

VIDEO To visit a family birthday party, watch **Diálogo en vivo.**

HABLAR

5 **Conversa.** Work in groups of four.

Use the diagram below to make up short conversations to find out what your friends have. Use the model as your guide.

MODELO   **muchos o pocos hermanos** →
—¿Tienen ustedes muchos o pocos hermanos?
—Tenemos muchos (pocos) hermanos.

ESCRIBIR

6 **Escribe un e-mail.** You have a key pal in the Canary Islands in Spain. Write your key pal an e-mail telling as much as you can about your family and yourself. Ask your key pal questions about his or her family.

Una plaza en Tenerife en las islas Canarias, España

LEER • ESCRIBIR

7 **Completa con tener.** Complete with **tener.** You will now have to use all forms of the verb.

CULTURA

Una familia en el jardín delante de su casa en un suburbio de Caracas, Venezuela

Aquí __1__ (nosotros) una fotografía de la familia Sánchez. La familia Sánchez __2__ una casa bonita en Caracas, Venezuela. Su casa __3__ siete cuartos. Los Sánchez __4__ dos hijos—Guadalupe y Daniel.

Guadalupe: ¡Hola! Soy Guadalupe Sánchez. Yo __5__ dieciséis años y mi hermano Daniel __6__ catorce. Nosotros __7__ mascotas, dos perros cariñosos.

Daniel: ¡Hola, amigo! Y tú, ¿cuántos años __8__? ¿__9__ hermanos? ¿Cuántos hermanos __10__ (tú)? ¿__11__ ustedes una mascota también? ¿Qué __12__? ¿Un perro o un gato?

HABLAR • ESCRIBIR

8 **¡Te toca a ti!** Using words from each of the boxes below, make up complete sentences telling what these people or places have or don't have.

Nosotros		dos pisos
Tú		un gato
Yo		un hijo único
Daniela	tener	quince años
La casa	no tener	pelo rubio
El jardín		ojos castaños
Mis primos		un garaje
Mi tía		dos mascotas
		plantas y árboles
		un carro nuevo

Conexiones

La genética

Todos nosotros tenemos genes de nuestros padres. Los genes determinan, por ejemplo, el color de nuestros ojos, de nuestro pelo y otras características físicas. Los factores genéticos son muy importantes en cada individuo.

Los adjetivos posesivos

1. A possessive adjective tells who owns or possesses something—*my* book and *your* pencil. Observe the possessive adjectives in Spanish. Note that, like other adjectives in Spanish, they agree with the noun they modify.

yo	**mi** padre	**mi** prima	**mis** padres	**mis** primas
tú	**tu** padre	**tu** prima	**tus** padres	**tus** primas

él
ella
ellos
ellas
usted
ustedes
} **su** padre   **su** prima   **sus** padres   **sus** primas

Es mi padre.   **Es tu padre.**   **Es su padre.**

2. The possessive adjectives **mi, tu,** and **su** have only two forms—singular and plural. As you can see from the examples above, **su** and **sus** can refer to many different people.

el perro de él	su perro
el perro de ella	su perro
el perro de usted	su perro
el perro de ellos	su perro
el perro de ustedes	su perro

3. The possessive adjective **nuestro** (and **vuestro**), like other adjectives that end in **-o,** has four forms.

nosotros(as) →

nuestro padre
nuestra prima
nuestros padres
nuestras primas

CULTURA

Elena y su hermano en casa en Buenos Aires

Práctica

 Personaliza. Answer about yourself.

1. ¿Es grande o pequeña tu familia?
2. ¿Cuántos años tiene tu hermano o tu hermana?
3. ¿Tiene tu familia un carro?
4. ¿Quién es tu profesor(a) de español?
5. ¿Es fácil o difícil tu curso de español?

 Personaliza. Work with a partner. Think of as many relatives as you can. Make up conversations as in the models and give personal answers.

MODELOS una prima →
—Yo tengo una prima.
—¿Ah, sí? ¿Quién es tu prima?
—Mi prima es _____.

dos primos →
—Yo tengo dos primos.
—¿Ah, sí? ¿Quiénes son tus primos?
—Mis primos son _____ y _____.

 Contesta según el modelo.
Answer according to the model.

MODELO el carro del señor González / nuevo →
—¿Es el carro del señor González?
—Sí, es su carro. Su carro es nuevo.

1. el hermano de Paco / inteligente
2. las hermanas de Eduardo / gemelas
3. los amigos de Mari / alumnos en la misma escuela
4. el perro de ellos / cariñoso
5. la casa de los Gómez / bonita

CULTURA
Unas amigas de la misma escuela en Puebla, México

FOLDABLES®
Study Organizer

MINIBOOK

See page SH28 for help with making this foldable. Practice vocabulary pertaining to the family and house. On the left, draw your family members and your house or apartment. On the right, describe what you have drawn. Share your Minibook with a partner and ask each other questions about it.

HABLAR • ESCRIBIR

12 **Personaliza.** Answer about your school and classes. Be careful to use the correct possessive adjectives in your answers.

1. ¿Es nueva o vieja la escuela de ustedes?
2. Su clase de español, ¿es grande o pequeña?
3. ¿Cuántos alumnos hay en su clase de español?
4. En general, ¿son grandes o pequeñas las clases en su escuela?
5. ¿Son interesantes sus cursos? ¿Cuáles son interesantes?

Comunicación

13 Get together with a classmate. Talk to him or her about some things that you have, he or she has, or some friends have. Use the verb **tener** and possessive adjectives. You may want to use words from the **banco de palabras.**

casa	apartamento	perro	gato
mascota	carro	amigos	pelo (color)
jardín	hermanos	bicicleta	ojos (color)

HABLAR • ESCRIBIR

14 **Juego** These words are all mixed up! Can you rearrange them to make sentences?

1. seis hermano **años** su tiene
2. **lámpara** al lado de **una** hay **cama** mi
3. **profesores** **de** **son** **dónde** nuestros
4. grande tiene **mi** cocina casa **una**
5. **son** **flores** bonitas **sus** **muy**
6. **perezoso** **padres** **gato** **un** tienen tus

15  **Rompecabezas**

Paco is related to Juana. Read what he says below about Juana. Figure out how Paco and Juana are related. After you solve this riddle, make up others to present to the class.

Su tía es la hija de nuestros abuelos. Mi tío es su padre.

CULTURA

Unos hermanos panameños

Las consonantes f, l, m, n, p

The pronunciation of the consonants **f, l, m, n,** and **p** is very similar in both Spanish and English. The **p,** however, is not followed by a puff of air as it often is in English. Repeat the following.

f	l	m	n	p
favor	la	mucho	no	Pepe
familia	Lola	menor	alumna	padre
fácil	Lupe	madre	nieto	piso
famoso	alumno	cómico	nuevo	Perú
sofá	abuela	amigo	sobrino	guapo

 Dictado

Pronounce the following sentences carefully. Then write them to prepare for a dictation.

> La familia de Felipe es francesa.
> Mi hermano menor es Fernando.
> Mis abuelos tienen un nieto nuevo.
> El apartamento de Pepe tiene dos pisos.
> Pepita es una peruana popular.
> Mi mascota Mona es mala.
> Perú es un país fabuloso.

Refrán

Can you guess what the following proverb means?

El mejor amigo, un perro.

¡Bravo!

You have now learned all the new vocabulary and grammar in this chapter. Continue to use and practice all that you know while learning more cultural information. ¡Vamos!

CULTURA

Plaza de Armas, Trujillo, Perú

¿Comprendes?

A Contesta. Answer based on the conversation.

1. ¿Tiene hermanos Federico?
2. ¿Cuántos tiene?
3. ¿Quién es una hermana de Federico?
4. ¿Es su hermana menor o mayor?
5. ¿Tiene muchas preguntas José?

B Completa. Complete the summary of the conversation between José and Federico.

Federico __1__ tres hermanos. __2__ familia es bastante grande. La hermana __3__ de Federico es Laura. Ella es __4__ amiga de Maricarmen. Son amigas __5__.

C Cuenta. In your own words give as much information as you can about each of the following people.

Federico	José	Laura	Maricarmen

D Dando opiniones Give an opinion.

¿Tiene José mucho interés en la hermana de Federico?
¿Cómo indica que tiene mucho interés o no?

Antes de leer

Skim the reading to see if there are any words that are unfamiliar to you.

Durante la lectura

As you read, look for the information around any unfamiliar word. It will help give you the meaning of the word.

✓ Reading Check

¿Cuántas personas hay en la familia Morales?

✓ Reading Check

¿Dónde tiene la familia Morales una casa privada?

Despúes de leer

Were you able to guess the meaning of any unfamiliar words using context clues? Which ones?

Una familia ecuatoriana

La familia Morales La familia Morales no es muy grande y no es muy pequeña. Es mediana. Los señores Morales tienen tres hijos—Jorge, Mari y Francisco. Jorge, el menor, tiene diez años. Mari tiene quince años y Francisco, el mayor, tiene diecisiete. Mari y Francisco son alumnos en un colegio en Quito, la capital de Ecuador. Pero no son alumnos en el mismo colegio. No van a un colegio mixto. Mari es alumna en un colegio para muchachas y Francisco es alumno en un colegio para muchachos. En Latinoamérica un colegio no es una universidad. Es una escuela secundaria.

La casa de los Morales Los Morales tienen una casa privada en un barrio residencial de Quito en las montañas, los Andes. En su barrio, hay casas privadas y edificios altos con condominios. Los edificios altos son muy modernos. Muchos tienen balcones con flores bonitas y de los balcones hay vistas fabulosas de la ciudad de Quito, de los picos andinos y del volcán Pichincha. La casa de los Morales tiene siete cuartos y detrás de la casa hay un jardín bonito con muchas plantas y flores. Alrededor de su casa hay un muro.

Una vista panorámica de Quito, Ecuador

CULTURA

¿Comprendes?

Más práctica

■ Workbook, pp. 2.10–2.12
● StudentWorks™ Plus

A **Recordando hechos** Answer the questions to see how much you remember about the Morales family from the story.

1. ¿Es grande la familia Morales?
2. ¿Cuántos hijos tienen los señores Morales?
3. ¿Cuántos años tiene el hijo menor?
4. ¿Cuántos años tiene el hijo mayor?
5. ¿Cuántos años tiene Mari?

B **Confirmando información**
Correct all the wrong information.

1. Los Morales son de un barrio residencial en la costa del Pacífico.
2. Muchos condominios en los edificios altos tienen jardines con flores bonitas.
3. Los Morales tienen un condominio.

C **Aumentando tu vocabulario** Match each word with its definition.

1. un colegio
2. fabuloso
3. andino
4. un suburbio
5. un pico
6. una casa privada
7. un balcón
8. los Andes

a. una casa de una sola familia
b. un tipo de terraza
c. un tipo de escuela
d. una zona residencial
e. muy bueno, extraordinario
f. montañas de Sudamérica
g. de los Andes
h. parte superior de una montaña

CULTURA

Un edificio de departamentos en el centro de Quito, Ecuador

D **Describiendo** Give as much information as you can about the following.

los miembros de la familia Morales	la casa de los Morales	la ciudad de Quito

Mascotas 🎧♻

Antes de leer

Think about the pets that people have. Are some rather exotic? Do you think people in different parts of the world may have different pets?

Cultura

Aquí tenemos un sato adorable. El sato es un perro especial de Puerto Rico. Los satos son muy cariñosos. No son todos del mismo color. Y no son todos del mismo tamaño. Unos son pequeños y otros son medianos. Pero no son grandes. Un sato puertorriqueño es un amigo sincero.

🌐 GeoVistas

To learn more about Peru, take a tour on pages SH56–SH57.

¿Tienes una mascota? Aquí en Estados Unidos, muchas familias tienen mascota, ¿no? En España y en Latinoamérica muchas tienen su mascota también. Como aquí, la mascota favorita es un perro o un gato. Los perros y los gatos son unos amigos buenos y sinceros.

En España y en Latinoamérica hay una cosa interesante. Hay unas excepciones pero en general las mascotas son populares en las ciudades y en los suburbios pero no en las zonas rurales. En las zonas rurales o en el campo, la gente no tiene un animal como un perro o un gato en casa.

Mascotas exóticas Hay también mascotas exóticas. Jorge es de Pisac en los Andes de Perú. Él tiene como mascota una llama. En Perú, Ecuador y Bolivia las llamas son domesticadas. Pero, ¡atención! Las llamas no tienen mucha paciencia y a veces son un poco desagradables, pero no peligrosas[1].

Andrea es de una zona tropical en Guatemala. Ella tiene un loro[2]. Su loro es bastante pequeño pero hay loros que son muy grandes. Los loros tienen muchos colores bonitos.

[1]peligrosas *dangerous*   [2]loro *parrot*

CULTURA

Los niños son de los Andes en Perú. Como Jorge en Pisac y Andrea en Guatemala ellos también tienen mascotas exóticas—un loro y una alpaca.

¿Comprendes?

Escoge. Select the correct answer or completion.

1. Muchas familias tienen una mascota porque _____.
   a. son de Estados Unidos, España o Latinoamérica
   b. las mascotas son amigos buenos
   c. las mascotas son animales

2. En España y en Latinoamérica, las mascotas son populares _____.
   a. en general
   b. en las zonas rurales
   c. en las zonas urbanas

3. ¿Por qué son desagradables a veces las llamas?
   a. Son domesticadas.
   b. Son peligrosas.
   c. No tienen mucha paciencia.

4. Un loro es _____ que tiene muchos colores bonitos.
   a. un perro
   b. un gato
   c. un pájaro

Conexiones

Las ciencias

¿Tienes interés en los animales exóticos? ¿Sí? Pues, las islas Galápagos en el océano Pacífico al oeste de Ecuador son para ti. En las islas Galápagos hay todo tipo de animales marinos y reptiles raros. Y no hay depredadores.

Una tortuga de las islas Galápagos

Vocabulario

1 **Completa.** Complete.

1. Mis padres tienen dos hijos. Yo soy Eduardo y mi _____ es Anita.

2–3. Yo soy el _____ de mis padres y Anita es su _____.

4. Mi padre tiene una hermana. Es mi _____ Isabel.

5. El _____ de Isabel es mi tío Enrique.

6. Tienen tres _____: Carlos, Susana y Teresa.

7. Sus hijos son mis _____.

8. Carlos tiene diez años y Susana y Teresa tienen quince. Las dos hermanas son _____.

9–10. Los padres de mis padres son mis _____ y yo soy su _____.

11. Mi hermana Anita es también su _____.

12. La esposa de mi abuelo es mi _____.

13. Nosotros somos todos _____ de la misma familia.

14–15. Mi primo tiene _____ castaño y _____ azules.

To review **Vocabulario 1,** turn to pages 58–59.

2 **Identifica.** Identify. Use **el** or **la**.

To review **Vocabulario 2,** turn to pages 62–63.

Gramática

3 **Contesta.** Answer.

23. ¿Cuántos años tienes?

24. ¿Cuántos hermanos tienes?

25. ¿Tienes una mascota?

To review the verb **tener,** turn to page 66.

4 **Crea una frase nueva.** Rewrite each sentence with the correct form of **tener** to agree with the new subject.

26. Elena tiene muchos primos.
Sus amigos _____.

27. Ustedes tienen un jardín bonito.
Nosotros _____.

28. Yo tengo un profesor muy bueno.
Ella también _____.

29. Ellos tienen un perro.
Ustedes _____.

30. Ella tiene dieciséis años.
Tú _____.

31. Nosotros tenemos ojos verdes.
Usted también _____.

5 **Completa.** Complete with the correct possessive adjective.

32. Nosotros tenemos un apartamento. _____ apartamento es bastante pequeño.

33. Yo tengo un hermano. _____ hermano tiene quince años.

34. Mi tío tiene hijos. _____ hijos son mis primos.

35. —Carlos y María, ¿tienen _____ padres un carro nuevo o viejo?

36. —José, ¿es de Puerto Rico _____ profesora de español?

37. Nosotros tenemos una casa en las afueras de la ciudad. Hay un muro alrededor de _____ casa.

To review **adjetivos posesivos,** turn to page 70.

Cultura

6 **Identifica.** Identify.

38. la capital de Ecuador

39. montañas altas de Sudamérica

40. un volcán cerca de Quito

To review this cultural information, turn to pages 76–77.

1 **Tu familia**

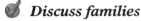 *Discuss families*

Conduct an interview with a friend. One of you will ask questions to get the following information and the other will answer. Then reverse roles.

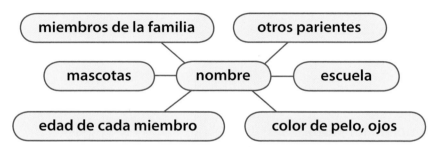

miembros de la familia

otros parientes

mascotas — nombre — escuela

edad de cada miembro

color de pelo, ojos

 2 **¿Cuál prefieres?**

Talk about housing

You are a realtor. You show your client (your partner) these two ads and describe the two properties. Your partner asks you questions about each of the dwellings.

ZONA RESIDENCIA
Piso 3 dormitorios, salón, cocina, baño nuevo.
Exterior. Reformado y amueblado.
99,165 €

ENTRADA CHICLANA
Chalet , 3 dorm, salón, cocina, baño.
87,000 €

 3 **Fotos de un álbum**

Describe families

Bring in a photo of a family from a magazine. Give them a family name. Identify the various members of the family. Then describe them.

 4 **Tu casa o apartamento**

Talk about your house or apartment

With a partner, describe your house or apartment. Ask each other questions. Compare and contrast the two homes.

Tarea

Write about your house or a house you dream of having someday—**la casa de mis sueños.**

Writing Strategy

Spatial ordering Always remember that when you write in the early stages of foreign language learning you have to "stick to" what you know how to say. Even though you may only be able to write a little, you have to give your writing some order.

One type of ordering is called "spatial ordering." This means that you will describe things as they actually appear from left to right, front to back, or top to bottom. You may wish to use spatial ordering for the topic you will now write about.

① Prewrite

Here are some suggestions to help you organize your writing.

- Draw a sketch of your dream house. Include the outside and the rooms on the inside. You will refer to this as a visual aid to organize your writing. Ask yourself, **¿Cómo es?**
- Begin to think of adjectives to describe your house. Begin with the outside. You may want to use the expressions **delante de, detrás de,** and **al lado de** with **hay.**
- Then move into your house. Make a list of the rooms. Go from room to room in a logical order. Think of words to use to describe each room. Include the furniture in each room.

Una casa en el lago Cuicocha en el norte de Ecuador

② Write

- Begin with a good introductory sentence, such as **La casa de mis sueños es...**
- Be sure your writing has a logical order. For example, do you describe the house in a logical fashion as you move through it?
- Give your composition a title.
- When you finish writing your description, proofread your work. Does it include the new vocabulary and the verbs **tener, ser, hay?** Did you use the right verb forms? Are the adjective endings correct? Did you check your spelling?
- You may wish to share your work with a classmate to have him or her edit your composition.

Evaluate

Don't forget that your teacher will evaluate you on your ability to organize your writing, to use correct grammar, and to present a vivid picture of your house that your readers will clearly understand.

Repaso del Capítulo ②

Gramática

- **El verbo tener** *(page 66)*
  Review the forms of the verb **tener**.

tener			
yo	tengo	nosotros(as)	tenemos
tú	tienes	*vosotros(as)*	*tenéis*
Ud., él, ella	tiene	Uds., ellos, ellas	tienen

- **Los adjetivos posesivos** *(page 70)*
  Review the forms of the possessive adjectives.

mi abuelo	mi abuela	mis abuelos	mis abuelas
tu abuelo	tu abuela	tus abuelos	tus abuelas
su abuelo	su abuela	sus abuelos	sus abuelas
nuestro abuelo	nuestra abuela	nuestros abuelos	nuestras abuelas

Note that **nuestro** has four forms rather than two.

Las mascotas son populares en Madrid. ¿Son grandes o pequeños los perros que tienen las señoras?

There are a number of cognates in this list. See how many you and a partner can find. Who can find the most? Compare your list with those of your classmates.

Vocabulario

Describing family members

la familia	el padrastro	el/la sobrino(a)	menor
el miembro	la madrastra	el/la gemelo(a)	mayor
los parientes	el/la hermano(a)	el nombre	cariñoso(a)
el padre	el/la hermanastro(a)	la mascota	el pelo castaño
la madre	el/la tío(a)	el/la perro(a),	(rubio, negro)
los padres	el/la primo(a)	el/la perrito(a)	los ojos castaños
el/la esposo(a)	el/la abuelo(a)	el/la gato(a),	(azules, verdes)
el marido	el/la nieto(a)	el/la gatito(a)	tener…años
la mujer	el/la hijo(a)		
	(único[a])		

Discussing housing

la casa	el jardín	los muebles	privado(a)
los cuartos	la flor	el sofá	viejo(a)
la sala	el árbol	la silla	la ciudad
el comedor	el edificio	la mesa, la mesita	las afueras
la cocina	la casa de	la lámpara	los suburbios
el cuarto de dormir,	apartamentos	la cama	
la recámara	el apartamento	el garaje	
el cuarto de baño	el piso	el carro	

Other useful words and expressions

la bicicleta	al lado de
hay	delante de
cada	detrás de
otro(a)	alrededor de

Repaso cumulativo

Repasa lo que ya has aprendido

These activities will help you review and remember what you have learned so far in Spanish.

1 **¿Sí o no?** Look at the photo below. Listen to each statement and indicate on a separate sheet of paper whether or not it describes the photo.

2 **Completa con ser o tener.** Complete with **ser** or **tener.**

1. ¡Hola! Yo _____ Emilia Castro. _____ quince años y _____ alumna en una escuela secundaria de Miami.

2. Mi hermano _____ alumno en la misma escuela que yo. Pero él _____ menor que yo. Él _____ trece años.

3. Mi hermano y yo _____ buenos amigos. _____ alumnos en la misma escuela. Nosotros _____ una mascota. ¿_____ ustedes una mascota también? ¿Qué _____?

4. Y tú, ¿quién _____? ¿De dónde _____? ¿_____ hermanos? ¿Cuántos _____? ¿_____ ustedes alumnos en la misma escuela?

3 **Escribe en el singular.** Write the sentences in the singular. Pay attention to the adjectives and the verb forms.

1. Los alumnos son inteligentes.

2. Las clases son pequeñas.

3. Los cursos son interesantes.

4. Pero los cursos son difíciles.

5. Las casas son bonitas.

6. Los edificios son altos.

Emilia es una alumna seria.

4 **Parea la pregunta con la(s) persona(s).**
Match the question and person(s).

a. b. c.

1. ¿De dónde eres?

2. ¿De qué nacionalidad es usted?

3. ¿Tiene usted hijos?

4. ¿Cuántos hermanos tienes?

5. ¿Son ustedes amigos?

6. ¿De dónde son ustedes?

7. ¿Cuántos años tienes?

8. ¿Tienen ustedes un apartamento en la capital?

5 **Parea los contrarios.** Match the opposites.

rubio   serio   alto   difícil   cómico

delante   BUENO   diferente   bajo

detrás   moreno   menor   feo

pequeño   mismo   GRANDE

fácil   malo   guapo   mayor

6 **Personaliza.** Answer and tell all about yourself. Make a
diagram like the one below to help organize your thoughts.

¿de dónde soy? ¿quién soy?

el color de mi pelo yo el color de mis ojos

¿cómo soy? mi edad

LA FAMILIA Y LA CASA

En clase
y después

Aquí y Allí

Vamos a comparar Think about your school day. What do you do during school and after school? As you study this chapter, you'll discover some things that you have in common with students in Spanish-speaking countries and some things that are different.

Objetivos

You will:

- talk about what you do in school
- identify some school clothes and school supplies
- talk about what you and your friends do after school
- compare school and after-school activities in Spanish-speaking countries and the United States

You will use:

- present tense of **-ar** verbs
- the verbs **ir, dar,** and **estar**
- the contractions **al** and **del**

◀ Los alumnos estudian español en una escuela de lenguas en las islas Canarias. Todos tienen su carpeta. Las escuelas donde los alumnos toman cursos de español son muy populares en España y Latinoamérica.

QuickPass

Go to glencoe.com
For: **Online book**
Web code: **ASD4003c3**

Introducción al tema
En clase y después

Look at these photographs to acquaint yourself with the theme of this chapter—school life in Spain and Latin America. You will learn about what students do in school and after school. As you proceed through the chapter, think about the many things that you and the students of the Spanish-speaking world have in common.

España ▲
El colegio San José es un colegio privado en Estepona, España, en la Costa del Sol. El colegio San José es un colegio mixto para muchachos y muchachas.

◄ Costa Rica
Las muchachas van a la escuela a pie en un suburbio de San José, Costa Rica. Llevan uniforme a la escuela—una blusa y una falda.

Ecuador Los dos amigos son alumnos en la misma escuela en Manta, Ecuador. Como las muchachas en Costa Rica, ellos también llevan uniforme a la escuela—un pantalón, una camisa y un suéter. ▼

▲ México Son alumnos de un colegio en Guadalajara, México. Hoy no tienen clases porque van con su profesora a visitar unos monumentos históricos en su ciudad. Observa que los alumnos llevan sus materiales escolares en una mochila.

◄ Ecuador
Como en Estados Unidos, muchos alumnos toman un bus escolar a la escuela. Aquí tenemos un minibus escolar en El Bosque, una zona residencial de Quito, Ecuador.

▲ **Cuba** Los alumnos aquí en La Habana, Cuba, prestan mucha atención cuando su profesora habla.

▲ **Perú** Cuando los alumnos necesitan un libro que no tienen, van a una biblioteca. La biblioteca aquí está en Barranco, una zona o barrio interesante de Lima, Perú.

▲ **Colombia** Los alumnos están en el pasillo de su escuela en Barranquilla, Colombia. En su escuela no tienen que llevar uniforme.

▲ **Panamá** Los alumnos van a regresar a casa en bus. La muchacha, como muchos alumnos en los países hispanos, lleva una carpeta.

Nicaragua Es un colegio moderno en Masaya, Nicaragua. ▶

En la sala de clase

enseñar

prestar atención

estudiar

el pupitre

Los alumnos están en la sala de clase.
La profesora enseña (el) español.
Los alumnos prestan atención cuando ella habla.

¡Así se dice!

- When you want to get a friend's attention to look at something, you can say **¡Mira!**
- **¿Qué pasa?** is a good expression you can use when you want to find out what's happening or what's going on.

Tlf: **917414653**

Ministerio de
Educación y Cultura

Grupo
B1D

Alumno: Tomás García

Materias	Calificaciones
Sociedad, Cultura y Religión	No Evaluable
Educación Física	7
Lengua Castellana y Literatura	6
Filosofía	7
Inglés	10
Historia Contemporánea	5
Matemáticas	1
Latín	9
Economía	5

una nota buena

una nota mala

Tomás saca una nota buena en inglés.
Saca una nota mala en matemáticas.

levantar la mano

La profesora da un examen
(una prueba).
Los alumnos toman el examen.

Julia tiene una pregunta.
Levanta la mano.
El profesor contesta la pregunta.

una camisa

una blusa

un pantalón

una falda

Los alumnos llevan uniforme a la escuela.
Los muchachos llevan un pantalón y una camisa.
Las muchachas llevan una falda y una blusa.

Carlos lleva una mochila. ¿Qué lleva en la mochila?

los materiales escolares

una hoja de papel

un libro

una calculadora

un bolígrafo

un lápiz

un cuaderno

la mochila

¡Ojo!

- Note that **la mano** ends in **o,** but it is feminine and takes the article **la.**
- The verb **llevar** can mean *to wear* or *to carry.*

En otras partes

The most common terms for *ballpoint pen* are **el bolígrafo** and **el lapicero.** In some countries you will hear **la pluma,** but **la pluma** is more frequently a *fountain pen.* Ask Spanish speakers in your class what word they use for *pen.*

ESCUCHAR

1 **Escucha y escoge.** Match each statement you hear with the photo it describes.

a.

b.

c.

d.

e.

LEER • HABLAR

2 **Parea.** Match the items below to describe José's busy day.

1. José estudia	**a.** en un laboratorio
2. José estudia biología	**b.** una nota mala
3. José contesta	**c.** español
4. José saca	**d.** la mano
5. José lleva	**e.** un pantalón y una camisa
6. José levanta	**f.** la pregunta

HABLAR • ESCRIBIR

3 **Mira y contesta.** Look at the photo and, based on what you see, answer **sí** or **no**.

1. ¿Está en clase la profesora?
2. ¿Miran los alumnos a la profesora?
3. ¿Prestan atención los alumnos?
4. ¿Da la profesora un examen?
5. ¿Levanta una muchacha la mano?
6. ¿Llevan los alumnos uniforme a la escuela?

CULTURA

Son alumnos en una escuela en La Habana, Cuba. Prestan mucha atención, ¿no?

EXPANSIÓN

Now, without looking at the questions, tell all you remember about the classroom. Your partner will add anything you forgot.

Más práctica

Workbook, pp. 3.3–3.4
StudentWorks™ Plus

ESCUCHAR • LEER

 Escoge. Choose the correct completion.

1. Los alumnos que estudian mucho sacan (notas buenas, notas malas).
2. Los alumnos llevan (sus uniformes, sus materiales escolares) en una mochila.
3. Los alumnos (hablan, prestan atención) cuando la profesora habla.
4. (El pupitre, La silla) es un tipo de mesa.
5. Cuando un alumno tiene una pregunta, el profesor (levanta, contesta) la pregunta.

HABLAR • ESCRIBIR

 Contesta. Make up answers about this  classroom in the Dominican Republic.

1. ¿Quiénes están en la sala de clase?
2. ¿Quién enseña?
3. ¿Enseña geografía o matemáticas?
4. ¿Cuándo levanta la mano un alumno?
5. ¿Qué llevan los muchachos a la escuela?
6. ¿Qué llevan los alumnos en su mochila?

CULTURA

La profesora está delante de su clase en Santo Domingo en la República Dominicana.

 Comunicación

 Ask if your partner has a certain item in his or her backpack. Your partner will answer and show you the item if it's there. Take turns.

 Say something about one of your friends or several friends using the following words.

estudiar   sacar   llevar   tomar   hablar

 **Comparaciones**

An important difference between English and Spanish is that in English we say *after school*. In Spanish we say **después de las clases** or **después de los cursos.**

HABLAR

 Juego Put school supplies in your backpack. With eyes closed, your partner takes out one item at a time and guesses what it is. Take turns.

VIDEO To practice your new words, watch **Vocabulario en vivo.**

Después de las clases

Los alumnos regresan a casa.
Van en el bus escolar.
Van en bus porque su casa está
  lejos de la escuela.

En la tienda

José y María están en la tienda.
Compran una carpeta.
Dan el dinero a la empleada.
Pagan en la caja.
La empleada trabaja en la tienda.

Los alumnos van a casa a pie porque
  su casa está cerca de la escuela.
Primero, van a una tienda.
Necesitan materiales escolares.

Para conversar

En casa

mirar un DVD

escuchar música

hablar en su móvil

usar la computadora

navegar la red (el Internet)

enviar correos electrónicos

Andrés está en su cuarto.
Navega la red.
Busca información en el Internet.

En otras partes

La computadora is used throughout Latin America to express *computer*. **El ordenador** is used in Spain.

QuickPass

Go to glencoe.com
For: **Vocabulary practice**
Web code: **ASD4003c3**

ESCUCHAR

1 **Determina cuándo.** You will hear a series of statements. On a sheet of paper make a chart like the one below. As you listen, determine when the activities take place.

antes de las clases	durante las clases	después de las clases

Conexiones

La tecnología

Cuando navegas el Internet tienes acceso al mundo entero. Es posible buscar información sobre la historia, el arte, la música—todo. Es posible enviar correos electrónicos y conversar con amigos en todas partes del mundo.

Con tu móvil además de hablar con amigos es posible sacar fotografías y bajar *(download)* música. Las posibilidades son infinitas.

HABLAR

2 **Contesta.** Answer using a word from the **banco de palabras.**

un DVD	un correo electrónico	su móvil
información	música	el dinero

1. ¿Qué busca José cuando navega la red?
2. ¿Qué compra Elena en la tienda de videos?
3. ¿Qué da a la empleada?
4. ¿Qué escucha Teresa?
5. ¿Qué envía Carlos a un amigo?
6. ¿Qué usa Mari cuando habla con sus amigos?

LEER

3 **Escoge.** Choose the correct word to complete each sentence.

1. Jorge _____ música en su MP3.
   a. escucha   **b.** envía   **c.** mira   **d.** navega

2. Mi hermana _____ la red.
   a. estudia   **b.** levanta   **c.** navega   **d.** habla

3. Elena _____ en su móvil.
   a. trabaja   **b.** mira   **c.** busca   **d.** habla

4. Mis amigos _____ correos electrónicos.
   a. envían   **b.** escuchan   **c.** compran   **d.** regresan

5. Ellos _____ información en el Internet.
   a. hablan   **b.** buscan   **c.** van   **d.** están

6. El empleado _____ en la tienda.
   a. paga   **b.** compra   **c.** trabaja   **d.** regresa

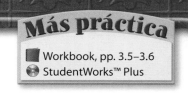
Más práctica

■ Workbook, pp. 3.5–3.6
● StudentWorks™ Plus

LEER • HABLAR • ESCRIBIR

4 **Pregunta.** Make up questions using the question words from the **banco de palabras.** The words in italics will help you figure out which question word to use.

¿Qué?	¿Cuándo?	¿Cómo?	¿Por qué?
¿Quiénes?	¿Quién?	¿Dónde?	¿Adónde?
¿Cuánto?			

1. Los alumnos van *a casa.*
2. Los amigos están *en la sala.*
3. *José* necesita una camisa nueva.
4. *Los amigos* van a una tienda.
5. Van a una tienda *después de las clases.*
6. Luis habla *muy bien* el español.
7. Luis compra *una carpeta.*
8. La carpeta cuesta *ocho pesos.*
9. Los alumnos regresan a casa a pie *porque su casa está cerca de la escuela.*

CULTURA

Las muchachas regresan a casa después de sus clases en Managua, Nicaragua.

 Comunicación

5 Get together with a classmate. He or she will take the role of a newly arrived exchange student from Nicaragua. Tell him or her what your friends typically do after school.

Después de las clases mis amigos…

LEER • HABLAR

6 **Parea.** Match the first part of each sentence with the best completion. Use **porque.**

1. Rafael va a la tienda
2. Teresa saca notas buenas
3. Enrique va a la caja
4. Él presta atención
5. Carlota levanta la mano
6. Sarita toma el bus escolar a casa

a. estudia mucho
b. el profesor habla
c. tiene una pregunta
d. necesita materiales escolares
e. tiene que pagar
f. su casa está lejos

QuickPass

Go to glencoe.com
For: **Grammar practice**
Web code: **ASD4003c3**

Presente de los verbos en -ar

1. Action words are verbs. Most verbs in Spanish belong to a family or conjugation. Verbs that have an infinitive (*to speak, to study*) that ends in **-ar (hablar, estudiar)** are called **-ar** verbs or first conjugation verbs. In this chapter you have learned the following **-ar** verbs:

> **estudiar, enseñar, levantar, contestar, hablar, tomar, mirar, escuchar, sacar, llevar, regresar, necesitar, navegar, buscar, enviar, comprar, pagar, trabajar**

2. All Spanish verbs change their endings according to the subject. Study the following forms of the verbs **hablar** and **mirar.**

infinitive	hablar		
stem	**habl-**		
yo	**hablo**	**nosotros(as)**	**hablamos**
tú	**hablas**	*vosotros(as)*	*habláis*
Ud., él, ella	**habla**	**Uds., ellos, ellas**	**hablan**

infinitive	mirar		
stem	**mir-**		
yo	**miro**	**nosotros(as)**	**miramos**
tú	**miras**	*vosotros(as)*	*miráis*
Ud., él, ella	**mira**	**Uds., ellos, ellas**	**miran**

3. Study the following.

Hablo español.

When you talk about yourself, you use the ending **-o.**

José, hablas muy bien.

When you speak to a friend, you use the ending **-as.**

Habla español.

When you talk about someone, you use the ending **-a.**

Comparaciones

El inglés

In English, it is necessary to use a subject such as *I, you, we*. However, in Spanish, you can often omit the subject because the verb ending indicates who the subject is.

Hablamos español.

Hablan español.

Hablan español.

When you speak about yourself and someone else, you use the ending **-amos**.

When you talk about two or more people, you use the ending **-an**.

When you speak to two or more people, you also use the ending **-an**.

Práctica

LEER • HABLAR • ESCRIBIR

1 **Forma frases.** Make up complete sentences by putting the words in order.

1. español / Juan / estudia
2. el mismo curso / los amigos / toman
3. en la clase de español / habla / el profesor / español
4. Anita / la red / navega / en casa
5. su música favorita / en su MP3 / escucha / Enrique
6. los amigos / miran / navegan / la red / un DVD / después de las clases / y
7. busca / Manuel / escolares / en la tienda / materiales
8. en / pagan / la caja

ESCUCHAR • HABLAR • ESCRIBIR

2 **Personaliza.** Answer about yourself.

1. ¿Estudias español?
2. ¿Hablas español en clase?
3. ¿Hablas bien?
4. ¿Usas la computadora?
5. ¿Navegas la red?
6. ¿Tomas cuatro o cinco cursos?
7. ¿Sacas notas buenas o malas?
8. ¿Llevas uniforme a la escuela?

VIDEO To visit a math class in Spain, watch **Diálogo en vivo.**

ESCUCHAR • HABLAR

3 Conversa. You didn't hear what your friend said. As in the model, ask your friend to repeat the information.

MODELO —Necesito un lápiz.
—Perdón, ¿qué necesitas?
—Un lápiz.

1. Busco mi cuaderno.
2. Necesito mi libro de español.
3. Escucho mi música favorita.
4. Necesito un bolígrafo.
5. Miro un DVD.
6. Compro una carpeta.

ESCRIBIR

4 **Juego** Compete with a partner. Copy this chart and see who can finish first with no mistakes. Correct each other's chart.

yo	tú	usted	él	nosotros	ellas
miro					
				estudiamos	
		paga			
	buscas				
					escuchan
		levanta			

Conexiones

La geografía
La geografía es el estudio de la Tierra y sus características—los océanos, las montañas, los desiertos, las junglas, etcétera. Cuando necesitas información sobre un punto geográfico, ¿navegas el Internet?

ESCUCHAR • HABLAR • ESCRIBIR

5 **Contesta.** Answer about yourself and a friend. Remember to use the **nosotros** form of the verb.

1. ¿Estudian ustedes geografía?
2. ¿Toman ustedes cuatro o cinco cursos?
3. ¿Navegan ustedes la red?
4. ¿Buscan información en la red?
5. ¿Toman ustedes muchos exámenes?
6. ¿Sacan ustedes notas buenas?

EXPANSIÓN

Now ask a classmate these same questions. Remember to use **tú**.

CULTURA
Dos amigas del mismo colegio en Guadalajara, México

ESCUCHAR • HABLAR

6 **Conversa.** Speak with some friends as in the model.

MODELO —Ustedes necesitan estudiar.
—Oye. ¿Hablas en serio? La verdad
es que estudiamos.

1. Ustedes necesitan estudiar mucho.
2. Ustedes necesitan escuchar.
3. Ustedes necesitan sacar notas buenas.
4. Ustedes necesitan prestar atención.

LEER

7 **Parea.** Read each sentence and determine to whom it refers.

1. Hablo en mi móvil.
2. Ellos llevan muchos libros.
3. Estudias mucho.
4. Navegamos la red.
5. Ustedes escuchan
música clásica.
6. Siempre presta atención.
7. Usted habla muy bien.

a. *myself*
b. *you (a friend)*
c. *you (an adult)*
d. *other people*
e. *you (several people)*
f. *myself and others*
g. *another person*

HABLAR • ESCRIBIR

8 **Completa.** Complete the following story about a student in Barcelona. You will now use all forms of the **-ar** verbs. **¡Cuidado!** Pay careful attention to the endings.

CULTURA

Barcelona, la ciudad de Emilio, es una ciudad grande en Cataluña en el nordeste de España. En Barcelona, Emilio habla español y catalán. En las escuelas los profesores enseñan en catalán.

To learn more about Spain, take a tour on pages SH44–SH45.

Emilio __1__ (ser) un muchacho español. Él __2__ (estudiar) en un colegio en Barcelona. Los amigos de Emilio __3__ (llevar) uniforme a la escuela. Uno de sus amigos __4__ (hablar):

—Sí, todos nosotros __5__ (llevar) uniforme a la escuela. ¿__6__ (Llevar) ustedes uniforme a la escuela en Estados Unidos?

Los amigos de Emilio __7__ (tomar) muchos cursos. Y Emilio también __8__ (tomar) muchos cursos. Unos cursos __9__ (ser) fáciles y otros __10__ (ser) difíciles. Los amigos de Emilio __11__ (hablar):

—Nosotros __12__ (tomar) nueve cursos. En algunos cursos nosotros __13__ (sacar) notas muy buenas y en otros __14__ (sacar) notas bajas.

Un amigo __15__ (preguntar):

—¡Oye, Emilio! ¿En qué cursos __16__ (sacar) tú notas buenas y en qué cursos __17__ (sacar) tú notas malas?

Emilio __18__ (contestar):

—Cuando yo __19__ (estudiar) yo __20__ (sacar) notas buenas en todos mis cursos.

Más práctica

Workbook, pp. 3.9–3.10
StudentWorks™ Plus

Los verbos ir, dar, estar

1. The verbs **ir, dar,** and **estar** are irregular, because they have a different form with **yo.** All the other forms are the same as those of a regular **-ar** verb.

	ir	dar	estar
yo	**voy**	**doy**	**estoy**
tú	vas	das	estás
Ud., él, ella	va	da	está
nosotros(as)	vamos	damos	estamos
vosotros(as)	*vais*	*dais*	*estáis*
Uds., ellos, ellas	van	dan	están

2. You use **estar** to tell how you feel.

> —**¿Cómo estás?**
> —**Estoy bien, gracias.**

You also use **estar** to tell where you are.

> —**¿Dónde estás?**
> —**Estoy en la escuela.**

CULTURA

Los alumnos dan un paseo con su profesor durante una excursión escolar en la Ciudad de Panamá. Están en el casco viejo (histórico) de la capital.

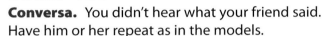

VIDEO To visit a dance class with Spanish students after school, watch **Cultura en vivo.**

Práctica

Diego es un alumno en una escuela en Colombia. Tiene una mochila pero cuando va de una clase a otra no lleva sus libros en la mochila.

ESCUCHAR • HABLAR • ESCRIBIR

9 **Personaliza.** Answer about yourself.

1. ¿Cómo estás hoy?
2. ¿Estás en la escuela ahora o estás en casa?
3. ¿En qué clase estás?
4. ¿Vas a casa después de las clases?
5. ¿Vas a casa a pie o en el bus escolar?

ESCUCHAR • HABLAR

10 **Conversa.** You didn't hear what your friend said. Have him or her repeat as in the models.

MODELOS   —**Voy a la escuela.**
　　　　　　 —**¿Adónde vas?**

　　　　　　 —**Vamos a la escuela.**
　　　　　　 —**¿Adónde van ustedes?**

1. Voy a la clase de español.
2. Voy al laboratorio de biología.
3. Voy a la cocina.
4. Voy al café.
5. Voy al gimnasio.
6. Voy a la tienda.

HABLAR • ESCRIBIR

11 **Forma frases.** Make up sentences using the following cues. You will use all forms of the verbs.

1. nosotros / ir / a la cocina
2. mis padres / estar / en la sala
3. yo / ir / a mi cuarto
4. mi computadora / estar / en mi cuarto
5. yo / navegar / la red / y / dar la información a mi hermanito
6. el profesor / dar / un examen
7. usted / ir / a la tienda
8. tú / estar / lejos de tu casa

InfoGap For more practice using **-ar** verbs and **ir, dar,** and **estar,** do Activity 3 on page SR5 at the end of this book.

Más práctica

Workbook, p. 3.11
StudentWorks™ Plus

Las contracciones al y del

1. The preposition **a** means *to* or *at.* **A** contracts with **el** to form one word—**al. A** does not contract with **la, las,** or **los.**

Él va **al** cuarto.	Voy **a la** tienda.
Vamos **al** gimnasio.	Ellos van **a la** sala.

2. The preposition **a** has another important use. Whenever the direct object of a verb is a person, you must put **a** before it. This **a** is not translated. It is called the **a personal.** Observe the following sentences.

Miro la televisión.	Miro **al** amigo de Teresa.
Escucho la música.	Escucho **a la** profesora.
Busco un bolígrafo.	Busco **a** mis amigas.

3. The preposition **de** means *of* or *from.* **De** contracts with **el** to form **del.** It does not contract with **la, las,** or **los.**

Es el libro **del** profesor.
Es la escuela **de la** amiga de Pablo.

4. **De** also forms a part of many other prepositions.

delante **del** jardín	antes **de los** exámenes
cerca **del** carro	detrás **de la** casa
después **de las** clases	lejos **de la** tienda

CULTURA

Los alumnos están en la clase de español. Ellos prestan atención al profesor. Ellos levantan la mano. Tienen muchas preguntas.

Práctica

HABLAR

 12 **Conversa.** With a partner prepare a conversation based on the model.

MODELO   el laboratorio →
—¡Oye! ¿Adónde vas?
—¿Quién? ¿Yo?
—Sí, tú.
—Pues, voy al laboratorio.

1. el gimnasio
2. la cafetería
3. el auditorio
4. la tienda

HABLAR • ESCRIBIR

 13 **Completa.** Complete each sentence with the correct form of the preposition **de.**

1. Ellos hablan _____ familia de José.
2. El profesor está delante _____ clase.
3. Cerca _____ casa hay un patio.
4. Detrás _____ patio hay un garaje.
5. ¿Qué opinión tienes _____ profesor?
6. Después _____ clases vamos a casa.

ESCUCHAR • HABLAR • ESCRIBIR

 14 **Contesta.** Answer.

1. ¿Miras la televisión?
2. ¿Miras a la profesora también?
3. ¿Escuchas un CD?
4. ¿Escuchas al profesor cuando él habla?
5. ¿Contestas la pregunta?
6. ¿Contestas a tu amigo?

HABLAR • ESCRIBIR

 15 **Forma frases.** Make up two sentences using each verb. Be sure to use the **a personal** when it is necessary.

yo	mirar	el profesor
tú	escuchar	los alumnos
él	enseñar	la lección
usted	buscar	un pantalón
nosotros		mi amigo
ellas		la música
		un DVD
		mi hermana
		el muchacho
		la profesora

FOLDABLES®
Study Organizer

POCKET BOOK
See page SH23 for help with making this foldable. Organize your new vocabulary. Label the pockets with topics such as school activities, after-school activities, and school supplies. Then with a partner make index cards with the words and phrases you have learned. Add to these pockets as you learn new words.

ESCRIBIR

16 **¡Te toca a ti!** E-mail your key pal in Mexico. Tell about what you do in school and after school.

HABLAR • ESCRIBIR

17 **Juego** Have a contest and see who can make up the most sentences in three minutes using the following verbs.

tomar   escuchar

hablar   **ir**   MIRAR

PRONUNCIACIÓN

La consonante t

You pronounce the **t** in Spanish with the tip of the tongue pressed against your upper teeth. No puff of air follows the **t** sound. It is very clear. Repeat the following.

ta	te	ti	to	tu
nota	Teresa	tío	toma	tú
está	interesante	tiene	levanto	estudia
carpeta	siete	tipo	momento	

Dictado

Pronounce the following sentences carefully. Then write them to prepare for a dictation.

Tito presta atención.
Tu tío Tito es simpático.
Tus tíos tienen tres tacos.
Tu gato Tigre está detrás de la terraza.

¡Bravo!

You have now learned all the new vocabulary and grammar in this chapter. Continue to use and practice all that you know while learning more cultural information. ¡Vamos!

CULTURA

Es la casa de la familia Duarte en Cotacachi, en el norte de Ecuador. Delante de la casa hay un jardín con flores bonitas.

Dos amigos

Diego	Linda, ¿a qué clase vas ahora?
Linda	Voy a la clase de español.
Diego	¿Qué tal tu clase de español?
Linda	Es bastante interesante y no muy difícil.
Diego	¿Hablas en serio?
Linda	Sí, sí. Hablo en serio. La señora Gómez es muy simpática.
Diego	¡Ay, Linda!
Linda	¿Qué pasa?
Diego	¿Mi móvil? ¿Dónde está?
Linda	¿Por qué no buscas en tu mochila?
Diego	¡Un momento! Ah, sí. Aquí está.
Linda	El viernes, ¿vas a la fiesta de Sandra?
Diego	Sí, ¿y tú?
Linda	Sí, voy. ¡Cómo no!

¿Comprendes?

A **¿Quién es?** Tell whether each statement is talking about Diego or Linda.

	Diego	Linda
1. Va a su clase de español.		
2. Probablemente no toma un curso de español. No estudia español.		
3. Busca su móvil.		
4. Su móvil está en su mochila.		
5. Va a la fiesta de Sandra.		

B **Contesta.** Answer based on the information in the conversation.

1. ¿A qué clase va Linda?
2. ¿Cómo es la clase de español?
3. ¿Cómo es la profesora?
4. ¿Quién es la profesora?
5. ¿Qué busca Diego?
6. ¿Dónde está?

C **Llegando a conclusiones** What does Linda say to Diego that surprises him? What tells you that he is surprised?

CULTURA

Una vista bonita de Miami, Florida

Antes de leer

Think of some cognates that you have already learned.

✓ Reading Check

¿Está Magalí ahora en Perú o en Estados Unidos?

✓ Reading Check

¿Qué es una escuela mixta?

Durante la lectura

As you read, write down all the cognates you recognize.

Después de leer

How many cognates did you find? Was it easy to guess their meaning?

✓ Reading Check

¿Cuáles son otras palabras para «escuela secundaria»?

READING STRATEGY

Recognizing cognates When you read in Spanish, it is possible that you will come across some new words. There are several strategies you can use to guess the meaning of these new words. One is to recognize cognates—words that look alike and mean the same thing in Spanish and English. In Spanish they are called **palabras afines.**

Escuelas aquí y en Latinoamérica 🎧 ♻️

Magalí es una alumna de intercambio[1]. Ella es de Arequipa, Perú, pero pasa un año con una familia en Nueva York. Ella va a la escuela con sus nuevos «hermanos». Magalí observa que hay diferencias entre su escuela en Perú y su nueva escuela en Nueva York.

En Perú muchos alumnos van a una escuela privada. La mayoría[2] de las escuelas privadas no son mixtas. Los muchachos van a una escuela y las muchachas van a otra. Pero la mayoría de las escuelas públicas son mixtas. Los alumnos de las escuelas privadas y públicas llevan uniforme. No van a clase en un blue jean y T-shirt.

CULTURA

Lupe y sus amigas, como Magalí, son peruanas. Ellas van a la misma escuela en una región rural cerca de Arequipa.

Las escuelas en Perú como en muchas partes de Latinoamérica tienen nombres diferentes que las escuelas en Estados Unidos. Por ejemplo, un colegio es una escuela secundaria. Una academia es una escuela primaria o secundaria. En la lengua de los alumnos o estudiantes, la escuela secundaria o *high school* es la prepa—una forma corta o abreviada de «la preparatoria».

[1]de intercambio   *exchange*   [2]mayoría   *majority*

¿Comprendes?

Más práctica

Workbook, pp. 3.12–3.14
StudentWorks™ Plus

A **Buscando información** Indicate which place(s) each statement refers to.

	Latinoamérica	Estados Unidos	los dos
1. La mayoría de los alumnos llevan uniforme a la escuela.			
2. Hay escuelas públicas y privadas.			
3. Un gran número de alumnos van a escuelas privadas.			
4. Son los profesores que enseñan.			
5. Un colegio es una escuela secundaria.			

B **Aumentando tu vocabulario** Complete each statement.

1. Otras palabras que significan «escuela» son _____, _____ y _____.
2. Otra palabra que significa «alumno(a)» es _____.
3. Otra expresión que significa «la mayoría» es _____.
4. Otra palabra que significa «elemental» es _____.

C **Contrastando** ¿Cuáles son unas diferencias entre las escuelas en Perú y en Estados Unidos?

Cultura

En muchas escuelas de Latinoamérica y también en España los alumnos no van de una sala a otra para cada clase. Son los profesores que van de una sala a otra.

CULTURA

Plaza de Armas en Arequipa, Perú

¿Quiénes trabajan? 🎧♻️

Antes de leer

You are going to read about the jobs or work of young people in the Spanish-speaking world. Before reading this selection, consider the answers to the following personal questions: **¿Trabajas después de las clases? ¿Qué tipo de trabajo tienes? ¿Cuántas horas trabajas? Y tus amigos, ¿trabajan muchos de ellos después de las clases o no?**

En Estados Unidos En Estados Unidos muchos alumnos trabajan después de las clases. Trabajan, por ejemplo, en un café, en un restaurante o en una tienda. No trabajan a tiempo completo, sólo a tiempo parcial.

En los países hispanos Hay jóvenes que trabajan en los países hispanos también. Son los jóvenes que terminan su educación después de la primaria o escuela elemental. Por lo general, los alumnos que van a la secundaria o prepa no trabajan. En unos colegios las clases no terminan hasta bastante tarde[1]. Y los alumnos de las escuelas secundarias toman muchos cursos en un semestre. Ellos trabajan mucho—pero no en un restaurante o una tienda. Trabajan en la escuela. Y de noche[2] cuando regresan a casa preparan sus tareas.

A veces unos alumnos trabajan durante el *weekend* o el fin de semana o durante sus vacaciones.

[1]bastante tarde   *rather late*   [2]de noche   *at night*

¿Comprendes?

Escoge. Choose the correct answer or completion.

1. ¿Quiénes trabajan en Latinoamérica?
   a. los alumnos secundarios
   b. los alumnos que no van a la secundaria
   c. los jóvenes en la escuela primaria
   d. por lo general, todos los jóvenes latinoamericanos

2. ¿Por qué no trabajan los alumnos que van a la secundaria en Latinoamérica?
   a. No trabajan.
   b. Sus clases terminan bastante tarde.
   c. Terminan con su educación.
   d. Sólo trabajan a tiempo parcial.

3. ¿Qué es la prepa?
   a. una escuela elemental o primaria
   b. una escuela privada
   c. una escuela secundaria
   d. un trabajo a tiempo parcial

4. De noche los alumnos hispanos _____.
   a. llevan uniforme
   b. van a clase
   c. trabajan a tiempo completo
   d. estudian y preparan sus tareas

CULTURA

Unos alumnos secundarios en un pasillo *(hallway)* de su escuela en León, en el norte de Nicaragua

Vocabulario

To review **Vocabulario 1,** turn to pages 92–93.

1 **Identifica.** Identify. Use **el** or **la.**

2 **Escoge.** Choose the correct word to complete each sentence.

va	toma	mira	compra
lleva	presta	escucha	da

9. José _____ un DVD en la tienda.

10. Él _____ el DVD en la sala.

11. Un alumno bueno _____ atención cuando el profesor habla.

12. Ella _____ uniforme a la escuela.

13. Elena _____ su música favorita.

14. El profesor _____ un examen hoy.

15. ¿Adónde _____ tu amigo?

To review **Vocabulario 1** and **Vocabulario 2,** turn to pages 92–93 and 96–97.

Gramática

3 **Completa.** Complete with the correct form of the indicated verb.

16. Yo _____ una nota buena en español. (sacar)

17. Nosotros _____ un examen. (tomar)

18. ¿En qué _____ (tú) tus materiales escolares? (llevar)

19. Todos ustedes _____ muchos materiales escolares en su mochila, ¿no? (llevar)

20. Ella _____ la computadora en clase. (usar)

21. Yo _____ la red. (navegar)

22. Ellos _____ información en el Internet. (buscar)

To review **-ar** verbs, turn to pages 100–101.

4 Contesta. Answer.

23. ¿Vas a la escuela en el bus escolar?

24. ¿Das tus tareas a la profesora?

25. ¿Estás en casa o en la escuela?

26. ¿Están ustedes en la escuela ahora?

27. ¿Van ustedes a casa a pie o en el bus escolar?

To review **ir, dar,** and **estar,** turn to page 105.

5 Escribe frases. Write a sentence using the following words.

28. nosotros / ir / tienda / después de / clases

29. alumnos / peruano / ir / colegio

To review **las contracciones,** turn to page 107.

6 Completa. Complete with the correct form of **a** or **de.**

30–31. Es el libro _____ profesor, no _____ profesora.

32. Ellos van _____ tienda, ¿no?

33. ¿Vas _____ colegio Bolívar?

34. Es la casa _____ familia Salas.

To review the **a personal,** turn to page 107.

7 Completa. Complete with the **a personal** when necessary.

35. Miro _____ la televisión.

36. Escucho _____ profesor.

To review this cultural information, turn to pages 112–113.

Cultura

8 ¿Sí o no? Indicate whether the following statements are true or false.

37. En Perú la mayoría de las escuelas privadas son mixtas.

38. Una prepa es una escuela primaria.

39. En Latinoamérica los alumnos de muchas escuelas públicas llevan uniforme.

40. Cuando los alumnos hablan, usan formas cortas de palabras como «la prepa» y «la tele».

CULTURA
Una muchacha peruana

1 La clase de español

Talk about your Spanish class

Tell a friend all the things you do in Spanish class. Tell him or her what you think about your Spanish class.

2 Un alumno bueno o malo

Describe different types of students

Work with a partner. Give some traits of a good student and a bad student. Think about the traits and tell what each type of student you are. Find out if your partner agrees.

CULTURA

Unos alumnos dominicanos en su escuela en Santo Domingo

3 Después de las clases

Talk about what you do after school

Work with a partner. Discuss the things you do after school.

4 En clase

Talk about what you and your classmates do in school

Look around your classroom and tell all that is going on. Tell some things your classmates are doing. Give your opinions about the class. Use the expression **a mi parecer** to introduce your opinions.

Tarea

Interview and write a report about an exchange student in your school.

Writing Strategy

Preparing for an interview An interview is a good way to gather information for a story or a report. Like any good interviewer you have to prepare questions ahead of time. To prepare the questions, think about what you want to learn from the person. Your questions should be open-ended, not just *yes/no* questions.

The following diagram gives you question words you can use to prepare your interview.

```
              ¿Quién?
     ¿Qué?            ¿Cuándo?

  ¿Quiénes?                 ¿Cómo?

            Preguntas

  ¿Dónde?                 ¿Cuánto(s)?

     ¿Adónde?           ¿Por qué?
              ¿De dónde?
```

❶ Prewrite

Here are some suggestions to help you prepare for your interview.

- Make a list of the verbs you know that you can use in your questions.
- Write the questions you want to ask him or her using the question words in the diagram.
- Look at the chart below for ideas about the information you want.

personal	actividades escolares
su familia	su escuela
su casa	un día típico en su escuela
su apariencia física	actividades con sus amigos
su personalidad	

❷ Write

- After you have prepared your questions, conduct the interview with a classmate.
- Write down his or her answers to your questions.
- Then organize the answers to your questions to write your article based on the interview.

Evaluate

Don't forget that your teacher will evaluate you on your ability to write meaningful, open-ended interview questions and on your ability to write a well-organized, grammatically correct article based on the person's answers to your questions.

Repaso del Capítulo ③

Gramática

- ### Presente de los verbos en -ar *(pages 100–101)*
  Study the following forms of the present tense of a regular **-ar** verb.

hablar			
yo	hablo	nosotros(as)	hablamos
tú	hablas	vosotros(as)	habláis
Ud., él, ella	habla	Uds., ellos, ellas	hablan

- ### Presente de ir, dar, estar *(page 105)*
  These three irregular verbs have the same endings as a regular **-ar** verb in all forms except **yo.** Study the following.

	ir	dar	estar
yo	voy	doy	estoy
tú	vas	das	estás
Ud., él, ella	va	da	está
nosotros(as)	vamos	damos	estamos
vosotros(as)	vais	dais	estáis
Uds., ellos, ellas	van	dan	están

- ### Las contracciones al y del *(page 107)*
  The prepositions **a** and **de** contract with **el** to form one word—**al, del.**

  Yo voy al colegio.
  Es el libro del profesor.

- ### A personal *(page 107)*
  Whenever the direct object of a verb is a person, you must put **a** before it. This **a** is not translated.

  Miro al amigo de Teresa.

CULTURA

Las muchachas regresan a casa después de las clases en Antigua, Guatemala. Una muchacha lleva flores que va a dar a su mamá. Las flores que tiene son del mismo color que el suéter del uniforme que lleva a la escuela.

Vocabulario

Talking about school and school activities

la escuela	estudiar	dar un examen, una	ir
la sala de clase	escuchar	prueba	dar
el pupitre	mirar	tomar un examen	estar
una pregunta	prestar atención	sacar una nota	
enseñar	levantar la mano	buena (alta)	
hablar	contestar	mala (baja)	

Identifying some school supplies

una mochila	un libro	un cuaderno	una calculadora
los materiales	un bolígrafo	un lápiz, unos	una carpeta
escolares	una hoja de papel	lápices	

Identifying some clothing

el uniforme	la camisa	la blusa
el pantalón	la falda	llevar

Talking about after-school activities

el móvil	la computadora,	ir a pie	enviar un correo
el MP3	el ordenador	en el bus escolar	electrónico
la música	regresar	navegar la red,	
un DVD		el Internet	

Talking about shopping

una tienda	la caja	buscar
un(a) empleado(a)	trabajar	comprar
el dinero	necesitar	pagar

Other useful words and expressions

antes de	¿adónde?	¡Mira!
durante	¿cuándo?	¿Cuánto cuesta?
después de	¿por qué?	¿Qué pasa?
cerca de	porque	usar
lejos de		

Literary Reader

You may wish to read about the epic poem *El Cid,* found on pages 398–401.

Repaso cumulativo

Repasa lo que ya has aprendido

These activities will help you review what you have learned so far in Spanish.

1 **Escucha y escoge.** Listen to each statement and identify the character it describes.

Felipe   Carlos   Ana   Mari   Diego   Sara

2 **Describe a tu profesor(a).** Describe your teacher. Answer the following questions.

1. ¿Quién es?
2. ¿De dónde es?
3. ¿Cómo es?
4. ¿Tiene una computadora en clase?

3 **Personaliza.** Answer about yourself.

1. ¿Quién eres?
2. ¿De qué nacionalidad eres?
3. ¿Cuántos años tienes?
4. ¿Tienes el pelo rubio, castaño o negro o eres pelirrojo(a)?
5. ¿Tienes ojos azules, castaños o verdes?
6. ¿Dónde eres alumno(a)?
7. ¿Cuántos cursos tienes?
8. ¿Eres hijo(a) único(a)?
9. ¿Tienes hermanos? ¿Cuántos?
10. ¿Quiénes son?
11. ¿Cómo son tus hermanos?
12. ¿Hay gemelos en tu familia?

CULTURA

El joven está en la plaza principal en Mérida en la península Yucatán en México. En el centro de la plaza está la bandera mexicana.

4 **Personaliza.** Describe your house or apartment.

5 **Da lo contrario.** Give the opposite.

1. serio
2. alto
3. bueno
4. rubio
5. ambicioso
6. antes de
7. delante de
8. grande

CULTURA

Es una casa de estilo colonial en Antigua, Guatemala. Las casas coloniales son muy bonitas. Tienen solamente un piso.

6 **Completa.** Complete with the verb **tener.**

1. Yo _____ mucho trabajo.
2. Mi hermano _____ cinco cursos.
3. Mi hermano y yo _____ una mascota.
4. Nuestra mascota _____ sólo dos meses.
5. ¿_____ tú hermanos?
6. ¿_____ ustedes una mascota también?

7 **Crea preguntas.** Make up questions.

1. *Los alumnos* hablan mucho.
2. *La profesora* enseña.
3. Los alumnos van *a la cafetería.*
4. Son *de Nueva York.*
5. Son *inteligentes.*
6. Tienen *cuatro* libros.

8 **Rompecabezas**

Choose the word in each group that does not belong. Then think of another word that fits the category.

1. ¡Buenos días! ¡Hasta luego! ¡Buenas tardes! ¡Hola!

2. alto bajo ambicioso guapo

3. la historia el francés el inglés el español

4. la profesora el curso la clase el amigo

5. norteamericana chilena Venezuela guatemalteco

ciento veintitrés **123**

¿Qué comemos y dónde?

Aquí y Allí

Vamos a comparar ¿Tienes una idea de lo que come la gente en otros países? En este capítulo vas a aprender lo que comen unas familias hispanas y donde. Compara la comida que comen las familias latinas con la comida que tu familia come.

Objetivos

You will:

- identify foods and discuss meals
- talk about places where you eat
- order food or a beverage at a café
- compare eating habits in Spain, Latin America, and the United States

You will use:

- present tense of regular **-er** and **-ir** verbs
- expressions with the infinitive— **ir a, tener que, acabar de**

◄ **Una familia mexicana come en el patio de su casa en Tepoztlán en el estado de Morelos.**

QuickPass

Go to glencoe.com
For: **Online book**
Web code: **ASD4003c4**

Introducción al tema

¿Qué comemos y dónde?

Los platos de muchos países latinoamericanos llevan pimientos que tienen nombres diferentes como chiles, ajíes, chipotles y morrones. ▶

Look at these photographs to acquaint yourself with the theme of this chapter—what we eat and where. You will notice here and throughout the chapter that in the Spanish-speaking world there is a great variety of interesting and delicious foods. What people eat in one area is different from what people eat in another area, just as in the United States. Do you recognize any of the foods you see here? Of all the foods, which would be your favorite?

Puerto Rico
La señora prepara unas frituras de Puerto Rico en un puesto de comida en Piñones cerca de San Juan. ▶

▲ **México** En su carrito en el famoso Parque de Chapultepec en la Ciudad de México, la señora prepara y vende bocadillos o sándwiches. En México son tortas.

El chocolate es un producto de las Américas. La palabra «chocolate» es de la palabra «xocoatl» en náhuatl, una lengua de los indígenas de México. Aquí vemos unos bombones de chocolate y una planta de cacao que produce el chocolate. ▶

▲ **Perú** La muchacha tiene un puesto en Huanchaco, Perú, donde prepara y vende raspadillas—un refresco de hielo granizado y el jugo de una fruta tropical.

◀ **España** Un mesón es un tipo de café adonde va la gente a comer tapas. Aquí vemos un jamón famoso de España—el jamón serrano—y un queso famoso—el queso manchego.

Argentina El delicioso bife argentino es famoso en el mundo entero. El señor prepara bife y pollo a la parrilla en un restaurante de Buenos Aires. ▶

Las comidas

El desayuno

el panecillo
la mantequilla

las tostadas,
el pan tostado

el cereal

el tocino,
el bacón

los huevos

El almuerzo

una hamburguesa

un sándwich de
jamón y queso,
un bocadillo

una pizza

una ensalada de
lechuga y tomates

La cena

un helado

el pollo

el pescado

el postre

el flan

las legumbres, los
vegetales, las verduras

las papas,
las patatas fritas

la carne

arroz y frijoles

Las bebidas

una gaseosa,
una cola

un vaso
de leche

un vaso
de agua fría

una taza
de chocolate
caliente

una taza
de café

un vaso de
jugo de naranja

En otras partes

Las papas is used throughout Latin America and **las patatas** is used in Spain. *Dessert* is usually **el postre,** but **la sobremesa** is used as well. In addition to **los frijoles,** you will also hear **las habichuelas. La torta** usually means *cake,* but you also hear **el pastel, la tarta,** and **el bizcocho.** In Mexico, **una torta** is a sandwich.

Para conversar

Tengo mucha hambre.
Voy a comer algo.

Tengo mucha sed.
Tengo que beber algo.

¿Dónde comemos?

Lidia toma el desayuno en casa.
¿Qué come para el desayuno?
Come cereal y bebe un vaso de
  jugo de naranja.

Los alumnos toman el almuerzo
  en la cafetería.
Comen un bocadillo o una pizza.

La familia Valdés es de Colombia.
Viven en Bogotá.
Esta noche cenan en casa.

Los Valdés reciben una sorpresa.
Abuelita llega con una torta grande.
¡Qué deliciosa!

QuickPass

Go to glencoe.com
For: **Vocabulary practice**
Web code: ASD4003c4

FOLDABLES®
Study Organizer

TAB BOOK

Como
No como
Bebo
No bebo

See page SH25 for help with making this foldable. Use this study organizer to tell what you do or do not eat and drink. Share your results with a partner. Find out if you have similar tastes.

ESCUCHAR

1 **Escucha y escoge.** Match each statement you hear with the photo it describes.

a.

b.

c.

d.

HABLAR

2 **Completa.** Tell at what meal José eats the following.

MODELO **José come un sándwich de queso. →**
José come un sándwich de queso para el almuerzo.

1. José come cereales.
2. José come carne, un biftec.
3. José come un bocadillo de jamón.
4. José come pan tostado.

HABLAR • ESCRIBIR

3 **Contesta.** Look at the picture of Anita. Make up answers about her.

1. Cuando Anita tiene hambre, ¿come algo o bebe algo?
2. Cuando Anita tiene sed, ¿come algo o bebe algo?
3. Anita es vegetariana. ¿Come ella carne? ¿Come arroz y frijoles?
4. ¿Qué come Anita cuando tiene hambre?
5. ¿Qué bebe Anita cuando tiene sed?
6. ¿Qué come Anita ahora?
7. ¿Dónde viven Anita y su amiga?

CULTURA

Anita come un helado con una amiga después de las clases. Anita y su amiga son de México. Viven en Guadalajara.

Más práctica

- Workbook, pp. 4.3–4.4
- StudentWorks™ Plus

LEER

④ **¿Sí o no?** Carmen doesn't know if she has put the following items in the correct categories. Create a chart similar to the one below on a piece of paper to record your answers. Put a check under **sí** if she is correct and **no** if she is wrong. Then help her out by indicating the correct categories for your **no** responses.

	sí	no	la categoría correcta
1. La naranja es una fruta.	✓		
2. El café es una bebida.			
3. La leche es una comida.			
4. El biftec es una carne.			
5. La lechuga es una fruta.			
6. El tocino es una carne.			
7. El helado es un pescado.			
8. La torta es un postre.			

HABLAR • ESCRIBIR

⑤ **Personaliza.** Tell what your favorite foods are for the following meals.

1. tu desayuno favorito
2. tu almuerzo favorito
3. tu cena favorita en casa
4. tu cena favorita en un restaurante
5. tu bebida favorita

ESCRIBIR

⑥ **Rompecabezas**

Join two pieces to form a word. When you have finished, you should have nine words. Do not use any piece more than once.

zo, cino, po, ne, almuer, be, to, mida, llo, hue, co, bre, car, so, ham, que, ber, vos

Conexiones

La salud
Es muy importante comer comidas que contienen vitaminas. Mira la tabla. Luego analiza tu dieta. ¿Contiene tu dieta vitaminas suficientes? ¿Qué comes para tener las vitaminas necesarias?

Vitamina

A	vegetales, leche, algunas frutas
B	carne, huevos, leche, cereales, vegetales verdes
C	frutas cítricas, tomates, lechuga
D	leche, huevos, pescado
E	vegetales, huevos, cereales

En otras partes

Jugo de naranja means *orange juice* and is universally understood in the Spanish-speaking world. **Zumo de naranja** is used exclusively in Spain. You will hear **jugo de china** in Puerto Rico. Ask Spanish speakers in your class if they use any other words to express *orange juice*.

VIDEO To practice your new words, watch **Vocabulario en vivo.**

En el café

Los refrescos

unos batidos de jugos tropicales

el agua mineral con gas

Las meriendas

Tapas, Antojitos

los camarones

las albóndigas

las aceitunas

las empanadas

los tostones

los pinchitos

el mesero

una mesa ocupada

una mesa libre

Los amigos van al café.
Marisol ve una mesa libre.

el menú

José Luis abre el menú.
Marisol lee el menú.

Antes de comer

Para conversar

Sí, señores. ¿Qué desean tomar?

Para mí, un batido de papaya.

Y para mí, una cola y una empanada de carne. Tengo hambre.

Los amigos hablan con el mesero.
El mesero escribe la orden.

VIDEO To visit a café watch **Diálogo en vivo.**

En otras partes

Small snacks are called **tapas** in Spain and in other countries. They are called **botanas** in Mexico and **antojitos** or **bocaditos** as well in parts of Latin America. **Tostones** in the Caribbean are called **patacones** in many areas of Latin America. **El mesero** is used throughout Latin America and **el camarero** is used in Spain.

Después de comer

Para conversar

La cuenta, por favor.

¿Está incluido el servicio?

Sí, señorita. Enseguida.

Sí, señorita.

Café Estrella

Mesa nº 4   Fecha 3 oct

Cantidad	CONCEPTO	
1	batido	12
1	empanadas	24
1	gaseosa	10
	SERVICIO INCLUIDO	
	TOTAL	46

QuickPass

Go to glencoe.com
For: **Vocabulary practice**
Web code: **ASD4003c4**

LEER

1 **Escoge.** Draw a chart similar to the one below. Indicate whether each item of food is a beverage, snack, or meal.

InfoGap For more practice using your new vocabulary, do Activity 4 on page SR6 at the end of this book.

	refresco	merienda	comida
1. una limonada			
2. antojitos			
3. una empanada			
4. carne y legumbres			
5. un batido			
6. huevos y jamón			

ESCUCHAR • HABLAR • ESCRIBIR

2 **Corrige.** Work with a partner. Read each sentence aloud and have your partner correct the wrong information. Take turns.

1. Los amigos buscan una mesa ocupada.
2. Anita escribe el menú en el café.
3. Jorge desea unos pinchitos porque tiene sed.
4. Los clientes escriben la orden.
5. Una empanada es una bebida con una fruta tropical.
6. Sarita lee el menú y luego abre el menú.

Un taco es una tortilla frita de carne o pollo con tomate, lechuga y queso.

LEER • HABLAR

3  **Rompecabezas**

Choose the word in each group that does not belong. Then think of another word that fits the category.

1. el batido | la cola | el pan | el agua mineral

2. el menú | la cuenta | la sorpesa | el mesero

3. las aceitunas | el pinchito | el tostón | el pollo

4. el helado | el flan | el refresco | la torta

Una enchilada es una tortilla blanda con carne, pollo o queso. Muchos platos mexicanos van acompañados de arroz y frijoles.

HABLAR • ESCRIBIR

4 Contesta. Answer the questions to tell a story about some friends in a café in Uruguay.

1. ¿Van los amigos al café antes de las clases o después de las clases? ¿Viven ellos en Uruguay?
2. Antes de comer, ¿qué tienen todos en la mano? ¿El menú o la cuenta?
3. ¿Leen el menú?
4. Carlos no tiene hambre. ¿Desea una merienda o sólo un refresco?
5. Teresa tiene hambre. ¿Va a comer algo? ¿Qué va a comer?
6. ¿Habla el mesero con los amigos?
7. ¿Escribe él su orden?

EXPANSIÓN

Now, without looking at the questions, tell all you remember about the friends from Uruguay.

 **CULTURA**

Hay muchos cafés en España y Latinoamérica. Aquí vemos un café típico en una calle de Colonia, Uruguay. El café tiene una terraza al aire libre.

HABLAR • ESCRIBIR

5 Pregunta. Make up questions using words from the **banco de palabras.** Be sure to pay attention to the italicized words so you choose the correct question word.

¿Qué?	¿Quién?	¿Quiénes?	¿Cómo?
¿Cuándo?	¿Dónde?	¿Adónde?	

🌐 **GeoVistas**

To learn more about Uruguay, take a tour on pages SH60–SH61.

1. *Los amigos* van al café.
2. Ellos van *al café.*
3. Van al café *después de las clases.*
4. Ven una mesa libre *en el café.*
5. Toman *una merienda.*
6. *Felipe* no come.
7. El mesero es *muy simpático* y *da un servicio bueno.*
8. *El servicio* está incluido en la cuenta.

❀ Comunicación

6 Get together in small groups as if you were at a café in a Spanish-speaking country. Talk all about your school activities, but don't forget to look at the menu and tell the server what you want. ● . . . .

QuickPass

Go to glencoe.com
For: **Grammar practice**
Web code: ASD4003c4

Presente de los verbos en -er, -ir

1. You have already learned the present tense of regular **-ar** verbs. There are two other families or conjugations of regular verbs. Verbs whose infinitives end in **-er** are second conjugation verbs. Verbs whose infinitives end in **-ir** are third conjugation verbs. Some verbs of the second and third conjugations that you will use frequently are **comer, beber, leer, ver, comprender** *(to understand)*, **aprender** *(to learn)*, **abrir, recibir, escribir,** and **vivir.**

2. Study the following forms of **-er** and **-ir** verbs.

infinitive	comer		
stem	**com-**		
yo	**como**	nosotros(as)	**comemos**
tú	**comes**	*vosotros(as)*	*coméis*
Ud., él, ella	**come**	Uds., ellos, ellas	**comen**

infinitive	vivir		
stem	**viv-**		
yo	**vivo**	nosotros(as)	**vivimos**
tú	**vives**	*vosotros(as)*	*vivís*
Ud., él, ella	**vive**	Uds., ellos, ellas	**viven**

Note that all forms of **-er** and **-ir** verbs are the same except **nosotros(as)** and **vosotros(as).**

3. Note also the forms of the verb **ver.**

ver	
veo	**vemos**
ves	*veis*
ve	**ven**

La familia Gómez vive en Texas. La familia come enchiladas. Esta noche papá prepara la comida. ▼

Práctica

ESCUCHAR

1 **Escucha y escoge.** Listen to the sentences. Determine whether each one refers to one person or more than one person. Make a chart like the one below to indicate your answers.

one person	more than one person

ESCUCHAR • HABLAR • ESCRIBIR

2 **Cambia según el modelo.** Redo each sentence using the new subject. Pay particular attention to the verb ending.

MODELO   Juan come en la cafetería. (Juan y Ana) →
          Juan y Ana comen en la cafetería.

1. María vive en California. (ellas)
2. Ella asiste a una escuela pública. (su hermano y ella)
3. Ella aprende español en la escuela. (ellas)
4. Ella lee y escribe mucho. (sus amigas)
5. A veces ella ve la televisión. (ellas)

HABLAR • ESCRIBIR

3 **Personaliza.** Answer about yourself.

1. ¿Qué comes para el desayuno?
2. ¿Qué bebes para el desayuno?
3. Cuando tienes sed, ¿bebes agua caliente o agua fría?
4. ¿Lees mucho?
5. ¿Recibes muchos correos electrónicos?
6. ¿A qué escuela asistes?
7. ¿Qué aprendes en la escuela?

HABLAR • ESCRIBIR

4 **Escribe tu nombre y dirección.** Write the information about yourself on a card like the one below. Trade cards with classmates. Present the information on your card to the class.

Nombre ___

Calle/Avenida ___

Pueblo/Ciudad ___

Estado ___

Zona postal ___

País ___

¡Ojo!

The verb **asistir** is a false cognate. It means *to attend*, not *to assist*.

Cultura

El ceviche
Comen ceviche en muchos países latino-americanos cerca de la costa. El ceviche es pescado crudo marinado en limón y otras hierbas y especias. ¡Qué rico! Donde tú vives, ¿es popular el ceviche?

Gramática

VIDEO Want help with the present tense of regular verbs? Watch Gramática en vivo.

Comunidades

Un restaurante mexicano

Aquí vemos un restaurante mexicano en Miami. Como en Estados Unidos, los restaurantes mexicanos son populares en España y Latinoamérica también. ¿Hay un restaurante mexicano donde vives? ¿Vas al restaurante? ¿Qué comes?

HABLAR

5 **Conversa según el modelo.**
Work with a partner and make up a conversation according to the model.

MODELO

— Oye, ¿qué ves?
— Veo la televisión.

1.   2.

3.   4.

HABLAR

6 **Conversa.** Work with a group of friends and find out who eats what as in the model.

MODELO

—¿Comen ustedes una hamburguesa cuando tienen hambre?
—Sí, (No, no) comemos una hamburguesa cuando tenemos hambre.

1.   2.   3.   4.

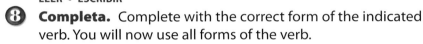
HABLAR

7 **Personaliza.** Work with a partner and talk about yourself and some friends. Remember to use **nosotros.**

1. ¿Dónde viven ustedes?
2. ¿A qué escuela asisten ustedes?
3. ¿Reciben notas buenas o malas?
4. ¿Qué aprenden ustedes en la escuela?
5. ¿Leen ustedes muchos libros?
6. ¿Escriben muchos correos electrónicos?

LEER • ESCRIBIR

8 **Completa.** Complete with the correct form of the indicated verb. You will now use all forms of the verb.

Yo ___1___ (vivir) en Colorado y mi amigo Alonso ___2___ (vivir) en Colorado también. Nosotros ___3___ (asistir) a la misma escuela. Nosotros ___4___ (aprender) mucho.

Nosotros ___5___ (comer) el almuerzo en la cafetería. Alonso ___6___ (comer) ensaladas y yo ___7___ (comer) bocadillos. Después de las clases vamos a un café. Yo ___8___ (ver) al mesero en el café. Yo ___9___ (leer) el menú y doy la orden al mesero. El mesero ___10___ (escribir) la orden.

Cuando mis amigos regresan a casa ellos ___11___ (leer) los correos electrónicos que ___12___ (recibir). ___13___ (Ver) la televisión también. Y tú, ¿___14___ (recibir) muchos correos electrónicos? Y, ¿___15___ (ver) la televisión?

Comunicación

9 You received an e-mail from a key pal in Spain in which he describes an afternoon with friends. Respond and let him know what you do after school. Do you go to a café or a fast-food restaurant **(restaurante de comida rápida)**? Tell him what you and your friends talk about.

CULTURA

Las hermanas compran un refresco antes de regresar a casa después de las clases en Ecuador.

¿Te acuerdas?

Remember that you have already learned the verbs **tener** and **ir**.

Expresiones con el infinitivo

1. You have already learned that the infinitive of a verb in Spanish ends in **-ar**, **-er**, or **-ir**. The infinitive often follows another verb or expression. You have already seen the infinitive used in the following sentences.

> **¿Qué desean ustedes tomar?**
> **Debes estudiar y aprender más.**

No tengo hambre porque acabo de comer.

2. Here are some other useful expressions that are followed by the infinitive.

> **tener que**   *to have to*
> **ir a**   *to be going to*
> **acabar de**   *to have just (done something)*

> —**Tengo que comer algo. Voy a ir a la cafetería.**
> —**Yo no. Acabo de comer y no tengo hambre.**

CULTURA

Las alumnas de un colegio de León en Nicaragua toman una merienda en un puesto de comida cerca de su escuela.

Práctica

HABLAR • ESCRIBIR

⑩ **Personaliza.** Answer the questions to tell what you are going or not going to do after school.

1. Después de las clases, ¿vas a ir a un café con tus amigos?
2. ¿Vas a regresar a casa?
3. ¿Vas a comer un bocadillo?
4. ¿Vas a tomar un refresco?
5. ¿Vas a enviar o recibir correos electrónicos?
6. ¿Vas a hablar en tu móvil?

ESCUCHAR • HABLAR

⑪ **Entrevista a un(a) amigo(a).** Work with a classmate. Interview each other. Ask the following questions.

1. ¿Tienes que estudiar?
2. ¿Tienes que prestar atención cuando la profesora habla?
3. ¿Tienes que leer y escribir mucho en clase?
4. ¿Tienes que llevar uniforme a la escuela?
5. ¿Tienes que recibir notas buenas?

HABLAR • ESCRIBIR

⑫ **Sigue el modelo.** Make up a sentence as in the model.

MODELO　**ver la televisión / trabajar →
No vamos a ver la televisión porque tenemos que trabajar.**

1. escuchar un CD / estudiar
2. hablar por teléfono / ver un programa importante
3. tomar seis cursos / sacar notas buenas
4. hablar / escuchar
5. ir a la fiesta / estudiar para un examen

Comparaciones

Inca Kola

Inca Kola es la bebida nacional de Perú. ¿Qué crees? ¿Cuál es la bebida nacional de Estados Unidos?

Comunicación

⑬ Tell a partner some things you're not going to do tomorrow because you have to do something else. Tell what you have to do. Your classmate will let you know if he or she is in the same situation.

CULTURA

Los alumnos no estudian más hoy porque acaban de tomar un examen y ahora conversan en una calle de Quito, Ecuador.

HABLAR • ESCRIBIR

14 Contesta. Answer telling what you or your friends have or have not just done.

1. ¿Acaban de comer ustedes?
2. ¿Acabas de hablar con tus abuelos?
3. ¿Acaban ustedes de tomar un examen?
4. ¿Acabas de ver un programa de televisión?
5. ¿Acaban tus amigos de navegar el Internet?

Comunicación

15 Tell your friends some things you're not going to do because you just did them. Take turns.

16 You and a friend decide to go to your favorite cafeteria. Look at the menu and tell each other what you are going to eat.

El Paseo

Ensaladas

Ensalada de Lechuga y Tomate 1.25
Ensalada Mixta (por persona) 2.95

Huevos

Tortilla de Queso 2.95
Tortilla de Chorizo 3.95
Tortilla de Papas 2.95
Tortilla de Jamón 3.25
Tortilla Combinación (2) 3.50
Dos Huevos Fritos ó Revueltos
con Papas 1.75
Dos Huevos con Tostadas 1.75

Postres

ESPECIALIDADES DE LA CASA

Flan 1.25
Pastel de Manzana 1.25
Helados 1.25
Fresa, Vainilla, Chocolate

CULTURA

En muchos países hispanos hay cafeterías como la cafetería que vemos aquí en San Juan, Puerto Rico. La gente va a la cafetería a tomar una merienda, un refresco o una comida completa.

PRONUNCIACIÓN

La consonante d

The pronunciation of **d** in Spanish varies according to its position in the word. When a word begins with **d** (initial position) or follows the consonants **l, n,** or **r,** the tongue gently strikes the back of the upper front teeth. Repeat the following.

da	de	di	do	du
da	debo	día	domingo	duda
falda	desayuno	diciembre	cuando	durante
merienda	depende	difícil	comprendo	verduras

When **d** appears within the word between two vowels (medial position), **d** is extremely soft. Your tongue should strike the lower part of your upper teeth, almost between the upper and lower teeth. Repeat the following.

da	de	di	do	du
tostada	modelo	estudio	helado	educado
ensalada	idea	adiós	sábado	educación
enchilada	decide	bocadillo	pescado	

 **Dictado**

Pronounce the following sentences carefully. Then write them to prepare for a dictation.

> **Diego da el helado a Donato.**
> **David Dávila debe dar el dinero a Diana.**
> **Debes comer una ensalada de verduras.**
> **Es un domingo de diciembre.**

Refrán

Can you guess what the following proverb means?

Cuatro ojos ven más que dos.

¡Bravo!

You have now learned all the new vocabulary and grammar in this chapter. Continue to use and practice all that you know while learning more cultural information. ¡Vamos!

 ## Cultura

El mate
El mate es una bebida muy popular en Argentina, Uruguay y Paraguay. Es un té herbal. La gente bebe o toma el mate de una bombilla. ¿Beben tus padres de una bombilla?

Al teléfono

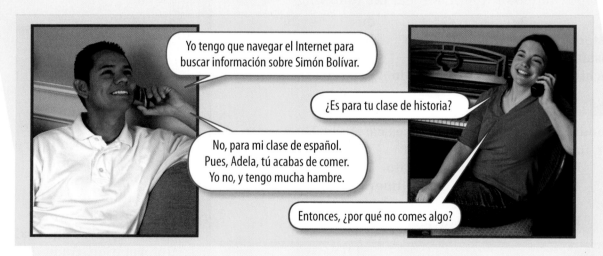

¿Comprendes?

A **Contesta.** Answer based on the information in the conversation between Diego and Adela.

1. ¿Hablan por teléfono Diego y Adela?
2. ¿Quién acaba de comer?
3. ¿Qué va a ver?
4. ¿Tiene ella tareas?
5. ¿Por qué tiene que navegar el Internet Diego?
6. ¿Para qué clase es?
7. ¿Quién tiene hambre?
8. ¿Por qué no tiene hambre Adela?

B **Escoge.** Choose the correct answer.

1. ¿Dónde está Adela?
   a. en la escuela
   b. en casa

2. ¿Quién es Diego?
   a. el amigo de Adela
   b. el hermano de Adela

3. ¿Por qué usa la computadora Diego?
   a. porque tiene que buscar información sobre un héroe latinoamericano
   b. porque tiene que escribir una composición para su clase de historia

4. ¿Qué va a comer Diego?
   a. una comida completa
   b. una merienda

C **Comparando** Make a diagram similar to the one below. Fill in the diagram with statements that apply to Diego, Adela, and both.

Diego | Adela
1.   1.   1.
2.   2.   2.
3.   3.

D **Resumiendo** Work with a partner. Summarize what you learned about Adela and Diego.

Conexiones

La historia

Diego indica en la conversación que tiene que escribir una composición sobre Simón Bolívar—el héroe latinoamericano que lucha contra España por la independencia de los países de la América del Sur. Simón Bolívar es el gran libertador de los países del norte del continente. ¿Quién es un héroe en la historia de Estados Unidos?

SIMON BOLIVAR

LIBERTADOR
DE SEIS NACIONES
PANAMÁ   BOLIVIA
COLOMBIA ECUADOR
PERÚ Y VENEZUELA
NACIÓ EN CARACAS VENEZUELA

Antes de leer

Look at the photographs that go with this story. What do you think the story might be about?

✓ **Reading Check**

¿Dónde viven las dos familias?

Durante la lectura

Look at the photograph that goes with the section you are reading. How does it help you understand what you are reading?

Después de leer

Were you correct in your predictions about the story based on what you saw in the photos?

✓ **Reading Check**

¿Cenan todos a la misma hora en las diferentes partes del mundo hispano?

READING STRATEGY

Using visuals Before you start to read, be sure to look at any illustrations, photographs, or graphic images that accompany the selection. Visuals provide clues to help you understand content. So remember, make it easy on yourself: look before you read.

La comida en otras partes

La familia de José Luis Aparicio vive en Madrid, la capital de España. La familia de Catalina Ayerbe vive en Granada, Nicaragua.

El desayuno Por la mañana, cada familia toma el desayuno. Los Aparicio en España comen pan con mantequilla o mermelada. A veces comen churros. Los padres toman café con leche y José Luis y sus hermanos toman chocolate caliente.

Los Ayerbe en Nicaragua también comen pan con mantequilla o mermelada. Y un plato muy popular es el gallopinto—una combinación de arroz con frijoles. Mucha gente come gallopinto con huevos para el desayuno. Y beben un jugo de una deliciosa fruta tropical.

El almuerzo Los Aparicio y los Ayerbe no regresan a casa a tomar el almuerzo. Los jóvenes comen en la cafetería de la escuela o en un café o cafetería cerca de la escuela o en un puesto o tenderete[1] de comida. Para el almuerzo comen simplemente una pizza o un bocadillo. En España comen a veces una tortilla a la española. No es como una tortilla mexicana. Es un tipo de *omelet* de patatas, cebolla[2] y huevos. A veces Catalina y sus amigos comen carne asada[3] con arroz y frijoles o unas bocas (tapas) como tostones con queso.

La cena Por lo general los Aparicio y los Ayerbe cenan en casa. Pero, ¿a qué hora? Pues, en España no cenan hasta las diez o diez y media. En Nicaragua como en otros países latinoamericanos cenan a eso de[4] las ocho.

[1]puesto, tenderete *stand*
[2]cebolla *onion*
[3]asada *roasted*
[4]a eso de *at about*

¿Comprendes?

A **Recordando hechos** Answer based on the information in the reading.

1. ¿Dónde vive la familia de José Luis Aparicio?
2. ¿Dónde viven los Ayerbe?
3. ¿Dónde toman los jóvenes el desayuno?
4. ¿Dónde toman el almuerzo?

B **Describiendo** Tell what you learned about the following.

1. el desayuno típico de una familia en España
2. el desayuno típico de una familia en Nicaragua
3. una tortilla a la española
4. un almuerzo típico de Catalina en Nicaragua

CULTURA

Aquí vemos unos edificios bonitos en Granada, Nicaragua. La familia de Catalina vive en Granada, una ciudad colonial.

C **Comparando** Create a chart like the one below and then discuss your answers with your classmates. You may check more than one column for each sentence.

	en España	en Nicaragua	donde vivo yo
1. Tomamos el desayuno por la mañana.			
2. Comemos churros.			
3. El gallopinto es un plato típico.			
4. Comemos tortillas de huevos, patatas y cebolla.			
5. Cenamos a las diez de la noche.			
6. Cenamos a eso de las ocho.			
7. A veces tomamos el almuerzo en un puesto de comida.			

D **Comparando y contrastando** Cuando comparas algo, citas cosas que son similares. Cuando contrastas algo, das diferencias. En la lectura, ¿cuáles son unas actividades de las familias de José Luis y de Catalina que son similares? Y, ¿cuáles son diferentes? ¿Cuáles de las actividades de las dos familias son similares o diferentes de las actividades de tu familia?

GeoVistas

To learn more about Nicaragua, turn to pages SH50–SH51.

Una merienda ¿Dónde? 🎧♻️

Antes de leer

Vas a aprender adonde van los jóvenes en España y Latinoamérica a tomar algo. Cuando tienes sed o hambre y deseas tomar algo, ¿adónde vas?

En un café Después de las clases en España y Latinoamérica muchos alumnos van a un café o una cafetería. Muchos cafés tienen una terraza al aire libre[1]. Cuando hace buen tiempo buscan una mesa libre en la terraza.

En el café toman un refresco si solo tienen sed o toman una merienda si tienen hambre. En el café ven a sus amigos y conversan con ellos. Hablan de muchas cosas.

En un mesón Los universitarios van a un mesón. Los mesones son muy populares en España pero hay mesones en Latinoamérica también. En el mesón los estudiantes hablan con sus amigos y comen tapas en España o antojitos en Latinoamérica. No tienen que leer un menú porque ven los antojitos o tapas en platos en una barra[2] y seleccionan los antojitos que desean comer.

Los tunos A veces entra en el mesón un grupo de tunos. Los tunos son músicos que tocan[3] la guitarra y cantan[4]. Los estudiantes cantan con ellos. Los tunos son populares sobre todo en España y en Guanajuato, México.

[1]al aire libre   *outdoors*
[2]barra   *counter*
[3]tocan   *play*
[4]cantan   *sing*

CULTURA

Los tunos tocan la guitarra y cantan. Son populares en España y Guanajuato, México.

¿Comprendes?

Escoge. Select the correct answer or completion based on the information in the reading.

1. ¿Adónde van muchos alumnos después de las clases?
   a. al café
   b. a casa
   c. a la escuela

2. La terraza del café está _____.
   a. en el interior del café
   b. delante del café
   c. en la cocina del café

3. ¿Quiénes toman una merienda?
   a. los alumnos que tienen un menú
   b. los alumnos que tienen hambre
   c. los universitarios

4. «Conversar» significa _____.
   a. leer
   b. tomar
   c. hablar

5. ¿Dónde comen tapas los universitarios?
   a. en el café
   b. en un mesón
   c. con los tunos

6. ¿Por qué no tienen que leer los universitarios un menú en el mesón?
   a. No comprenden el menú.
   b. No necesitan comida en el mesón.
   c. Ven los platos de tapas en la barra.

7. ¿Qué son los tunos?
   a. meseros
   b. mesones
   c. músicos

CULTURA

Las jóvenes toman una merienda y un refresco en un café en la Plaza Mayor en Madrid.

Vocabulario

1 **Completa.** Complete.

1. Yo tengo _____. Voy a tomar una gaseosa.
2. Elena tiene _____. Va a comer algo.
3. Paco es vegetariano. No come _____.
4. Normalmente los alumnos toman el desayuno en casa, pero toman _____ en la escuela.
5. Viven cerca de la costa. Así comen mucho _____.

To review **Vocabulario 1,** turn to pages 128–129.

2 **Contesta.** Answer.

6. ¿Cuáles son tres cosas que comemos para el desayuno?
7. ¿Cuáles son tres cosas que comemos para el almuerzo?
8. ¿Cuáles son tres cosas que comemos para la cena?

3 **Parea.** Match each statement with the illustration it describes. Then fill in the missing words.

a.   b.   c.

d.   e.

To review **Vocabulario 2,** turn to pages 132–133.

9. Los amigos van _____.
10. Teresa ve _____ libre.
11. Tomás lee _____.
12. Tomás tiene sed. Toma _____.
13. El mesero escribe _____.

Gramática

4 **Completa.** Complete with the correct form of the verb.

14. Ellos _____ muchas legumbres. (comer)

15. Nosotros _____ en Estados Unidos. (vivir)

16. Nosotros _____ el español en la escuela. (aprender)

17–18. Yo _____ y _____ mucho. (leer, escribir)

19. ¿Qué _____ tú en la televisión? (ver)

20. ¿Qué _____ ustedes? (beber)

21. ¿_____ (tú) una sorpresa a veces? (recibir)

22. Los amigos _____ el menú. (leer)

23. José tiene que estudiar. Él _____ su libro. (abrir)

24. Todos los parientes _____ a la fiesta. (asistir)

25. El mesero _____ la orden. (escribir)

To review the present tense of **-er** and **-ir** verbs, turn to page 136.

5 **Completa.** Complete with the correct form of **ir a, tener que,** or **acabar de.**

26. Yo no tengo hambre porque _____ comer.

27. Es necesario. Yo _____ estudiar porque mañana tengo un examen importante.

28. Voy al café donde _____ tomar un refresco.

To review the expressions **ir a, tener que,** and **acabar de,** turn to page 140.

6 **Escribe con nosotros.** Write with **nosotros.**

29–33. Después de las clases tengo que ir a casa. Voy a usar la computadora porque recibo muchos correos electrónicos. Leo los correos. Luego escribo muchos correos electrónicos.

To review the present tense of **-er** and **-ir** verbs and **ir a** and **tener que,** turn to pages 136, 140.

Cultura

7 **Contesta.** Answer.

34. ¿Cuál es un desayuno típico en España?

35. ¿Cuál es un desayuno típico en Nicaragua?

36. ¿Dónde toman los alumnos el almuerzo en España y Nicaragua?

37. ¿En qué país cenan muy tarde?

To review this cultural information, turn to pages 146–147.

8 **Corrige.** Correct the following false statements.

38. La tortilla mexicana lleva huevos, patatas y cebolla.

39. El gallopinto es una mezcla de papas y frijoles.

40. Los jóvenes toman el desayuno en la cafetería o en un café.

Un desayuno típico en España y muchas partes de Latinoamérica

Prepárate para el examen
Practice for oral proficiency

1 **¿Qué comes?**

✔ *Talk about eating habits*

Work in groups of three or four. Find out what each of you eats for different meals.

2 **En un café**

✔ *Tell about your friends and school*

Get together with several friends and pretend you are chatting in a café. Have a lively conversation talking about typical topics such as your friends, your teachers, your school activities, your after-school activities, etc. There's quite a bit you can say.

CULTURA

Los alumnos y los profesores toman el almuerzo en la cafetería de una escuela en Barranquilla, Colombia.

3 **En otras partes**

✔ *Compare eating habits in Spanish-speaking countries with your own*

Get together with several friends. Discuss what you learned about some of the eating habits in Spain and Nicaragua. Are they similar to yours or different?

4 **Debo, pero no voy a...**

✔ *Tell what you should do and what you have to do*

Tell some things you should do but aren't going to do because you have to do something else.

5 **Ahora no, porque...**

✔ *Tell what you have just done and what you are going to do*

Tell some things you don't have to do now because you just did them. Continue by telling some things you are going to do.

Prepárate para el examen
Practice for written proficiency

Tarea

Write an essay in Spanish comparing and contrasting some foods and eating habits of Hispanic families you have learned about. Then think about your family's eating customs and discuss ways your family's habits are similar to or different from those of the families in Spain and Nicaragua.

Writing Strategy

Organizing To present ideas you must give some organization to what you write. Here are two possible choices as to how to organize your writing.

• Write all the information you know about a particular person or group before moving on to the next one.

• Write about one topic and compare the people or groups before going on to the next topic.

CULTURA

Tapas en una barra de una cafetería en España

① Prewrite

Remember to write using only Spanish you have learned. Stick to what you know. Here are some ideas to help you. You may wish to use charts similar to the ones below to help you organize.

• List the Spanish verbs that you will want to use.

• List the meals and foods you plan to discuss.

• List the habits or customs you plan to discuss.

② Write

• Create sentences using words in your lists.

• Organize your sentences following one of the suggestions given in the Writing Strategy.

• Prepare a draft. Read it and correct any errors.

• Give your composition an attention-grabbing title.

Evaluate

Don't forget that your teacher will evaluate you on organization, use of vocabulary, correctness of grammar, and completeness of information.

Comidas

Estados Unidos   España

Nicaragua

Costumbres

Estados Unidos   España

Nicaragua

Gramática

- ### Presente de los verbos en -er, -ir *(page 136)*
  Verbs of the second and third conjugations have the same endings in all forms except **nosotros(as)** and **vosotros(as)**.

comer			
yo	como	nosotros(as)	comemos
tú	comes	vosotros(as)	coméis
Ud., él, ella	come	Uds., ellos, ellas	comen

escribir			
yo	escribo	nosotros(as)	escribimos
tú	escribes	vosotros(as)	escribís
Ud., él, ella	escribe	Uds., ellos, ellas	escriben

Note the forms of the verb **ver.**

ver			
yo	veo	nosotros(as)	vemos
tú	ves	vosotros(as)	veis
Ud., él, ella	ve	Uds., ellos, ellas	ven

- ### Expresiones con el infinitivo *(page 140)*
  Ir a *(to be going to)*, **tener que** *(to have to)*, and **acabar de** *(to have just)* are frequently used expressions in Spanish that are followed by the infinitive—the form of the verb that ends in **-ar, -er,** or **-ir.**

  Acabo de llegar a Masaya. Yo voy a ir al café.
  Tengo que comer algo.

CULTURA

Aquí vemos un café interesante en Masaya, Nicaragua. El café ofrece deliciosos batidos de muchas frutas tropicales. Si tienes hambre, ofrecen meriendas también.

There are a number of cognates in this list. See how many you and a partner can find. Who can find the most? Compare your list with those of your classmates.

Vocabulario

Talking about meals

la comida	vegetariano(a)	comer
el desayuno	tener hambre	beber
el almuerzo	tener sed	cenar
la cena	tomar	

Identifying some foods

las tostadas, el pan tostado	el jamón	los frijoles	el postre
el panecillo	el queso	las legumbres, los vegetales, las verduras	el helado
la mantequilla	una ensalada		el flan
el cereal	una pizza	la lechuga	la torta
el huevo	una hamburguesa	el tomate	
el tocino, el bacón	la carne	las papas, las patatas fritas	
un sándwich, un bocadillo	el pollo		
	el pescado		
	el arroz		

Identifying some drinks

el refresco	la gaseosa	el chocolate	el vaso
la bebida	el agua (mineral) (con gas)	el café	la taza
un jugo de naranja		el batido	caliente
la leche		la cola	frío(a)

Talking about a café

la merienda	los camarones	el/la cliente(a)	abrir
las tapas, los antojitos	las aceitunas	el menú	recibir
la empanada	las albóndigas	la orden	escribir
los tostones	una mesa ocupada	la cuenta	¿Qué desean tomar?
los pinchitos	una mesa libre	ver	¿Está incluido el servicio?
	el/la mesero(a)	leer	

Other useful words and expressions

una sorpresa	tener que	aprender	deber
enseguida	ir a	comprender	vivir
	acabar de	creer que sí (que no)	

Repaso cumulativo

Repasa lo que ya has aprendido

These activities will help you review
what you have learned so far in Spanish.

 ¿Sí o no? Look at the family tree below of **la familia Hernández.** Listen to each statement and indicate on a separate sheet of paper whether each statement is true or false.

Aquí vemos a una madre con su bebé durante una fiesta en Cotacachi, Ecuador.

 Personaliza. Answer the questions giving information about yourself.

1. ¿Cuántos años tienes?
2. ¿Cuántos hermanos tienes?
3. ¿Cuántos años tienen ellos?
4. ¿Tiene tu familia una casa privada o un apartamento?
5. ¿Cuántos cuartos tiene tu casa o apartamento?
6. ¿Tienen ustedes una mascota?
7. ¿Qué tienen? ¿Un perro o un gato?

 Escribe cada frase de nuevo. Rewrite each sentence with the new subject. Pay particular attention to the verb ending.

1. Yo estudio español. (nosotros)
2. Ellos sacan notas buenas. (tú)
3. Los alumnos prestan atención. (el alumno)
4. Tú hablas mucho. (ustedes)
5. Nosotros miramos un DVD. (yo)
6. Carlos escucha un CD. (ellos)

Unas alumnas colombianas regresan a casa después de las clases.

Lee y escribe. Read the story and then redo it changing Carlos to your own name. Tell all about yourself.

Yo soy Carlos. Soy de Caracas, Venezuela. Tengo diecisiete años. Ahora estoy en clase. Después de las clases voy a un café con mis amigos.

 Escribe. Rewrite Activity 4 changing **yo** to **él**.

 Personaliza. Answer about yourself.
1. ¿Quién eres?
2. ¿De dónde eres?
3. ¿Cómo eres?
4. ¿Quién es tu amigo(a)?
5. ¿Cómo es él o ella?

 Inventa. Look at the illustrations of a typical day in the life of Rafael and his younger brother, Jaime. Describe their day. Include as many details as possible.

Deportes

Aquí y Allí

Vamos a comparar Los deportes son populares en casi todas partes del mundo. Pero la popularidad o importancia de cierto deporte puede variar de un país a otro. En unas culturas son muy apreciados los deportes de equipo y en otras los deportes individuales. ¿Juegan un papel o rol importante los equipos deportivos en tu escuela? ¿Qué deporte es muy popular? Vas a aprender si los mismos deportes que nos interesan mucho a nosotros son populares también en España y Latinoamérica.

Un grupo de amigos juegan fútbol en la isla de Ometepe en el lago de Nicaragua. Al fondo podemos ver los volcanes Concepción y Maderas.

Objetivos

You will:

- talk about sports
- describe a soccer uniform
- identify colors
- compare team sports in the U.S. and Spanish-speaking countries

You will use:

- present tense of stem-changing verbs
- verbs such as **interesar, aburrir,** and **gustar**

Go to glencoe.com
For: **Online book**
Web code: **ASD4003c5**

Introducción al tema
Deportes

Honduras Aquí vemos a un pelotero—un joven que juega pelota—durante la época de los mayas. La estatua del pelotero está en Copán, Honduras. Los deportes son populares aun en la época de los mayas. ▼

▲ **República Dominicana**
Es una carrera de ciclistas durante los Juegos Panamericanos en Santo Domingo, en la República Dominicana.

Look at these photographs to acquaint yourself with the theme of this chapter—sports. In this chapter you will learn to discuss sports that are played throughout Spain and Latin America. What do these photos tell you about sports in Spanish-speaking countries? Are the same sports popular in the United States? Can you think of a major sport in the United States that is not shown here?

Argentina Un tenista argentino juega contra un tenista español en una competición en la Avenida Nueve de Julio en Buenos Aires, Argentina. ▼

Guatemala Las dos muchachas juegan básquetbol en una cancha delante de unas ruinas de una iglesia en Antigua, Guatemala. ▼

▲ **Cuba** En unos países hispanos, pero no en todos, el béisbol es muy popular. Aquí vemos a un joven beisbolista cubano.

México El fútbol es el deporte número uno. Aquí el equipo brasileño juega contra el equipo mexicano. ▼

Chile Es una entrada a un juego de fútbol en que juega la Universidad de Chile. ▼

ESTADIO LIGA DEPORTIVA UNIVERSITARIA
LIGA
vs.
UNIVERSIDAD DE CHILE 11:30
Domingo 6 de Julio
N° 8968
US$ 2.00
GENERAL SUR

México Aquí vemos el Estadio Azul en la Ciudad de México. Muchas ciudades españolas y latinoamericanas tienen grandes estadios deportivos. ▶

El fútbol

In Chapter 3 you learned the expressions **ir a pie** and **levantar la mano.** Do you remember the meanings of **el pie** and **la mano?**

el equipo

la portería

el portero

lanzar el balón

Los jugadores juegan (al) fútbol.
El portero guarda la portería.
El jugador puede lanzar (tirar) el balón con el pie.
Pero no puede tocar el balón con la mano.

el campo de fútbol

TIGRES 40:00 TOROS

el tanto   0   2   0

Hay dos tiempos en el partido de fútbol.
Cuando empieza el segundo tiempo, los jugadores vuelven al campo.

los aficionados

meter un gol

El portero no puede bloquear el balón.
El balón entra en la portería.
El jugador marca un tanto.
Los aficionados aplauden.

Cada equipo quiere ganar el partido.
Pero no puede ser.
Un equipo pierde.

- When you want to express disappointment over an event or situation, you can say: **¡Qué pena! Lo siento mucho.**
- When you want to find out what a friend thinks about something, you can ask: **¿Qué piensas?**
  —**¿Qué piensas del equipo?**
  —**Pienso que es fantástico. Siempre gana.**

la jugadora

la camiseta

el pantalón corto

los calcetines largos

las zapatillas

¿De qué color es?

rosado(a)

amarillo(a)

negro(a)

gris

anaranjado(a)

de color marrón

blanco(a)

verde

azul

rojo(a)

El uniforme de cada equipo tiene su propio color o colores.

Para conversar

A mí me gusta el fútbol. Y a ti, ¿te gusta también? ¿Te interesa o no?

No, no me interesa el fútbol, pero me gusta el tenis.

ESCUCHAR

1 **Escucha y decide.** Listen to each statement. Indicate whether each one is correct or not. Make a chart similar to the one below to indicate your answers.

correcto	incorrecto

Comunidades

¿Viven muchos hispanos o latinos en tu comunidad o cerca de tu comunidad? ¿Son ellos muy aficionados al fútbol? ¿Que tipo de fútbol juegan más—el fútbol americano o el soccer? ¿Hay brasileños donde vives? ¡Los brasileños son fanáticos del fútbol!

HABLAR • ESCRIBIR

2 **Identifica.** Identify the clothing that the player is wearing and give the correct color.

ESCUCHAR • HABLAR • ESCRIBIR

3 **Contesta.** Answer the questions about a sporting event.
1. ¿Qué llevan los jugadores de fútbol?
2. En un partido de fútbol, ¿quiénes vuelven al campo cuando empieza el segundo tiempo?
3. ¿Cuándo mete un gol o marca un tanto un jugador?
4. En un juego de fútbol, ¿con qué pueden lanzar el balón los jugadores?
5. ¿Son futbolistas los jugadores?
6. ¿Quieren ganar los dos equipos?
7. ¿Pueden ganar los dos equipos?

EXPANSIÓN

Now, without looking at the questions, tell all you remember about the game. Your partner will add any information you forgot.

Más práctica

Workbook, pp. 5.3–5.4
StudentWorks™ Plus

HABLAR

4 Ask your partner these questions. Develop brief conversations by giving your own opinions as well. When you agree with your partner's opinion, you can add **Estoy de acuerdo.**

1. ¿Qué piensas del fútbol?
2. ¿Qué piensas del equipo de fútbol de tu escuela?
3. ¿Qué piensas de tu clase de español?
4. ¿Qué piensas de tus amigos?
5. ¿Qué piensas de tus profesores?

LEER • HABLAR

5 **Lee y completa.** Cuando los equipos juegan en la Copa Mundial, todos los jugadores del equipo son de la misma nacionalidad. Cada equipo tiene la bandera de su país. Da los colores de las banderas de los siguientes países.

México

Argentina

Chile

Perú

Comparaciones

6 Con un(a) amigo(a), compara y contrasta el fútbol americano y el fútbol que juegan en Europa y Latinoamérica.

fútbol americano

fútbol en Europa y Latinoamérica

El béisbol

la jardinera

la bateadora

la pelota

la pícher, la lanzadora

batear

lanzar

el bate

la cátcher, la receptora

el platillo

el campo de béisbol

La pícher lanza la pelota.   La bateadora batea.

el guante

atrapar

correr

El jugador (beisbolista) corre de una base a otra.

El jugador atrapa la pelota.
Atrapa la pelota con el guante.

El básquetbol, El baloncesto

driblar con el balón

el cesto, la canasta

la cancha

El jugador dribla con el balón.

El jugador tira el balón.
Cuando mete el balón en el cesto, encesta.

El tenis

la pelota

por encima de

la raqueta

la red

una cancha de tenis

Las amigas juegan (al) tenis.
Una jugadora golpea la pelota.
Otra jugadora devuelve la pelota.
La pelota tiene que pasar por encima de la red.
Juegan individuales. No juegan dobles.

¡Ojo!

Note that the verb
volver means *to return
to a place* and **devolver**
means *to return
something.*

¡Así se dice!

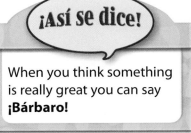

When you think something
is really great you can say
¡Bárbaro!

Go to glencoe.com
For: **Vocabulary practice**
Web code: **ASD4003c5**

ESCUCHAR

1 **Escucha y escoge.** Match each statement you hear with the sport being played in the photo.

a.

b.

c.

Conexiones

La arqueología

La arqueología es el estudio de los artefactos de las civilizaciones antiguas. En Copán, Honduras, hay ruinas de una cancha de pelota de los mayas—los indígenas de gran parte de Centroamérica. La cancha data del año 755 después de Cristo. Para jugar la pelota los mayas usan una pelota muy grande y pesada *(heavy)* y no pueden tocar la pelota con las manos.

LEER • ESCRIBIR

2 **Escoge y completa.** Choose the correct word from the **banco de palabras** to complete each sentence.

atrapa	devuelve	marca
corre	dribla	batea

1. La jugadora _____ un jonrón.
2. El beisbolista _____ la pelota con un guante.
3. El beisbolista _____ de una base a otra.
4. Cuando el jugador de básquetbol mete el balón en el cesto, _____ un tanto.
5. El jugador de básquetbol _____ con el balón.
6. En un juego de tenis un jugador _____ la pelota al otro.

ESCUCHAR • HABLAR • ESCRIBIR

3 **Contesta.** Answer the questions about a basketball game.

1. ¿Es el baloncesto un deporte de equipo o un deporte individual?
2. ¿Cuántos jugadores juegan en un equipo de básquetbol? ¿Cinco o nueve?
3. Durante un partido de baloncesto, ¿driblan los jugadores con el balón o lanzan el balón con el pie?
4. ¿El jugador de básquetbol tira el balón en el cesto o en la portería?
5. ¿Marca un tanto el jugador cuando encesta?
6. Cuando marca un tanto, ¿aplauden los aficionados?

Más práctica

Workbook, pp. 5.5–5.7

StudentWorks™ Plus

LEER

④ **Rompecabezas**

Choose the word in each group that does not belong.
Then switch the wrong words to make each group correct.

1. campo   guardar   raqueta   portero

2. receptor   platillo   guante   portería

3. pelota   canasta   red   golpear

4. bate   cesto   balón   driblar

ESCUCHAR • HABLAR • ESCRIBIR

⑤ **Confirma.** Correct the false statements.

1. Los beisbolistas juegan con un balón.
2. Los beisbolistas juegan en una cancha.
3. Los futbolistas llevan un guante.
4. Juegan básquetbol con una pelota.
5. El jugador de básquetbol mete el balón en un guante para marcar un tanto.
6. En el tenis la pelota tiene que tocar (rebosar) la red.
7. Hay dos tenistas en un partido de dobles.

LEER • ESCRIBIR

⑥ **Completa.** Complete with the correct color.

1. Las zapatillas del jugador de béisbol son _____.
2. El guante de béisbol es de color _____.
3. La camiseta del jugador de básquetbol es _____.
4. El pantalón corto del jugador de básquetbol es _____.
5. Los calcetines del jugador de tenis son _____.
6. La camiseta del jugador de tenis es _____.

Cultura

El jai alai
El jai alai o la pelota vasca es un juego del País Vasco (Euskadi) en el norte de España. Los jugadores de jai alai, «los pelotaris», usan una cesta para lanzar y atrapar la pelota. Mira el uniforme que lleva un jugador de jai alai.

Comunicación

⑦ Work with a partner. Give some information about a sport. Your partner will tell what sport you're talking about. Take turns.

Gramática

Los verbos de cambio radical e → ie

1. Some verbs in Spanish are called stem-changing verbs. The verbs **empezar, pensar, perder, querer,** and **preferir** are examples of stem-changing verbs. All forms, except the **nosotros** (and **vosotros**) forms, change the **e** of the infinitive to **ie.** The endings of these verbs are the same as those of a regular verb.

querer			
yo	quiero	nosotros(as)	queremos
tú	quieres	vosotros(as)	queréis
Ud., él, ella	quiere	Uds., ellos, ellas	quieren

2. Read the following verbs across. Observe the stem change and note that the endings are the same as those of a regular verb.

	empezar	perder	preferir
yo	empiezo	pierdo	prefiero
tú	empiezas	pierdes	prefieres
Ud., él, ella	empieza	pierde	prefiere
nosotros(as)	empezamos	perdemos	preferimos
vosotros(as)	empezáis	perdéis	preferís
Uds., ellos, ellas	empiezan	pierden	prefieren

¡Ojo!

Remember that if you pronounce the verb form correctly, you will write it correctly. It is always important to pay attention to the pronunciation.

¿Te acuerdas?

Review the verb **tener,** which you learned in Chapter 2. It follows this same pattern except for the **yo** form **tengo.**

CULTURA

Los amigos compran un helado en Zafra, España. Pedro y Antonio quieren un helado de vainilla pero Francisco prefiere el chocolate.

Práctica

ESCUCHAR • HABLAR • ESCRIBIR

 1 **Personaliza.** Answer about yourself and some friends.

1. ¿Quieren ustedes jugar fútbol?
2. ¿Empiezan ustedes a jugar a las tres y media?
3. ¿Quieren ustedes ganar?
4. ¿Pierden ustedes a veces?
5. ¿Dónde prefieren ustedes jugar?

LEER • HABLAR • ESCRIBIR

2 **Forma frases.** Form sentences.

1. los jugadores / empezar a jugar
2. los dos equipos / querer ganar
3. el equipo de Javier / querer ganar
4. Javier / querer meter un gol
5. el portero / querer bloquear el balón
6. el equipo de Javier / perder

¿Lo sabes?

Empezar and **comenzar** *(to begin)* require **a** before an infinitive.

Empiezan a jugar.
Comienzan a jugar.

 Comunicación

3 You're at a school sporting event. A friend calls you on your cell phone and asks about how things are going for the team. Try to use the following verbs.

empezar   **pensar**   **perder**   **querer**   **preferir**

HABLAR • ESCRIBIR

4 **Personaliza.** Answer about yourself.

1. ¿Prefieres jugar béisbol o fútbol?
2. ¿Prefieres jugar con un grupo de amigos o con un equipo organizado?
3. ¿Prefieres jugar o ser espectador(a)?
4. ¿Siempre quieres ganar?
5. ¿Pierdes a veces?

LEER • ESCRIBIR

5 **Completa.** Complete with the correct form of the verb(s).

1. Tú no _____ perder y no _____. (querer, perder)
2. Ustedes _____ ganar y nosotros _____ ganar también. (preferir, preferir)
3. ¿Qué _____ usted? ¿_____ empezar ahora o no? (pensar, querer)

CULTURA

El padre y su hijo no quieren jugar en el parque. Prefieren jugar en una calle cerca de su casa en Cádiz, España.

Los verbos de cambio radical o → ue

1. The verbs **poder, volver, devolver,** and **dormir** *(to sleep)* are also stem-changing verbs. The **o** of the infinitive changes to **ue** in all forms except **nosotros** (and **vosotros**).

poder			
yo	puedo	nosotros(as)	podemos
tú	puedes	vosotros(as)	podéis
Ud., él, ella	puede	Uds., ellos, ellas	pueden

2. Read the following verbs across. Observe the stem change and note that the endings are the same as those of a regular verb of the same conjugation.

	volver	dormir
yo	vuelvo	duermo
tú	vuelves	duermes
Ud., él, ella	vuelve	duerme
nosotros(as)	volvemos	dormimos
vosotros(as)	volvéis	dormís
Uds., ellos, ellas	vuelven	duermen

3. The **u** in the verb **jugar** also changes to **ue** in all forms except **nosotros** (and **vosotros**).

jugar			
yo	juego	nosotros(as)	jugamos
tú	juegas	vosotros(as)	jugáis
Ud., él, ella	juega	Uds., ellos, ellas	juegan

CULTURA

Los alumnos son de León, Nicaragua. Ellos vuelven a casa después de las clases.

¿Lo sabes?

Jugar is sometimes followed by **a** when a sport is mentioned. Both of the following are acceptable.

Juegan al fútbol.
Juegan fútbol.

Práctica

VIDEO Want help with the present tense of stem-changing verbs? Watch **Gramática en vivo.**

Más práctica
Workbook, pp. 5.10–5.11
StudentWorks™ Plus

ESCUCHAR • HABLAR • ESCRIBIR

6 Personaliza. Answer about yourself and some friends.

1. ¿Juegan ustedes tenis?
2. ¿Pueden ustedes jugar tenis en la escuela?
3. Cuando juegan tenis, ¿prefieren ustedes jugar individuales o dobles?
4. ¿Duermen ustedes bien después de muchas actividades físicas?

LEER • ESCRIBIR

7 Personaliza. Answer about yourself.

1. ¿A qué hora empieza tu clase de español?
2. ¿Puedes hablar inglés en la clase de español?
3. A veces, ¿juegas Bingo en la clase de español?
4. ¿Duermes en clase?
5. Cuando tomas un examen, ¿devuelve tu profesor(a) los exámenes pronto?
6. ¿A qué hora vuelves a casa después de las clases?

GeoVistas

To learn more about Mexico, take a tour on pages SH46–SH47.

HABLAR • ESCRIBIR

8 Sigue el modelo. Make up sentences as in the model.

MODELO   ellas / jugar básquetbol →
          Ellas juegan básquetbol.

1. juego / empezar ahora
2. jugadoras / volver a la cancha
3. tú / tener que driblar
4. Catalina / querer encestar
5. su equipo / no poder perder
6. nosotros / tener que ganar

HABLAR

9 Dramatiza. Stand up and act out soccer, basketball, baseball, and tennis moves. Have someone tell you what you're doing.

CULTURA

Es una cancha de baloncesto en Zihuatanejo, México. Cuando juegas baloncesto aquí, puedes disfrutar también de una vista de Zihuatanejo y del océano Pacífico.

FOLDABLES®
Study Organizer

front

El fútbol

FORWARD-BACKWARD BOOK
See page SH22 for help with making this foldable. Use this study organizer to talk about sports. Work with a partner. You and a partner will each create a Forward-Backward Book with terminology and pictures for two sports. Then ask questions about the content of your partner's book.

LEER • ESCRIBIR

10 Completa. Complete with the correct form of the indicated verb. You will use all verb forms.

Yo ___1___ (jugar) mucho al fútbol y mi amiga Carla ___2___ (jugar) mucho también pero ahora no ___3___ (poder).

Vamos a hablar con Carla.

—Carla, ¿por qué no ___4___ (poder) jugar con nosotras?

—Yo ___5___ (querer) pero no ___6___ (poder). ___7___ (Querer) volver a casa.

—¿Por qué ___8___ (querer) ir a casa?

—Porque ___9___ (tener) dos amigos que ___10___ (volver) hoy de España y ___11___ (querer) estar en casa.

EXPANSIÓN

Now, without looking at the conversation, tell all you remember about it. Your partner will add anything you forgot.

Comunicación

11 A classmate will ask you if you want to do something or go somewhere. Tell him or her that you want to but can't because you have to do something else. Take turns asking and answering the questions. Remember to use **querer, poder,** and **tener que.**

HABLAR

12 **Juego** Work with a partner. The people below all want to play a certain sport, but there is a problem. Tell why they cannot do what they want to do. Take turns.

Quiero jugar básquetbol.

Quiero jugar béisbol.

Quiero jugar fútbol.

Quiero jugar tenis.

Los verbos interesar, aburrir, gustar

1. The verbs **interesar** and **aburrir** function the same in English and in Spanish. Study the following examples.

¿Te aburre el béisbol?	*Does baseball bore you?*
No, el béisbol me interesa.	*No, baseball interests me.*
¿Te aburren los deportes?	*Do sports bore you?*
No, los deportes me interesan.	*No, sports interest me.*

2. The verb **gustar** in Spanish functions the same as **interesar** and **aburrir**. **Gustar** conveys the meaning *to like*, but its true meaning is *to please*. The Spanish way of saying *I like baseball* is *Baseball pleases me.*

¿Te aburre el béisbol? No. Me interesa.
¿Te gusta el béisbol? Sí, me gusta mucho el béisbol.
¿Te gustan los deportes en general? Sí, me gustan todos.

3. **Gustar** is often used with an infinitive to tell what you like to do.

¿Te gusta ganar? Sí. No me gusta perder.
¿Te gusta comer? Sí, me gusta comer.

¿Lo sabes?

Mí and **ti** are used after a preposition: **a mí** and **a ti.** You will frequently use **a mí** and **a ti** to add emphasis.

—**A mí me gusta. ¿A ti también?**
—**Sí, a mí también.**

—**A mí no me gusta. ¿Y a ti?**
—**(No.) Ni a mí tampoco.**

CULTURA

Aquí vemos a unos miembros del equipo de básquetbol de una escuela secundaria en Mérida, Venezuela.

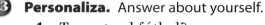

Práctica

Los alumnos tienen mucho interés en la biología. ¿A ti te interesa también?

HABLAR • ESCRIBIR

13 **Personaliza.** Answer about yourself.

1. ¿Te gusta el fútbol?
2. ¿Qué te gusta más? ¿El fútbol o el béisbol?
3. En general, ¿te gustan los deportes o no?
4. ¿Te gustan el tenis y el golf?
5. ¿Te gusta más practicar un deporte o ser espectador(a)?

ESCUCHAR • HABLAR • ESCRIBIR

14 **Contesta según el modelo.** Answer according to the model.

MODELO —¿**Te gustan los tomates?**
—**Sí, a mí me gustan y como muchos. ¿Y a ti?**

1. ¿Te gustan las hamburguesas?
2. ¿Te gusta la carne?
3. ¿Te gustan los cereales?
4. ¿Te gusta el helado?
5. ¿Te gustan las frutas?
6. ¿Te gusta el arroz?

ESCUCHAR • HABLAR • ESCRIBIR

15 **Personaliza.** Answer about yourself.

1. ¿Te interesa el curso de historia? ¿Te gusta la historia?
2. ¿Te interesa el curso de español? ¿Te gusta el español?
3. ¿Te interesa la biología? ¿Te gustan las ciencias?

 Comunicación

16 Work with a partner. Tell which courses interest you and which courses bore you. Also, tell which ones you really like and the ones you don't like very much. Take turns.

InfoGap For more practice using **interesar, aburrir,** and **gustar,** do Activity 5 on page SR7 at the end of this book.

HABLAR • ESCRIBIR

17 **¡Te toca a ti!** Tell your classmates all the things you like to do.

HABLAR

18 **¡Manos a la obra!** Make a collage of some things you like and don't like. Use your collage to explain your likes and dislikes to the class. You may want to include pictures of the following: **comidas, deportes, actividades.**

PRONUNCIACIÓN 🎧

Las consonantes s, c, z

The consonant **s** is pronounced the same as the *s* in *sing.* Repeat the following.

sa	se	si	so	su
sala	seis	sí	sobre	su
pasa	base	decisión	solo	Susana
mesa	serio	siete	ambicioso	suburbio
interesa	mesero	siento	curso	
rosado	camiseta	televisión		
piensa	segundo	física		

The consonant **c** in combination with **e** or **i** (**ce, ci**) is pronounced the same as an **s** in all areas of Latin America. In many areas of Spain, **ce** and **ci** are pronounced like the *th* in English. Likewise, the pronunciation of **z** in combination with **a, o, u** (**za, zo, zu**) is pronounced as an **s** throughout Latin America and as *th* in most areas of Spain. Repeat the following.

za	ce	ci	zo	zu
lanza	cesto	cinco	empiezo	Venezuela
empieza	cena	recibe	lanzo	azul
zapatillas	necesita	aficionado	perezoso	zumo
comienza	calcetines	encima	almuerzo	
		ciento	venezolano	

 **Dictado**

Pronounce the following sentences carefully. Then write them to prepare for a dictation.

> El señor González enseña en la sala de clase.
> El aficionado lleva una camiseta, zapatillas y calcetines largos.
> Toma el almuerzo a las doce y diez en la cocina.
> Los venezolanos empiezan a volver al campo.
> Sí, Susana recibe seis camisetas.

 **¡Bravo!**

You have now learned all the new vocabulary and grammar in this chapter. Continue to use and practice all that you know while learning more cultural information. **¡Vamos!**

¿Quiénes juegan?

Sara	Hola, Esperanza. ¿Qué hay?
Esperanza	¿Qué piensas? ¿Quieres jugar fútbol?
Sara	¡Bárbaro! Me gusta mucho el fútbol. ¿Cuándo jugamos? ¿Ahora?
Esperanza	Ahora, sí.
Sara	¡Oye, Esperanza! ¿Puede jugar mi amiga Teresa? Es muy buena jugadora.
Esperanza	Ay, ¡qué pena! Lo siento mucho pero ya tenemos las once jugadoras. Ella puede jugar mañana si quiere.
Sara	¡Cómo no! ¿A qué hora empiezan a jugar mañana?
Esperanza	A la misma hora.

¿Comprendes?

VIDEO To observe a lesson on how to play **pato**, a popular sport in Argentina, watch **Diálogo en vivo**. To visit a **pato** match, watch **Cultura en vivo**.

A **Contesta.** Answer based on the conversation.

1. ¿Quiénes hablan?
2. ¿Quiere jugar Sara?
3. ¿Qué piensa? ¿Es una buena idea?
4. ¿Cuándo van a jugar?
5. ¿Quién más quiere jugar?
6. ¿Puede o no?
7. ¿Por qué no puede?
8. ¿Cuándo puede jugar?

B **Resumiendo** Retell the events in the conversation in your own words.

C **Analizando** Trabaja con un(a) compañero(a). En la conversación hay un problema. ¿Cuál es? ¿Cómo resuelven el problema las muchachas?

CULTURA

El fútbol es un deporte muy popular en Perú. Aquí vemos el Estadio Nacional en Lima, la capital.

Antes de leer

Think about sports teams and sporting events in your school. Does your school have organized teams? What sports are popular?

✓ Reading Check

¿Dónde practican los deportes los jóvenes en Latinoamérica?

Durante la lectura

Think about the role of school sports in Hispanic countries compared with the role of sports in your school.

✓ Reading Check

¿Qué deporte es muy popular en España y Latinoamérica?

✓ Reading Check

¿Dónde es popular el béisbol?

Después de leer

Can you relate to the information in the reading? Do sports play a role in your life?

Los deportes de equipo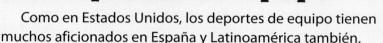

Como en Estados Unidos, los deportes de equipo tienen muchos aficionados en España y Latinoamérica también.

El fútbol El deporte número uno en la mayoría de los países hispanos es el fútbol—el *soccer* en Estados Unidos. Cuando no hay clases, grupos de amigos organizan un partido espontáneo de fútbol en un parque, en la calle o en el patio de la escuela. Cada vez que un jugador mete un gol los otros miembros del equipo aplauden. Son ellos sus mismos porristas[1].

CULTURA

Los jóvenes juegan fútbol en las afueras de La Paz, Bolivia.

El fútbol profesional El fútbol profesional es muy popular. Muchas ciudades tienen su propio equipo como el Real Madrid, por ejemplo. Y cada país tiene su equipo nacional. Cada equipo tiene sus colores. Cuando el equipo de un país juega contra el equipo de otro país, van miles de aficionados al estadio para ver el partido.

El béisbol El béisbol es muy popular en el Caribe—Puerto Rico, Cuba, la República Dominicana—y también en Venezuela, Panamá y Nicaragua. El pequeño pueblo de San Pedro de Macorís en la República Dominicana es el pueblo que produce más beisbolistas de las Grandes Ligas que cualquier[2] otro pueblo.

[1]mismos porristas *own cheerleaders* [2]cualquier *any*

¿Comprendes?

Más práctica

📓 Workbook, pp. 5.14–5.15
🌐 StudentWorks™ Plus

A Confirmando información ¿Correcto o no?

1. En Latinoamérica el fútbol tiene muchos aficionados. Es muy popular.
2. Los jóvenes en los países hispanos solo juegan partidos organizados de fútbol en la escuela.
3. El fútbol que juegan en España y Latinoamérica es el mismo fútbol que jugamos en Estados Unidos.
4. No hay equipos de fútbol profesionales en Latinoamérica.
5. El béisbol es muy popular en varios países latinoamericanos.

B Recordando hechos Contesta.

1. ¿Dónde juegan fútbol los jóvenes?
2. ¿Dónde juegan los equipos profesionales?
3. ¿Cuál es el deporte número uno en muchas partes de Latinoamérica?
4. ¿En qué países es el béisbol el deporte número uno?

GeoVistas

To learn more about the Dominican Republic, take a tour on pages SH62–SH63.

C Analizando

¿Por qué es el pequeño pueblo de San Pedro de Macorís un pueblo importante y famoso?

D Infiriendo

An inference is something that is not explicitly stated; it is a hidden message. Based on what you just read, how would you answer the following? **¿Dónde son más populares o importantes los deportes escolares organizados? ¿En Estados Unidos o en España y Latinoamérica? ¿Por qué contestas así?**

CULTURA

Es una vista del pueblo de San Pedro de Macorís en la República Dominicana. Es un pueblo pequeño pero produce muchos beisbolistas famosos de las Grandes Ligas.

Roberto Clemente 🎧♻

Antes de leer

Vas a leer una biografía corta del famoso beisbolista puertorriqueño Roberto Clemente. Piensa en unos jugadores de béisbol famosos. Hay unos que son héroes. Vas a leer sobre las hazañas, o buenas acciones, de Roberto Clemente. Luego decide si él es héroe.

Roberto Clemente es de Carolina, Puerto Rico. Cuando tiene sólo diecisiete años ya es jugador profesional de béisbol. Clemente juega con los Piratas de Pittsburgh. Cuatro veces es campeón de los bateadores y diez veces recibe el premio[1] del Guante de Oro por ser el mejor jardinero derecho[2] de su liga.

Es diciembre en Puerto Rico. Hace calor en la isla tropical. Clemente va a Puerto Rico donde pasa unas vacaciones con su familia. Pero algo ocurre. En Managua, la capital de Nicaragua, hay un terremoto desastroso. Clemente recibe las noticias del desastre el día de Nochebuena[3]. Tiene que actuar. Organiza ayuda[4] para sus hermanos nicaragüenses. Los puertorriqueños contribuyen generosamente. Clemente busca un avión[5]. Solo puede encontrar un avión viejo. Llena el avión de medicinas, comida y otras provisiones para las víctimas del terremoto. Clemente está en la cabina de mando con el piloto. El avión despega[6]. Momentos después—otro desastre. El avión cae[7] en las aguas del Caribe. Clemente muere—pierde su vida.

Aquí tenemos el comentario de un famoso entrenador[8]: «Es imposible producir un filme sobre la vida de Roberto. No hay otro Roberto. No hay actor para tomar el papel (el rol) de Roberto Clemente».

Hoy hay un gran centro deportivo para los jóvenes de Puerto Rico que lleva el nombre de Roberto. La calle donde está la casa de Roberto lleva su nombre. Pero la señora de Clemente y sus hijos prefieren el nombre original. Cuando la calle lleva el nombre original, Clemente vive.

CULTURA

La pobre ciudad de Managua, Nicaragua, después de la destrucción causada por el terremoto del 27 de diciembre de 1972

[1]premio *prize*
[2]mejor jardinero derecho *best right fielder*
[3]Nochebuena *Christmas Eve*
[4]ayuda *help*

[5]avión *airplane*
[6]despega *takes off*
[7]cae *falls*
[8]entrenador *manager*

¿Comprendes?

Escoge. Choose the correct completion or answer.

1. Roberto Clemente es de _____.
   a. Pittsburgh
   b. Puerto Rico
   c. Nicaragua
   d. Estados Unidos

2. ¿Qué son los Piratas?
   a. aficionados de Pittsburgh
   b. hombres malos
   c. un equipo profesional de béisbol
   d. un premio

3. Clemente juega la posición de _____.
   a. pícher
   b. jardinero
   c. cátcher
   d. bateador

4. Un terremoto es _____.
   a. una ocurrencia
   b. un desastre natural
   c. un accidente
   d. ¡Bárbaro!

5. ¿Por qué busca Clemente un avión?
   a. Busca ayuda.
   b. Quiere estar en la cabina de mando.
   c. Quiere enviar provisiones a Nicaragua.
   d. Quiere comprar un avión.

6. ¿Cuál es la idea principal de las palabras del famoso entrenador?
   a. Roberto Clemente es Roberto Clemente.
   b. Roberto Clemente es un actor muy bueno.
   c. No hay otro hombre como Roberto Clemente.
   d. No hay filme sobre su vida.

ROBERTO W. CLEMENTE MIDDLE SCHOOL

CULTURA

Hay escuelas que llevan el nombre de Roberto Clemente como la escuela que vemos aquí en Germantown, Maryland. ¿Hay una escuela cerca de donde tú vives que lleva el nombre de una persona famosa?

183

Vocabulario

1 **Completa.** Complete.

1. Los beisbolistas atrapan la pelota en _____.
2. Los calcetines pueden ser _____ o cortos.
3. El béisbol y el básquetbol son dos _____.
4. _____ guarda la portería.
5. Un equipo _____ y otro equipo pierde.
6. El jugador _____ un gol y marca un tanto.
7–8. El _____ de básquetbol mete el balón en el _____.

 To review **Vocabulario 1** and **Vocabulario 2,** turn to pages 162–163 and 166–167.

2 **Identifica el deporte.** Identify the sport.

9. Corren de una base a otra.
10. Tienen que driblar con el balón.
11. La pelota tiene que pasar por encima de la red.
12. El balón tiene que entrar en la portería.

3 **Identifica.** Identify.

 To review **Vocabulario 2,** turn to pages 166–167.

13.

14.

15.

16.

Gramática

4 **Completa.** Complete.

17. Los jugadores _____ al campo. (volver)

18–19. Nosotros _____ jugar pero no _____.
(querer, poder)

20. Nuestro equipo no _____. (perder)

21. ¿Cuándo _____ tú? (empezar)

22. Ustedes _____ bastante bien. (jugar)

23. Yo lo _____ mucho. (sentir)

24. ¿_____ usted jugar béisbol o fútbol con sus amigos?
(preferir)

25. Después del partido, tú _____ bien. (dormir)

26. Nosotros _____ a formar un equipo de béisbol.
(comenzar)

27. Yo _____ la pelota pero no pasa por encima
de la red. (devolver)

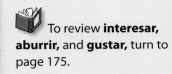 To review **los verbos de cambio radical,** turn to pages 170 and 172.

5 **Completa.** Complete.

28–29. ¿A ti _____ gust_ los deportes?
—Sí, a mí _____ gust_ mucho.

30–31. A ti _____ gust_ la ensalada
y comes mucha. Pero a mí no _____
gust_.

32. Me gust_ comer frijoles.

33. El arte me interes_ mucho.

34. No me interes_ las matemáticas.

35–36. —¿A ti _____ aburr_ tus clases?
—No, a mí _____ interes_ todas.

To review **interesar, aburrir,** and **gustar,** turn to page 175.

To review this cultural information, turn to pages 180–181.

Cultura

6 **Corrige.** Correct any wrong information.

37. El deporte número uno en todas partes de
España y Latinoamérica es el béisbol.

38. Los jóvenes latinoamericanos organizan partidos
espontáneos de fútbol en el gimnasio de su escuela,
no en un parque o en la calle.

39. El béisbol es muy popular en Puerto Rico, Cuba
y Venezuela.

40. El Real Madrid es un equipo de béisbol.

CULTURA

La fuente de fútbol delante del edificio de la Confederación Sudamericana de Fútbol en Asunción, Paraguay

Prepárate para el examen
Practice for oral proficiency

1 **El uniforme del equipo**

Discuss team uniforms

Your team is choosing its uniform and you have to decide on the colors for the shirts, shorts, socks, and shoes. Find out what a friend thinks of your choices. He or she will respond with **Me gusta(n) (mucho)…** or **No me gusta(n)… Prefiero…**

2 **¿Qué piensas?**

Ask for an opinion

Have a conversation with a friend. Ask the friend what he or she thinks about certain sports. Your friend will answer and will ask you what you think.

3 **Intereses**

Talk about your interests

Work with a classmate. Share some things that interest and/or bore you.

4 **Un deporte favorito**

Describe a sport

Describe your favorite sport to a friend. Then ask your friend about his or her favorite sport.

CULTURA

Aficionados en un evento deportivo en Argentina

5 **Un reportaje televisivo**

Announce a sporting event

You are a sports announcer for a Spanish-speaking television station. Give a brief description of a sporting event that you are attending at your school.

Prepárate para el examen
Practice for written proficiency

Tarea

Describe one of your school's sports teams. You may want to include the number of players, the captains, the team's colors, and the team's win-loss record. Also, tell what happens during a typical game.

Writing Strategy

Clustering Think about the information you want to include. "Brainstorm" by writing down whatever ideas come into your mind. Then organize these random ideas into groups or "clusters" such as the one below. Clustering helps you present your information in a clear and organized fashion.

① Prewrite

- Write your brainstorming ideas in Spanish. Write the verbs, adjectives, and nouns that you have learned and that you want to include in your essay.
- Create a cluster similar to the one below.
- Decide on the order of your paragraphs.

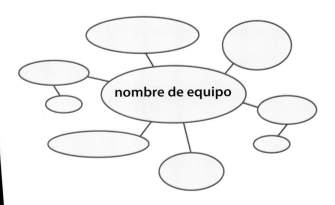

nombre de equipo

Los jóvenes juegan fútbol en el patio de su escuela en Chichicastenango, Guatemala.

② Write

- Begin with a brief introduction to capture the reader's attention. You could start with a question or an interesting fact about the team.
- Start each paragraph with a topic sentence. Then write sentences that focus and expand on that information.
- Write a brief conclusion to summarize or to express your opinion about the team.
- Give your composition an interest-grabbing title.
- Proofread your work. Did you use the correct words and endings? Did you spell correctly?
- Read your composition one final time. You may want another student to read it also.

Evaluate

Don't forget that your teacher will evaluate you on your organization, spelling, correct use of vocabulary and grammar, and completeness of your message.

Repaso del Capítulo 5

Gramática

- ### Los verbos de cambio radical e → ie, o → ue *(pages 170, 172)*
  Review the forms of stem-changing verbs. Note that in all forms except **nosotros** (and **vosotros**) the **e** of the infinitive changes to **ie** and the **o** of the infinitive changes to **ue**.

querer (e → ie)	
quiero	queremos
quieres	*queréis*
quiere	quieren

poder (o → ue)	
puedo	podemos
puedes	*podéis*
puede	pueden

- ### Los verbos interesar, aburrir, gustar *(page 175)*
  The verbs **interesar** and **aburrir** function the same in English and Spanish. **Gustar** in Spanish conveys the meaning *to like,* but its literal meaning is *to please.* Therefore, it functions the same as **interesar** and **aburrir.**

  —**Me interesa el béisbol. ¿Te interesa a ti también?**
  —**A mí, no. Me aburre.**
  —**A mí me gustan todos los deportes.**

  Note that **mí** and **ti** are used following a preposition.

  A mí me gusta el tenis.
  ¿A ti te gusta?

CULTURA

Dos equipos de jóvenes juegan durante un partido de básquetbol en Bilbao, en el País Vasco (Euskadi) en el norte de España.

There are a number of cognates in this list. See how many you and a partner can find. Who can find the most? Compare your list with those of your classmates.

Vocabulario

Identifying sports
los deportes	el béisbol	el básquetbol,	el tenis
el fútbol		el baloncesto	

Talking about a sporting event in general
el partido, el juego	el/la espectador(a)	volver	perder
el equipo	el tanto	poder	ganar
el/la jugador(a)	jugar (a)	querer	aplaudir
el/la aficionado(a)	empezar, comenzar		

Describing a soccer (el fútbol) game
el campo de fútbol	la portería	guardar	volver
el tiempo	el gol	entrar	meter (un gol)
el balón	lanzar	bloquear	
el/la portero(a)	tocar		

Describing a baseball game
el campo de béisbol	el/la cátcher,	el guante	batear
el/la beisbolista	el/la receptor(a)	el platillo	correr
el/la bateador(a)	el/la jardinero(a)	la base	atrapar
el/la lanzador(a),	la pelota	el jonrón	
el/la pícher	el bate		

Describing a basketball game
la cancha	el balón	driblar (con)
el cesto, la canasta	tirar	encestar

Describing a tennis game
la cancha	la red	golpear	por encima de
la raqueta	individuales	pasar	
la pelota	dobles	devolver	

Identifying a soccer team uniform
la camiseta	el pantalón corto	los calcetines largos	las zapatillas

Identifying colors
¿De qué color es?	anaranjado(a)	de color marrón	rojo(a)
el color	azul	gris	rosado(a)
amarillo(a)	blanco(a)	negro(a)	verde

Expressing likes and dislikes
gustar	interesar	aburrir

Other useful words and expressions
pensar	preferir	¡Qué pena!	¿Qué piensas de…?
dormir	propio(a)	Lo siento (mucho).	¡Bárbaro!

Repaso cumulativo

Repasa lo que ya has aprendido

These activities will help you review
what you have learned so far in Spanish.

 Escucha. Look at the illustrations. You will hear two
statements about each one. On a separate sheet of paper,
indicate whether the statement accurately describes the
illustration.

a.

b.

c.

2 Contesta. Answer.

1. ¿Qué comes para el desayuno?
2. ¿Qué come tu familia para la cena?
3. ¿Qué comida toman tú y tus amigos en la cafetería?
4. ¿Qué aprendes en la escuela?
5. ¿Comprendes bien cuando tu profesor(a) habla en español?
6. ¿Reciben tú y tus amigos notas buenas?

3 Completa con el adjetivo posesivo. Complete with the possessive adjective.

1. Nosotros tenemos un buen equipo. El equipo de _____ escuela gana muchos partidos.
2. Me gusta mucho el básquetbol. Es _____ deporte favorito.
3. Oye, Enrique. ¿Cuál es _____ deporte favorito?
4. Aprendemos mucho en la clase de español. _____ profesor es muy bueno.
5. La familia de José tiene un carro nuevo. _____ carro está en el garaje.
6. Yo tengo muchos amigos. _____ amigos son muy simpáticos.
7. María, ¿tienes muchos primos? ¿Dónde viven _____ primos?

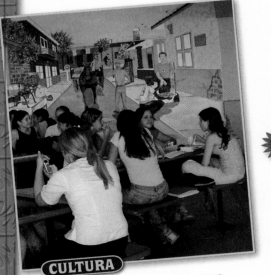

CULTURA

Los jóvenes comen y conversan (charlan) en la cafetería de su escuela en Barranquilla, Colombia. Una muchacha chequea (verifica) mensajes en su móvil.

Habla con la señora Vargas. Change the questions to speak with Mrs. Vargas. Remember to use **usted**.

1. ¿Vas con Juan?
2. ¿Hablas español?
3. ¿Usas la computadora?
4. ¿Tienes un carro nuevo?
5. ¿Lees mucho?
6. ¿Ves la televisión?
7. ¿Dónde vives?
8. ¿Puedes ir?
9. ¿Quieres comer ahora?
10. ¿Qué piensas?

Personaliza. Get together with a classmate. Tell your partner all about yourself. Some information you may want to give is:

mi nacionalidad

mi escuela

donde vivo

mi familia

yo

mis deportes favoritos

cuantos años tengo

color de mis ojos y de mi pelo

mis comidas favoritas

Parea los contrarios. Match the opposites.

1. bonito, guapo
2. gracioso
3. ambicioso
4. alto
5. grande
6. difícil
7. interesar
8. interesante

a. pequeño
b. aburrir
c. serio
d. aburrido
e. feo
f. bajo
g. perezoso
h. fácil

Juego Tell where each of the following might take place.
¡Cuidado! Some might happen in more than one place.

escuchar la música   mirar un DVD   enviar correos electrónicos
tomar el desayuno   llevar uniforme   preparar la comida
usar la computadora   prestar atención   tomar un examen
escuchar a la profesora   cenar con la familia   hablar en el móvil

EN CASA	EN LA ESCUELA
_____	_____
_____	_____

El bienestar

Aquí y Allí

Vamos a comparar Vas a aprender unas características de personalidad y unas emociones que tenemos de vez en cuando. En general no hay grandes diferencias en la personalidad y las emociones entre los seres humanos de las muchas partes del mundo. Las generalizaciones sobre tales aspectos de la naturaleza humana son casi siempre estereotípicas. Pero sabemos que las personas en todas partes del mundo quieren estar contentas y gozar de buena salud.

Objetivos

You will:

- describe people's personality, conditions, and emotions
- explain minor illnesses
- talk about a doctor's appointment
- learn about a literary genre—the picaresque novel

You will use:

- **ser** and **estar**
- indirect object pronouns

◄ El médico le da su diagnóstico a la paciente quien le presta mucha importancia. A ella le importan mucho su salud y bienestar.

QuickPass

Go to glencoe.com
For: **Online book**
Web code: **ASD4003c6**

Introducción al tema
El bienestar

◀ **Venezuela** ¿Cómo está la muchacha venezolana? ¿Qué expresiones tiene en la cara?

Look at these photographs to acquaint yourself with the theme of this chapter—well-being. In this chapter you will talk about your and others' personality, emotions, and health. What emotions do you see on the girl's face at the left? Personality, emotions, and health are universal themes. It doesn't matter who we are or where we're from—we all have personalities, feel emotions, and strive for good health.

Estados Unidos Todos los alumnos que vemos aquí están contentos, ¿no? ¿De dónde son? Pues son de muchos países pero ahora están en Estados Unidos. Cuatro de ellos son hispanos o latinos. ▼

Clínica

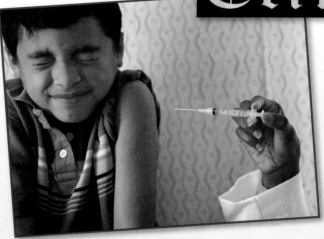

◄ Puerto Rico Los dos niños visitan una clínica en Puerto Rico. La muchacha tiene fiebre y le toman la temperatura. El muchacho necesita una inyección. No le gusta. Pica.

España Muchas farmacias son bastante bonitas. Aquí vemos una decoración en el exterior de una farmacia en Barcelona, España. ►

Chile La médica es muy seria, ¿no? Como todos los médicos ella tiene muchas responsabilidades. ▼

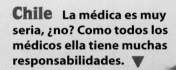

▲ España Es una farmacia antigua en la Gran Canaria, una de las islas Canarias. Las Canarias son islas españolas en el Atlántico al oeste de África. En las farmacias tradicionales venden solo medicamentos. No venden productos cosméticos. Pero en las farmacias modernas venden productos de belleza también.

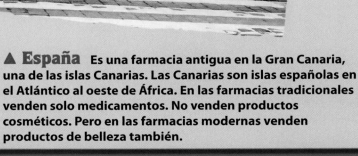

contento, alegre

triste, deprimida

de mal humor

de buen humor

¡Ojo!

Note that the adjectives **bueno** and **malo** are often shortened to **buen** and **mal** when placed before a masculine noun. **Buena** and **mala** are not shortened.

energética

cansado

José está muy contento. Acaba de recibir una A en español.
Elena está triste porque acaba de recibir una nota mala.

Susana está de buen humor.
Tiene una sonrisa en la cara.
Tiene también un buen sentido de humor.
Julia está de mal humor. Está enojada (enfadada).

Tomás está lleno de energía y tiene mucho entusiasmo.
Felipe está cansado.

obstinado, terco

flexible

Alejandro no es flexible. Es muy terco y obstinado. Es un tipo muy difícil.

Lupe es ambiciosa. Siempre quiere tener éxito—quiere tener buenos resultados.

Maripaz es bien educada. Siempre tiene buena conducta. Pero su hermano es mal educado. Tiene malos modales.

Para conversar

A Rubén le falta paciencia. Es muy impaciente. A veces su comportamiento me molesta (enfada, enoja).

¿Lo sabes?

Muchas palabras relacionadas con la personalidad y las emociones son palabras afines.

calmo	**paciente**
tranquilo	**dinámico**
nervioso	**la energía**

QuickPass

Go to glencoe.com
For: **Vocabulary practice**
Web code: **ASD4003c6**

ESCUCHAR • HABLAR

1 Personaliza. Da respuestas personales.

1. ¿Eres flexible o terco(a)?
2. Por lo general, ¿estás de buen humor o estás de mal humor?
3. ¿Estás cansado(a) cuando no duermes bien?
4. ¿Estás lleno(a) de energía hoy?
5. ¿Siempre quieres tener éxito?

LEER • HABLAR • ESCRIBIR

2 Escoge la palabra correcta.

1. Una persona (paciente, impaciente) pierde control con frecuencia.
2. Una persona (de buen humor, de mal humor) está contenta.
3. Cuando una persona está enojada, (está de buen humor, está de mal humor).
4. Una persona está (contenta, triste) cuando recibe notas buenas.
5. Él duerme bien y está (cansado, lleno de energía).
6. Le gusta mucho el plan y está muy (deprimido, entusiasmado).
7. Él es un tipo (flexible, terco) y siempre toma en cuenta los deseos y opiniones de otros.
8. Él es muy (bien educado, mal educado). Tiene buena conducta.

CULTURA

Las alumnas están en una sala de clase en Madrid. Una parece que tiene estrés. Pero la otra tiene una sonrisa y expresión alegre, ¿no?

LEER

3 Parea los contrarios.

1. contento
2. cansado
3. tranquilo
4. ambicioso
5. flexible
6. positivo

a. energético
b. perezoso
c. terco
d. triste
e. nervioso
f. negativo

4 **Rompecabezas**

Make as many words as possible from the letters below.

t	i	m	a	r	e	j
o	s	n	d	u	c	h

LEER

5 Parea los sinónimos.

1. calmo   a. alegre
2. enojado   b. conducta
3. contento   c. enfadado
4. molestar   d. tranquilo
5 comportamiento   e. enojar
6. terco   f. obstinado

ESCRIBIR

6 Categoriza. Haz una lista de características positivas y características negativas.

características	
positivas	**negativas**

CULTURA

Marisa es bastante graciosa, ¿no? Tiene una sonrisa bonita en la cara. ¿De dónde es Marisa? Es de California y es de ascendencia mexicana.

ESCRIBIR

7 Personaliza. Prepara una autoevaluación. ¿Cuáles consideras unas características de tu personalidad?

HABLAR • ESCRIBIR

8 Da la característica de cada persona.

1. Él tiene buena conducta. Es _____.
2. Las opiniones de otros no le tienen mucha importancia. Es _____.
3. Ella siempre tiene una _____ agradable en la cara.
4. Siempre quiere ir en adelante y tener éxito. Es _____.
5. Él escucha a todos y luego toma una decisión. Es muy _____.
6. Ella es bastante cómica. Tiene un buen _____ de humor.

9 Trabajen en grupos. Hagan una encuesta. Hablen de las características que buscan o consideran importantes en un(a) amigo(a) bueno(a). Indiquen las respuestas en una tabla como la de al lado. Compartan los resultados con la clase.

buen sentido de humor

simpático(a)

paciente

flexible

🌸 **Comunicación**

10 Work with a classmate. Tell some typical things people do. Each of you will determine whether you think it's **buen comportamiento** or **mal comportamiento**.

En la consulta del médico

Está bien.

Está enferma.

En otras partes

In addition to **la consulta** you will also hear **el consultorio. El paciente** is also referred to as **el enfermo.** Another word for **un catarro** is **un resfrío.**

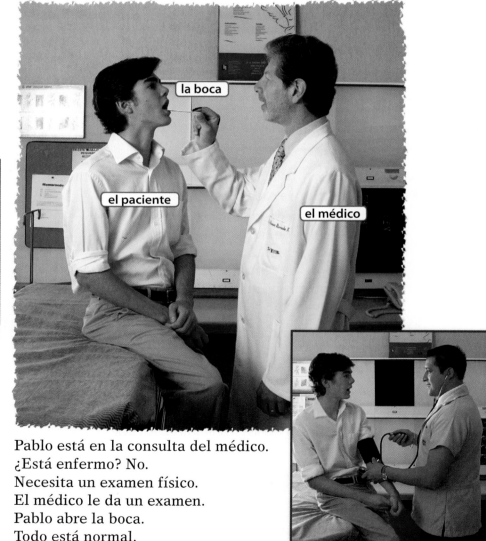

la boca

el paciente

el médico

Pablo está en la consulta del médico.
¿Está enfermo? No.
Necesita un examen físico.
El médico le da un examen.
Pablo abre la boca.
Todo está normal.

El enfermero le toma la
tensión arterial.
También toma el pulso.

¿Estás bien o no?

VIDEO To visit a sick friend, watch **Diálogo en vivo.**

Enrique tiene fiebre.
Tiene que guardar cama.

Inés tiene catarro.
Está resfriada.

Adolfo tiene mucho estrés.
Tiene dolor de cabeza.

Lupe tiene dolor de estómago.
Le duele el estómago.

Luis tiene tos.
Tose mucho.

Teresa tiene dolor de garganta.
Le duele la garganta.

La médica le da una receta.
Le receta una medicina para la tos.

Teresa y su madre van a la farmacia.
En la farmacia venden medicamentos (medicinas).

201

ESCUCHAR

 1 Escucha. Indica si la frase es correcta o no.

correcta	incorrecta

ESCUCHAR • HABLAR • ESCRIBIR

 2 Contesta.

1. Sonia tiene la temperatura normal. ¿Tiene fiebre?
2. Sonia quiere jugar en el equipo de fútbol. ¿Por qué tiene que ir a la consulta del médico?
3. ¿Qué le da el médico?
4. ¿Quién le toma el pulso?
5. ¿Cuál es el diagnóstico del médico?

EXPANSIÓN

Ahora, sin mirar las preguntas, cuenta la información en tus propias palabras. Si no recuerdas todo, un(a) compañero(a) te puede ayudar.

LEER • HABLAR • ESCRIBIR

 3 Completa.

1. El niño tiene que _____ porque tiene fiebre.
2. Tiene _____. Tose mucho.
3. Le duele la cabeza. Tiene _____ de cabeza.
4. El enfermero le toma la _____ arterial.
5. El médico examina a sus pacientes en _____.
6. El médico le da un examen completo. Le da un examen _____.
7. Tiene que ir a la farmacia porque el médico le da una _____.

HORARIO DE FARMACIA
DE LUNES A SABADO
DE: 9 A.M. A 9 P.M.
DOMINGOS
DE: 8 A.M. A 8 P.M.

CULTURA

Es una farmacia típica en Baños, Ecuador. En la farmacia venden muchos productos médicos. Si tienes una pregunta sobre tu salud, la farmacéutica te puede ayudar. En España y Latinoamérica los farmacéuticos les dan atención médica a sus clientes para condiciones no muy graves.

Más práctica

📖 Workbook, pp. 6.5–6.6
⊙ StudentWorks™ Plus

HABLAR

 4 **Dramatiza.** Dramatize some of the ailments and activities in the vocabulary. Call on a friend to tell what you are doing.

ESCRIBIR

5 Da una palabra o expresión relacionada.

1. duele
2. la medicina
3. toser
4. enfermo
5. consultar
6. resfriado

HABLAR • ESCRIBIR

6 **¡Manos a la obra!** Work in groups of three. Draw your own **Para conversar.** Include a doctor, a nurse, and a patient. Write at least one speech bubble for each. Then perform your dialogue for the class.

Para conversar

ESCRIBIR

7 **Rompecabezas**

 ¡Qué pena! Letters have broken off these words. Can you put them back where they belong?

gar anta   far acia   d lor

fie re   cabe a   e trés   ca arro

m   o   s   t   g   z   b

Conexiones

La salud mental
La salud física es muy importante y también es muy importante la salud mental. Todos tenemos emociones y a veces estamos tristes o enojados si nos ocurre algo desagradable. Es normal. Pero si un individuo está muy triste o deprimido con frecuencia, tiene que identificar el porqué. Es importante hablar de nuestros problemas emocionales y buscar ayuda. En el ambiente escolar podemos hablar con un(a) consejero(a). Nos puede ayudar.

 Go to glencoe.com
For: **Grammar practice**
Web code: **ASD4003c6**

Ser y estar

Características y condiciones

1. Spanish has two verbs that mean *to be.* They are **ser** and **estar.** These verbs have distinct uses. **Ser** expresses an inherent trait or characteristic that does not change.

> **El edificio es muy alto.**
> **Ella es sincera.**

2. **Estar** expresses a temporary state, emotion, or condition.

> **Juan no está bien hoy. Está enfermo.**
> **La joven está cansada.**
> **José, ¿por qué estás nervioso?**
> **El agua está fría.**

3. You can often use either **ser** or **estar** depending upon what you mean to say. Note the different messages in the following.

> **Él es agresivo.** *He is naturally an aggressive type.*
> **Él está muy agresivo.** *He's not normally that way but now he's acting in an aggressive way.*
> **Ella es muy obstinada.** *She's a very obstinate type.*
> **Ella está muy obstinada.** *She's being very obstinate now.*

El joven no está enfermo pero tiene dolor de cabeza. Le duele mucho.

Práctica

ESCUCHAR

1 Escucha las frases. Indica si es una característica o una condición.

característica	condición

ESCUCHAR • HABLAR • ESCRIBIR

2 Personaliza. Da una respuesta personal.

1. ¿Es grande o pequeña tu casa?
2. ¿Es bonita?
3. ¿De qué color es tu casa?
4. ¿Es nuevo o viejo el carro de tu familia?
5. ¿Es bien educada o mal educada tu mascota?
6. ¿Cómo es tu hermano(a)?

CULTURA

La casa está en el Pueblito. El Pueblito es un museo al aire libre en la Ciudad de Panamá. La casa es de madera. En el Pueblito hay casas típicas de todas las regiones de Panamá.

Más práctica

Workbook, pp. 6.7–6.9
StudentWorks™ Plus

ESCUCHAR • HABLAR • ESCRIBIR

 3 Personaliza. Da una respuesta personal.

 1. ¿Cómo estás hoy? ¿Estás bien o estás enfermo(a)?
2. ¿Estás contento(a)?
3. ¿Estás triste?
4. ¿Estás nervioso(a)?
5. ¿Estás de buen humor o de mal humor?

LEER • HABLAR • ESCRIBIR

 4 Completa. Completa con la emoción o característica apropiada.

1. Ramón _____ porque acaba de marcar un tanto.
2. Luisa _____ porque acaba de dormir mucho.
3. Lucas _____ porque su abuelo está enfermo.
4. Su padre _____ porque tiene mucho estrés.
5. Maricarmen _____ y siempre quiere trabajar y tener éxito.

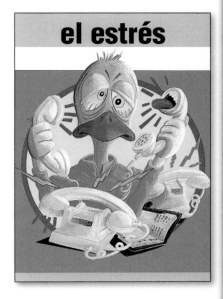

el estrés

Comunicación

 5 Create a chart like the one below on a separate sheet of paper. List some emotions similar to the ones below. Give an instance of when you feel a certain way. Present your results to the class.

Estoy enojado(a) cuando…

contento(a) ¿Cuándo?

triste ¿Cuándo?

calmo(a) ¿Cuándo?

yo

nervioso(a) ¿Cuándo?

de buen humor ¿Cuándo?

HABLAR • ESCRIBIR

 6 **Juego** Compete with a partner. In one minute, list as many adjectives as you can that use **ser.** Then do the same for **estar.** Check each other's lists. The one with the most correct words wins. Then compare your adjectives and how many you found with those of the others in the class.

Ser y estar

Origen y colocación

1. You use **ser de** to tell where someone or something is from and what something is made of.

> **La profesora es de Puerto Rico.**
> **El café es de Colombia.**
> **La casa es de adobe.**

2. You use **estar** to express where someone or something is located. It is important to remember that **estar** expresses both temporary and permanent location.

> **Los alumnos están en la escuela.**
> **Madrid está en España.**

CULTURA

El joven es de San Juan, Puerto Rico.

CULTURA

Las casas están en una aldea de los emberá—un grupo indígena de Panamá. La aldea está en una zona tropical. Las casas de los indígenas de las zonas tropicales son de paja.

Práctica

ESCUCHAR • HABLAR • ESCRIBIR

7 ¿De dónde es? Contesta según el modelo.

MODELO —¿**Es cubano el muchacho?**
—**Sí, creo que es de Cuba.**

1. ¿Es colombiana la muchacha?
2. ¿Es guatemalteco el joven?
3. ¿Es puertorriqueña la señora?
4. ¿Es española la profesora?
5. ¿Es peruano el médico?
6. ¿Son venezolanos los amigos?
7. ¿Son chilenas las amigas?
8. ¿Son costarricenses los jugadores?

ESCUCHAR • LEER • HABLAR

 8 Practica la conversación y presta atención al uso de
ser y **estar.**

—¿Es de Nicaragua Nora?

—No, Teresa. Creo que es venezolana.

—¿Ella es de Venezuela? Yo también soy de Venezuela
y ahora aquí estamos en la Florida.

—Nora está en tu clase de inglés, ¿no?

—Sí, y es muy inteligente. Y algo más que me gusta,
siempre está de buen humor.

HABLAR • ESCRIBIR

9 Contesta según la conversación.

1. ¿Es de Nicaragua Nora?
2. ¿De qué nacionalidad es?
3. ¿Quién más es de Venezuela?
4. ¿Dónde están las dos muchachas ahora?
5. ¿Están ellas en la misma clase de inglés?
6. ¿Cómo es Nora?
7. ¿Siempre está contenta?

EXPANSIÓN

Ahora, sin mirar las preguntas, relata la información en la
conversación en tus propias palabras. Si no recuerdas algo,
un(a) compañero(a) te puede ayudar.

InfoGap For more practice
using **ser** and **estar,** do
Activity 6 on page SR8 at
the end of this book.

GeoVistas

To learn more about
Venezuela, take a tour on
pages SH54–SH55.

CULTURA

Es una plaza bonita en
San Juan, Venezuela.

VIDEO Want help with **ser** and **estar**? Watch **Gramática en vivo.**

HABLAR • ESCRIBIR

10 ¿De dónde es y dónde está ahora?
Contesta. Presta atención a la diferencia entre el uso de **ser** y **estar.**

1. Bernardo es de Argentina pero ahora está en España.
   ¿De dónde es Bernardo?
   ¿Dónde está ahora?
   ¿De dónde es y dónde está?

2. Linda es de Estados Unidos pero ahora está en Colombia.
   ¿De dónde es Linda?
   ¿Dónde está ahora?
   ¿De dónde es y dónde está?

3. La señora Martín es de Cuba pero ahora está en Puerto Rico.
   ¿De dónde es la señora Martín?
   ¿Dónde está ahora?
   ¿De dónde es y dónde está?

CULTURA

Los jóvenes están en una placita en La Palma, una de las islas Canarias. Las islas Canarias están en el océano Atlántico al oeste de África.

ESCUCHAR • HABLAR • ESCRIBIR

11 Personaliza. Da una respuesta personal.

1. ¿Dónde está tu escuela?
2. ¿Está tu escuela cerca o lejos de tu casa?
3. ¿Estás en la escuela a las diez de la mañana?
4. ¿En qué clase estás después del almuerzo?
5. ¿De dónde es tu profesor(a) de español?
6. ¿Y de dónde eres tú?
7. ¿Cómo estás hoy?
8. Y el/la profesor(a), ¿cómo está?

LEER • HABLAR

12 Parea el verbo con la expresión.

ser **estar**	enfermo en casa inteligente cerca de sincero enojado en México de Madrid alto

FOLDABLES®
Study Organizer

PAPER FILE FOLDER
See page SH29 for help with making this foldable. Make two folders, one with **ser** on the tab and **estar** on the other. Write sentences using each verb. On the back, explain your reason for your verb choice. Place the sentences in the correct folders. Trade folders with a friend and check each other's work.

Los pronombres me, te, nos

1. In Chapter 5 you learned the pronouns **me** and **te** with the expressions **me gusta, te interesa, te aburre.** Note that **nos** is the object pronoun that corresponds to **nosotros.**

> No **nos** aburre el curso. **Nos** gusta.
> **Nos** interesa bastante.

2. Me, te, and **nos** are object pronouns. They can be used as either direct or indirect objects. Note that unlike in English, you put the object pronoun right before the verb.

> El médico **me** ve. **Me** examina.
> ¿**Te** habla el médico?
> Sí, **me** habla.
> El médico **nos** examina y **nos** da una receta.

Práctica

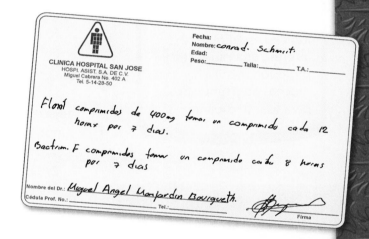

HABLAR • ESCRIBIR

 Personaliza. Da una respuesta personal.

1. A veces, cuando estás enfermo(a), ¿tienes que ir al médico?
2. Cuando estás en su consultorio, ¿te habla la recepcionista?
3. ¿Te examina el médico?
4. ¿Te habla también?
5. ¿Qué te duele?
6. ¿Te da un diagnóstico el médico?
7. ¿Te da una receta?
8. ¿Te receta medicina?

ESCUCHAR • HABLAR • ESCRIBIR

 Crea frases según el modelo.

MODELO ver →
   Cuando estamos enfermos, el médico nos ve.

1. examinar
2. mirar
3. hablar
4. dar una receta

HABLAR • ESCRIBIR

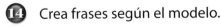 Trabaja con un(a) compañero(a) de clase.
Forma frases con las siguientes expresiones.

 me molesta **me enoja** **me enfada** **me duele**

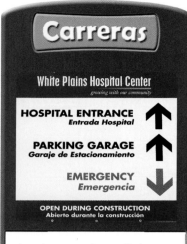

Carreras

White Plains Hospital Center
growing with our community

HOSPITAL ENTRANCE
Entrada Hospital ↑

PARKING GARAGE
Garaje de Estacionamiento ↑

EMERGENCY
Emergencia ↓

OPEN DURING CONSTRUCTION
Abierto durante la construcción

Aquí vemos las señales para una sala de emergencia en un hospital en Nueva York. Los anuncios son en inglés y español. Si te interesa una carrera en la profesión médica hay muchas oportunidades para usar tu español.

Los pronombres le, les

1. **Le** and **les** are indirect object pronouns. That means they are the indirect receivers of the action of the verb. They answer the question *to whom* or *for whom*.

> La médica **le** da una receta.
> La médica **les** habla.

2. The indirect object pronouns **le** and **les** are both masculine and feminine. **Le** and **les** are often used with another phrase to clarify to whom they refer.

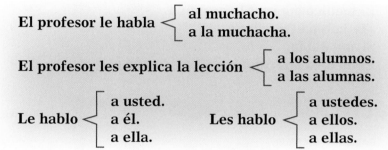

El profesor **le** habla ⎰ al muchacho.
⎱ a la muchacha.

El profesor **les** explica la lección ⎰ a los alumnos.
⎱ a las alumnas.

Le hablo ⎰ a usted.
⎨ a él.
⎱ a ella.

Les hablo ⎰ a ustedes.
⎨ a ellos.
⎱ a ellas.

Práctica

HABLAR • ESCRIBIR

16 Contesta las preguntas sobre el pobre Nando que está enfermo.

1. ¿Está Nando en el consultorio?
2. ¿Le habla el médico?
3. ¿Nando le explica sus síntomas?
4. ¿Le duele la garganta?
5. ¿El médico le examina la garganta?
6. ¿El médico le da una receta?
7. ¿Le receta unos medicamentos?

17 Prepara una conversación según el modelo.

MODELO   A mí me gusta mucho el arte. →
      Y a tu amiga Rosa le gusta también, ¿verdad?

1. los deportes
2. la clase de español
3. el color verde
4. las legumbres
5. el helado
6. la comida mexicana

CULTURA

Una muchacha le habla a su amiga en Antigua, Guatemala. Parece ser una conversación seria.

Comunicación

18 Make a list of things you like. Interview some friends and find out if they like them, too. Report the results to the class.

HABLAR • ESCRIBIR

19 Juego ¿Es una frase? These words are all mixed up! Can you rearrange them to make logical sentences?

1. una receta médico da me el
2. les habla madre sus la a hijos
3. casa nos su gusta
4. profesor le a usted el lección la explica
5. ¿enfada te hermana tu?
6. dan perro un ellos ella a le

PRONUNCIACIÓN

Las consonantes c, g

The consonant **c** in combination with **a, o, u** (**ca, co, cu**) has a hard **k** sound. **C** changes to **qu** with **e** or **i** (**que, qui**) in order to maintain the hard **k** sound. Repeat the following.

ca	que	qui	co	cu
cama	que	aquí	como	cubano
casa	queso	equipo	cocina	cuando
cámara	parque	quiero	médico	Cuzco
cancha	raqueta	tranquilo	terco	
catarro	pequeño		físico	

Dictado

Pronounce the following sentences carefully. Then write them to prepare for a dictation.

> **Yo practico el básquetbol en el parque pequeño.**
> **El cubano come el queso aquí en el parque.**
> **Él es muy terco y físico, no tranquilo.**

The consonant **g** in combination with **a, o, u** (**ga, go, gu**) is pronounced somewhat like the **g** in **go**. To maintain this same sound **g** changes to **gu** before **e** or **i** (**gue, gui**). Repeat the following.

ga	gue	gui	go	gu
paga	guerra	amiguito	juego	guante
gana			golpea	seguro

Dictado

Pronounce the following sentences carefully. Then write them to prepare for a dictation.

> **Góngora gana el Guante de oro.**
> **El amiguito quiere jugar.**
> **El médico examina la boca y la garganta.**

Refrán

Can you guess what the following proverb means?

Entre salud y dinero, salud quiero.

¡Bravo!

You have now learned all the new vocabulary and grammar in this chapter. Continue to use and practice all that you know while learning more cultural information. **¡Vamos!**

QuickPass
Go to glencoe.com
For: **Conversation practice**
Web code: ASD4003c6

UN ALUMNO DE COLOMBIA

MAGALÍ, TE PRESENTO LUIS. ES UN ALUMNO NUEVO AQUÍ.

MUCHO GUSTO, LUIS. ¿DE DÓNDE ERES?

SOY DE COLOMBIA.

LUIS ESTÁ EN MI CLASE DE ESPAÑOL. Y, ¡QUÉ BIEN HABLA! ME ENCANTA SU ACENTO.

CON PERMISO. TENGO QUE IR A MI CLASE DE BIOLOGÍA. EMPIEZA AHORA.

CIAO, LUIS. ¡HASTA PRONTO!

LUIS ME PARECE UN BUEN TIPO.

TIENE UNA PERSONALIDAD QUE ME GUSTA.

ES BIEN EDUCADO Y SIEMPRE ESTÁ DE BUEN HUMOR.

¿VES LA SONRISA QUE TIENE?

¡SÍ, SÍ! Y, ¿QUÉ PIENSAS? ES BASTANTE GUAPO, ¿NO?

¿Comprendes?

A Contesta según la información en la conversación.

1. ¿De dónde es Luis?
2. ¿En qué clase está con Elena?
3. ¿A qué clase tiene que ir ahora?
4. ¿Qué piensa Elena de Luis?
5. ¿Qué le gusta a Magalí?
6. ¿Qué te parece? ¿Les interesa Luis a las muchachas?

B Cuenta lo que pasa en la conversación en tus propias palabras.

C Da la siguiente información.

características positivas de Luis	la apariencia de Luis

D **Interpretando** ¿Qué piensas?

¿Tiene Magalí mucho interés en Luis? ¿Por qué?

¿Y Elena? ¿Tiene ella interés también? ¿Por qué?

CULTURA

Bogotá, la capital de Colombia, es una gran ciudad con avenidas anchas y edificios modernos de muchos pisos—rascacielos. Un rascacielos es un edificio muy alto que rasca (toca) el cielo.

READING STRATEGY

Skimming Skimming is looking over an entire reading selection quickly to get a general idea of what it is about. Once you have a general idea of the reading, you can go back and read it again to find out more of the details.

Antes de leer

Skim the selection by looking for key words and reading the first and last sentence of each paragraph. Determine what you think this reading is about.

 **Reading Check**

¿Qué es un pícaro?

Durante la lectura

Think about those characteristics of Periquillo that make him **un antihéroe.**

 **Reading Check**

¿Dónde trabaja Periquillo?

Después de leer

Did skimming the reading give you a general sense of what the reading would be about?

El Periquillo Sarniento

La literatura picaresca La literatura tiene sus héroes y también sus antihéroes. En la literatura hispana hay un antihéroe especial—el pícaro. El pícaro es un muchacho humilde que no tiene dinero. Como es muy pobre su vida es una lucha[1] continua.

El Periquillo Sarniento *El Periquillo Sarniento* es del autor mexicano Fernández de Lizardi. Periquillo no es como los otros pícaros típicos. Él no es pobre y asiste a la universidad. Pero no le gusta trabajar. Le falta ambición. Es perezoso y pasa de una aventura a otra.

Trabaja como criado[2] en casa de un médico. Habla mucho con el médico y lee sus libros sobre la medicina. Decide que el médico no es bueno y que no les trata bien a sus pacientes. Periquillo le roba al médico. Toma sus libros, una cantidad de dinero y su mula. En la mula va a un pueblo pequeño donde no hay médico. Finge[3] ser médico y muy pronto tiene muchos pacientes. Creen que Periquillo es un médico auténtico.

Un día ve a un señor que está muy enfermo. Su familia está muy deprimida. Para aliviar el dolor de estómago que tiene el enfermo, Periquillo prepara una mezcla[4] de cosas horribles. El enfermo bebe. Y, ¿qué pasa? El señor abre los ojos, reconoce a su familia y les habla. La familia está muy alegre y todos le dan las gracias a su «médico».

Periquillo tiene otras aventuras pero poco a poco él cambia[5] su mala conducta y vive como una persona responsable.

[1]lucha *struggle*
[2]criado *housekeeper*
[3]Finge *He pretends*

[4]mezcla *mixture*
[5]cambia *changes*

¿Comprendes?

Más práctica

Workbook, pp. 6.11–6.13
StudentWorks™ Plus

A Confirmando información Corrige la información que no es correcta.

 1. El pícaro es un héroe.
 2. *El Periquillo Sarniento* es una novela romántica.
 3. Como todos los pícaros, Periquillo es pobre.
 4. No tiene educación.
 5. Periquillo trabaja como médico en casa de un criado.

B Describiendo Describe los defectos que tiene Periquillo.

C Recordando hechos Contesta.

 1. ¿Qué lee Periquillo en casa del médico?
 2. ¿Qué piensa Periquillo del médico?
 3. ¿Cuáles son tres cosas que Periquillo toma del médico?
 4. ¿Adónde va Periquillo?

D Describiendo Describe.

 1. a la familia del paciente
 2. la condición del paciente
 3. el tratamiento que le da Periquillo

E Analizando Contesta.

 1. ¿Por qué cree Periquillo que el médico no es bueno?
 2. Cuando Periquillo llega al pueblo, ¿por qué tiene muchos pacientes inmediatamente?
 3. ¿Por qué creen que Periquillo es un buen médico?
 4. ¿Debe Periquillo tratar de curar a los enfermos? Explica por qué contestas que sí o que no.

Una litografía de José Joaquín Fernández de Lizardi

Lazarillo de Tormes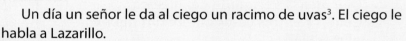

Antes de leer

Vas a leer un episodio en la vida de Lazarillo, un pícaro español. Como todos los pícaros, Lazarillo tiene que ser muy astuto. Es una característica importante para los pícaros. Vas a ver por qué.

La primera novela picaresca es *Lazarillo de Tormes* de un autor anónimo español. Lazarillo es un niño pobre de Salamanca. No tiene dinero y siempre tiene que confrontar muchos obstáculos. Pero el joven no pierde su sentido de humor.

La madre de Lazarillo no tiene marido. Es viuda[1]. Ella gana muy poco dinero. Un día, llega al hotel donde trabaja un señor ciego[2]. La pobre madre está muy triste pero como ella no tiene dinero le da a su hijo al señor ciego.

Lazarillo es muy astuto y no tiene confianza en el ciego. Es un hombre cruel y trata muy mal a Lazarillo.

Un día un señor le da al ciego un racimo de uvas[3]. El ciego le habla a Lazarillo.

—Lazarillo, yo voy a comer una uva. Cada vez que yo como una, tú puedes comer una también. ¿Me prometes[4] comer solamente una?

—Sí, señor.

El ciego empieza a comer. Y, ¿cuántas uvas come? ¿Una? ¡No! Come dos.

Luego el ciego le da el racimo a Lazarillo y Lazarillo empieza a comer. ¿Cuántas uvas come? ¿Una? ¿Dos? ¡No! Lazarillo come tres.

—Lazarillo, tú no comes solamente una uva. Comes tres.

—No, señor.

—Lazarillo, tú ves que yo como dos uvas y no me dices nada[5]. Por eso, estoy seguro que tú comes tres y rompes[6] nuestra promesa.

—Sí, señor. Pero, ¿quién rompe nuestra promesa primero? ¡Yo, no! ¡Usted, sí!

Una vista de la Plaza Mayor en Salamanca, la ciudad natal de Lazarillo

[1]viuda   *widow*
[2]ciego   *blind*
[3]racimo de uvas   *bunch of grapes*

[4]prometes   *promise*
[5]dices nada   *say nothing*
[6]rompes   *break*

¿Comprendes?

A Escoge.

1. Lazarillo tiene que confrontar muchos obstáculos en la vida porque es _____.
  a. ciego
  b. pobre
  c. perezoso

2. Lazarillo siempre está _____.
  a. de buen humor
  b. de mal humor
  c. triste

3. La pobre madre le da a su hijo al ciego porque _____.
  a. no le gusta
  b. no tiene dinero y está desesperada
  c. el ciego es un buen hombre

4. ¿Por qué come Lazarillo tres uvas a la vez?
  a. porque quiere romper la promesa que tiene con el ciego
  b. porque tiene mucha hambre
  c. porque el ciego rompe su promesa primero

5. ¿Por qué tienen que ser astutos los pícaros?
  a. Son bastante maliciosos.
  b. No son muy inteligentes.
  c. Son pobres y viven solos.

B **Analizando** Explica por qué el primero que rompe la promesa es el ciego y no Lazarillo.

CULTURA

El monumento a Lazarillo de Tormes en la ciudad de Salamanca. Lazarillo es un personaje famoso, ¿no?

Vocabulario

1 **Parea.**

A B C D E F

1. Le duele la cabeza.
2. Está cansada.
3. Está triste.
4. Tose.
5. Es dinámico y ambicioso.
6. Tiene catarro.

2 **Parea.**

7. Él no es flexible.
8. Es mal educado.
9. Es perezoso.
10. Siempre está enojado.
11. Le examina la garganta.
12. Tiene que guardar cama.
13. Le falta paciencia.

a. No le gusta trabajar.
b. Tiene que abrir la boca.
c. Es terco.
d. Está enfermo. Tiene fiebre.
e. No me gusta su conducta.
f. Todo le molesta.
g. Es un tipo impaciente.

3 **Completa con una palabra apropiada.**

14. Ella siempre tiene una _____ en la cara. Siempre está de buen humor.
15. Tiene mucho estrés y tiene dolor de _____.
16. Tiene _____ y le duele la garganta.
17. El médico ve a sus pacientes en _____.
18. Siempre come cosas malas y después tiene dolor de _____.
19. _____ me toma el pulso y la tensión arterial.
20. En la farmacia _____ muchos medicamentos.

To review **Vocabulario 1** and **Vocabulario 2,** turn to pages 196–197 and 200–201.

CULTURA

La señora está siempre de muy buen humor porque le gusta su trabajo. Vende dulces en su bodega en Antigua, Guatemala.

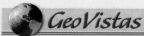 *GeoVistas*

To learn more about Guatemala, take a tour on pages SH48–SH49.

Gramática

4 **Completa con ser o estar.**

21. Lima _____ en Perú.

22. Nuestra escuela _____ grande.

23. Él no trabaja. _____ perezoso.

24. Ella _____ nerviosa porque tiene un examen.

25–26. Sus amigos _____ de México pero ahora _____ en la Florida.

27. José _____ enfermo.

28. Clara, ¿_____ cansada porque acabas de jugar tenis?

29. Yo tengo mucha energía hoy. _____ muy energético(a).

30. Yo _____ ambicioso(a) y quiero sacar buenas notas.

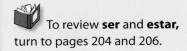To review **ser** and **estar,** turn to pages 204 and 206.

5 **Completa con el pronombre apropiado.**

31. ¿_____ va a hablar Juan?
—Sí, siempre me habla.

32–33. ¿_____ explica (a ustedes) la lección la profesora?
—Sí, ella _____ explica la lección.

34. El médico _____ da una receta a su paciente.

35–36. —¿A ustedes _____ enoja su conducta?
—Sí, _____ molesta.

To review indirect object pronouns, turn to pages 209–210.

Cultura

6 **Describe.**

37. Describe a Periquillo Sarniento.

7 **¿Sí o no?**

38. *El Periquillo Sarniento* es de un autor español.

39. Periquillo tiene su doctorado en medicina y es un médico excelente.

40. Todos los pícaros cambian su mala conducta.

To review this cultural information, turn to pages 214–215.

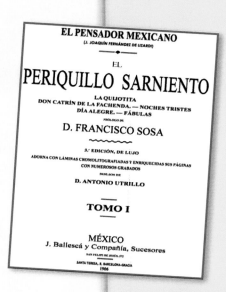

EL PENSADOR MEXICANO
(J. JOAQUÍN FERNÁNDEZ DE LIZARDI)

EL
PERIQUILLO SARNIENTO

LA QUIJOTITA
DON CATRÍN DE LA FACHENDA. — NOCHES TRISTES
DÍA ALEGRE. — FÁBULAS

PRÓLOGO DE
D. FRANCISCO SOSA

3.ª EDICIÓN, DE LUJO

ADORNA CON LÁMINAS CROMOLITOGRAFIADAS Y ENRIQUECIDAS SUS PÁGINAS
CON NUMEROSOS GRABADOS

DIBUJOS DE
D. ANTONIO UTRILLO

TOMO I

MÉXICO
J. Ballescá y Compañía, Sucesores
1906

1 **¿Quién es sincero(a)?**

 Talk about personality traits

Con un(a) compañero(a) de clase discute quien o quienes tienen las siguientes características. ¿Qué indica que tiene las siguientes características?

> **Es muy energético(a).**
> **Tiene mucha paciencia.**
> **Es bastante perezoso(a).**
> **Es bien educado(a).**
> **Es dinámico(a) y ambicioso(a).**

2 **Mis emociones**

 Talk about your feelings

Indica cuando tienes las siguientes emociones o sentimientos. Puedes incluir otras.

> **Estoy nervioso(a) cuando...**
> **Estoy contento(a) cuando...**
> **Me enoja cuando...**

CULTURA

El joven está contento y siempre está de buen humor. Tiene una personalidad agradable. A todos les gusta su sonrisa.

3 **¡A tu éxito!**

 Tell how you are going to be successful

Habla de como vas a tener éxito.

> **Como quiero tener éxito, voy a...**

4 **¿Qué tienes?**

 Role-play a visit to a doctor's office

Estás en la consulta del médico. Habla con el médico (tu compañero[a]) de tus enfermedades. Luego cambien de rol.

Prepárate para el examen
Practice for written proficiency

Tarea

Write a complete description of yourself. If you prefer, however, you can write about a fictitious character—someone you read about or made up.

Writing Strategy

Writing a personal essay One of the best ways to start to write something personal is to sit down and begin to jot down random ideas. Write down what comes to your mind about yourself or your fictitious person. Be sure that you use only words and grammar you have learned in Spanish.

❶ Prewrite

Fill in a chart similar to the one below. Give as much information about yourself or your fictitious person as you can under each category. Feel free to create additional categories. Use as much of this chapter's vocabulary as possible. Include interesting details to make your description interesting and lively and maybe even funny.

❷ Write

- Begin with an introduction that explains whom you are describing.
- Decide the order you wish to give to the categories suggested in the chart. Use a separate paragraph for each category.
- Give your composition a title that will grab the readers' attention.
- Edit your work. Check spelling, grammar, punctuation, and sentence structure.

Evaluate

Don't forget that your teacher will evaluate you on your organization, correct use of vocabulary and grammar, understandability, ability to hold the interest of the reader, and completeness of your message.

Repaso del Capítulo ⑥

Gramática

- ### Ser y estar *(pages 204 and 206)*

  The verbs **ser** and **estar** have distinct uses.

Característica	Él **es** muy ambicioso.
Origen	Ella **es** de la República Dominicana.
Condición	Ella **está** muy cansada hoy.
Colocación	Él **está** en San Juan esta semana.
	San Juan **está** en Puerto Rico.

- ### Los pronombres **me, te, nos** *(page 209)*

  The object pronouns **me**, **te**, and **nos** can be either a direct object or an indirect object.

direct object	*indirect object*
El médico **me** ve.	El médico **me** habla.
El médico **te** examina.	El médico **te** da una receta.

- ### Los pronombres **le, les** *(page 210)*

  Review the indirect object pronouns **le** and **les**.

  Le hablo ⎰ a usted.
  ⎱ a él.
  ⎱ a ella.

  Les escribo ⎰ a ustedes.
  ⎱ a ellos.
  ⎱ a ellas.

CULTURA

El niño les da de comer a las palomas en la Plaza Central de Mérida, México. En muchas plazas y parques de España y Latinoamérica, a los niños les encanta dar de comer a las palomas.

222 *doscientos veintidós*

CAPÍTULO 6

There are a number of cognates in this list. See how many you and a partner can find. Who can find the most? Compare your list with those of your classmates.

Vocabulario

Describing emotions and feelings

alegre
contento(a)
triste
deprimido(a)

enojado(a)
enfadado(a)
energético(a)

calmo(a),
   tranquilo(a)
nervioso(a)

cansado(a)
de mal (buen)
   humor

Discussing personality and behavior

la personalidad
el comportamiento
la conducta
los modales
la energía

el entusiasmo
la paciencia
dinámico(a)
ambicioso(a)
perezoso(a)

paciente
impaciente
flexible
terco(a),
   obstinado(a)

agradable
bien (mal)
   educado(a)

Describing some minor health problems

la salud
un catarro
una fiebre
una tos
el estrés
el dolor
   de garganta
   de estómago
   de cabeza

el examen físico
la tensión arterial
el pulso
la consulta
el/la médico(a)
el/la enfermero(a)
el/la paciente

la farmacia
el/la farmacéutico(a)
la receta
el medicamento, la
   medicina
enfermo(a)
resfriado(a)

examinar
abrir
toser
doler
recetar
vender

Other useful words and expressions

la sonrisa
la cara
la boca
el/la niño(a)
el tipo

lleno(a) de
me falta
me enfada
me enoja
me molesta

guardar cama
tener éxito
ser
estar

 **Literary Reader**

You may wish to read the Mexican legend *Iztaccíhuatl y Popocatépetl,* found on pages 402–405.

Repaso cumulativo

Repasa lo que ya has aprendido

These activities will help you review
what you have learned so far in Spanish.

 1 Escucha las frases. Indica en una tabla como
la de abajo si las frases son correctas o no.

sí	no

 2 Completa con el verbo **ser**.

1. Yo _____ alumno(a) en la clase de la señora
   Lugones.

2. La clase _____ bastante grande.

3. Los alumnos de la señora Lugones _____ bastante
   buenos.

4. Nosotros _____ alumnos serios.

5. ¿Tú _____ un(a) alumno(a) serio(a) también?

6. ¿En qué escuela _____ ustedes alumnos?

3 Escribe frases. Presta atención a las terminaciones
(*endings*) de los adjetivos.

1. muchacha / rubio
2. clase / pequeño
3. lecturas / fácil
4. edificio / alto

5. departamentos / grande
6. carro / viejo
7. jardín / bonito
8. flores / bonito

 4 Personaliza. Da respuestas personales.

1. ¿Cuántos años tienes?

2. ¿Cuántos años tienen tus hermanos si no eres
   hijo(a) único(a)?

3. ¿Tienen ustedes una mascota? ¿Qué tienen?

4. ¿Cuántos cuartos tiene su casa o apartamento?

5. ¿Tienes muchos primos?

6. ¿Tienen ustedes una familia grande o pequeña?

Muchas personas tienen como
mascota un loro como el loro
aquí de Antigua, Guatemala.

Completa personalmente.

1. Soy de _____.
2. Tengo el pelo _____.
3. Tengo ojos _____.
4. Soy _____.
5. Y estoy _____.

 Da el antónimo.

1. alto
2. cansado
3. feo
4. ambicioso
5. malo
6. interesante
7. contento
8. pequeño
9. mucho
10. antes de
11. interesar
12. delante de

Contesta según el dibujo.

1. ¿Qué muebles hay en la sala?
2. ¿Qué muebles hay en el comedor?
3. ¿Qué muebles hay en los cuartos de dormir?

 Forma preguntas.

1. *El joven* es ambicioso.
2. El joven es *ambicioso.*
3. Él es *médico.*
4. Vive *en Salamanca.*
5. Tiene *dos* hijos.
6. Él va *a su consultorio.*
7. Él va a su consultorio *de lunes a viernes.*

De vacaciones

Vamos a comparar ¿Cuándo tiene tu escuela las grandes vacaciones? ¿En verano o en invierno? En unos países hispanos las vacaciones— de unos dos o tres meses—coinciden con la Navidad. Vas a ver como pasan unos jóvenes sus vacaciones. Muchas veces depende del clima de la región donde viven.

◄ La gente nada y practica la plancha de vela en el lago Pucón, en el famoso distrito de los lagos en la frontera entre Chile y Argentina.

Objetivos

You will:

- talk about summer and winter weather and activities

- discuss summer and winter resorts in Spanish-speaking countries

You will use:

- preterite tense of regular **-ar** verbs

- preterite of **ir** and **ser**

- direct object pronouns

QuickPass

Go to glencoe.com
For: **Online book**
Web code: **ASD4003c7**

Introducción al tema
De vacaciones

Look at these photographs to acquaint yourself with the theme of this chapter. Who doesn't enjoy taking a summer or winter vacation? In this chapter you will learn that the opportunities for a fabulous vacation in the Spanish-speaking world are limitless. Which of these vacation spots do you find the most enticing? All kinds of wonderful experiences await you. **¡Vamos!**

▲ **México** Una familia va a nadar en el agua turquesa de un cenote o cueva subterránea en la península de Yucatán.

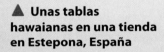

▲ Unas tablas hawaianas en una tienda en Estepona, España

▲ **España** Es la playa de Illetas en la isla de Mallorca en España. El mar Mediterráneo es famoso por sus aguas cristalinas.

◀ **México** Es una playa bonita en Puerto Vallarta, México.

República Dominicana Aquí vemos muchas planchas de vela en una playa de la costa norte de la República Dominicana. La plancha de vela es un deporte acuático popular en muchas partes del mundo. ▶

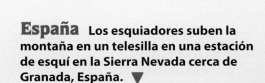

▲ **Honduras** Un delfín en el Instituto de Ciencias Marinas en Roatán, Honduras

España Los esquiadores suben la montaña en un telesilla en una estación de esquí en la Sierra Nevada cerca de Granada, España. ▼

▲ **Argentina, Paraguay** Las famosas cataratas del Iguazú en la frontera entre Brasil, Argentina y Paraguay

España Una estación de esquí en Aragón en el norte de España ▶

229

El verano

¿Qué tiempo hace en el verano?

Hace buen tiempo.   A veces llueve.
Hace (Hay) sol.   Cuando llueve está nublado.
Hace calor.   Hay nubes.

En otras partes

Tomar fotos is used throughout Latin America. **Sacar fotos** is used in Spain.

In Spain and other countries you will hear **la piscina.** In Mexico it is **la alberca.** You will also hear **la pila.**

la playa, el balneario
el mar
tomar el sol
la ola
una cámara digital
el traje de baño, el bañador
la toalla
la arena

Los amigos fueron a la playa.
Pasaron el fin de semana en la playa. Tomaron el sol.
Elena tomó (sacó) fotos con su cámara digital.

practicar la plancha de vela

el surfing

la tabla hawaiana

el buceo

bucear

los anteojos de sol, las gafas para el sol

la piscina, la alberca

una crema solar, una loción bronceadora

Jaime nadó en la piscina.

el esquí acuático (náutico)

un barquito

esquiar en el agua

Los amigos alquilaron (rentaron) un barquito.
Carlos esquió en el agua.

la cancha de voleibol

Hay una cancha de voleibol en la playa.
Un jugador lanza el balón.
Otro jugador del equipo contrario lo devuelve.

VIDEO To visit a beautiful beach in Puerto Rico, watch **Cultura en vivo.**

QuickPass

Go to glencoe.com
For: **Vocabulary practice**
Web code: **ASD4003c7**

ESCUCHAR

1 Escucha las frases. Parea cada frase con la foto que describe.

a.

b.

c.

d.

HABLAR • ESCRIBIR

2 Contesta sobre unos amigos que pasaron un rato (unos momentos) en la playa.

1. ¿Fueron los amigos a la playa ayer?
2. ¿Pasaron el fin de semana en la playa?
3. ¿Nadó José en el mar?
4. ¿Tomó Adela el sol?
5. ¿Usó una loción bronceadora protectora?
6. ¿Buceó ella o esquió en el agua?

EXPANSIÓN

Ahora, sin mirar las preguntas, da toda la información en tus propias palabras. Si no recuerdas algo, un(a) compañero(a) te puede ayudar.

ESCUCHAR • HABLAR • ESCRIBIR

3 Confirma. ¿Sí o no?

1. Hay playas en un balneario.
2. Hay olas grandes en una piscina.
3. El Caribe es un mar y el Pacífico es un océano.
4. A todos les gusta ir a la playa cuando está nublado y llueve.
5. Es importante usar una crema o loción bronceadora protectora cuando uno toma el sol.
6. Una persona lleva un traje de baño cuando juega tenis.
7. Alquilaron un barquito porque van a nadar.

ESCUCHAR • HABLAR • ESCRIBIR

 4 Con un(a) compañero(a) de clase, prepara una conversación según el modelo.

 MODELO —¿Qué compró Elisa?
—Compró un traje de baño.
—Y, ¿cuánto le costó?
—Ni idea.

1. **2.** **3.** **4.**

Comunicación

 5 Tú y un(a) amigo(a) planean una excursión a la playa. ¿Qué tienen que llevar a la playa? ¿Cómo van a pasar la tarde en la playa?

HABLAR • ESCRIBIR

6 Contesta sobre un grupo de amigos en la playa.

1. ¿Hay una cancha de voleibol en la playa?
2. ¿Juegan los amigos voleibol?
3. ¿Cuántas personas hay en la cancha?
4. ¿Golpeó Luis el balón?
5. ¿Pasó por encima de la red el balón?
6. ¿Marcó él un tanto?

CULTURA

Los jóvenes juegan voleibol en una playa en España. El voleibol es una actividad playera popular.

VIDEO To practice your new words, watch **Vocabulario en vivo.**

El invierno

¿Qué tiempo hace en el invierno?

Hace frío. Nieva.
A veces hay mucha nieve.
Ayer la temperatura bajó a cero.

el pico

la montaña

una estación de esquí

la pista

el telesquí, el telesilla

el gorro

la esquiadora

el bastón

el esquí

la snowboarder

el casco

los guantes

la chaqueta de esquí, el anorak

la bota

¡Así se dice!

If you want to say *perhaps* or *maybe,* you can use the expressions **¡Quizás!, ¡Quizá!,** or **¡Tal vez!**

la ventanilla, la boletería

EL PICO
19 FEB
09:30 am
Todo día
No alquilar

el boleto, el ticket

VIDEO To go shopping for ski clothes with friends, watch **Diálogo en vivo.**

Los amigos compraron los tickets para el telesquí. Los compraron en la ventanilla.

Tomaron el telesilla. Lo tomaron para subir la montaña.

Hugo tiene miedo. No quiere bajar la pista avanzada. Prefiere las pistas para principiantes.

el/la patinador(a)

la pista de patinaje al aire libre

el patín

Julio y su amiga fueron a patinar sobre el hielo ayer.

En otras partes

El boleto is used throughout Latin America to mean *ticket*. In Spain it is **un billete.** A small ticket such as for a lift, bus, or subway is called **un ticket.** Variations are **el tiquete, el tique.**

doscientos treinta y cinco **235**

Los esquiadores suben los Pirineos en un telesilla en una estación de esquí en Andorra entre Francia y España.

Comunidades

¿En qué parte de Estados Unidos vives? ¿Hay balnearios o estaciones de esquí? ¿Qué atracciones hay? ¿Visitan muchos turistas tu estado? ¿Qué quieren ver o visitar? Si de vez en cuando hay unos turistas que hablan español, les debes hablar para practicar tu español.

HABLAR • ESCRIBIR

1 Identifica todo lo que ves en la foto. ¿Qué tiempo hace?

LEER

2 Categoriza. ¿Son palabras relacionadas con el esquí, el patinaje o los dos?

	esquí	patinaje	los dos
1. el pico			
2. el invierno			
3. la ventanilla			
4. el patín			
5. el hielo			
6. la pista			
7. el telesilla			
8. el bastón			

HABLAR • ESCRIBIR

3 Contesta sobre un grupo de amigos en una estación de esquí.

1. ¿Fueron los amigos a una estación de esquí?
2. ¿Compraron tickets para subir la montaña en el telesilla?
3. ¿Tomaron el telesilla para subir?
4. Cuando llegan al pico de la montaña, ¿ven muchas pistas?
5. ¿Hay pistas para expertos y principiantes?
6. ¿Tiene miedo Guillermo?
7. ¿Qué no quiere bajar?

EXPANSIÓN

Ahora, sin mirar las preguntas, da toda la información en tus propias palabras. Si no recuerdas algo, un(a) compañero(a) te puede ayudar.

HABLAR • ESCRIBIR

4 Prepara una lista de todo lo que necesitas cuando vas a esquiar. Luego prepara una lista de lo que necesitas cuando vas a la playa.

Más práctica
Workbook, pp. 7.5–7.6
StudentWorks™ Plus

ESCUCHAR • HABLAR • ESCRIBIR

5 Personaliza. Da respuestas personales.

1. Donde tú vives, ¿es popular el patinaje sobre hielo?
2. ¿Hay pistas de patinaje?
3. ¿Hay pistas al aire libre o cubiertas?
4. ¿Tienes patines?
5. ¿Hace mucho frío donde vives?
6. ¿Tienes miedo a veces cuando participas en ciertas actividades?
7. ¿Cuándo tienes miedo?

HABLAR • ESCRIBIR

6 Describe una de las fotografías.

LEER • ESCRIBIR

7

Work in pairs to solve the puzzle. Unscramble the words. Then, unscramble the circled letters. The first to discover the secret word wins.

LIHOE _____ _____ _____ ⭕ _____

TANÓBS _____ ⭕ _____ _____ _____ _____

YEAR _____ _____ ⭕ _____

MOPITE _____ _____ _____ _____ _____ ⭕

APTSI _____ _____ _____ ⭕ _____

SOCCA _____ _____ _____ ⭕ _____

Palabra secreta: _____

QuickPass

Go to glencoe.com
For: **Grammar practice**
Web code: **ASD4003c7**

Pretérito de los verbos en -ar

1. To express an action that began and ended at a specific time in the past you use the preterite tense. The endings of the preterite tense are different from those of the present tense.

2. You form the preterite of regular **-ar** verbs as follows.

infinitive	mirar		
stem	mir-		
yo	miré	nosotros(as)	miramos
tú	miraste	vosotros(as)	mirasteis
Ud., él, ella	miró	Uds., ellos, ellas	miraron

infinitive	nadar		
stem	nad-		
yo	nadé	nosotros(as)	nadamos
tú	nadaste	vosotros(as)	nadasteis
Ud., él, ella	nadó	Uds., ellos, ellas	nadaron

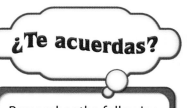

¿Te acuerdas?

Remember the following spelling patterns.
**ca, que, qui, co, cu
ga, gue, gui, go, gu
za, ce, ci, zo, zu**

3. Note the spelling of the **yo** form of verbs that end in **car**, **gar**, and **zar**.

c → qué	g → gué	z → cé

¿Marcaste un tanto?   Sí, marqué un tanto.
¿Llegaste a tiempo?   Sí, llegué a tiempo.
¿Empezaste a bucear?   Sí, empecé a bucear.

CULTURA

Aquí en Puerto Madryn, Argentina, puedes rentar todos los artículos necesarios para el buceo.

Práctica

ESCUCHAR

1 Escucha y determina si es el presente o el pretérito. Indica tus respuestas en una tabla como la de abajo.

presente	pretérito

ESCUCHAR • HABLAR

2 Contesta sobre Gustavo quien pasó una tarde en la playa.

1. Ayer, ¿pasó Gustavo la tarde en la playa?
2. ¿Con quiénes pasó la tarde?
3. ¿Tomó Gustavo mucho sol?
4. ¿Usó una loción bronceadora protectora?
5. ¿Nadó en el mar?
6. ¿Esquió en el agua?
7. ¿Tomó fotos con su cámara digital?

EXPANSIÓN

Ahora, sin mirar las preguntas, cuenta la información en tus propias palabras. Si no recuerdas todo, un(a) compañero(a) te puede ayudar.

ESCRIBIR

3 Forma frases en el pasado.

MODELO **amigos / comprar / raqueta**
Los amigos compraron una raqueta.

1. jóvenes / jugar / tenis
2. ellos / jugar / cancha cubierta
3. ellos / golpear / pelota
4. los jóvenes / jugar / dobles
5. Alicia y Paco / marcar / primer tanto
6. ellos / ganar / partido

EXPANSIÓN

Ahora, sin mirar las frases que formaste, relata toda la información en tus propias palabras.

Los dos amigos jugaron individuales en una cancha de tenis al aire libre.

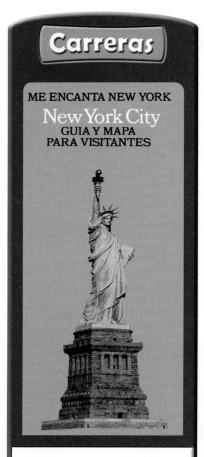

Carreras

ME ENCANTA NEW YORK

New York City
GUIA Y MAPA
PARA VISITANTES

Si hablas español hay muchas oportunidades para usar la lengua en la industria del turismo. ¿Por qué? Pues, porque hay mucha gente de ascendencia latina que vive en Estados Unidos y hay muchos turistas de España y Latinoamérica que visitan nuestro país.

 4 Personaliza. Da una respuesta personal.

1. Ayer, ¿a qué hora llegaste a casa?
2. ¿Preparaste la comida?
3. ¿Estudiaste?
4. ¿Escuchaste música?
5. ¿Miraste la televisión?
6. ¿Hablaste con un(a) amigo(a)?
7. ¿Le hablaste por teléfono en tu móvil?
8. ¿Te gustó la conversación?

 5 Trabajando en grupos, preparen una conversación sobre un juego de básquetbol según el modelo.

MODELO   —¿Jugó Pablo?
          —A ver, Pablo. ¿Jugaste?
          —Sí, jugué.

1. ¿Jugó Pablo básquetbol?
2. ¿Dribló con el balón?
3. ¿Pasó el balón a un amigo?
4. ¿Tiró el balón a su amigo?
5. ¿Entró el balón en el cesto?
6. ¿Marcó un tanto?

 6 Cambia **nosotros** a **yo.** Presta atención a la ortografía.

Ayer nosotros llegamos a la playa y empezamos a jugar fútbol. Jugamos muy bien. No tocamos el balón con las manos. Lo lanzamos con el pie o con la cabeza. Marcamos tres tantos.

CULTURA

Los jóvenes jugaron fútbol en una playa de Puerto Vallarta en México.

HABLAR

7 Conversa con un grupo de amigos que fueron a una fiesta anoche.

MODELO hablar →

—¿Hablaron ustedes durante la fiesta?
—Sí, hablamos.

1. jugar juegos de video
2. tomar una merienda
3. sacar fotos
4. rentar un DVD
5. tomar un refresco
6. escuchar música

LEER • ESCRIBIR

8 Completa en el pretérito. Tienes que usar todas las formas de los verbos.

Un grupo de amigos y yo __1__ (pasar) unos días en un balneario. Nosotros __2__ (llegar) el viernes por la noche y __3__ (pasar) dos noches en la casa de nuestro amigo Andrés.

En la playa todos nosotros __4__ (tomar) el sol. Yo __5__ (nadar) en el mar pero a Teresa no le gusta el mar y ella __6__ (nadar) en la piscina. Rubén __7__ (alquilar) un barquito y él y yo __8__ (esquiar) en el agua.

Y tú, ¿__9__ (nadar) la última vez que __10__ (pasar) algunos días en la playa? Y tus amigos, ¿__11__ (nadar) ellos también o solo __12__ (tomar) el sol?

Un anuncio publicitario en Valencia, España

InfoGap For more practice using the preterite of **-ar** verbs, do Activity 7 on page SR9 at the end of this book.

LEER • HABLAR • ESCRIBIR

9  Rompecabezas

First choose the word in each group that does not belong. Then think of another word that fits the category. Using all four words, create a sentence in the preterite.

1. el mar   la ola   el invierno   la playa

2. la toalla   las gafas   la crema protectora   la bota

3. el bañador   el gorro   los guantes   el anorak

4. nadar   patinar   bucear   tomar el sol

Pretérito de ir y ser

The verbs **ir** and **ser** are irregular in the preterite. Note that they have the same forms. You can determine the difference in meaning by the context of the sentence.

ir, ser	
yo	fui
tú	fuiste
Ud., él, ella	fue
nosotros(as)	fuimos
vosotros(as)	*fuisteis*
Uds., ellos, ellas	fueron

Yo fui a la playa y él fue también.
I went to the beach and he went, too.

Yo fui presidente y él fue vicepresidente.
I was president and he was vice president.

Los alumnos fueron a la escuela a pie in Oaxaca, México.

Un grupo de señores fueron a la playa de las Canteras en Las Palmas de Gran Canaria. Pasaron unos días agradables.

Práctica

 10 Escucha y determina quién habla.

yo	él, ella

HABLAR • ESCRIBIR

11 Personaliza. Da una respuesta personal.

1. Ayer, ¿fuiste a la escuela?
2. ¿Cómo fuiste? ¿En carro, en bus o a pie?
3. ¿Fuiste a las montañas el invierno pasado?
4. ¿Fuiste a una estación de esquí?
5. ¿Fuiste a la playa el verano pasado?
6. ¿Fuiste a un balneario?
7. ¿Fuiste al partido de fútbol el sábado pasado?

(EXPANSIÓN)

Ahora, sin mirar las preguntas, relata toda la información en tus propias palabras. Si no recuerdas algo, un(a) compañero(a) te puede ayudar.

ESCRIBIR

12 Completa con el pretérito de **ir.**

1. Yo _____ a la escuela ayer.
2. Mis amigos _____ también.
3. Nosotros _____ juntos.
4. Nosotros _____ a las ocho de la mañana.
5. Yo _____ a la cafetería para tomar el almuerzo pero Elena no _____.
6. ¿_____ (tú) a la cafetería ayer también?

(CULTURA)

La muchacha fue a la costa en San Juan, Puerto Rico, donde patinó en línea a lo largo de la playa.

 Comunicación

 13 Get together in groups of three or four. You will ask one another where you went in the past year. After you all have given your answers, determine how many of you went to the same places. Present your results to the class.

Los pronombres lo, la, los, las

1. The direct object is the word in the sentence that receives the direct action of the verb. It answers the question *what* or *whom*. The direct object can be either a noun or a pronoun. **Lo, la, los,** and **las** are direct object pronouns.

2. The direct object pronouns can replace either a thing or a person. The pronoun must agree with the noun it replaces and it comes right before the verb.

Ella compró el casco.	Ella **lo** compró.
Compró los guantes.	**Los** compró.
¿Miró Juan la pelota?	Sí, **la** miró.
¿Miró las raquetas?	Sí, **las** miró.
¿Invitaste a Juan?	Sí, **lo** invité.
¿Invitaste a María?	Sí, **la** invité.
¿Invitaste a sus amigos?	Sí, **los** invité.

La señora vende anteojos de sol. Los vende en una calle de Baños, Ecuador. Ahora no tiene clientes y charla con una amiga.

Práctica

VIDEO Want help with direct and indirect object pronouns? Watch **Gramática en vivo.**

Más práctica
Workbook, p. 7.11
StudentWorks™ Plus

ESCUCHAR • HABLAR

14 Con un(a) compañero(a), prepara una conversación según el modelo.

MODELO el bañador →
—¿Tienes el bañador?
—Sí, lo tengo. Lo compré ayer.

1. los anteojos de sol
2. el boleto
3. la toalla
4. el gorro
5. las botas
6. los guantes
7. la chaqueta de esquí
8. el casco

ESCUCHAR • HABLAR • ESCRIBIR

15 Contesta con el pronombre apropiado.

1. ¿Tienes tus botas nuevas?
2. ¿Tienes tu raqueta nueva?
3. ¿Tienes tu bañador nuevo?
4. ¿Tienes tus patines nuevos?
5. ¿Tienes tu cámara nueva?
6. ¿Tienes tu móvil nuevo?

LEER • HABLAR

16 Rompecabezas

Work with a partner and see who can solve each riddle first.

1. la usas cuando sacas fotos
2. la usas después de nadar
3. la necesitas cuando practicas el surfing
4. lo alquilas para esquiar en el agua
5. lo tomas para subir la montaña
6. la llevas cuando hace frío
7. lo debes comprar si quieres tomar el telesquí
8. los lleva una persona que patina

FOLDABLES®
Study Organizer

LARGE SENTENCE STRIPS
See page SH31 for help with making this foldable. Practice using direct object pronouns. On the front of each flap, write sentences with direct objects. Trade sentence strips and under the flaps replace the objects with pronouns. Check each other's work.

HABLAR

 17 Piensa en cosas que quieres comprar. Luego, con un(a) compañero(a) de clase, prepara una conversación según el modelo.

MODELO —¿Cuándo compraste los esquís?
—Los compré ayer.
—Me gustan. ¿Dónde los compraste?
—Los compré en la tienda Galerías.
—¿Cuánto te costaron?
—Me costaron 150 pesos.

LEER • ESCRIBIR

 18 Completa con un pronombre.

Ayer yo fui a buscar una raqueta de tenis para Elena. ___1___ compré en el Corte Inglés. A Elena le gustó mucho. Ella ___2___ usó ayer cuando jugamos tenis. Ella me enseñó unas fotos. José ___3___ sacó con su nueva cámara digital. Él ___4___ compró ayer porque él también fue al Corte Inglés.

HABLAR

 19 Work with a partner. Make up a conversation based on what you see in the photograph and use as many object pronouns as you can.

PRONUNCIACIÓN

Las consonantes b, v

There is no difference in pronunciation between a **b** and a **v** in Spanish. The **b, v** sound is somewhat softer than the sound of an English *b*. When making the sound, the lips barely touch.

Since **b** and **v** sound the same, people very often have trouble spelling words with a **b** or a **v**. They will often ask:

¿B de burro?   ¿V de vaca?

ba	be	bi	bo	bu
balón	béisbol	bien	recibo	bus
base	bebe	recibimos	árbol	aburre
batea	recibe	biftec	bonito	abuela
bajo	bebida	billete	fútbol	buceo
bárbaro	nube		boleto	
bastón			bota	

va	ve	vi	vo	vu
va	vela	vive	vosotros	vuelve
nieva	verano	vivimos	huevo	vuestro
nueva	verde	viejo	volver	
vamos	joven	vista	voy	
vaso	ventanilla	invierno	voleibol	
	venezolano		nuevo	

✏ Dictado

Pronounce the following sentences carefully. Then write them to prepare for a dictation.

> Va a visitar a sus abuelos en Bolivia.
> No nieva en Venezuela donde vivimos.
> Bárbara bebe un batido en el bus.
> Víctor ve la televisión.
> David vive en una casa nueva, no vieja.
> El joven alquila un barco de vela en verano.
> Lleva bañador cuando bucea.

Refrán

Can you guess what the following proverb means?

A invierno lluvioso, verano abundoso.

¡Bravo!

You have now learned all the new vocabulary and grammar in this chapter. Continue to use and to practice all that you know while learning more cultural information. **¡Vamos!**

Un día en la playa

Nando	¿Fuiste a la playa ayer?
Teresa	Sí, fui con Naida. Pasamos una tarde agradable. Naida nadó mucho y yo tomé el sol.
Nando	¿Esquiaron en el agua?
Teresa	No, yo tomé (llevé) mi plancha de vela pero no la usé.
Nando	¿No la usaste? ¿Por qué?
Teresa	Poco viento.
Nando	Ah, verdad. Si no hay mucho viento no puedes practicar la plancha de vela. No vale.
Teresa	¡Quizás, mañana!
Nando	Debes ir a Rincón. Allí las olas son más grandes y hay más viento.

¿Comprendes?

A Contesta según la información en la conversación.

1. ¿Quién fue a la playa?
2. ¿Con quién fue?
3. ¿Cómo pasaron la tarde?
4. ¿Quién nadó?
5. ¿Quién tomó el sol?
6. ¿Usó su plancha de vela Teresa?
7. ¿Adónde debe ir Teresa para practicar la plancha de vela?
8. ¿Cuáles son dos cosas necesarias para poder practicar la plancha de vela?

GeoVistas

To learn more about Puerto Rico, take a tour on pages SH62–SH63.

B **Resumiendo** Cuenta lo que pasó en la conversación en tus propias palabras.

C **Analizando** Si estás en Puerto Rico y quieres practicar la plancha de vela, ¿adónde debes ir? ¿Por qué?

CULTURA
En la playa de Tres Palmas en Rincón, Puerto Rico, las olas son bastante grandes.

Antes de leer

Before reading the selection, look at the two subtitles. Make a chart with a subtitle at the top of each column.

Durante la lectura

As you read, fill in your chart with information you want to remember. You don't need to use complete sentences.

✓ Reading Check

¿Adónde fueron a comer los amigos?

Un día en una playa de España 🎧 ♻️

La playa de Estepona El otro día Juan Carlos y un grupo de sus amigos del colegio fueron a Estepona donde pasaron el día entero en la playa. Estepona tiene muchos balnearios y cuando el día está muy claro, es posible ver la costa de África.

Los amigos lo pasaron muy bien en la playa. Conversaron de muchas cosas. Nadaron y tomaron el sol. Sandra y Felipe alquilaron un barquito y esquiaron en el agua. Y Tomás practicó la plancha de vela.

A eso de las tres y media todos fueron a un chiringuito—un restaurante pequeño al aire libre en la playa. Como[1] están en la costa tienen que comer pescado y mariscos. Todos picaron de varios platos—gambas al ajillo[2], arroz con camarones, calamares[3]—y una tortilla a la española. La tortilla fue para Maripaz porque a ella no le gustan los mariscos ni el pescado.

CULTURA
Un chiringuito en Estepona

✓ Reading Check

¿Para quiénes es un paraíso Tarifa?

Después de leer

Use your notes to help with the ¿Comprendes? activities. Were your notes helpful?

Tarifa Durante el almuerzo habló Fernando. Les habló a sus amigos de su día en Tarifa. Tarifa no está muy lejos de Estepona. En Tarifa el Mediterráneo entra en el Atlántico. Hay mucho viento y el mar está casi siempre bravo[4]. Las olas son muy grandes y por consecuencia Tarifa es un paraíso para los aficionados a la plancha de vela.

[1]Como *As, Since*
[2]gambas al ajillo *shrimp in garlic sauce*
[3]calamares *squid*
[4]bravo *rough*

250

¿Comprendes?

Más práctica

Workbook, pp. 7.12–7.15
StudentWorks™ Plus

A **Recordando hechos** Contesta.

1. ¿Adónde fueron Juan Carlos y un grupo de sus amigos?
2. ¿De qué hablaron los amigos?
3. ¿En qué actividades participaron?
4. ¿Adónde fueron a eso de las tres y media?
5. ¿Qué platos picaron?
6. ¿A quién no le gustan los mariscos ni el pescado?

B **Describiendo** Describe.

1. un chiringuito
2. Tarifa
3. Estepona

C **Analizando** Contesta.

¿Por qué a los aficionados a la plancha de vela les gusta ir a Tarifa?

CULTURA

A mucha gente le gusta practicar la plancha de vela en Tarifa, España.

CULTURA

El joven esquió en el agua en Puerto Banús, Marbella, España.

Antes de leer

Vas a leer sobre una estación de esquí. Antes de leer piensa en la información que ya tienes de tus cursos de ciencias sobre las estaciones en las diferentes partes del mundo.

Julio en Argentina 🎧♻

Es el mes de julio y Miguel y sus amigos de su colegio en Buenos Aires están de vacaciones. No hay clases porque tienen sus vacaciones de invierno. Miguel y varios amigos fueron a Bariloche a esquiar. Bariloche es un pueblo en los Andes de Argentina.

Pero, una pregunta: ¿Esquiaron en julio? ¿Cómo es posible? ¿Hay nieve en julio? Como Argentina está en el hemisferio sur, las estaciones son contrarias a las estaciones del hemisferio norte.

Bariloche está en el distrito de los famosos lagos[1] en la frontera de Argentina y Chile. Cerro Catedral está a veinte kilómetros de Bariloche y es la estación de esquí más popular de Argentina. Tiene una infinidad de pistas para todos los niveles[2] de esquiadores.

No importa si no te gusta esquiar. Tienes que visitar la región de Bariloche. Si no te fascinan las pendientes nevadas[3] seguramente te va a encantar el panorama magnífico que puedes observar de un telesilla que te sube hasta los 2.400 metros de altura. ¿Vas a tener miedo?

[1]lagos   *lakes*
[2]niveles   *levels*
[3]pendientes nevadas   *snow-covered slopes*

CULTURA

Cerro Catedral en el Parque Nacional Nahuel Huapi cerca de Bariloche en la frontera de Argentina y Chile

¿Comprendes?

CULTURA
El lago Nahuel Huapi y
la catedral en San Carlos
de Bariloche, Argentina

Escoge.

1. «Las estaciones son contrarias» significa que son _____.
   a. las mismas
   b. cortas
   c. opuestas
   d. al mismo tiempo

2. «Cerro Catedral tiene una infinidad de pistas» significa
   que _____.
   a. las pistas en Cerro Catedral son infinitas
   b. hay muchas pistas
   c. hay un número definido de pistas
   d. las pistas en Cerro Catedral son famosas

3. ¿Por qué debe uno visitar la región de Bariloche aun si no
   le gusta esquiar?
   a. Hay pistas para todos los niveles de esquiadores.
   b. Cerro Catedral no está muy lejos de Bariloche.
   c. Bariloche está en los Andes en la frontera de Argentina
      y Chile.
   d. Las vistas son estupendas y les encantan a todos.

4. ¿Quién puede tener miedo?
   a. una persona a quien no le gusta la nieve
   b. una persona que no puede esquiar
   c. una persona a quien no le gusta el invierno
   d. una persona a quien no le gusta subir muy alto

Vocabulario

1 **Identifica.**

 To review **Vocabulario 1** and **Vocabulario 2,** turn to pages 230–231 and 234–235.

1.

2.

3.

4.

5.

2 **Contesta.**
6. ¿Qué tiempo hace en verano?
7. ¿Qué tiempo hace en invierno?

3 **Contesta.**
8. ¿Qué lleva una persona cuando va a la playa?
9. ¿Qué lleva una persona que esquía?
10. ¿Dónde puede nadar una persona?
11. ¿Dónde puede esquiar una persona?
12. ¿Dónde puede patinar una persona?

Gramática

4 **Completa con el pretérito.**

13. Carlos _____ en el agua. (esquiar)

14. Ellos _____ un barquito. (alquilar)

15. La temperatura _____ a cero. (bajar)

16. ¿_____ (tú) fotos? (tomar)

17. Yo _____ español con mis amigos. (hablar)

18–19. Nosotros _____ las fotos que Elena _____.
(mirar, tomar)

20. Yo _____ un CD. (escuchar)

To review **el pretérito,** turn to pages 238 and 242.

5 **Escribe en el pretérito.**

21–22. Yo voy y él va también.

23. Yo llego a la playa.

24. Empiezo a jugar voleibol con mis amigos.

25. Yo marco tres tantos.

26. Y tus amigos, ¿juegan bien también?

27. Vamos a la playa después del almuerzo.

6 **Contesta con un pronombre.**

28. ¿Tiene José el gorro?

29. ¿Compró María la crema solar?

30. ¿Tiene Carolina los boletos?

31. ¿Alquilaron los amigos el barquito?

32. ¿Alquilaron las planchas de vela también?

33. ¿Ves a los gemelos en el telesilla?

34. ¿Escucharon los niños a sus padres cuando esquiaron?

35. ¿Miraste a tu hermana en la piscina?

36. ¿Invitaron los amigos a Alicia a la playa?

To review **los pronombres,** turn to page 244.

Cultura

7 **Completa.**

37. De Estepona en la Costa del Sol es posible ver la costa de _____.

38. _____ es un restaurante pequeño al aire libre en la playa.

39. En los restaurantes en la playa comen mucho _____ porque están en la costa.

40. Tarifa está en un punto de tierra donde el mar Mediterráneo entra en _____.

To review this cultural information, turn to pages 250–251.

1 **El tiempo**

Describe the weather where you live

What are the summers like? What are the winters like? Which do you prefer? Why?

2 **Mis vacaciones de verano**

Talk about a summer vacation

Work with a classmate. Tell him or her where you like to go on a summer vacation. Tell what you do and give some reasons why you like it so much. Your classmate will then tell what he or she does. Are your summer vacations similar?

3 **Donde vivo yo**

Tell about vacations where you live

Work with a classmate. He or she will take the role of an exchange student from Argentina. Tell him or her where people from your area tend to vacation. Give reasons. Your classmate will then tell what they do in Argentina based on what you have learned in this chapter. Argentina also has many beaches such as Mar del Plata.

4 **Un paraíso**

Discuss two beautiful resorts

Look at this ski resort in the Sierra Nevada mountains in Spain and this beach resort in Taboga Island, Panama. Which one do you prefer for a vacation? Explain why.

La estación de esquí de Pradollano en la Sierra Nevada en España

Una playa tranquila en la isla Taboga en Panamá

5 **Ayer**

Tell what you did

Work with a classmate. Tell the things you did yesterday. Compare and see whether you did the same things. Use the following verbs.

estudiar	trabajar	mirar un DVD	escuchar música	hablar
tomar	sacar	nadar	esquiar	llevar

Prepárate para el examen
Practice for written proficiency

Tarea

Write an e-mail about what you did during a real or imaginary vacation in a Spanish-speaking country.

El malecón a lo largo de la playa en Cádiz, España

Writing Strategy

Writing an e-mail You often write an e-mail to a friend or family member to tell them about something you did. You want to give them information that will interest them. So that they can share and enjoy your experience, remember to write with enthusiasm using expressions such as **¡Bárbaro! ¡Fabuloso! ¡Estupendo!**

1 Prewrite

- Decide on the resort you are going to say you visited. You may want to re-read some information about the place in your textbook.

- Since you're going to describe what you did, you must use the past tense. Make a list of all the **-ar** verbs you know that relate to your vacation. You will also want to use **ir** and **ser.**

- Use the verbs in your list to write sentences about what you did or what others did who were with you. Use the diagram below to help organize your sentences.

```
            with
           whom
            |
when ——— place ——— what
you went   name and   you did
           location
          /        \
  what              what
  you did          a friend or
  together        friends did
```

2 Write

- Begin the e-mail with an attention-grabbing introduction that tells where, when, and with whom you went.

- Organize your writing. You may want to use chronological order, or you may prefer to organize by activity or people involved.

- Write a conclusion. End by telling why you had a great time. **Lo pasé muy bien porque…**

- Read over your e-mail and correct any errors you find. Errors in grammar or spelling could lead to confusion on the part of the reader.

- Click SEND!

Evaluate

Don't forget that your teacher will evaluate you on the correct use and spelling of the verbs in the past tense as well as on how organized, understandable, and interesting your e-mail is.

Repaso del Capítulo 7

Gramática

- ### Pretérito de los verbos en -ar *(page 238)*
  The preterite tense is used to express actions that began and ended at a specific time in the past. Review the forms of the preterite of regular **-ar** verbs.

hablar			
yo	hablé	nosotros(as)	hablamos
tú	hablaste	*vosotros(as)*	*hablasteis*
Ud., él, ella	habló	Uds., ellos, ellas	hablaron

- ### Pretérito de ir y ser *(page 242)*
  Review the preterite forms of **ir** and **ser**. Note that their forms are identical.

ir, ser			
yo	fui	nosotros(as)	fuimos
tú	fuiste	*vosotros(as)*	*fuisteis*
Ud., él, ella	fue	Uds., ellos, ellas	fueron

- ### Pronombres lo, la, los, las *(page 244)*
  The direct object pronouns **lo, la, los, las** can replace either a thing or a person. The pronoun comes right before the verb.

  ¿Ves a Juan? ¿**Lo** ves?

  ¿Tienes el móvil? ¿**Lo** tienes?

  Tengo los tickets. **Los** tengo.

  ¿Invitaste a Marisol? ¿**La** invitaste?

  ¿Quieren la cámara? ¿**La** quieren?

  José compró las botas. **Las** compró.

CULTURA

Los jóvenes pasaron una tarde agradable en una de las isletas en el lago de Nicaragua.

There are a number of cognates in this list. See how many you and a partner can find. Who can find the most? Compare your list with those of your classmates.

Vocabulario

Describing weather

el verano	la nieve	Nieva.	Hace calor (frío).
el invierno	la nube	Hace buen (mal)	Hace (Hay) sol.
la temperatura	Llueve.	tiempo.	nublado(a)

Describing the beach and summer activities

el balneario	la piscina, la alberca	el esquí acuático	pasar
la playa	el surfing	(náutico)	nadar
la arena	la plancha de vela	el barquito	bucear
el mar	la tabla hawaiana	el voleibol	
la ola	el buceo	practicar	
el sol		alquilar, rentar	

Identifying beach gear

la toalla	los anteojos de sol,	una crema (loción)	una cámara digital
el traje de baño,	las gafas para el	solar, una loción	
el bañador	sol	bronceadora	

Describing a ski resort and winter activities

una estación de	el/la esquiador(a)	el patinaje sobre el	esquiar
esquí	el/la snowboarder	hielo	subir
la montaña	la ventanilla, la	la pista de patinaje	bajar
el pico	boletería	el/la patinador(a)	patinar
la pista	el boleto, el ticket	el/la experto(a)	
el telesquí, el	el hielo	el/la principiante	
telesilla			

Describing winter gear and equipment

el esquí	las botas	la chaqueta de esquí	el snowboard
el bastón	los guantes	el anorak	el patín
el gorro	el casco		

Other useful words and expressions

ayer	este año	tener miedo
esta noche	el año pasado	No vale.
anoche	esta semana	¡Quizás! ¡Quizá!
esta tarde	la semana pasada	¡Tal vez!
ayer por la tarde	el fin de semana	

Repaso cumulativo

Repasa lo que ya has aprendido

These activities will help you review
what you have learned so far in Spanish.

HORARIO DE FARMACIA
DE LUNES A SABADO
DE: 9 A.M. A 9 P.M.
DOMINGOS
DE: 8 A.M. A 8 P.M.

1 Escucha las frases. Indica si la frase es correcta o no según la información en el anuncio.

2 Contesta.
1. ¿Van ustedes a veces a la playa?
2. ¿A ti te gusta la playa?
3. ¿Nadas? ¿Dónde nadas?
4. ¿Tomas el sol? ¿Usas una loción bronceadora?
5. ¿Vas a la playa con tus amigos?
6. ¿Toman tus amigos una merienda en la playa?
7. ¿Esquían ustedes en el agua?
8. ¿Pasan ustedes un día agradable en la playa?

3 Cambia al presente.
1. Esquié en las montañas.
2. Mi amigo Carlos compró los tickets para el telesilla.
3. Tomamos el telesilla para subir la montaña.
4. Yo llevé un casco.
5. Bajé una pista avanzada.
6. Carlos bajó una pista más fácil.

4 Rompecabezas

Choose the word in each group that does not belong and tell why it is **el intruso.** Then think of another word that could replace **el intruso.**

1. la madre   el sobrino   el postre   la prima
2. driblar   toser   patinar   correr
3. perezoso   sincero   paciente   pelirrojo
4. el otoño   la profesora   el médico   la mesera

Completa en el presente.

1. Ricardo _____ en una tienda. (estar)
2. Unos amigos _____ con él. (estar)
3. Ricardo _____ una camisa. (necesitar)
4. Él _____ una camisa blanca. (buscar)
5. Ricardo, yo también _____ una camisa. (necesitar)
6. Ricardo y yo _____ con la empleada. (hablar)
7. La empleada _____ en la tienda. (trabajar)
8. Ella nos pregunta, «¿Qué _____ ustedes?» (desear)
9. Ricardo y yo _____ la camisa que _____. (comprar, necesitar)
10. Luego nosotros _____ a la caja y _____. (ir, pagar)

 ¡Te toca a ti! **Crea frases con las siguientes expresiones.**

Me gusta   **Me interesa**   **Me enoja**

 Mira los dibujos de un día que Marta y Juan pasaron en la playa. Describe el día.

En tu tiempo libre

Aquí y Allí

Vamos a comparar Los eventos culturales como *shows* o espectáculos folklóricos, conciertos y exposiciones artísticas son muy populares en los países hispanos. La gente asiste con frecuencia a los eventos culturales. ¿Qué piensas? ¿Son populares aquí en Estados Unidos también?

Objetivos

You will:

- talk about a birthday party
- discuss concerts, movies, and museums
- discuss Hispanic art and music

You will use:

- preterite of **-er** and **-ir** verbs
- the verbs **oír** and **leer**
- affirmative and negative words

El Museo Guggenheim en Bilbao, España, es famoso por su estilo arquitectónico y sus exposiciones de arte moderno y contemporáneo.

QuickPass

Go to glencoe.com
For: **Online book**
Web code: **ASD4003c8**

Introducción al tema
En tu tiempo libre

Look at these photographs to acquaint yourself with the theme of this chapter. We all love free time, **¿no?** In this chapter you'll see some of the things your counterparts in the Spanish-speaking world do when they have free time. You will learn that culture plays an important role in their activities. Do you see activities on this page that you also enjoy during your free time?

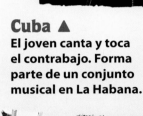

Cuba ▲
El joven canta y toca el contrabajo. Forma parte de un conjunto musical en La Habana.

◀ **Argentina** Una pareja joven baila el famoso tango en una calle de San Telmo en Buenos Aires.

España La Gran Vía es una de las avenidas principales de Madrid. En la Gran Vía hay muchos cines y teatros. ▶

México El museo de la famosa artista mexicana Frida Kahlo está en Coyoacán al sur de la Ciudad de México. El museo es la antigua casa de la familia de Frida Kahlo. Ella vivió en la casa también durante los años de su matrimonio con Diego Rivera, un pintor y muralista mexicano. ▼

▲ **Argentina** La Boca en Buenos Aires es un barrio o zona pintoresca de la ciudad donde hay muchos artistas. La Boca es famosa por sus casas de muchos colores.

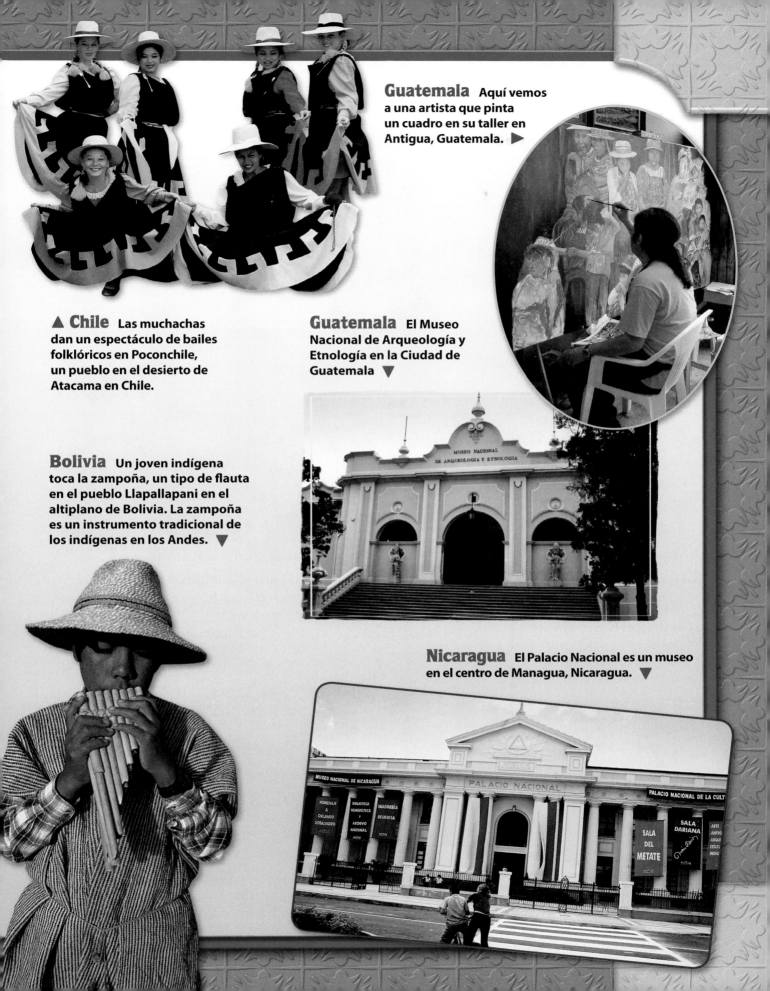

Guatemala Aquí vemos a una artista que pinta un cuadro en su taller en Antigua, Guatemala. ▶

▲ **Chile** Las muchachas dan un espectáculo de bailes folklóricos en Poconchile, un pueblo en el desierto de Atacama en Chile.

Guatemala El Museo Nacional de Arqueología y Etnología en la Ciudad de Guatemala ▼

Bolivia Un joven indígena toca la zampoña, un tipo de flauta en el pueblo Llapallapani en el altiplano de Bolivia. La zampoña es un instrumento tradicional de los indígenas en los Andes. ▼

Nicaragua El Palacio Nacional es un museo en el centro de Managua, Nicaragua. ▼

Una fiesta en casa

las velas

la torta, la tarta, el pastel

el regalo

En otras partes

Cacahuates is used in most areas of Latin America; in Spain it is **cacahuetes. El maní** is used in Puerto Rico.

Felipe dio una fiesta en casa para el cumpleaños de Sarita.
Todos los amigos dieron regalos a Sarita.
Ella recibió muchos regalos y los abrió.
Carlos le dio boletos (entradas) para un concierto.

las galletas

los vegetales crudos

los cacahuates, el maní

Durante la fiesta, los jóvenes picaron.
Comieron vegetales crudos, galletas con queso y cacahuates.

Un concierto

Sarita salió ayer.
Ella asistió a un concierto.

¡Ojo!

The verb **salir** means
to *leave* or *to go out.*
It can also convey the
meaning *to go out with
someone* in the sense of
to date.
> **Ella salió para
> España.
> Ella salió anoche.
> Salió con Roberto.**

la banda

los músicos

los cantantes

un conjunto, un grupo musical

Sarita oyó el concierto.
La banda tocó bien.
Los cantantes cantaron bien.

Después del concierto,
  Sarita volvió a casa.
  Volvió a casa a pie.

ESCUCHAR

1 Escucha y parea. Parea lo que oyes con el dibujo que describe.

a.

b.

¿Te acuerdas?

You have already learned the verb **perder** meaning *to lose.*

Perdieron el juego.

Perder can also mean *to miss.*

Perdió el autobús.

HABLAR

2 Contesta sobre un concierto según se indica.

1. ¿A qué asistió Tomás? (un concierto)
2. ¿Quiénes dieron el concierto? (su grupo favorito)
3. ¿Fue un concierto de jazz, rock o pop? (pop)
4. ¿Qué recibieron los músicos y cantantes? (muchos aplausos)
5. ¿Cómo volvió Tomás a casa? (a pie)
6. ¿Por qué volvió a pie? (perdió el bus)

EXPANSIÓN

Ahora, sin mirar las preguntas, cuenta la información en tus propias palabras. Si no recuerdas algo, un(a) compañero(a) te puede ayudar.

HABLAR

3 Contesta según las fotos.
¿Qué comió José?

1.

2.

3.

HABLAR • ESCRIBIR

④ Personaliza. Da respuestas personales.

Los nombres de muchos instrumentos musicales son palabras afines. Aquí tienes unos ejemplos: **el piano, el violín, la viola, la guitarra, la trompeta, el clarinete, la flauta.** ¿Tocas un instrumento musical? ¿Cuál? ¿Tocas en una orquesta o banda? ¿Qué tipo de orquesta o banda es?

LEER • ESCRIBIR

⑤ Da una palabra apropiada.

1. los que cantan
2. los que tocan instrumentos musicales
3. lo que da o presenta un grupo musical
4. un grupo o conjunto de músicos
5. algo que puedes comer
6. lo que recibes para tu cumpleaños
7. lo que hay sobre una torta de cumpleaños

la guitarra

el violín

CULTURA

La Banda Municipal de Las Palmas de Gran Canaria de España dio un concierto al aire libre.

El cine

una película

la taquilla

Ana fue al cine.
Ana compró las entradas en la taquilla.

Vio una película.   Ella la vio en español.

En otras partes

In addition to **una película,** you will also hear **un filme** or **un film.**

¡Así se dice!

If suddenly something comes to your mind and you want to say *by the way* you can say **¡A propósito!**
¡A propósito! ¿Te interesa ir al museo?

Para conversar

¿Comprendió (Entendió) Ana la película?

Sí, la entendió bastante bien. Pero su amigo no entendió nada.

El museo

VIDEO To witness a discussion on culture, watch **Diálogo en vivo.**

un cuadro

una estatua de bronce

En otro salón vieron una estatua de bronce.

Los amigos visitaron el museo.
Vieron una exposición de arte hispano.

Eduardo siempre va al museo.
Le gusta mucho el arte.

Pero a su amigo José no le gusta nada.
Él no va casi nunca al museo.

La pintora tiene algo en la mano.

Ahora no tiene nada en la mano.

Anita ve a alguien. Ve a su amiga.

Ahora Anita no ve a nadie.

Comunidades

El Museo del Barrio en la Ciudad de Nueva York tiene exposiciones sobre muchos aspectos de la cultura puertorriqueña.

En el *Hispanic Institute* en Nueva York hay una exposición permanente de los cuadros de artistas famosos de España.

ESCUCHAR • HABLAR • ESCRIBIR

 Escucha las frases. Indica en una tabla como la de abajo si cada frase es verdad o no.

verdad	falso

LEER

2 Escoge la palabra apropiada.
 1. La muchacha (vio, oyó) un filme.
 2. La muchacha (vio, oyó) el concierto.
 3. El artista pinta (un cuadro, una estatua).
 4. Vieron una exposición en (el cine, el museo).
 5. (El pintor / El escultor) pinta.

HABLAR • ESCRIBIR

3 Contesta.
 1. ¿Qué visitó la clase del señor Salas?
 2. ¿Qué vieron?
 3. ¿Qué tipo de exposición fue?
 4. ¡A propósito! ¿Fue Ana al cine?
 5. ¿Qué vio?
 6. ¿Entendió la película?

CULTURA

Un grupo de estudiantes en un museo de arte contemporáneo en Vitoria en el País Vasco (Euskadi) en España

ESCRIBIR

④ Da el contrario.

1. siempre
2. alguien
3. algo
4. nada
5. nunca
6. nadie

HABLAR • ESCRIBIR

⑤ Personaliza. Da respuestas personales.

1. ¿Te gusta el arte?
2. ¿Eres aficionado(a) al arte?
3. ¿Vas con frecuencia a un museo?
4. ¿Qué puedes ver en un museo?
5. ¿Vas con frecuencia al cine?
6. ¿Te gustan las películas?
7. ¿Qué piensas? ¿Puedes entender películas en español?
8. ¿Entiendes películas en inglés?

CULTURA

Un museo de arte moderno en Palma de Mallorca

⑥ **Rompecabezas**

Can you figure out what the following movie titles are in English?

Rompiendo el Hielo

Lo que el viento se llevó

Piratas del Caribe

LA GUERRA DE LAS GALAXIAS

El Señor de los Anillos

El Rey León

La Bella y La Bestia

Blanca Nieves

Comunicación

⑦ Tell the class whether you prefer to go to an art museum or a movie theater. Explain why.

⑧ In small groups, discuss activities you like to do in your free time. In addition to going to a party, movie, concert, or museum, you may wish to discuss some of your other activities. Some expressions you may want to use are: **escuchar música, ver la tele, leer, navegar la red, practicar un deporte, ir a un café, tocar un instrumento musical, ir a la playa.**

InfoGap For more practice using your new vocabulary, do Activity 8 on page SR10 at the end of this book.

QuickPass

Go to glencoe.com
For: **Grammar practice**
Web code: **ASD4003c8**

Pretérito de los verbos en -er, -ir

1. You have already learned the preterite forms of regular **-ar** verbs. Study the preterite forms of regular **-er** and **-ir** verbs: **-í, -iste, -ió, -imos, -isteis, -ieron.** The preterite endings of regular **-er** and **-ir** verbs are the same.

infinitive	comer		
stem	com-		
yo	comí	nosotros(as)	comimos
tú	comiste	vosotros(as)	comisteis
Ud., él, ella	comió	Uds., ellos, ellas	comieron

infinitive	asistir		
stem	asist-		
yo	asistí	nosotros(as)	asistimos
tú	asististe	vosotros(as)	asististeis
Ud., él, ella	asistió	Uds., ellos, ellas	asistieron

2. The preterite forms of the verbs **dar** and **ver** are the same as those of regular **-er** and **-ir** verbs. However, note that there are no accent marks.

	dar	ver
yo	di	vi
tú	diste	viste
Ud., él, ella	dio	vio
nosotros(as)	dimos	vimos
vosotros(as)	disteis	visteis
Uds., ellos, ellas	dieron	vieron

3. Remember that the preterite is used to tell about an event that began and ended at a specific time in the past.

Ellos **salieron anoche.**
Ayer no **comí** en casa. **Comí** en el restaurante.
¿**Viste** una película **la semana pasada**?

Práctica

HABLAR • ESCRIBIR

1 Contesta sobre una fiesta de cumpleaños que dio Miguel.

1. ¿Dio Miguel una fiesta?
2. ¿La dio para celebrar el cumpleaños de Alejandra?
3. ¿Escribió Miguel las invitaciones?
4. ¿Vio Alejandra a todos sus amigos en la fiesta?
5. ¿Le dieron regalos a Alejandra?
6. ¿Recibió ella muchos regalos?
7. ¿A qué hora salieron sus amigos de la fiesta?
8. Según sus padres, ¿volvieron a casa bastante tarde?

EXPANSIÓN

Ahora, sin mirar las preguntas, relata toda la información en tus propias palabras. Si no recuerdas algo, un(a) compañero(a) te puede ayudar.

HABLAR • ESCRIBIR

2 Personaliza. Da respuestas personales.

1. ¿A qué hora saliste de casa esta mañana?
2. ¿Perdiste el bus escolar o no?
3. ¿Aprendiste algo nuevo en español?
4. ¿Comprendiste lo que aprendiste?
5. ¿Viste un DVD en clase?
6. ¿A qué hora saliste de la escuela?
7. ¿A qué hora volviste a casa?

ESCUCHAR • HABLAR

3 Con un(a) compañero(a) de clase, prepara una miniconversación según el modelo.

MODELO ir al cine →
—¿Fuiste al cine?
—Sí, fui al cine.

1. ver una película americana
2. entender la película
3. salir del cine a las diez
4. perder el autobús
5. volver a casa a pie

CULTURA

Dos amigos compraron una bebida y luego vieron una película en un cine en Santiago de Chile.

VIDEO Want help with the preterite of regular verbs? Watch **Gramática en vivo.**

Las guaguas escolares esperan el regreso de los alumnos que gozan de una excursión escolar en La Habana.

FOLDABLES®
Study Organizer

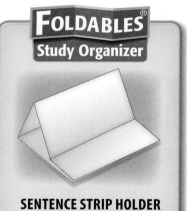

SENTENCE STRIP HOLDER

See page SH33 for help with making this foldable. Practice the preterite form of verbs by making flashcards of verbs. Then, with a partner, take turns using these verbs in sentences. Ask each other questions about the sentences.

LEER

④ Completa en el pretérito sobre una visita a un restaurante mexicano.

—¿ __1__ ustedes a un restaurante mexicano? (Ir)

—Sí.

—¿Qué __2__ ustedes? (comer)

—Pues, todos nosotros no __3__ la misma cosa. Yo __4__ tacos y otros __5__ enchiladas. Pero todos nosotros __6__ arroz y frijoles. (comer)

—¿A qué hora __7__ ustedes del restaurante? (salir)

— __8__ a eso de las ocho y media. (Salir)

—¿ __9__ ustedes una propina al mesero? (Dar)

—Sí, le __10__ una propina porque él nos __11__ un servicio bueno. (dar)

EXPANSIÓN

¡Adivina! Según el contexto, ¿qué es una propina?

ESCRIBIR

⑤ Cambia el párrafo al pretérito.

Esta mañana, José sale de casa y ¡qué pena! Pierde el bus escolar. Así va a la escuela a pie. En la escuela yo como en la cafetería. José y yo no comemos juntos porque él sale de la escuela y come en un café cerca de la escuela. Hoy la profesora nos enseña una lección difícil. Los alumnos no la comprenden enseguida. La profesora nos da otra explicación y luego todos la comprendemos. Aprendemos mucho en su clase. ¿Y tú? ¿Aprendes mucho en tu clase de español? ¿Qué aprendes?

 Comunicación

⑥ With a partner, make up a conversation telling what you did in the past week. Find out if you did the same things.

Gramática

Los verbos oír, leer

1. Note the forms of the present and preterite of **oír**. Pay particular attention to the spelling.

oír	presente	pretérito
yo	oigo	oí
tú	oyes	oíste
Ud., él, ella	oye	oyó
nosotros(as)	oímos	oímos
vosotros(as)	*oíste*	*oísteis*
Uds., ellos, ellas	oyen	oyeron

2. The verb **leer** follows the same pattern as **oír** in the preterite.

leer	
leí	leímos
leíste	*leísteis*
leyó	leyeron

Práctica

LEER • ESCRIBIR

7 Completa con la forma correcta del presente de **oír.**

1. Yo _____ la música de una guitarra.
2. Nosotros no _____ nada.
3. Tú, ¿me _____ bien?
4. Él _____ todo.
5. Ustedes _____ lo que explico, ¿no?

LEER • ESCRIBIR

8 Cambia **yo** a **Raúl.**

1. Yo leí el anuncio del concierto.
2. Lo leí en la revista *Gente.*
3. Yo oí el concierto.
4. Oí a Shakira. Ella cantó muy bien.

EXPANSIÓN

Cambia **yo** a **Raúl y yo.** Luego cambia **yo** a **Raúl y Ana.**

Cultura

Shakira es una cantante colombiana de ascendencia libanesa. Sus canciones en español y también en inglés tienen mucho éxito. Shakira es también compositora, instrumentista y bailadora.

Además de ser una figura famosa es una persona caritativa. Estableció varias escuelas especiales para niños pobres en el norte de Colombia.

Palabras afirmativas y negativas

1. Study the following affirmative and negative words.

Algo está en la mesa.
Hay **algo** en la mesa.
Vi **algo** allí.

Nada está en la mesa.
No hay **nada** en la mesa.
No vi **nada** allí.

Alguien canta.
Oí a **alguien**.

Nadie canta.
No oí a **nadie**.

Él siempre va al cine.

Ella nunca va al cine.
Ella no va **nunca** al cine.

2. Note that in Spanish you can use more than one negative word in the same sentence.

Él **nunca** habla mal de **nada** ni de **nadie**.

Práctica

LEER • HABLAR • ESCRIBIR

9 Cambia a la forma negativa.

1. Siempre como comida mexicana.
2. Siempre uso mi móvil.
3. Alguien me enoja.
4. Veo a alguien delante de la clase.
5. Tengo algo en mi mochila.
6. El profesor tiene algo en la mano.

ESCUCHAR • HABLAR • ESCRIBIR

10 Contesta con **no.**

1. ¿Tienes algo en la mano?
2. ¿Hay algo en tu mochila?
3. ¿Ves a alguien?
4. ¿Hay alguien delante de ti?
5. ¿Vas siempre al museo?
6. ¿Siempre lees algo a alguien?
7. ¿Siempre les escribes algo a tus amigos?

 CULTURA
¿Tiene algo la muchacha? Sí, tiene un libro y una mochila.

Las consonantes j, g

The Spanish **j** sound does not exist in English. In Spain, the **j** sound is very guttural. It comes from the throat. In Latin America, the **j** sound is much softer. Repeat the following.

ja	je	ji	jo	ju
hija	garaje	Jiménez	José	junio
roja		antojitos	ojo	julio
trabaja			joven	jugar
jardín			frijol	jugo
caja				

In combination with **e** or **i**, **g** has the same sound as the Spanish **j**. For this reason, you must pay particular attention to the spelling of words with **ge** and **gi**.

ge	gi
gemelos	gigante
gente	biología
generoso	energía

Dictado

Pronounce the following sentences carefully. Then write them to prepare for a dictation.

El hijo de José Jiménez trabaja en el garaje.
El joven jugador tiene ojos azules.
La clase de biología cultiva vegetales en un jardín.
Los gemelos José y Julián son dos jóvenes generosos.
El viejo general trabaja con alguien en julio.

¡Ojo!

Garaje can also be written **garage.**

Refrán

Can you guess what the following proverb means?

¡FELIZ CUMPLEAÑOS, ANA!

Más vale tarde que nunca.

¡Bravo!

You have now learned all the new vocabulary and grammar in this chapter. Continue to use and practice all that you know while learning more cultural information. **¡Vamos!**

CULTURA

Los jóvenes son gemelos. Son inteligentes los dos y también son muy generosos.

QuickPass

Go to glencoe.com
For: **Conversation practice**
Web code: **ASD4003c8**

Anoche

¿Comprendes?

A Contesta según la información en la conversación.

1. ¿Por qué no contestó su móvil Julia?
2. ¿Adónde fue?
3. ¿Qué vio?
4. ¿Le gustó?
5. ¿Lo entendió?
6. ¿Salió Roberto?
7. ¿Qué vio?
8. ¿Con quién vio el DVD?

B **Resumiendo** Cuenta la información de la conversación en tus propias palabras.

C **Analizando** ¿Qué te indica que Julia tiene interés en Roberto?

D **Interpretando** En la conversación, ¿quién es hispano y quién no lo es? Por qué?

CULTURA

Clientes delante de la taquilla del Cine Corrientes en Buenos Aires, Argentina

Antes de leer

Think about any cultural events you have attended that you enjoyed.

Durante la lectura

As you read each section, decide which interests you more and why.

> ✓ **Reading Check**
>
> ¿Durante qué guerra luchó Zapata?

> ✓ **Reading Check**
>
> ¿Cuáles son dos instrumentos andinos?

Después de leer

What aspect of culture in this reading did you personally find the most or least interesting?

Un día de cultura latina

Ayer pasaste un día de cultura latina. Viste una exposición de arte hispano. Comiste en una churrasquería—un restaurante argentino donde comiste el famoso bife argentino. Luego oíste un concierto de música latina.

Arte En el museo, viste un cuadro del famoso muralista mexicano José Clemente Orozco— *Zapatistas*. Tiene un motivo político emocionante. Emiliano Zapata fue un líder revolucionario. Durante la Revolución mexicana los zapatistas lucharon[1] con Zapata contra las injusticias del gobierno. En el cuadro, ¿ves como los peones[2] caminan (van a pie) de una manera pausada y laboriosa? ¿Puedes ver la inclinación de los cuerpos[3]? ¿Te parece que los peones participan en una marcha determinada para derrocar[4] a sus opresores?

Música Durante el concierto oíste varios tipos de música latina. Un conjunto de los Andes tocó la flauta y la zampoña—instrumentos populares entre los indígenas andinos.

Un grupo guatemalteco tocó marimbas. En Guatemala las orquestas de marimbas van de un pueblo a otro para tocar durante las fiestas locales.

Un grupo de jóvenes tocan zampoñas y flautas.

Un grupo de músicos tocan marimbas en Antigua, Guatemala.

[1]lucharon   *fought*
[2]peones   *peasants*

[3]cuerpos   *bodies*
[4]derrocar   *overthrow*

282

¿Comprendes?

Más práctica

Workbook, pp. 8.10–8.11
StudentWorks™ Plus

A Recordando hechos Contesta.

1. ¿Qué viste en el museo durante tu visita imaginaria?
2. ¿Dónde comiste?
3. ¿Qué comiste?
4. Después de comer, ¿adónde fuiste?
5. ¿Qué oíste?

B Explicando Contesta.

1. ¿Contra qué lucharon los peones en el cuadro de Orozco?
2. ¿A quiénes quieren derrocar? ¿Por qué?

Zapatistas de José Clemente Orozco

C Describiendo

Describe el cuadro *Zapatistas* en tus propias palabras.

D Describiendo Describe.

1. la música indígena andina
2. la música indígena guatemalteca

doscientos ochenta y tres **283**

LECTURA
UN POCO MÁS

Antes de leer

Vas a leer sobre una excursión escolar. A veces, ¿hay excursiones escolares en tu escuela? ¿Adónde van? ¿Visitan un parque especial, un museo, un teatro? Antes de leer piensa en una posible excursión con tu clase de español.

CULTURA
El Zócalo y la Catedral Metropolitana en la Ciudad de México

GeoVistas

To learn more about Mexico, take a tour on pages SH46–SH47.

Domingo, día 18 de febrero

La señora Ocampo acompañó a su clase de español a hacer una excursión escolar a su capital, la Ciudad de México. Visitaron muchos sitios de interés histórico en la capital.

¿Por qué fueron el domingo? Fueron el domingo porque los domingos a las nueve y media de la mañana hay un espectáculo del Ballet Folklórico de México en el magnífico Palacio de Bellas Artes. Los alumnos de la señora Ocampo vieron el espectáculo y les gustó mucho. Después subieron al tercer piso donde vieron unos murales de los famosos muralistas mexicanos Rivera, Orozco y Siqueiros. En sus murales de protesta social los artistas critican las injusticias que sufrieron los peones mexicanos.

Cuando salieron del Palacio de Bellas Artes, pasaron por el centro histórico de la capital. En el Zócalo, la plaza principal de la capital y la más grande de Latinoamérica, visitaron la Catedral Metropolitana.

Después de su visita a la catedral, fueron a la famosa Casa de los Azulejos[1] donde tomaron el almuerzo. Casi todos comieron tacos y enchiladas acompañadas de arroz y frijoles refritos. ¡Qué rico!

Cuando volvieron a casa después de pasar un día muy agradable, todos decidieron que quieren volver otra vez a la capital para visitar el Bosque de Chapultepec y el Museo de Antropología. ¡A ver si la señora Ocampo está conforme!

[1]Azulejos   *Tiles*

CULTURA
Un domingo en el Bosque de Chapultepec

¿Comprendes?

Escoge.

1. ¿Cuál es la profesión de la señora Ocampo?
   a. guía turística
   b. agente
   c. profesora
   d. excursionista

2. ¿Qué es el Palacio de Bellas Artes en México?
   a. un palacio privado
   b. la residencia del presidente
   c. un espectáculo
   d. un museo y un teatro

3. Los grandes muralistas mexicanos critican _____.
   a. el arte surrealista
   b. las injusticias sociales
   c. a los peones y campesinos
   d. la protesta social

4. ¿Qué es la Casa de los Azulejos?
   a. una casa privada
   b. un restaurante
   c. una catedral
   d. un museo de azulejos

5. ¿Qué quieren los alumnos de la señora Ocampo?
   a. volver a visitar la capital una vez más
   b. ver un espectáculo del Ballet Folklórico
   c. pintar unos murales
   d. tomar el almuerzo en un restaurante mexicano

VIDEO To see **una charreada**—a favorite Mexican cultural event—watch **Cultura en vivo.**

CULTURA

La Casa de los Azulejos en el centro histórico de la Ciudad de México. Es una tienda y un restaurante.

Conexiones

La geografía

La Ciudad de México es una gran metrópoli. Hay muy pocas ciudades con mayor población que la Ciudad de México. ¿Puedes adivinarse su población? Pues la zona metropolitana de la ciudad tiene unos veinte millones de habitantes. ¿Cuántos habitantes hay en tu ciudad o pueblo?

Vocabulario

1 Identifica.

1.

2.

3.

4.

5.

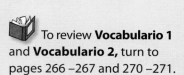 To review **Vocabulario 1** and **Vocabulario 2,** turn to pages 266–267 and 270–271.

2 Corrige.

6. Dan o presentan una película en un museo.

7. Los pintores dieron un concierto.

8. Ellos bebieron vegetales crudos.

9. Ellos oyeron una exposición de arte.

10. No hay nadie en la mochila.

11. Hay regalos en la torta.

12. Vieron una estatua en el cine.

13. Anoche los cantantes tocaron muy bien.

14. José dio un concierto para su cumpleaños.

15. Los músicos dieron muchos aplausos.

Gramática

3 **Completa con el pretérito.**

16. Yo _____ una película muy buena. (ver)

17. El público _____ mucho. (aplaudir)

18. Nosotros _____ ir al concierto. (decidir)

19. Los cantantes _____ muchos aplausos. (recibir)

20. ¿A qué hora _____ tú del estadio? (salir)

21. ¿Dónde _____ ustedes? (comer)

22. Teresa _____ el concierto y le gustó mucho. (oír)

23. Ellos _____ la novela *Lazarillo de Tormes*. (leer)

24. Ayer yo les _____ las entradas a mis amigos. (dar)

25. ¿_____ tú al concierto la semana pasada? (asistir)

26. Nosotros _____ muchos regalos para nuestro cumpleaños. (recibir)

27. ¿_____ ustedes el nuevo CD de su grupo favorito? (oír)

28. Sarita _____ tres gaseosas. (beber)

To review **el pretérito,** turn to pages 274 and 277.

4 **Da la forma negativa.**

29. Ellos oyeron a alguien.

30. Hay algo en la mesa.

31. Ellos van siempre al mismo cine.

32. Ellos siempre hablan a alguien de algo.

33. Hay siempre algo nuevo en el museo.

34. Ella tiene algo en la mano.

35. Alguien habla.

To review **palabras afirmativas y negativas,** turn to page 278.

To review this cultural information, turn to pages 282–283.

Un mural de Orozco en un edificio de la Universidad de México

Cultura

5 **¿Sí o no?**

36. Una churrasquería es un restaurante mexicano.

37. Muchos murales de los muralistas mexicanos tienen motivos políticos.

38. Orozco es un muralista mexicano.

39. La marimba es un instrumento popular entre los indígenas en los Andes de Sudamérica.

40. Emiliano Zapata pintó el cuadro *Zapatistas*.

CULTURA

Prepárate para el examen
Practice for oral proficiency

1 **Anoche**

Talk about a birthday party

Work with a classmate. Each of you went to a different birthday party last night. Tell each other about the party you attended. Whose birthday was it? Who attended? What did you eat and drink? What music did you listen to?

2 **Una visita al museo**

Discuss a museum visit

Work in groups of three or four. Two of you spent last Saturday at a museum. Your friends have some questions. Describe your museum visit and answer all their questions.

3 **Un conjunto musical**

Describe a musical group

Work with a classmate. Tell each other about your favorite musical group. Tell why you like their music.

4 **Volviste tarde.**

Explain why you got home late

You got home really late last night. One of your parents (your partner) wants to know why. He or she will ask how you spent your evening. You'd better have some good answers.

Tarea

Prepare a poster announcing a cultural event that is going to take place at your school or in your town. You have already seen a preview of the event, so as part of your poster you will write a brief review of what you saw.

Writing Strategy

Writing publicity Publicity includes posters and ads. The first goal of publicity writing is to capture the attention of your audience. Publicity should:

- attract attention
- include all the important information
- get the results you want

1 Prewrite

- Decide the event for which you want to prepare the poster. It can be a movie at your school, *a school show*, «espectáculo» or «drama», a musical concert, or exposition of work by members of the art club.
- Think about the important information you have to include—event, participants, place, date and time, and price.

2 Write

- Write an attention-grabbing heading for your poster.
- Give all the necessary information about the event.
- Write your brief paragraph about the preview you saw. Remember to use the preterite.
- Check to make sure your facts are accurate.
- Check to make sure you haven't made any spelling or grammatical errors.

Evaluate

Don't forget that your teacher will evaluate you on your poster's design and completeness of information, and on your paragraph's organization, use of vocabulary, and correctness of spelling and grammar.

Repaso del Capítulo 8

Gramática

- ### Pretérito de los verbos en -er, -ir *(page 274)*

  The preterite endings of regular **-er** and **-ir** verbs are the same. Review the forms below.

comer			
yo	comí	nosotros(as)	comimos
tú	comiste	*vosotros(as)*	*comisteis*
Ud., él, ella	comió	Uds., ellos, ellas	comieron

escribir			
yo	escribí	nosotros(as)	escribimos
tú	escribiste	*vosotros(as)*	*escribisteis*
Ud., él, ella	escribió	Uds., ellos, ellas	escribieron

  The preterite forms of the verbs **dar** and **ver** are the same as those of regular **-er** and **-ir** verbs. Review the following forms.

DAR	di	diste	dio	dimos	*disteis*	dieron
VER	vi	viste	vio	vimos	*visteis*	vieron

- ### Los verbos oír, leer *(page 277)*

  The verbs **leer** and **oír** have a spelling change in the **él** and **ellos** forms of the preterite tense.

Ud., él, ella	leyó	oyó
Uds., ellos, ellas	leyeron	oyeron

- ### Palabras afirmativas y negativas *(page 278)*

  Review the following words.

AFFIRMATIVE	NEGATIVE
algo	nada
alguien	nadie
siempre	nunca

  Él nunca le dio nada a nadie.
  Ella no compró nada en la tienda.

CULTURA

Los jugadores gritaron y aplaudieron cuando un miembro de su equipo marcó un gol.

Vocabulario

Describing a concert

el concierto	el/la cantante	cantar	recibir (muchos)
el/la músico(a)	dar un concierto	asistir a un concierto	aplausos
el grupo, el conjunto	tocar un	oír un concierto	
la banda	instrumento		

Going to the movies

el cine	la taquilla	el boleto, la entrada
la película		

Describing a museum visit

el museo	una estatua	una exposición	el/la pintor(a)
un cuadro	(de bronce)	de arte	el/la escultor(a)

Describing a party

el cumpleaños	la torta, la tarta,	el regalo	el maní
la fiesta	el pastel	las galletas	los vegetales crudos
el/la invitado(a)	las velas	los cacahuates	picar

Other useful words and expressions

todos	nunca	volver	decidir
casi	algo	visitar	¡A propósito!
nada	alguien	salir	
nadie	siempre	perder (el autobús)	

Repaso cumulativo

Repasa lo que ya has aprendido

These activities will help you review
what you have learned so far in Spanish.

 1 **Escucha las frases. Indica el dibujo que cada frase describe.**

a.　　　　　　　　　　　　b.

 2 **Completa en el presente.**

1. Nosotros _____ a un concierto. (asistir)
2. Mi grupo favorito _____ el concierto. (dar)
3. Todos los aficionados _____ mucho. (aplaudir)
4. Yo no _____ cacahuates. (comer)
5. Tú _____ una película en español. (comprender)
6. ¿A quién _____ ustedes? (ver)

 3 **Completa con la letra que falta.**

1. Nosotros _i_imos en Estados Unidos.
2. Nosotros _e_emos leche.
3. Él _e la tele_isión.
4. El paciente a_re la _oca.
5. Ellos _an al consultorio y yo _oy también.
6. Ella _ende camisas.

A ella no le interesa nada la clase de matemáticas.

 4 **Identifica.**

a. las cosas que te gustan
b. las cosas que te interesan
c. las cosas que te aburren

5 **Categoriza. Organiza las palabras en las siguientes categorías.**

alto	bajo	serio	ambicioso
bonito	moreno	rubio	gracioso
inteligente	malo	interesante	enfermo
tímido	honesto	triste	generoso
nervioso	guapo	bueno	cansado
contento			

personalidad	características físicas	emociones	condiciones físicas o mentales

 6 **Describe a un(a) de tus amigos(as).**

 7 **Personaliza. Contesta.**

1. ¿Quién eres?
2. ¿De dónde eres?
3. ¿Cómo eres?
4. ¿Cómo estás hoy?
5. ¿Cuántos años tienes?
6. Por lo general, ¿estás de buen humor o estás de mal humor?

 8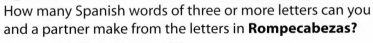

How many Spanish words of three or more letters can you and a partner make from the letters in **Rompecabezas?**

20+	¡Estupendo!
12–19	¡Excelente!
6–11	¡Bien!
0–5	No muy bien. ☹

¡Vamos de compras!

Aquí y Allí

Vamos a comparar Vas a aprender como va de compras la gente en España y Latinoamérica. En los países latinos hay varios tipos de mercados que son muy interesantes. Algunos son muy pintorescos. ¿Qué tipo de tiendas hay cerca de donde tú vives? ¿Dónde va de compras tu familia? ¿En un mercado, un supermercado, tiendas pequeñas o tiendas grandes?

Objetivos

You will:

- talk about buying clothes
- talk about buying food
- compare shopping in Spanish-speaking countries with shopping in the United States

You will use:

- more numbers
- the present tense of **saber** and **conocer**
- comparatives and superlatives
- demonstrative adjectives and pronouns

Una estudiante universitaria en un mercado de flores en Cuenca, Ecuador

Go to glencoe.com
For: **Online book**
Web code: **ASD4003c9**

Introducción al tema
¡Vamos de compras!

Look at these photographs to acquaint yourself with the theme of this chapter. Shopping is something we all do. We shop for basic everyday needs and we shop for some things that are not so necessary. As you will learn in this chapter, there are many interesting and fun types of shopping venues in Spain and Latin America. At which of the places shown here would you most like to shop?

▲ **Chile** El joven vende pescado en una pescadería en Puerto Montt en la Patagonia chilena.

México Es una panadería en La Condesa, una zona o colonia de la Ciudad de México. ¿Tienes hambre? ¿Quieres comprar algo? ▼

◀ **Argentina** Las muchachas en Buenos Aires regresan a casa después de las clases. Pero antes, van de compras.

◀ **Argentina** Es una vista del centro comercial Galerías Pacífico en el centro de Buenos Aires.

Ecuador Aquí vemos una tienda en Ecuador. En la tienda venden de todo—máscaras, cerámicas, tejidos, etc. ▼

◄ Nicaragua La señora tiene un puesto de frutas y verduras (legumbres) en León, Nicaragua. Tales puestos o tenderetes son populares en todas partes de Latinoamérica.

▲ Perú Es la galería de un mercado grande en Lima, Perú.

España Las muchachas van de compras en el Rastro— un antiguo mercado famoso en Madrid los domingos por la mañana. ►

España ¿Quieres comprar algo en el Centro Villalobos en la Gran Canaria? ¿A qué piso tienes que ir para comprar lo que quieres? ►

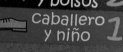
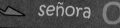

◄ España Venden cangrejos de río en el mercado municipal de San Sebastián en el País Vasco (Euskadi).

España La joven es empleada en una tienda de ropa en el País Vasco en el norte de España. ►

297

Un centro comercial

En otras partes

Un blue jean is universally understood but you will also hear **un (pantalón) vaquero** in many areas and **los mahones** in Puerto Rico. In addition to **la chaqueta** you will also hear **un saco** and, less commonly, **una americana** for a sports jacket.

el escaparate

Hay muchas tiendas en un centro comercial.
Mucha gente va de compras en el centro comercial.

La ropa

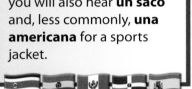

la talla

el número

un vestido

un par de zapatos

una camisa de manga corta

una corbata

una chaqueta

un blue jean

un par de tenis

un pantalón largo

Para conversar

José, esta chaqueta no te queda bien.

Es verdad. Es muy grande, ¿no? Necesito una talla más pequeña.

José quiere comprar una chaqueta.
Pero no sabe su talla.

Para conversar

Quiero un par de zapatos.

Y, ¿qué número calza usted?

37.

¿Le gustan estos?

Elena habla con la empleada.

¡Así se dice!

When you want to say how lucky you are about something, you can say **¡Qué suerte tengo!**

¿Cuál es el precio?

50%

TODO AL 50%

50

250 pesos

500 pesos

Estas blusas (aquí) cuestan 500 pesos. Cuestan mucho. Son caras.
Aquellas camisetas (allá) cuestan 250 pesos. Cuestan poco. Son baratas.

Hoy hay un saldo (una liquidación).
Cuando una tienda tiene un saldo, rebajan los precios.
Todo te sale más barato.
Te cuesta menos.

ESCUCHAR

1 Escucha. Escoge la frase correcta. Prepara una tabla como la de abajo para indicar tus respuestas.

a	b

HABLAR • ESCRIBIR

2 Personaliza. Da respuestas personales.

1. ¿Hay un centro comercial donde ustedes viven?
2. ¿Qué hay en este centro comercial?
3. ¿Cuándo rebajan las tiendas los precios?
4. Cuando rebajan los precios, ¿cómo te sale todo?
5. ¿Qué talla necesitas cuando compras una camisa o una blusa?
6. ¿Qué número calzas?

ESCRIBIR

3 Repasa los colores. Indica todos los artículos de ropa de color rojo, amarillo, negro, gris, blanco, verde, anaranjado y azul.

Diego   **Teresa**   **Ernesto**   **Graciela**

HABLAR • ESCRIBIR

4 Personaliza. Da respuestas personales.

1. ¿A ti te gusta mirar en los escaparates de las tiendas?
2. ¿Te gusta ir de compras o no?
3. ¿Prefieres llevar una camisa o una blusa de mangas largas o de mangas cortas?
4. Si eres muchacho, ¿te gusta llevar chaqueta y corbata? Si eres muchacha, ¿te gusta llevar vestido?
5. ¿Prefieres llevar un pantalón más formal y zapatos o un blue jean y tenis a la escuela?

CULTURA

Es un centro comercial moderno en Barcelona, España.

Más práctica
Workbook, pp. 9.3–9.4
StudentWorks™ Plus

LEER • HABLAR

5 Escoge la respuesta correcta del **banco de palabras**.

con la empleada	treinta y ocho
en la caja	ciento cincuenta pesos
una camisa	no, barata
el dinero	

1. ¿Con quién habla Esteban en la tienda de ropa?
2. ¿Qué quiere comprar Esteban?
3. ¿Qué talla usa?
4. ¿Cuánto cuesta la camisa que mira?
5. ¿Es cara?
6. ¿Dónde paga Esteban?
7. ¿Qué le da al cajero?

EXPANSIÓN

Ahora, sin mirar las preguntas, da toda la información en tus propias palabras. Si no recuerdas algo, un(a) compañero(a) te puede ayudar.

CONVERSION DE TALLAS

Ropa de señora – Vestidos y abrigos						
Estados Unidos	6	8	10	12	14	16
España	36	38	40	42	44	46
Sudamérica	34	36	38	40	42	44
Ropa de señora – Blusas y jersey						
Estados Unidos	30	32	34	36	38	40
España	38	40	42	44	46	48
Sudamérica	38	40	42	44	46	48
Ropa de caballeros – Trajes						
Estados Unidos	34	36	38	40	42	44
España	44	46	48	50	52	54
Sudamérica	44	46	48	50	52	54
Calzado – señoras						
Estados Unidos	4	5	6	7	8	9
España	34/35	35/36	36/37	38/39	39/40	41/42
Sudamérica	2	3	4	5	6	7
Calzado – caballeros						
Estados Unidos	8	$8^{1/2}$	9	$9^{1/2}$	10	$10^{1/2}$
España	41	42	43	43	44	45
Sudamérica	6	$6^{1/2}$	7	$7^{1/2}$	8	$8^{1/2}$

6 **R o m p e c a b e z a s**

Change one letter in each word to form a new word.

habla   par   cara   corta   más

nada

allá   sale   hoy   menor

Comunicación

7 Con un(a) compañero(a) de clase, preparen una conversación entre los jóvenes en la fotografía. Presenten su conversación a la clase.

CULTURA

La pareja miró en el escaparate de una tienda de ropa en el barrio de Salamanca, Madrid. Este barrio tiene muchas tiendas elegantes.

VIDEO To practice your new words, watch **Vocabulario en vivo.**

En el mercado

un puesto, un tenderete

En el mercado hay muchos puestos.
En cada puesto los vendedores venden un producto diferente.

Las señoritas van de compras.
Ellas van de un puesto a otro.

Un puesto de legumbres, una verdulería

las judías verdes

las zanahorias

los pimientos

los guisantes

el maíz

las cebollas

En otras partes

In addition to **el maíz,** you will hear **el elote** in Mexico and parts of Central America. You will hear **el choclo** in areas of South America. **Las judías verdes** are also called **chauchos, porotos,** and, in some areas, **frijoles.**

Un puesto de frutas, una frutería

las naranjas

la piña

las uvas

las manzanas

los plátanos

En el supermercado

un carrito lleno de compras

un paquete de vegetales congelados

ocho tajadas de jamón

una botella de agua mineral

un bote (una lata) de atún

un frasco de mayonesa

¡Así se dice!

When asking how much something costs, such as fruits and vegetables whose prices vary frequently, you most often ask:

—**¿A cuánto están los tomates?**

—**Están a cincuenta el kilo.**

When a vendor asks if you want something else (**¿Algo más?**), you can say what you want or respond **No, nada más, gracias.**

En un mercado indígena

tejidos

artesanía

sandalias

cerámicas

En el mercado indígena venden de todo.
La cliente no paga el precio que le da el vendedor.
Quiere pagar menos.
Quiere un precio más bajo.
En el mercado todos regatean.

QuickPass

Go to glencoe.com
For: **Vocabulary practice**
Web code: **ASD4003c9**

FOLDABLES®
Study Organizer

PROJECT BOARD WITH TABS
See page SH32 for help
with making this foldable.
Practice using vocabulary
related to shopping.
Create an illustrated tab for
different shopping venues.
Under each tab, list what
you would purchase at that
particular shopping place.
Compare your purchases
with a partner's.

ESCUCHAR

1 Escucha las frases. Parea cada frase con la foto que describe.

a.

b.

c.

HABLAR

2 Contesta sobre el mercado y el supermercado.

1. ¿Qué hay en un mercado?
2. ¿Hablan los clientes con los vendedores?
3. ¿Van los clientes con frecuencia a los mismos puestos?
4. ¿Tienen precios buenos?
5. ¿Qué tipo de productos hay en un mercado indígena?
6. ¿Regatean los clientes en un mercado indígena?
7. ¿Vas al supermercado para comprar comida?
8. ¿Usas un carrito cuando estás en el supermercado?

ESCRIBIR

3 Categoriza. Prepara una lista de frutas y legumbres.

frutas	legumbres

CULTURA

Una pastelería en Antigua,
Guatemala. Tiene un buen
surtido de dulces, ¿no?

Más práctica

■ Workbook, pp. 9.5–9.6
● StudentWorks™ Plus

LEER • HABLAR

4 Completa la conversación en un mercado o verdulería.

—¿_____ están los tomates hoy?

—Están a cincuenta _____ kilo.

—Un kilo, por _____.

—¿_____ más, señora?

—No, _____, gracias.

LEER • ESCRIBIR

5 Escoge del **banco de palabras** para completar las frases.

carnicería	pastelería	panadería
verdulería	pescadería	frutería

1. Necesito pan. Voy a la _____.
2. Vamos a comer sardinas. Voy a la _____.
3. Necesito carne picada para preparar hamburguesas. Voy a la _____.
4. Quiero comprar un postre. Voy a la _____.
5. Quiero guisantes, maíz y brócoli. Voy a la _____.
6. Voy a preparar una ensalada de manzanas, naranjas y plátanos. Voy a la _____.

LEER • ESCRIBIR

6 Completa la lista de compras de la señora Vázquez.

HABLAR

7 **Juego** Play this game with a partner. Name one item you want to buy and your partner will tell you where you can buy it. Choose from the following shopping venues. Take turns.

un supermercado

un mercado indígena

una tienda de ropa

¿Dónde lo compro?

un puesto de legumbres

un puesto de frutas

Conexiones

Las matemáticas
La medida tradicional para peso en Estados Unidos es la libra. En el sistema métrico, la medida para peso está basada en el kilogramo, o kilo. Hay mil gramos en un kilo. El kilo es igual a 2,2 libras. Una libra estadounidense es un poco menos de medio kilo.

Lista de compras

un _____ de tomates frescos

un _____ de atún en aceite

dos _____ de guisantes congelados

un _____ de mayonesa

seis _____ de jamón

dos _____ de agua mineral

Gramática

¿Te acuerdas?

You have already learned the numbers **uno a cien(to)** on page 8.

Comparaciones

En muchos de los países hispanos usan un punto en los números donde en Estados Unidos usamos una coma. Nota los siguientes números.

1,480 (Estados Unidos)
1.480 (países hispanos)

¿Cómo escribes el número 2482 si vives en Estados Unidos? ¿Y si vives en un país hispano?

Los números

1. **Cien** is used when followed by a noun. When followed by another number it is **ciento**.

   cien euros
   ciento cincuenta pesos

2. The numbers from 200 to 1000 are as follows. Pay particular attention to the spelling of 500, 700, and 900. Numbers, when used as adjectives, must agree with the nouns they modify.

   doscientos
   trescientos
   cuatrocientos
   quinientos
   seiscientos
   setecientos
   ochocientos
   novecientos
   mil

   el año mil cuatrocientos noventa y dos   1492
   el año mil setecientos setenta y seis   1776

TODOS ESTOS REGALOS PUEDEN SER SUYOS

1955 PUNTOS — MALETA TIPO TROLLEY

1.785 PUNTOS — MOCHILA

3945 PUNTOS — BICICLETA DE MONTAÑA

3. **Mil** when used in counting does not have a plural form. **Un millón** does. Note the following.

   mil dólares   **un millón de dólares**
   dos mil dólares   **dos millones de euros**
   cien mil dólares   **un millón quinientos mil pesos**
   dos mil nueve

   Note that when stating the year after 2000, you should use the article.

   en el dos mil diez

4. **Mil** has a plural form when not used in counting.

   Miles de turistas visitan Guatemala cada año.

Más práctica

Workbook, p. 9.7
StudentWorks™ Plus

Práctica

HABLAR

① Cuenta de cien a mil por cientos.

HABLAR

② Indica el precio según el modelo.

MODELO   **tomates / quinientos pesos / el kilo →**
          Los tomates están a quinientos pesos el kilo.

1. huevos / dos euros / la docena
2. papas / doscientos pesos / el kilo
3. manzanas / setecientos pesos / el kilo
4. cebollas / sesenta y dos pesos / el kilo

HABLAR • ESCRIBIR

③ Da las siguientes fechas.

1. 1492	**5.** 1810
2. 1808 a 1814	**6.** 1776
3. 718	**7.** 1898
4. 1936	**8.** 2001

LEER • HABLAR

④ **Investigación** Look up the important event that took place in each of the years listed in Activity 3. Discuss your findings with the class.

CULTURA

Un puesto de legumbres en un mercado municipal en Guadalajara, México

---

Comunicación

⑤ You work in a clothing store after school. You must do the inventory. Tell another employee (your partner) how many of the following items the store has in stock. Take turns.

vestidos 842   camisas 15,445
pantalones 9,850   blue jean 6,100
zapatos 10,049   chaquetas 577

Presente de saber y conocer

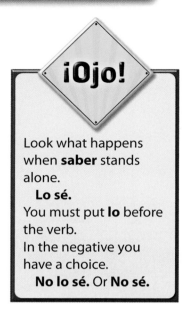

1. The verbs **saber** and **conocer** both mean *to know*. Note that like many Spanish verbs they have an irregular **yo** form in the present tense. All other forms are regular.

saber			
yo	sé	nosotros(as)	sabemos
tú	sabes	vosotros(as)	sabéis
Ud., él, ella	sabe	Uds., ellos, ellas	saben

conocer			
yo	conozco	nosotros(as)	conocemos
tú	conoces	vosotros(as)	conocéis
Ud., él, ella	conoce	Uds., ellos, ellas	conocen

2. The verb **saber** means *to know a fact* or *to have information about something*. It also means *to know how to do something*.

> **Yo sé donde está el mercado.**
> **No sabemos a qué hora vamos al mercado.**
> **Ellos saben regatear.**

3. The verb **conocer** means *to know* in the sense of *to be acquainted with*. It is used with people and complex or abstract concepts rather than simple facts.

> **Yo conozco a Luis.**
> **Ella conoce a su hermano.**
> **Los alumnos conocen bien la arquitectura española.**

CULTURA

¿Sabes que hay mucha influencia árabe en la arquitectura española? Aquí vemos un ejemplo de la influencia de los moros en Granada.

Práctica

HABLAR • ESCRIBIR

6 Personaliza. Da respuestas personales.

1. ¿Sabes el número que calzas?
2. ¿Sabes la talla que usas?
3. ¿Sabes dónde está el mercado?
4. ¿Sabes el número de tu móvil?
5. ¿Conoces España?
6. ¿Conoces la historia de España?
7. ¿Conoces al primo de José Luis?

ESCUCHAR • HABLAR • ESCRIBIR

7 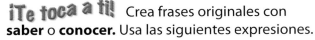 Crea frases originales con **saber** o **conocer.** Usa las siguientes expresiones.

1. a tu amigo
2. donde vive
3. su número de teléfono
4. su dirección de correo electrónico
5. a sus padres
6. a toda la familia de José
7. el precio
8. la talla
9. jugar tenis
10. donde está la cancha
11. a Picasso

CULTURA

Estos tunos en la Ciudad de México saben tocar muy bien la guitarra. ¿Sabes tú tocar un instrumento musical? ¿Cuál?

8 Completa con las formas correctas de **saber** o **conocer.**

1. Yo _____ a Mari y _____ donde vive.
2. ¿_____ si ella tiene el número de tu móvil?
3. Yo no _____ si lo tiene o no.
4. Aquí está Felipe. Tú lo _____, ¿no?
5. Sí, yo lo _____. Y _____ que es el hermano de Mari.

✿ Comunicación

9 Trabaja con un(a) compañero(a) de clase. Indiquen todo lo que saben hacer. ¿Saben hacer las mismas cosas o no?

LEER • ESCRIBIR

10 Completa con la forma correcta de **saber** o **conocer.**

Pepita	Sandra, ¿__1__ tú a Sarita Álvarez?
Sandra	Claro que __2__ a Sarita. Ella y yo somos muy buenas amigas.
Pepita	¿__3__ tú que ella va a Argentina?
Sandra	¿Ella va a Argentina? No, yo no __4__ nada de sus planes. ¿Cuándo va a salir?
Pepita	Pues, ella no __5__ exactamente qué día va a salir. Pero __6__ que va a salir en junio.
Sandra	¿Sarita __7__ Argentina?
Pepita	Creo que sí. Yo no __8__ definitivamente. Pero yo __9__ que ella __10__ a mucha gente en Argentina.
Sandra	¿Cómo es que ella __11__ a mucha gente allí?
Pepita	Pues, tú __12__ que ella tiene parientes en Argentina, ¿no?
Sandra	Ay, sí es verdad. Yo __13__ que tiene familia en Argentina porque yo __14__ a su tía Lola. Y __15__ que ella es de Argentina.

CULTURA

Durante los fines de semana hay un mercado al aire libre en el parque de la Recoleta en Buenos Aires. Muchos artistas venden sus cuadros.

> **GeoVistas**
>
> To learn more about Argentina, take a tour on pages SH58–SH59.

11 **Juego ¿A quién conoces?** Think of someone in the class whom you know quite well. Tell your partner some things you know about this person. Don't say who it is. Your partner will guess. Take turns.

Comparativo y superlativo

1. To express the comparative in Spanish, you put **más** or **menos** before the adjective or adverb and **que** after it.

> **Ella es más alta que su hermana.**
> **Es también más ambiciosa que ella.**

After **que**, you use the subject pronouns or **nadie**.

> **Ella sabe más que yo, tú y ella.**
> **Ella sabe más que nadie.**

2. To express the superlative, you use the definite article plus **más. De** always follows the superlative.

> **Ella es la muchacha más simpática de todas.**
> **Su hermano es el más inteligente de la clase.**

3. Study the comparative and superlative forms of **bueno, malo, bien,** and **mal.**

bueno	mejor	el/la mejor
malo	peor	el/la peor
bien	mejor	
mal	peor	

> **Carlos es el mejor alumno de la clase de español.**
> **Él habla mejor que nadie.**

CULTURA

El sencillo cuesta menos que el súper y el doble cuesta más que el súper. El doble es el más caro de los tres.

Práctica

HABLAR • ESCRIBIR

12 Contesta.

1. ¿Es más grande tu clase de historia o tu clase de español?
2. ¿Cuál es tu clase más pequeña de todas?
3. En tu escuela, ¿es más popular el fútbol o el béisbol?
4. ¿Cuál es el deporte más popular de todos?
5. Cuando hay una liquidación, ¿son los precios más bajos o más altos?

HABLAR • ESCRIBIR

13 Forma frases completas según el modelo.

> MODELO alto   Luis / Jaime / Andrés →
> **Luis es alto. Jaime es más alto que Luis y Andrés es el más alto de todos.**

1. graciosa   Susana / Adela / Lupe
2. interesantes   los Gómez / los García / los Ramos
3. dinámico   Paco / Tadeo / Carlos

CULTURA

Una joven con su hermana menor en el pueblo pequeño de Subtanjalla en el sur de Perú. Las dos muchachas tienen un gatito.

Más práctica

Workbook, p. 9.11
StudentWorks™ Plus

HABLAR • ESCRIBIR

14 Personaliza. Da respuestas personales.

1. En tu familia, ¿quiénes son mayores que tú?
2. ¿Tienes un(a) hermano(a) menor?
3. ¿Eres tú el (la) menor o no?
4. ¿Quién es el (la) mejor estudiante?
5. ¿Quién es tu mejor amigo(a)?
6. ¿En qué clase recibes las mejores notas?
7. ¿En qué clase recibes las peores notas?

Demostrativos

1. In Spanish the demonstratives are **este, ese,** and **aquel.** Note that the demonstratives can be either adjectives or pronouns. **Este** *(this, this one)* indicates something close to you. **Ese** *(that, that one)* indicates something close to the person you're speaking with. **Aquel** *(that, that one over there)* indicates something far away from both of you.

InfoGap For more practice using the comparative and superlative, do Activity 9 on page SR11 at the end of this book.

2. Study the forms of the demonstratives.

este libro	estos libros	esta mesa	estas mesas
ese libro	esos libros	esa mesa	esas mesas
aquel libro	aquellos libros	aquella mesa	aquellas mesas

esta camisa y esa (que tú tienes)
estas tiendas aquí y aquellas (en las afueras)

Práctica

HABLAR

15 Prepara una conversación con un(a) compañero(a) según el modelo.

MODELO   los zapatos →
   —¿Cuál es el precio de los zapatos?
   —¿Cuáles? ¿Estos zapatos aquí?
   —No, aquellos allá.

1. los guantes
2. las blusas
3. el vestido
4. los pantalones
5. el gorro
6. las botas
7. la chaqueta
8. la camisa

CULTURA

En este parque de la Ciudad de México, el Bosque de Chapultepec, hay puestos donde venden globos y algodón de azúcar.

ESCUCHAR • HABLAR • ESCRIBIR

16 Cambia al singular o viceversa.

1. Estas ideas son muy buenas.
2. Ese carro es nuevo.
3. Esos niños son inteligentes.
4. Aquella casa es moderna.
5. Estos cuadros son interesantes.
6. Aquel museo es fabuloso.

PRONUNCIACIÓN

Las consonantes ñ, ch, x

The **ñ** is a separate letter of the Spanish alphabet. The mark over it is called a **tilde.** Note that it is pronounced similarly to the *ny* in the English word *canyon.* Repeat the following.

señor	otoño	España	niño
señora	pequeño	cumpleaños	compañía
año	mañana	baño	piña

Ch is pronounced much like the *ch* in the English word *church.* Repeat the following.

coche	chaqueta	champú
chocolate	muchacho	churro

An **x** between two vowels is pronounced much like the English *x* but a bit softer. It's like a **gs: examen →
eg-samen.** Repeat the following.

exacto	examen
éxito	próximo

When **x** is followed by a consonant, it is pronounced like an **s.** Repeat the following.

extremo	explicar	exclamar

Dictado

Pronounce the following sentences carefully. Then write them to prepare for a dictation.

> El señor español compra una chaqueta cada año en el otoño.
> Va a tener éxito en su próximo examen.
> La señora exclama «¡Qué pena!» cuando el señor explica la situación extrema.

Refrán

Can you guess what the following proverb means?

Más vale pájaro en mano que cien volando.

¡Bravo!

You have now learned all the new vocabulary and grammar in this chapter. Continue to use and practice all that you know while learning more cultural information. **¡Vamos!**

En una tienda de ropa

¿Comprendes?

VIDEO To go shopping with two friends, watch **Diálogo en vivo.**

A Contesta según la información en la conversación.

1. ¿Con quién habla José en la tienda de ropa?
2. ¿Qué quiere comprar?
3. ¿Sabe su talla?
4. ¿Le queda bien la chaqueta?
5. ¿Qué necesita?
6. ¿Cuánto cuesta la chaqueta?
7. ¿Por qué tiene suerte José?
8. ¿Qué más quiere él?
9. ¿A qué departamento tiene que pasar?

B Resumiendo Cuenta la información en la conversación en tus propias palabras.

C Llegando a conclusiones

1. ¿Qué piensas? Cuando José pasa al departamento de calzados, ¿sabe qué número calza? ¿Tiene el empleado un par de zapatos que le quedan bien? ¿Compra José zapatos?

2. ¿Por qué quiere José comprar una chaqueta nueva y un par de zapatos? ¿Por qué los necesita? ¿Adónde va a ir?

CULTURA
Una tienda de ropa para caballeros en la Ciudad de México

Antes de leer

Think of your family's shopping habits. What types of stores do you and your family prefer for buying food?

✓ **Reading Check**

¿Cuándo tienen mercado los pueblos indígenas de Latinoamérica?

✓ **Reading Check**

¿Por qué son famosos los otavaleños?

CULTURA

Esta señora en el mercado de Chichicastenango en Guatemala no tiene un puesto. Vende sus productos de una canasta en el suelo.

Durante la lectura

Compare and contrast these shopping habits with yours. Do you bargain to get the best prices?

Mercados indígenas

Es un domingo y estamos en Chichicastenango, Guatemala. Son las seis de la mañana y llega mucha gente a pie y en bus para ir al mercado. En muchos pueblos indígenas de Latinoamérica hay mercado uno o dos días a la semana.

Los sábados hay un mercado célebre en Otavalo en Ecuador. En Otavalo como en «Chichi» hay muchos puestos en el centro donde venden de todo—artesanía, ropa, tejidos y ¡claro!, comestibles—la comida es muy importante.

En los mercados la mayoría de los vendedores son mujeres y ellas saben que sus compradores nunca quieren pagar el primer precio y van a regatear. Todos quieren un precio más bajo. En los mercados hay unos turistas también que quieren comprar y llevar a casa un buen recuerdo. Y como recuerdo no hay nada mejor que un tejido de Otavalo. Los indígenas otavaleños tienen fama mundial de ser los mejores tejedores y es la comunidad indígena más próspera de toda América.

CULTURA

Como ves en la foto, hay vendedores que colocan sus productos en el suelo y hay otros que tienen puestos o tenderetes. Este mercado está en Otavalo.

¿Comprendes?

Más práctica

■ Workbook, p. 9.12
● StudentWorks™ Plus

CULTURA

En Mérida, México, como en muchas otras ciudades, hay un gran mercado municipal y en las calles alrededor del mercado hay más puestos como los que ves aquí.

A Recordando hechos

1. ¿Qué hay en muchos pueblos de Latinoamérica?
2. ¿Cuántas veces a la semana hay mercado?
3. ¿Qué hay en los mercados?

B Confirmando información Corrige.

1. Los mercados indígenas son por la noche.
2. En los mercados indígenas la mayoría de los vendedores son hombres.
3. Los compradores pagan el primer precio que les da la vendedora.
4. Solo los habitantes del pueblo van al mercado.
5. Los indígenas de Chichicastenango son la comunidad más próspera de toda América.

C Describiendo

Describe un mercado indígena.

D Explicando

¿Qué es el regateo? ¿A ti te gusta regatear?

E Analizando

¿Por qué es el mercado en Otavalo, Ecuador, un mercado célebre (famoso)?

VIDEO To visit an indigenous market in Peru, watch **Cultura en vivo.**

De compras 🎧♻️

Antes de leer

Piensa en como los miembros de tu familia van de compras y el tipo de comidas que ustedes toman.

CULTURA

El mercado municipal en Estepona en el sur de España

Mercado municipal En muchas ciudades de España y Latinoamérica hay un mercado municipal. En el mercado hay muchos puestos—carnicerías, panaderías, verdulerías, etc. A mucha gente le gusta ir al mercado municipal porque saben que todo lo que compran es fresco. Y, ¡una cosa más! Como suelen[1] ir de compras a diario (todos los días), conocen a los vendedores y pueden tener confianza en ellos.

CULTURA

Hay muchos pasillos en este supermercado moderno en Mérida, Venezuela.

Supermercado Además de mercados municipales hay supermercados donde la gente toma un carrito y lo empuja[2] de pasillo a pasillo donde pueden comprar comestibles en paquetes, latas y frascos. Y como no quieren o no pueden ir de compras todos los días compran muchas cosas congeladas.

Centro comercial En las afueras de las ciudades hay grandes centros comerciales modernos. Tienen tiendas de ropa, videojuegos y electrodomésticos. Y si tienes hambre hay también una zona de comedores. ¿Quieres ver una película? Hay cines también.

[1]**suelen** *they are used to*   [2]**empuja** *push*

318

¿Comprendes?

Escoge.

1. ¿Qué es un mercado municipal?
   a. un mercado de la ciudad
   b. un mercado indígena
   c. un mercado en un centro comercial
   d. un supermercado

2. Las carnicerías, panaderías, etc., en los mercados son _____.
   a. centros
   b. puestos
   c. tiendas
   d. mercados

3. ¿Cuándo va la gente de compras en un mercado municipal?
   a. un día a la semana
   b. casi nunca
   c. casi todos los días
   d. cuando hay mercado

4. Los clientes en un supermercado usan _____.
   a. un pasillo
   b. un carrito
   c. una lata
   d. un puesto

5. En los centros comerciales hay _____.
   a. puestos indígenas
   b. solo ropa
   c. muchas tiendas
   d. comida congelada

CULTURA

Los clientes empujan sus carritos por los pasillos de este hipermercado en la Ciudad de México.

Vocabulario

1 **Completa.**

1–2. Esa chaqueta no le _____ bien. Necesita una _____ más grande.

3. ¿Qué _____ calzas?

4–5. Rebajan los precios cuando hay un _____ y todo le sale más _____.

6. Hay muchos _____ en un mercado.

7–8. Él compra _____ de agua mineral y _____ de atún.

9–10. Ayer en el supermercado compré un _____ de mayonesa y cinco _____ de jamón.

11–12. En el carrito de Pablo hay siempre muchas frutas. Le gustan _____ y _____.

13. Yo pregunté al vendedor, «¿_____ están las zanahorias?»

14. Cuando la señora necesita comida, va _____ en el mercado.

15. Hay muchas tiendas de todos tipos en un _____.

To review **Vocabulario 1** and **Vocabulario 2,** turn to pages 298–299 and 302–303.

2 **Parea los contrarios.**

16. largo	**a.** barato
17. mucho	**b.** compro
18. menos	**c.** más
19. caro	**d.** corto
20. vendo	**e.** poco

Gramática

3 **Contesta.**

21. ¿Sabes quién es?

22. ¿Lo conoces?

23. ¿Sabes dónde vive?

To review **saber** and **conocer,** turn to page 308.

Cerámicas de México

4 **Escoge.**

24. Ella _____ que hay una diferencia.

    a. sabe   **b.** conoce

25. Ellos _____ donde vivimos.

    a. saben   **b.** conocen

26. Él me _____ bien.

    a. sabe   **b.** conoce

27. Él _____ que tengo móvil.

    a. sabe   **b.** conoce

28. Le gusta el arte y _____ bien la historia del arte mexicano.

    a. sabe   **b.** conoce

5 **Completa.**

29. Este centro comercial es _____ moderno _____ el otro.

30. A mi parecer, este centro comercial es _____ _____ moderno _____ todos.

31. Te va a salir _____ barato si regateas.

32. Él tiene veinte años y yo tengo dieciséis. Él es _____ _____ _____.

33. Ella es muy inteligente. Ella sabe _____ _____ nadie.

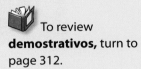
To review **comparativo y superlativo,** turn to page 311.

6 **Cambia al singular.**

34. Aquellos pantalones son caros.

35. Estos juegos de computadora me gustan mucho.

36. Esas frutas son muy frescas.

37. ¿Dónde compraste esos?

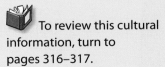
To review **demostrativos,** turn to page 312.

Cultura

7 **Contesta.**

38. ¿Qué venden en un mercado indígena?

39. ¿Qué pasa cuando el cliente y el vendedor regatean?

40. ¿De qué tienen fama los otavaleños?

To review this cultural information, turn to pages 316–317.

1 **En una tienda de ropa**

✓ *Shop for clothes* •·············
Work with a classmate. One will be the shopper
and the other the clerk. Make up conversations
to buy the items you see in the photo.

2 **De compras**

✓ *Discuss your shopping preferences*
Have a conversation with a friend. Tell whether or
not you like to shop. Tell why. When you do shop,
what types of things do you buy and what types of
stores do you go to? Do you go to individual stores
or large ones such as **un supermercado** or **una
tienda de departamentos?**

3 **En el mercado**

✓ *Shop in a market*
You are spending a summer with a family in Spain. You are going
to prepare a dinner for your Spanish family. Decide what you have
to buy at the market. Then have a conversation with a classmate
who will be the clerk at the store or stores.

CULTURA

El escaparate de una tienda de
moda femenina en Santiago,
Chile

CULTURA

Una pescadería
en Valencia, España

4 **En el centro comercial**

✓ *Describe a shopping mall*
Work with a classmate who will be an exchange student from
Chile. Tell him or her about a mall near you that you are both
going to go to.

5 **En el mercado indígena**

✓ *Talk about shopping at an indigenous market*
Imagine that you just returned from a visit to Ecuador or
Guatemala. Tell a friend all about your experience **en un
mercado indígena.**

Tarea

You have learned about stores and markets in Spain and Latin America. Write an essay in which you compare and contrast the different types of shopping venues in the Spanish-speaking world. Then continue your essay by comparing and contrasting them with shopping areas and customs that you are familiar with in the United States.

CULTURA

Una tienda de ropa en Arrecife, Lanzarote, una de las islas Canarias

Writing Strategy

Comparing and contrasting When writing, it is often necessary to compare people, places, or things. To do this you must write in such a way that your readers can be made aware of how they are alike and different. When you compare two things you explain how they are similar. When you contrast two things, you explain how they are different. Before you start, it is often a good idea to make a diagram or list of similarities and differences.

❷ Write

- Begin with an introduction that will explain the purpose of the essay and grab the readers' attention.
- Decide how you want to order your paragraphs.
- Use the information from your diagram to compare and contrast the different shopping venues.
- Choose an interesting title.
- Proofread your essay and correct errors.
- Invite a classmate to read your essay and to edit it or give you feedback.

❶ Prewrite

The following diagram will help you organize your ideas. Each circle shows aspects of one shopping venue. Where the circles overlap, write aspects the different venues have in common.

un centro comercial **un supermercado**

un mercado indígena

Evaluate

Don't forget that your teacher will evaluate you on your use of vocabulary, correctness of grammar and sentence structure, ability to compare and contrast shopping venues and customs, and the completeness of your message.

Repaso del Capítulo 9

Gramática

- ### Presente de saber y conocer *(page 308)*
  The verb **saber** means *to know a fact* or *to know how to do something*.
  The verb **conocer** means *to know* in the sense of *to be acquainted with*.
  Review the forms below.

saber		
yo **sé**	nosotros(as)	sabemos
tú sabes	*vosotros(as)*	*sabéis*
Ud., él, ella sabe	Uds., ellos, ellas	saben

conocer		
yo conozco	nosotros(as)	conocemos
tú conoces	*vosotros(as)*	*conocéis*
Ud., él, ella conoce	Uds., ellos, ellas	conocen

- ### Comparativo y superlativo *(page 311)*
  To form the comparative in Spanish, you put **más** or **menos** before
  the adjective or adverb and **que** after it.

Ella es más inteligente que yo.	*She is smarter than I am.*
Es menos ambiciosa que yo.	*She is less ambitious than I am.*

  To form the superlative in Spanish, you use the appropriate definite
  article **el, la, los, las** plus **más** and the adjective.

Él es el más serio de todos.	*He is the most serious of all.*
Él es el muchacho más alto de la clase.	*He is the tallest boy in the class.*

  The adjectives **bueno** and **malo** and the adverbs **bien** and **mal** have
  irregular comparative and superlative forms.

bueno	mejor	el/la mejor	los/las mejores
malo	peor	el/la peor	los/las peores
bien	mejor		
mal	peor		

  The adjectives **mayor** and **menor** most
  often refer to age.

  Yo soy mayor que mi hermana.
  Mi hermana es la menor de la familia.

- ### Demostrativos *(page 312)*
  Demonstrative adjectives and pronouns
  indicate location. In Spanish there are
  three demonstratives: **este, ese,** and **aquel.**

CULTURA

Los vegetales en este puesto en Barcelona son algunos
de los mejores del mercado.

Juego There are a number of cognates in this list. See how many you and a partner can find. Who can find the most? Compare your list with those of your classmates.

Vocabulario

Identifying some more articles of clothing

una camisa	un pantalón	una blusa	una corbata
de manga corta	un par de zapatos	una chaqueta	un blue jean
(larga)	una falda	un vestido	un par de tenis

Shopping for clothes

el centro comercial	la talla	rebajar	barato(a)
la tienda de ropa	el número	usar	caro(a)
el escaparate	un saldo,	calzar	mucho
el/la empleado(a)	una liquidación	costar	poco
	el precio		

Shopping for food

el mercado	el supermercado	las manzanas	una botella
el puesto,	los guisantes	los plátanos	un frasco
el tenderete	las judías verdes	las uvas	una tajada
el/la vendedor(a)	las zanahorias	la piña	la mayonesa
el producto	las cebollas	un carrito	el atún
el kilo	los pimientos	las compras	congelado(a)
la verdulería	el maíz	un bote, una lata	ir de compras
la frutería	las naranjas	un paquete	

Shopping in an indigenous market

el mercado indígena	las sandalias	regatear
la artesanía	las cerámicas	
los tejidos		

Other useful words and expressions

la gente	todos(as)	Te sale más barato.	¿A cuánto está(n)?
el/la cliente	Es verdad.	Te queda bien.	¿Algo más?
diferente			Nada más.

Literary Reader

You may wish to read the adaptation of *La camisa de Margarita* by Ricardo Palma, found on pages 406–409.

Repaso cumulativo

Repasa lo que ya has aprendido

These activities will help you review
what you have learned so far in Spanish.

Un mercado al aire libre en Mérida, Venezuela

1 Escucha las frases. Indica en una tabla como la de abajo si la frase describe la foto o no.

sí	no

2 Completa con el pretérito.

1. Nosotros _____ de compras. (ir)
2. Yo _____ a la tienda de ropa. (ir)
3. (Yo) _____ un blue jean. (buscar)
4. El empleado me _____. (hablar)
5. ¿_____ tú al concierto? (asistir)
6. ¿Te _____ el concierto? (gustar)
7. ¿Quién _____? (cantar)
8. ¿_____ el público? (aplaudir)
9. ¿Dónde _____ ustedes después? (comer)
10. ¿Te _____ el menú el mesero? (dar)

3 Sigue el modelo.

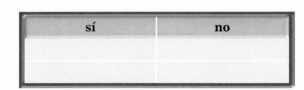

MODELO ¿Quién compró los muebles? →
Yo los compré.

1. ¿Quién compró la computadora?
2. ¿Quién creó la página Web?
3. ¿Quién compró la cámara digital?
4. ¿Quién tomó las fotos?
5. ¿Quién comió los chocolates?
6. ¿Quién vio la telenovela?
7. ¿Quién recibió los correos electrónicos?
8. ¿Quién no comprendió el menú?

Las amigas fueron de compras y tomaron el almuerzo. Lo tomaron en la zona de comedores en el centro comercial.

4 **Cambia a la forma negativa.**

1. Alguien lo sabe.

2. Ellos conocen a alguien.

3. Ellos compraron algo.

4. Algo está en el pupitre.

5. Ellos van siempre al centro comercial.

6. Ellos siempre compran algo.

5 **Describe el plan del apartamento.**

6 **Completa con expresiones apropiadas.**

1. Yo voy a _____.

2. Tenemos que _____.

3. No puedo _____.

4. No puedo porque tengo que _____.

5. Debes _____.

6. Ellos tomaron lecciones de tenis y saben _____.

7. Empiezan a _____.

7 **Juego** Play this game with a partner. Tell your partner what you do in your free time. Your partner will try to guess where you do it. Take turns. You may use the following as suggestions.

Navego la red. Ceno con mi familia. MIRO UNA PELÍCULA.

Compro las zapatillas. Toco la guitarra.

Corro después de las clases. Nado con mis amigos(as).

En avión

Aquí y Allí

Vamos a comparar Los medios de transporte más importantes varían de una región del mundo a otra. En España, por ejemplo, el servicio de trenes es excelente. No lo es en Latinoamérica donde mucha gente toma un autobús para ir de un lugar a otro. Pero vas a aprender por qué el avión es el medio de transporte más importante. Donde tú vives, ¿qué medios de transporte públicos hay? ¿Tienen muchos usuarios?

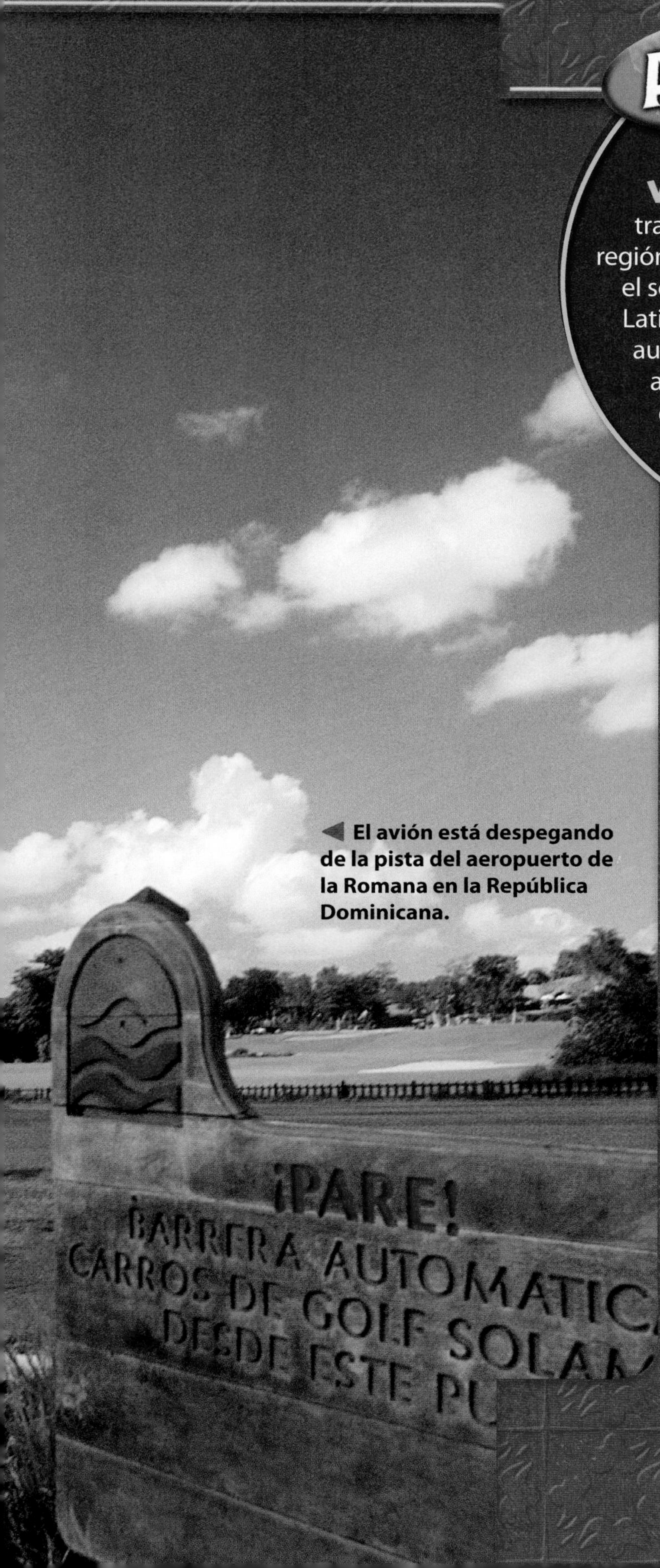

◄ El avión está despegando de la pista del aeropuerto de la Romana en la República Dominicana.

Objetivos

You will:

- talk about packing for a trip and getting to the airport
- tell what you do at the airport
- talk about being on an airplane
- discuss air travel in South America

You will use:

- verbs that have **g** in the **yo** form of the present tense
- the present progressive tense

QuickPass

Go to glencoe.com
For: **Online book**
Web code: **ASD4003c10**

Introducción al tema
En avión

Look at these photographs to acquaint yourself with the theme of this chapter. Air travel is the most important means of transportation in the world today. As you learn to use your Spanish in an airport and on an airplane, you will also learn why air travel is so extremely important in Latin America.

España ▶
Aquí vemos una terminal nueva en el aeropuerto internacional de Barajas, el aeropuerto que sirve a Madrid.

DEPARTING TO	AIRLINE	FLIGHT	GATE	TIME
CARACAS	American	935	C7	12:30P
HOUSTON-IAH	American	1391	C3	12:07P
SANTO DOMINGO	American	783	C5	1:20P
KEY WEST	American	4987		2:00P
BALTIMORE	American	1060	C7	4:19P
QUITO	American	967	C5	4:30P
INDIANAPOLIS, IN	American	1682	C9	6:21P
SAN JOSE, C.R.	American	2171	C7	6:24P

◀ **Estados Unidos**
Aquí vemos una pantalla de salidas. ¿Para qué ciudades latinoamericanas hay vuelos?

Chile El agente de la línea aérea está revisando los documentos de una pasajera que está tomando un vuelo internacional. ▼

330

▲ Perú El avión está en el aeropuerto de Arequipa en el sur de Perú. En el fondo vemos los Andes.

Argentina ▲
Los pasajeros tienen que esperar en fila delante del mostrador de una línea aérea en el aeropuerto de Ezeiza en Buenos Aires.

▲ República Dominicana Es el aeropuerto en Santo Domingo, la República Dominicana. Podemos ver también la torre de control.

México ▶
Los pasajeros están pasando por el control de seguridad en León, México.

◀ Colombia La asistenta de cabina está demostrando el uso de una máscara de oxígeno abordo de un avión colombiano.

331

Antes de salir para el aeropuerto

<blockquote>
¿Te acuerdas?

You will want to be able to discuss packing a suitcase. To review summer and winter clothing, see Chapter 7. To review general clothing, see Chapter 9.
</blockquote>

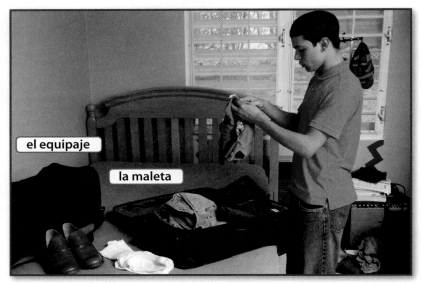

el equipaje

la maleta

Juan va a hacer un viaje.
Antes hace la maleta.
¿Qué pone en la maleta?

Pone la ropa que necesita para el viaje.

Al aeropuerto

el baúl, la maletera

el taxi

Juan sale para el aeropuerto en taxi.
Trae su equipaje.

Pone su equipaje en la maletera del taxi.
El taxista lo ayuda con su equipaje.

En el aeropuerto

Nueva Generación de asientos de clase ejecutiva en el 767

el boleto (billete) electrónico

el agente

el mostrador

la tarjeta de embarque

AEROMEXICO
aeromexico.com

NOMBRE/NAME
PAYTI/ANDREWMR
ORIGEN/ORIGIN
MEXICO CITY
DESTINO/DESTINATION
OAXACA

VUELO/FLIGHT CLASE FECHA/DATE
AM 2046 L   04JUN07
SALA/GATE HORA/TIME ASIENTO/SEA
-7A-   1140
NON-SMOKING
CONTROL 28   5C
FTKT 704

el nombre del pasajero

el número del vuelo

la hora de salida

el número del asiento

Juan está en el mostrador de la línea aérea.
Está haciendo un viaje internacional en avión.
Tiene que facturar su equipaje.
Pero no tiene que facturar su equipaje de mano.

Su tarjeta de embarque sale de un distribuidor automático.

En otras partes

In addition to **la tarjeta de embarque** you will also hear **la tarjeta de abordar** and **el pasabordo**.

práctica

QuickPass

Go to glencoe.com
For: **Vocabulary practice**
Web code: **ASD4003c10**

ESCUCHAR

1 Escucha las frases. Parea cada frase con el dibujo que describe.

a.

b.

c.

d.

e.

f.

HABLAR • ESCRIBIR

2 Contesta sobre un viaje que Teresa va a hacer a México.

1. ¿Hace Teresa un viaje a México?
2. Antes de hacer su viaje, ¿qué pone en la maleta?
3. ¿Para dónde sale Teresa para empezar su viaje?
4. ¿Cómo va al aeropuerto?
5. ¿Quién la ayuda con su equipaje?
6. ¿Dónde lo pone?

EXPANSIÓN

Ahora, sin mirar las preguntas, relata toda la información en tus propias palabras. Si no recuerdas algo, un(a) compañero(a) te puede ayudar.

LEER • ESCRIBIR

3 Elisa está en el aeropuerto. Va a las Galápagos. Completa con una palabra apropiada.

1. En el aeropuerto Elisa tiene que _____ su equipaje.
2. Va al mostrador de la _____.
3. Elisa tiene un _____ electrónico.
4. El agente le da su _____ para poder abordar el avión.

CULTURA

La señora está en el mostrador de la línea aérea. Va a volar a México.

CULTURA

Una vista de las islas Galápagos, Ecuador

LEER • ESCRIBIR

4 Completa. Escoge del **banco de palabras.**

pone	sale	trae	hace

1. Eduardo _____ un viaje a España.
2. Él _____ su ropa en la maleta.
3. Eduardo no _____ mucho equipaje.
4. _____ solamente una maleta y una mochila.
5. _____ el equipaje en la maletera del taxi.
6. _____ para el aeropuerto.
7. Su vuelo para España _____ a las ocho y media de la tarde.

InfoGap For more practice using your new vocabulary, do Activity 10 on page SR12 at the end of the book.

CULTURA

El famoso acueducto romano de Segovia, España, construido a fines del primer siglo después de Cristo

HABLAR • ESCRIBIR

5 Prepara una pregunta sobre cada frase en la Actividad 4. Usa las siguientes palabras.

¿quién?   ¿cuándo?
¿adónde?   ¿qué?   ¿dónde?

LEER • ESCRIBIR

6 Completa la tarjeta de embarque.

7 **Rompecabezas**

Unscramble the letters to reveal words related to airplane travel.

1. a l t a m e
2. n o t i s e a
3. j a q u e p i e
4. r a d o r o m t s
5. s o a r j e p a

En el control de seguridad

hacer cola

el pasaporte

Los pasajeros están pasando por el control de seguridad.
Su equipaje de mano tiene que pasar por el control de seguridad.
Hay que mostrar una forma de identidad con una fotografía.

En la puerta de salida

¡Así se dice!

- **Hay que** is a useful expression that means **Es necesario.**
- **A veces** and **de vez en cuando** are expressions to tell what you do every so often.

La pasajera está en la puerta de salida.
Está esperando la salida de su vuelo.
El avión está saliendo a tiempo. No sale tarde.
No hay un retraso (una demora).
Ella va a embarcar (abordar) dentro de poco.

Abordo del avión

el compartimiento superior

el servicio

la ventanilla

el asistente de vuelo

el pasillo

el asiento

el cinturón de seguridad

abrochados

Los pasajeros tienen que poner su equipaje de mano en el compartimiento superior o debajo del asiento.

Durante el despegue y el aterrizaje, los pasajeros tienen que tener sus cinturones abrochados.

la señal de no fumar

la máscara de oxígeno

el despegue

El avión está despegando.
Está despegando con destino a Madrid.
El avión acaba de despegar de la pista.

el aterrizaje

El avión está aterrizando.
Es un vuelo (procedente) de Lima.

ESCUCHAR • HABLAR • ESCRIBIR

 Personaliza. Da respuestas personales.

1. ¿Tomas un vuelo de vez en cuando?
2. ¿Te gusta volar?
3. ¿Quieres tomar un vuelo un día?
4. ¿Quieres hacer un viaje nacional o internacional?
5. ¿Adónde quieres ir?
6. ¿Hay un aeropuerto cerca de tu casa? ¿Cuál?
7. ¿Es un aeropuerto nacional o internacional?
8. Si tienes que tomar un vuelo, ¿prefieres un asiento en el pasillo o en la ventanilla?

LEER

 Escoge la palabra apropiada.

1. Los pasajeros hacen cola en (el asiento, la puerta) de salida.
2. Están (esperando, haciendo) la salida del vuelo.
3. El avión sale con un retraso de cinco minutos. Sale (tarde, a tiempo).
4. Los pasajeros toman su (pasillo, asiento) en el avión.
5. El avión despega de la (cola, pista).
6. Un vuelo (procedente de, con destino a) Panamá llega ahora.

LEER

 Verifica. ¿Sí o no?

1. Los pasajeros tienen que pasar por el control de seguridad abordo del avión.
2. Los pasajeros esperan la salida de su vuelo en la puerta de salida.
3. Los pasajeros embarcan después del aterrizaje.
4. Los pasajeros desembarcan después del aterrizaje.
5. Los pasajeros pueden poner su equipaje en el pasillo.
6. Los pasajeros tienen que tener sus cinturones de seguridad abrochados durante el despegue y el aterrizaje.
7. Un vuelo que sale tarde sale a tiempo.
8. En una cola o fila hay mucha gente.

CULTURA

La gente está llegando al aeropuerto de Ixtapa-Zihuatanejo en la costa del Pacífico en México.

Comunicación

4 Habla con un(a) compañero(a). Discutan todo lo que necesitan si hacen un viaje internacional.

LEER • ESCRIBIR

5 Pon las actividades en orden.

Llega al aeropuerto.

Toma su asiento.

Pone su ropa en la maleta.

Factura su equipaje y toma su tarjeta de embarque.

Sale de casa para ir al aeropuerto.

Espera el avión en la puerta de salida.

Pone su equipaje en la maletera del taxi.

Pasa por el control de seguridad.

Embarca el avión.

El avión despega.

CULTURA

El mostrador de una línea aérea centroamericana en el aeropuerto de la Ciudad de Guatemala. Es de noche y hay muy poca gente.

Comunicación

6 You are flying to Mexico to visit your key pal. You have never flown before. Once on the plane, you have some questions for the flight attendant (your partner) about the flight and where to put your things. Take turns.

7 **¡Manos a la obra!** Make up a name for a Spanish airline. Create a fun and colorful travel poster advertising the airline and where it flies. See how many new words you can include.

QuickPass

Go to glencoe.com
For: **Grammar practice**
Web code: **ASD4003c10**

Presente de hacer, poner, traer, salir

1. The verbs **hacer** *(to do, to make)*, **poner** *(to put, to place)*, **traer** *(to bring)*, and **salir** *(to leave)* have an irregular **yo** form. The **yo** form has a **g**. All the other forms are regular.

	hacer	poner	traer	salir
yo	hago	pongo	traigo	salgo
tú	haces	pones	traes	sales
Ud., él, ella	hace	pone	trae	sale
nosotros(as)	hacemos	ponemos	traemos	salimos
vosotros(as)	*hacéis*	*ponéis*	*traéis*	*salís*
Uds., ellos, ellas	hacen	ponen	traen	salen

2. Remember that the verb **tener** has a **g** in the **yo** form. The verb **venir** *(to come)* follows the same pattern. Note the **g** and the stem change.

venir			
yo	vengo	nosotros(as)	venimos
tú	vienes	*vosotros(as)*	*venís*
Ud., él, ella	viene	Uds., ellos, ellas	vienen

CULTURA

Las señoritas tienen equipaje porque van a hacer un viaje de Puerto Rico a Nueva York. Salen pronto pero antes toman un refresco en un café en San Juan.

Práctica

Más práctica
Workbook, pp. 10.7–10.8
StudentWorks™ Plus

HABLAR • ESCRIBIR

1 Imagina que vas a hacer un viaje a Ecuador.
Contesta las preguntas.

1. ¿Haces un viaje?
2. ¿Haces un viaje a Ecuador?
3. ¿Haces el viaje con un grupo de tu escuela?
4. ¿Sales para el aeropuerto con tus padres?
5. ¿Traes mucho equipaje?
6. ¿Traes tu cámara digital?
7. ¿Pones tu boleto y tu pasaporte en tu mochila?

EXPANSIÓN

Ahora, sin mirar las preguntas, relata toda la información
en tus propias palabras. Si no recuerdas algo, un(a)
compañero(a) te puede ayudar.

HABLAR • ESCRIBIR

2 Personaliza. Da respuestas personales.

Cuando haces un viaje a la playa donde hace calor,
¿qué pones en la maleta? Y cuando haces un viaje
a una estación de esquí, ¿qué pones en la maleta?

ESCUCHAR • HABLAR • ESCRIBIR

3 Sigue el modelo. Presta atención a las terminaciones
-emos, -imos.

MODELO **Ellos hacen un viaje. →**
**Sí, ellos hacen un viaje y nosotros
también hacemos un viaje.**

1. Ellos hacen un viaje a España.
2. Ellos salen para el aeropuerto.
3. Ellos traen mucho equipaje.
4. Ellos salen en el mismo vuelo.
5. Ellos vienen al aeropuerto en autobús.

CULTURA

La Plaza de Armas en el casco antiguo
de Quito, Ecuador

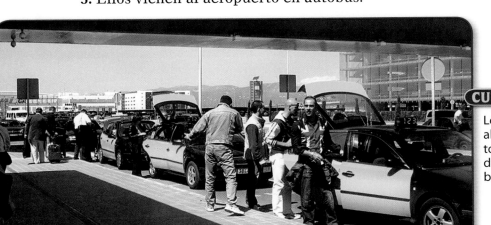

CULTURA

Los pasajeros acaban de llegar
al aeropuerto de Barcelona y
toman un taxi para ir al centro
de la ciudad. Hay una fila de taxis
bastante larga, ¿no?

LEER • ESCRIBIR

④ Completa con la forma correcta del presente del verbo. Ahora tienes que usar todas las formas.

Yo __1__ (hacer) un viaje a Palma. Palma __2__ (estar) en la isla de Mallorca en el Mediterráneo. __3__ (Estar) al este de España no muy lejos de Barcelona. Mi amiga Luisa __4__ (hacer) el viaje también. Nosotros __5__ (hacer) el viaje en avión hasta Barcelona y luego __6__ (ir) en barco, un ferry, desde Barcelona a Palma. Claro que podemos __7__ (hacer) el viaje en avión pero preferimos tomar el barco.

—¡Ay, Luisa! Pero tú __8__ (traer) mucho equipaje.

—No, yo no __9__ (traer) mucho. __10__ (Tener) solo dos maletas. Tú exageras. Tú también __11__ (venir) con mucho equipaje.

—¡Oye! ¿A qué hora __12__ (salir) nuestro vuelo para Barcelona?

—No __13__ (salir) hasta las seis y media. Nosotros __14__ (tener) mucho tiempo.

—¡Vamos ya! ¡Con permiso, señora!

CULTURA

Una playa en Palma de Mallorca. Mallorca es una de las islas Baleares en el mar Mediterráneo.

Comunicación

⑤ Tell a friend all the things you do the day of a flight from packing your suitcase to boarding the plane. Your friend will then ask you questions.

HABLAR

⑥ **Juego** Play this **Diez preguntas** game with a partner. Think of something related to airline travel for your partner to guess. If your partner guesses in ten questions or less, he or she wins. Take turns.

El presente progresivo

VIDEO To see a humorous experience at an airport, watch **Diálogo en vivo.**

1. You use the present progressive tense in Spanish to express an action in progress, an action that is currently taking place.

2. To form the present progressive you use the verb **estar** and the present participle. Study the forms of the present participle.

INFINITIVE	hablar	comer	vivir	hacer	salir
STEM	habl-	com-	viv-	hac-	sal-
PARTICIPLE	hablando	comiendo	viviendo	haciendo	saliendo

The verbs **leer, traer, oír,** and **caer** have a **y.**

leyendo   **trayendo**   **oyendo**   **cayendo**

3. Study the following examples of the present progressive.

José **está haciendo** un viaje a México.
Ahora **está esperando** la salida de su vuelo.
José **está mirando** su tarjeta de embarque.

Una pantalla de llegadas y salidas en el aeropuerto de la Ciudad de Guatemala. Hace buen tiempo hoy y la mayoría de los vuelos salen a tiempo. ¡Qué suerte para todos!

Práctica

HABLAR

7 Con un(a) compañero(a), practica la conversación en voz alta. Presta atención a todos los verbos en el tiempo progresivo.

Sandra, ¡qué sorpresa! ¿Qué estás haciendo aquí en el aeropuerto?

Estoy esperando a mi padre. Está volviendo de Puerto Rico. ¿Y tú, Julia? ¿Qué estás haciendo aquí?

Pues, estoy viajando a Costa Rica.

¡A Costa Rica! ¡Qué suerte tienes!

Sí, toda mi familia está haciendo el viaje para visitar a nuestros abuelos.

No, no. Son de aquí pero ahora están viviendo en Costa Rica. Les gusta mucho.

Ah, tus abuelos son de Costa Rica.

GeoVistas

To learn more about Costa Rica, take a tour on pages SH52–SH53.

HABLAR • ESCRIBIR

8 Contesta según la conversación.

1. ¿Por qué está en el aeropuerto Sandra?
2. ¿De dónde está volviendo el padre de Sandra?
3. Y, ¿para dónde está saliendo Julia?
4. ¿Quién está viajando con ella?
5. ¿A quiénes van a visitar?
6. ¿Qué están haciendo sus abuelos en Costa Rica?

EXPANSIÓN

Ahora, sin mirar las preguntas, relata toda la información en tus propias palabras. Si no recuerdas algo, un(a) compañero(a) te puede ayudar.

Más práctica

Workbook, p. 10.9
StudentWorks™ Plus

Gramática

HABLAR • ESCRIBIR

9 Contesta según se indica.

1. ¿Adónde están llegando los pasajeros? (al aeropuerto)
2. ¿Cómo están llegando? (en taxi)
3. ¿Adónde están viajando? (a Argentina en la América del Sur)
4. ¿Cómo están haciendo el viaje? (en avión)
5. ¿Dónde están facturando el equipaje? (en el mostrador de la línea aérea)
6. ¿Qué está mirando el agente? (los boletos y los pasaportes)
7. ¿De qué puerta están saliendo los pasajeros para Buenos Aires? (número siete)
8. ¿Qué están abordando? (el avión)

Comunicación

10 Use the conversation between Julia and Sandra as a guide to role-play a conversation between two friends who run into each other at an airport.

CULTURA

La Casa Rosada en Buenos Aires. Es aquí donde tiene el presidente argentino sus oficinas.

SINGLE PICTURE FRAME

See page SH27 for help with making this foldable. Work in groups. Each member of the group will make a foldable with a drawing (or magazine picture) related to airplane travel. Create a story about each picture by passing the picture around, with each person adding a sentence in the present progressive. An alternative would be to do this same activity as a writing activity.

HABLAR • ESCRIBIR

11 Forma frases según el modelo. Escoge palabras del **banco de palabras.**

MODELO   viajar →
Sí, estoy viajando.
No, no estoy viajando.

hablar español	usar mi móvil	hacer una tarea
leer una novela	estudiar	jugar fútbol
aprender mucho	salir ahora	comer

HABLAR

12 **Juego** Form small groups. Take turns pantomiming activities that might take place at an airport or on an airplane. The others will guess what you're doing, using the present progressive.

HABLAR • ESCRIBIR

13 Describe lo que ves en los dibujos. Usa el presente progresivo.

La consonante r

When a word begins with **r** (initial position), the **r** is trilled in Spanish. Within a word, this trilled **r** sound is spelled **rr**. The Spanish trilled **r** sound does not exist in English. Repeat the following.

ra	re	ri	ro	ru
rápido	receta	Ricardo	Roberto	Rubén
raqueta	red	aterriza	rojo	rubio
párrafo	corre	río	perro	

The sound for a single **r** within a word (medial position) does not exist in English either. It is trilled less than the initial **r** or **rr**. Repeat the following.

ra	re	ri	ro	ru
verano	arena	boletería	número	Perú
maletera	quiere	consultorio	pasajero	Aruba
para		periódico	cinturón	

Dictado

Pronounce the following sentences carefully. Then write them to prepare for a dictation.

> **El perro de Rubén corre en la arena.**
> **El avión para Puerto Rico aterriza con un retraso de una hora.**
> **El pasajero corre rápido por el aeropuerto.**
> **Ricardo pone su raqueta en la maletera del carro.**

CULTURA
El avión está aterrizando en el aeropuerto de Buenos Aires, Argentina.

Refrán

Can you guess what the following proverb means?

Mal hace quien nada hace.

¡Bravo!

You have now learned all the new vocabulary and grammar in this chapter. Continue to use and practice all that you know while learning more cultural information. **¡Vamos!**

QuickPass

Go to glencoe.com
For: **Conversation practice**
Web code: ASD4003c10

En el aeropuerto

Susana	¡Oye, Pedro! Está saliendo nuestro vuelo.
Pedro	Sí, ¡vamos ya! Tenemos que pasar por el control de seguridad y siempre hay una cola larga.
Susana	¿Tienes nuestras tarjetas de embarque?
Pedro	Sí, sí. Las tengo. ¿Necesitas ayuda con tu equipaje de mano?
Susana	No, no traigo mucho. Lo puedo llevar. ¿De qué puerta salimos?
Pedro	De la puerta 11. ¿A qué hora empieza el embarque?
Susana	Ahora mismo. ¡Vamos!

¿Comprendes?

A Contesta según la información en la conversación.

1. ¿Dónde están Pedro y Susana?
2. ¿Qué están anunciando?
3. ¿Ya pasaron por el control de seguridad Pedro y Susana?
4. ¿Qué hay siempre en el control de seguridad?
5. ¿Quién tiene las tarjetas de embarque?
6. ¿De qué puerta de salida salen?
7. ¿Está empezando el embarque?

B **Resumiendo** Relata toda la información en la conversación en tus propias palabras.

C **Prediciendo** ¿Piensas que Susana y Pedro van a perder su vuelo? ¿Por qué contestas que sí o que no?

CULTURA

Una vista panorámica de San Juan de Puerto Rico desde el Viejo San Juan hasta el Condado

LECTURA CULTURAL

Antes de leer

Scan the reading to find the most important idea in each section. Look for topic sentences.

✓ Reading Check

¿Cuál es un medio de transporte muy importante en Sudamérica?

✓ Reading Check

¿Dónde es muy densa la vegetación? ¿En las montañas o en las selvas?

Durante la lectura

Note each topic sentence. Think about the one idea that all the sentences and sections are about.

Después de leer

What was the main idea of the reading and of each section? What do you think was the author's purpose here?

READING STRATEGY
Identifying the main idea It is important to identify the main idea of a reading. Topic sentences—usually the first sentence in a paragraph—help you determine the main idea of a reading.

El avión en la América del Sur

El continente sudamericano es vasto. Las distancias entre ciudades son largas. Por eso el avión es un medio de transporte importante. A veces es imposible viajar por tierra[1] de un lugar a otro. ¿Por qué?

Montañas Una gran parte del oeste del continente es montañosa. Los altos picos nevados de los Andes parecen tocar el cielo[2]. Unas ciudades como Bogotá, Quito y La Paz están en los Andes. Y claro que hay también pequeños pueblos aislados en las montañas.

Selvas Al este de los Andes en Colombia, Ecuador, Perú, Bolivia y Brasil hay grandes selvas tropicales del río Amazonas. En las selvas la vegetación es muy densa y una gran parte de la cuenca[3] amazónica es inhóspita e impenetrable.

Desiertos La región a lo largo de la costa desde Perú hasta el centro de Chile es desierto. El Atacama en Chile es el desierto más árido (seco) del mundo—una región de arena y rocas (piedras).

Día y noche los aviones sobrevuelan los picos, selvas y desiertos para enlazar[4] las ciudades y pueblos de Sudamérica.

[1]por tierra *by land*
[2]cielo *sky*
[3]cuenca *basin*
[4]enlazar *connect*

CULTURA
Un pueblo aislado en los Andes de Venezuela

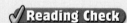

¿Comprendes?

Más práctica
Workbook, pp. 10.10–10.12
StudentWorks™ Plus

A Recordando hechos Contesta.

1. ¿Qué montañas corren del norte al sur a lo largo del océano Pacífico en la América del Sur?
2. ¿Qué hay al este de los Andes?
3. ¿Qué región de Sudamérica es desierto?

B Describiendo Describe.

1. los picos andinos
2. las selvas tropicales
3. el desierto

C Analizando Contesta.

1. ¿Por qué es el avión un medio de transporte muy importante?
2. En muchas regiones de Sudamérica, ¿por qué es difícil viajar por tierra?

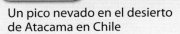

CULTURA

Un pico nevado en el desierto de Atacama en Chile

D Categorizando Completa la tabla de abajo. Luego, relata la información en la tabla en tus propias palabras.

	a lo largo de la costa peruana y chilena	al este de las montañas	en las montañas
desiertos			
picos cubiertos de nieve			
selvas tropicales			
la cuenca amazónica			
vegetación densa			
tierra árida			
Botogá, Quito, La Paz			

Un viaje interesante 🎧♻

Antes de leer

Vas a leer sobre un misterio famoso que hay en Perú. ¿Te gustan los misterios? ¿Hay algún misterio donde vives?

Reading Check

¿Qué son las líneas de Nazca?

Un vuelo interestante Si quieres hacer un viaje interesante en avión tienes que sobrevolar las líneas de Nazca. ¿Qué son las líneas de Nazca? Pues, en el desierto árido del sur de Perú hay una serie de dibujos o figuras misteriosas. Hay figuras geométricas—rectángulos, triángulos y líneas paralelas. Hay también representaciones perfectas de varios animales. A pesar de[1] muchas investigaciones el origen de las líneas o figuras que tienen más de 1.500 años queda[2] un misterio.

Y son tan grandes que la única manera de ver las figuras es tomar un vuelo. Las avionetas salen de Lima o del aeropuerto de la pequeña ciudad de Ica, muy cerca de las figuras.

[1]A pesar de   *In spite of*   [2]queda   *remains*

CULTURA

Las líneas de Nazca

¿Comprendes?

Escoge o completa.

1. Las líneas de Nazca están _____.
   a. en el pico de una montaña
   b. en una selva
   c. en un desierto

2. ¿Qué son las líneas?
   a. animales
   b. figuras misteriosas
   c. solamente figuras geométricas

3. El origen de las líneas de Nazca es _____.

4. ¿Por qué es necesario ver las líneas de un avión?
   a. porque hay avionetas que salen de Ica y Lima
   b. porque están en un desierto
   c. porque son tan inmensas

5. Un avión pequeño es _____.

CULTURA

Recientemente los arqueólogos descubrieron otras figuras delineadas en el costado rocoso no muy lejos de Nazca. Estas figuras son de la civilización de los paracas y son anteriores a las famosas líneas de Nazca.

CULTURA
Una avioneta que sobrevuela las líneas de Nazca

Vocabulario

1 **Completa.**

1–2. El agente trabaja en el _____ de la línea aérea en el _____.

3. La tarjeta de embarque indica el número del _____ y el número del asiento del pasajero.

4. Antes de ir a la puerta de salida los pasajeros tienen que pasar por el _____ donde inspeccionan su equipaje de mano.

5. El avión no sale a tiempo. Sale _____.

6. Los pasajeros tienen que _____ una forma de identidad.

7. Abordo del avión, hay que poner su equipaje en el _____.

8. Estamos esperando nuestro vuelo en la _____.

9. Antes de facturar mi equipaje, tomo mi tarjeta de embarque del _____.

10. Estás abordo del avión. ¿Sabes el número de tu _____?

To review **Vocabulario 1** and **Vocabulario 2,** turn to pages 332–333 and 336–337.

2 **Identifica.**

11.

12.

13.

14.

15.

Gramática

3 **Contesta.**

16. ¿Haces un viaje?

17. ¿Vienes en junio para mi cumpleaños?

18. ¿Qué pones en tu maleta o mochila?

19. ¿A qué hora sales?

20. ¿Traes mucho equipaje?

To review verbs with a **g** in the **yo** form, turn to page 340.

4 **Completa en el presente.**

21. Ellos _____ mañana. (venir)

22. Nosotros _____ mucho trabajo. (hacer)

23. José _____ su mochila debajo del asiento. (poner)

24. Yo lo _____. (oír)

25. ¿Tú _____ tu equipaje de mano? (traer)

26. Señor, ¿usted _____ esta mañana o esta tarde? (salir)

27. Nosotros _____ al aeropuerto con nuestros padres. (venir)

To review **el presente progresivo,** turn to page 343.

5 **Escribe en el presente progresivo.**

28. El avión despega.

29. Nosotros hacemos cola.

30. Ellos salen a tiempo.

31. Los pasajeros esperan en la puerta de salida.

32. Yo leo mi libro favorito.

33. Juan y Marisol, ¡ustedes nadan en el mar!

34. Tú vives cerca de mi casa ahora.

35. ¿Qué oyen tus primos?

Cultura

6 **Escoge.**

36. El continente sudamericano es _____.

   a. pequeño   **b.** alto   **c.** inmenso

37. Hay selvas tropicales en _____.

   a. las montañas   **b.** el desierto   **c.** la cuenca amazónica

38. El Amazonas es _____.

   a. un pico andino   **b.** un río   **c.** un desierto

7 **Contesta.**

39. ¿Por qué es difícil viajar por tierra en muchas partes de la América del Sur?

40. ¿Cuáles son unas características geográficas de la América del Sur?

CULTURA

La canoa es el medio de transporte más importante de la selva tropical de Latinoamérica. Aquí la madre y su hija van a Iquitos en la selva peruana.

To review this cultural information, turn to pages 350–351.

Prepárate para el examen

Practice for oral proficiency

1 Preparar para un viaje

✓ *Tell about packing for a trip*

You're getting ready to leave on a trip. Tell what you're going to pack. Will you use a suitcase, carry-on, or backpack? Does the weather where you're going influence what you are going to pack?

2 En el mostrador de la línea aérea

✓ *Converse with a ticket agent*

You are at the ticket counter at the airport. You are talking with the ticket agent (your partner). You want to find out details about the flight and check your luggage. The ticket agent asks for confirmation of your e-ticket and passport and answers any questions you have.

3 Un billete para Madrid

✓ *Buy an airplane ticket*

Work with a classmate. You want to fly with your family from somewhere in the United States to Madrid and you will be returning from Barcelona. Call the airline to get a reservation. Your classmate will be the reservation agent. Before you call, think about all the information you will need to provide or get from the airline agent: date of departure, departure time, arrival time in Madrid, flight number, and price.

4 ¿Quién está haciendo qué?

✓ *Tell what people are doing in your classroom*

Who's doing what? Look around you and tell what everyone is doing.

CULTURA

La profesora está enseñando y los alumnos están prestando atención en una clase de matemáticas en San Juan, Puerto Rico.

5 El continente sudamericano

✓ *Tell about travel in South America*

Work in small groups. Your aunt and uncle's family is thinking about traveling around South America. You have already been there. Tell them why it can be difficult to travel from one place to another by land. They will ask you questions.

Tarea

Write a letter to a service organization interested in international relations. Your goal is to win an all-expense-paid trip to spend two weeks living with a Spanish-speaking family in a country of your choice.

Writing Strategy

Answering an essay question Many types of applications contain or expect you to answer questions concerning your qualifications or reasons for applying. This requires you to write an essay that convinces that you are the right person.

❶ Prewrite

- Think of your overall goal—to convince all concerned why you are the right person to be sent to a foreign country.

- Look at the list of some types of questions you may have to answer. **¿Qué quieres visitar? ¿Por qué quieres ir allí? ¿Qué esperas hacer, ver o aprender allí? ¿Cómo quieres viajar? ¿Qué tipo de persona eres? ¿Qué estás haciendo ahora?**

- Think of other information the organization may want to know about you.

❷ Write

You really want to go on this trip, so be sure to plan your essay carefully.

- Write an introduction that will make the organization want to find out more about you.

- Start a new paragraph for the answer to each question.

- When you finish writing, check your work. Check spelling, grammar, and verb endings. Make sure your sentences are complete and understandable.

- Read over your work again to make sure all errors are corrected and to make sure that you have effectively communicated your message to the organization.

Evaluate

Don't forget that your teacher will evaluate you on your organization, use of vocabulary and grammar, and on how clear, complete, and convincing your essay is.

Repaso del Capítulo 10

Gramática

- ### Presente de **hacer, poner, traer, salir** *(page 340)*
  The verbs **hacer, poner, traer, salir,** and **oír** have a **g** in the **yo** form. All other forms are regular. Review the following forms.

  | yo | **ha**g**o** | **pon**g**o** | **trai**g**o** | **sal**g**o** | **oi**g**o** |

  Venir has a **g** in the **yo** form as well as a stem change just like the verb **tener,** which you have already learned.

venir	
veng**o**	venimos
v**ie**nes	*venís*
v**ie**ne	v**ie**nen

- ### El presente progresivo *(page 343)*
  The present progressive expresses an action that is taking place at the moment. It is formed with the verb **estar** and the present participle. Review the following forms.

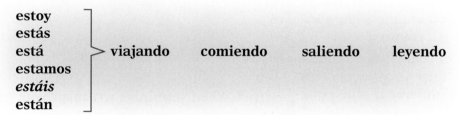

  estoy
  estás
  está } **viajando** **comiendo** **saliendo** **leyendo**
  estamos
  estáis
  están

CULTURA

La señorita está escuchando música en su MP3 mientras regresa a casa después de un viaje.

Vocabulario

Leaving for a trip

el equipaje de mano
la maleta
el taxi

el/la taxista
la maletera, el baúl
poner

hacer
  un viaje
  la maleta

Describing airport activities

el aeropuerto
el avión
el/la agente
el mostrador
la línea aérea
el boleto, el billete
  (electrónico)

el distribuidor
  automático
la tarjeta de
  embarque
el pasaporte
el nombre
el/la pasajero(a)

el número del vuelo
la hora de salida
la hora de embarque
el número del asiento
la forma de identidad
la puerta de salida
facturar el equipaje

pasar por el control
  de seguridad
hacer cola
mostrar
esperar
embarcar, abordar

Describing a flight

el/la asistente(a)
  de vuelo
el asiento
el pasillo
la ventanilla
el compartimiento
  superior

la máscara de
  oxígeno
el cinturón de
  seguridad
la señal de no fumar
el servicio

un retraso, una
  demora
el despegue
el aterrizaje
la pista
despegar
aterrizar

internacional
abordo
tarde
a tiempo
con destino a
procedente de

Other useful words and expressions

hay que
a veces
de vez en cuando

dentro de poco
debajo de

¡Con permiso!
abrochado(a)

Repaso cumulativo

Repasa lo que ya has aprendido

These activities will help you review and remember
what you have learned so far in Spanish.

 1 Escucha las expresiones. Indica en una tabla como la
de abajo si tienes que usar el verbo **saber** o **conocer**.

saber	conocer

 2 **Completa con verbos apropiados.**

Álvaro Irizarry ___1___ un muchacho alto y guapo.
Él ___2___ de San Juan, la capital de Puerto Rico. Puerto
Rico ___3___ una isla tropical en el mar Caribe. En la isla
siempre ___4___ calor y el tiempo ___5___ muy bueno con
mucho sol. A Álvaro y a sus amigos les ___6___ mucho ir
a la playa donde ___7___ una tarde agradable. Si ___8___
hambre, ___9___ a uno de los carritos que ___10___ en la
playa donde ___11___ una empanada deliciosa.

CULTURA
Una playa en la isla de Vieques en
Puerto Rico

 3 **Repasa tu vocabulario. Prepara una lista de todos los
artículos de ropa que ya aprendiste en español.**

 4 **Contesta.**

1. Va a hacer calor. ¿Qué vas a llevar?
2. Va a hacer frío. ¿Qué vas a llevar?
3. ¿Qué te gusta comer cuando tienes hambre?
4. ¿Qué te gusta beber cuando tienes sed?

 5 **Escribe las frases y cambia las palabras indicadas
a pronombres.**

1. Juan vio *a Ana* después de las clases.
2. Él dio *los boletos* a Ana porque es su amiga buena.
3. Habló también *a Mateo y Gabriela*.
4. Ellos compraron un refresco *para Juan*.

6 **Identifica el deporte.**

1. El portero quiere bloquear el balón.
2. Es posible bajar una pista fácil para principiantes o una pista difícil para expertos.
3. Los jugadores corren de una base a otra.
4. El balón tiene que pasar por encima de la red.
5. Juegan con una pelota y una raqueta y la pelota tiene que pasar por encima de la red.

7 **Rompecabezas**

El intruso Choose the word in each group that does not belong and tell why it is **el intruso.**

1. banda   avión   carro   autobús

2. siempre   a veces   nunca   nadie

3. mar   pelota   ola   piscina

4. cama   silla   falda   mesa

5. leer   patinar   escribir   estudiar

8 **Contesta.**

1. Ellos están jugando voleibol. ¿Tiene que pasar el balón por encima de la red o debajo de la red?

2. Mi padre está trabajando en nuestro jardín. ¿Él está cerca de nuestra casa o lejos de nuestra casa?

3. La agente trabaja en el mostrador de la línea aérea en el aeropuerto. ¿Está delante del mostrador o detrás del mostrador?

4. La pasajera está facturando su equipaje en el aeropuerto. ¿Está delante del mostrador o detrás del mostrador?

5. Abordo del avión, ¿es necesario poner el equipaje de mano debajo del asiento o sobre el asiento?

CULTURA

Los pasajeros están esperando delante del mostrador de una línea aérea en el aeropuerto de Ezeiza en Buenos Aires, Argentina.

¡Una rutina diferente!

Aquí y Allí

Vamos a comparar ¿Qué haces cada día desde el momento que te levantas hasta que te acuestas? Muchas cosas de la rutina diaria pueden ser aburridas, ¿no? Vas a ver si los jóvenes en España y Latinoamérica tienen la misma rutina. Pero vas a observar también que hay maneras de cambiar la rutina—sobre todo si decides viajar con un grupo de jóvenes por un país hispano.

Objetivos

You will:

- identify more parts of the body
- talk about your daily routine
- talk about backpacking and camping

You will use:

- reflexive verbs
- commands with **favor de**

◀ **Estos jóvenes están viajando por España con sus mochilas. A muchos jóvenes les gusta ser excursionistas o mochileros. De estas dos parejas, una es escandinava y la otra es norteamericana.**

QuickPass

Go to glencoe.com
For: **Online book**
Web code: **ASD4003c11**

Introducción al tema

¡Una rutina diferente!

Look at these photographs to acquaint yourself with the theme of this chapter. What activities are part of your daily routine? What activities do you enjoy doing occasionally? What do you think **una rutina diferente** refers to? In this chapter you will learn to talk about daily activities, but you will also see that many fun opportunities in Spain and Latin America await anyone with a spirit of adventure.

México La muchacha mexicana se cepilla. Tiene el pelo largo, ¿no? ▶

Perú El cartel que vemos aquí se encuentra delante de un albergue juvenil en Barranca, un barrio de Lima, Perú. ▼

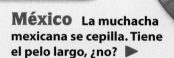

▲ **México** Mochileros en Oaxaca, México

España El joven da una caminata por los picos de Europa en Asturias en el norte de España. ▶

Argentina Un camping rodeado de un paisaje espectacular en el Parque Nacional Los Glaciares en la Patagonia, Argentina ▶

OBELISCO CAMPING
- MOCHILAS
- BOLSAS de DORMIR
- CARPAS
- ART. P/ESCALADA
- ACCESORIOS

Argentina
Una mochila puede llevar muchas cosas—aun un saco de dormir o, como indica el cartel en una tienda de camping en Buenos Aires, una bolsa de dormir. ▶

Chile La muchacha tiene su saco de dormir y su carpa en un camping en una reserva natural en Chile. ▼

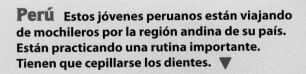

Perú Estos jóvenes peruanos están viajando de mochileros por la región andina de su país. Están practicando una rutina importante. Tienen que cepillarse los dientes. ▼

El cuerpo humano

la cabeza

la espalda

el codo

el brazo derecho

el dedo

la pierna

la rodilla

el pie

la mano izquierda

Para mantenerse en forma, Cristina se estira.

La rutina diaria

despertarse

tomar una ducha

lavarse la cara

lavarse el pelo

cepillarse (lavarse) los dientes

peinarse

el espejo

mirarse

sentarse

¡Hola!
Me llamo Roberto.
¿Y tú? ¿Cómo te llamas?

El muchacho se llama Roberto.

Ana se levanta temprano.
No se queda en la cama.
Se levanta enseguida. Ella es madrugadora.
Le gusta levantarse temprano.

Roberto se acuesta tarde.
Se acuesta a las once y media de la noche.
Él se duerme enseguida.
Él duerme ocho horas.

Elena tiene frío.
Se pone un suéter.

Elena tiene calor.
Se quita el suéter.

QuickPass

Go to glencoe.com
For: **Vocabulary practice**
Web code: **ASD4003c11**

ESCUCHAR

1 Escucha las frases. Parea cada frase con el dibujo que describe.

a.

b.

c.

d.

e.

f.

HABLAR • ESCRIBIR

2 Contesta.

1. Cuando Marisol se despierta, ¿se levanta enseguida?
2. Cuando Carlos se despierta, ¿se queda en la cama?
3. Cuando Vicente se peina, ¿se mira en el espejo?
4. Cuando Juanita se lava el pelo, ¿usa agua caliente?
5. Cuando Tomás toma el desayuno, ¿se sienta a la mesa?
6. Cuando Julia se acuesta, ¿se duerme enseguida?
7. ¿Cuándo se levanta un madrugador? ¿Temprano por la mañana o tarde?
8. Cuando Ricardo se levanta, ¿se estira?

3 **Rompecabezas**

Cambia una letra en cada palabra para formar una palabra nueva.

1. como
2. dolor
3. cada
4. coche

5. tocar
6. peso
7. gano
8. hola

Más práctica

📖 Workbook, pp. 11.3–11.4
💿 StudentWorks™ Plus

LEER

4 Parea para hacer una frase larga.

1. Él se pone un suéter
2. Ella se lava las manos
3. Ella se cepilla los dientes
4. Él se mira en el espejo
5. Ella se quita el suéter

a. porque va a comer.
b. porque se peina.
c. porque tiene calor.
d. porque acaba de comer.
e. porque tiene frío.

InfoGap For more practice using your new vocabulary, do Activity 11 on page SR13 at the end of this book.

HABLAR • ESCRIBIR

5 **Juego** ¡Corrige todas las frases absurdas!

1. Cada pierna tiene una mano y la mano tiene un dedo.
2. El codo está en la pierna y la rodilla está en el brazo.
3. La cara está en la espalda.
4. Los dientes están en el pelo.
5. La boca y los ojos están en la rodilla.

🌸 Comunicación

6 Pick someone in your family and describe his or her weekday routine to the class.

LEER

7 **Juego** Race with a partner to see who can be the first to put José's activities in the correct order.

José se levanta.
José se duerme enseguida.
José se lava la cara y los dientes en el cuarto de baño.
José va al comedor y toma el desayuno.
José se despierta.
José se acuesta.
José se quita la ropa.

CULTURA

La muchacha se mira en el espejo para ver si el pantalón le queda bien.

VIDEO To practice your new words, watch Vocabulario en vivo.

El camping

una carpa, una tienda de campaña

un saco (una bolsa) de dormir

Los amigos van de camping.
Lo están pasando bien. Se divierten mucho.
Los jóvenes arman (montan) una carpa.

Para conversar

¡Ya voy!

Alex, favor de venir acá. Favor de ayudarme con la carpa.

En otras partes

- In addition to **una barra** you will also hear **una pastilla.** You will also hear **pasta dentífrica** as well as **crema dental.**
- Una **tienda de campaña** is more common in Spain, **una carpa** in Latin America.

¿Qué llevan en su mochila?

una barra de jabón

un peine

un cepillo

un rollo de papel higiénico

el champú

un tubo de crema dental

un cepillo de dientes

VIDEO To go hiking with new friends, watch **Diálogo en vivo.**

Los mochileros dan una caminata.
Dan una caminata por un parque nacional.

Andrea se acuesta en la carpa.
Duerme en un saco de dormir.

¡Así se dice!

Note that when someone calls and you want to respond *I'm coming* you say: **¡Ya voy!**

ESCUCHAR

1 Escucha las frases. Indica en una tabla como la de abajo si cada frase es correcta o no.

sí	no

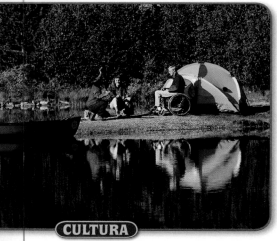

CULTURA

Los amigos están de camping en Chile durante el mes de abril. En Chile es el otoño.

HABLAR • ESCRIBIR

2 Contesta sobre un grupo de amigos que van de camping.

1. ¿Van de camping los amigos?
2. ¿Se divierten en el camping?
3. ¿Qué montan (arman)?
4. ¿En qué duermen?
5. ¿Dónde ponen sus sacos de dormir?
6. ¿Quiere José ayuda para montar la carpa?
7. ¿A ti te gusta el camping?

EXPANSIÓN

Sin mirar las preguntas, da toda la información que recuerdas en tus propias palabras. Si no recuerdas algo, un(a) compañero(a) te puede ayudar.

LEER • HABLAR • ESCRIBIR

3 Completa con una palabra apropiada.

1. María va a cepillarse los dientes. Necesita _____ y _____.
2. Tomás va a tomar una ducha. Necesita _____.
3. Carlos quiere peinarse. Necesita _____.
4. Julia quiere lavarse el pelo. Necesita _____.
5. Claudia va a cepillarse el pelo. Necesita _____.

El joven toma una ducha en agua fría pero no le molesta.

LEER

4 Parea las palabras que significan lo mismo.

1. la carpa
2. armar
3. los que llevan una mochila
4. lo pasa bien
5. el paseo largo

a. los mochileros
b. se divierte
c. la tienda de campaña
d. montar
e. la caminata

Comunicación

5 Estás en una farmacia. Quieres comprar los siguientes objetos. Conversa con el/la empleado(a).

ESCRIBIR

6 Rompecabezas

Join two puzzle pieces to form a word. When you have finished, you should have nine words. Do not use any piece more than once.

jo   nata   ce   pa

pú   pillo   espe   ro   cami

ja   cham   recho

car

de   tes   dien   dilla   bón

CULTURA

Los mochileros dan una caminata.

QuickPass

Go to glencoe.com
For: **Grammar practice**
Web code: **ASD4003c11**

Verbos reflexivos

1. Read the following sentences as you look at the illustrations.

Federico lava el carro.
Federico lo lava.

Federico se lava.

Julia cepilla al perro.
Julia lo cepilla.

Julia se cepilla.

Pedro mira a su amigo.
Pedro lo mira.

Pedro se mira en el espejo.

In the sentences to the left, one person performs the action and another person or thing receives the action. In the sentences to the right, the same person performs and receives the action of the verb. For this reason the pronoun **se** must be used. **Se** is called a reflexive pronoun because it refers back to the subject—**Federico, Julia, Pedro.**

2. Study the forms of a reflexive verb. Pay particular attention to the pronoun that goes with each form of the verb. It is called a "reflexive pronoun."

lavarse			
yo	**me** lavo	nosotros(as)	**nos** lavamos
tú	**te** lavas	*vosotros(as)*	*os laváis*
Ud., él, ella	**se** lava	Uds., ellos, ellas	**se** lavan

levantarse			
yo	**me** levanto	nosotros(as)	**nos** levantamos
tú	**te** levantas	*vosotros(as)*	*os levantáis*
Ud., él, ella	**se** levanta	Uds., ellos, ellas	**se** levantan

3. In the negative form, **no** is placed before the reflexive pronoun.

> **¿No te lavas las manos?**
> **La familia Martínez no se levanta tarde.**

4. In Spanish, when you refer to parts of the body and articles of clothing in a reflexive sentence, you often use the definite article, not the possessive adjective.

> **Me lavo la cara.**
> **Ella se cepilla los dientes.**
> **Él se pone el suéter.**

5. Note that the reflexive pronoun is added to the infinitive.

> **El niño quiere acostarse.**
> **Voy a lavarme las manos.**
> **¿Quieres quitarte la chaqueta?**

CULTURA

Los aficionados van a divertirse mucho durante el concierto que va a dar Enrique Iglesias en la Ciudad de México.

Práctica

 1 Contesta.

1. ¿Se levanta tarde o temprano Gregorio?

2. ¿Se lava por la mañana o por la noche?

3. ¿Se lava los dientes antes o después del desayuno?

4. ¿Se pone un suéter cuando hace frío?

5. ¿Se quita el suéter cuando tiene calor?

 2 Completa las conversaciones con un pronombre.

1. ¿A qué hora _____ levantas?
Soy madrugador(a). _____ levanto temprano, a las seis y media.

2. ¿_____ cepillas los dientes con frecuencia?
Sí, _____ cepillo los dientes unas cuatro veces al día.

3. ¿_____ peinas con frecuencia?
No, no _____ peino con frecuencia.

4. ¿A qué hora _____ despertaste esta mañana?
_____ desperté a las siete.

5. Y, ¿a qué hora _____ acostaste anoche?
Anoche _____ acosté a las diez y media.

 3 Trabaja con un(a) compañero(a). Preparen una conversación según el modelo.

MODELO

—¿Te cepillas?
—Sí, me cepillo.

Conexiones

La salud

Aquí tienes unas sugerencias importantes para mantenerte en buena salud. Debes

- dormir entre siete y ocho horas cada noche
- tomar un buen desayuno
- lavarte las manos antes de comer
- cepillarte los dientes después de comer

 **1.**

 **2.**

 **3.**

 **4.**

HABLAR • ESCRIBIR

4 Personaliza. Da respuestas personales.

1. ¿Cómo te llamas?
2. Y tu(s) hermano(s), ¿cómo se llama(n)?
3. ¿Cómo se llama tu profesor(a) de español?

CULTURA

Es una clase de español en Santa Fe, Nuevo México. La profesora se llama señora Brown. Parece que los alumnos se divierten mucho en clase, ¿no?

LEER • ESCRIBIR

5 Completa con un pronombre reflexivo y la forma correcta del verbo.

Hola. Yo __1__ llam__2__ Jorge y mi amigo __3__ llam__4__ Felipe. Felipe y yo no __5__ levant__6__ a la misma hora porque él es madrugador y yo no. Él __7__ levant__8__ temprano y yo __9__ levant__10__ tarde. Y tú, ¿__11__ levant__12__ tarde como yo o __13__ levant__14__ temprano como Felipe?

LEER • ESCRIBIR

6 Completa con un pronombre.

1. Quiero levantar__ temprano.
2. Niño, tienes que peinar__.
3. Vamos a lavar__ las manos.
4. ¿No quieres poner__ un suéter? Está haciendo frío.
5. Tienen que cepillar__ los dientes después de cada comida.

HABLAR

7 **Juego** Think of an object from this chapter. Your partner will ask **sí / no** questions which you will answer in complete sentences. If your partner guesses it in five questions or less, he or she wins. If you stump your partner, you win. Then reverse roles.

trescientos setenta y siete **377**

Gramática

VIDEO Want help with reflexive verbs? Watch **Gramática en vivo.**

Verbos reflexivos de cambio radical

1. The reflexive verbs **acostarse** (o → ue), **dormirse** (o → ue), **sentarse** (e → ie), **despertarse** (e → ie), and **divertirse** (e → ie) are stem-changing verbs.

acostarse			
yo	me acuesto	nosotros(as)	nos acostamos
tú	te acuestas	*vosotros(as)*	*os acostáis*
Ud., él, ella	se acuesta	Uds., ellos, ellas	se acuestan

divertirse			
yo	me divierto	nosotros(as)	nos divertimos
tú	te diviertes	*vosotros(as)*	*os divertís*
Ud., él, ella	se divierte	Uds., ellos, ellas	se divierten

2. Many verbs in Spanish can be used with a reflexive pronoun. Often the reflexive pronoun gives a different meaning to the verb. Study the following examples.

Ana pone su blusa en su mochila.	*Ana puts her blouse in her backpack.*
Ana se pone la blusa.	*Ana puts on her blouse.*
Ana duerme ocho horas.	*Ana sleeps eight hours.*
Ana se duerme enseguida.	*Ana falls asleep immediately.*
Ana llama a Carlos.	*Ana calls Carlos.*
Ella se llama Ana.	*She calls herself Ana. (Her name is Ana.)*
Ana divierte a sus amigos.	*Ana amuses her friends.*
Ana se divierte.	*Ana amuses herself. (Ana has a good time.)*

CULTURA

La joven ciclista se divierte en el Parque de la Ciudadela en Barcelona.

Práctica

ESCUCHAR • HABLAR • ESCRIBIR

 8 Personaliza. Da respuestas personales.

1. ¿Duermes en una cama o en un saco de dormir?
2. Cuando te acuestas, ¿te duermes enseguida?
3. Por la mañana, ¿te quedas en la cama cuando te despiertas?
4. A veces, ¿despiertas a tus hermanos?
5. ¿Ellos se enfadan cuando los despiertas?
6. ¿Te sientas a la mesa para tomar el desayuno?
7. ¿Te diviertes en la escuela?
8. ¿Diviertes a tus amigos?

CULTURA
El muchacho acaba de despertarse pero está cansado y no quiere levantarse. Quiere quedarse en la carpa.

LEER • ESCRIBIR

9 Completa sobre un día que María pasa en la playa.

1. María _____ su traje de baño en su mochila. Cuando llega a la playa ella _____ el traje de baño.
2. En la playa María ve a un amigo. Su amigo _____ Luis. Ella _____ a su amigo.
3. María y sus amigos lo pasan muy bien en la playa. Ellos _____ mucho y como María es muy cómica ella también _____ mucho a sus amigos.
4. Después de pasar el día en la playa, María está muy cansada. Cuando ella se acuesta, _____ enseguida y _____ más de ocho horas.

LEER • ESCRIBIR

10 Completa.

Cuando yo __1__ (acostarse), yo __2__ (dormirse) enseguida. Cada noche yo __3__ (dormir) ocho horas. Yo __4__ (acostarse) a las once y __5__ (levantarse) a las siete de la mañana. Cuando yo __6__ (despertarse), __7__ (levantarse) enseguida. Pero cuando mi hermana __8__ (despertarse), ella no __9__ (levantarse) enseguida. Y mi hermano, cuando él __10__ (acostarse), no __11__ (dormirse) enseguida. Él pasa horas escuchando música en la cama. Así él __12__ (dormir) solamente unas seis horas.

 Comunicación

 11 Work with a partner and discuss your typical daily routines. Share your results with your classmates.

CULTURA
La playa de Nerja en el sur de España

Más práctica

Workbook, p. 11.9
StudentWorks™ Plus

Mandatos con favor de

1. The expression **favor de** followed by the infinitive is a very useful way to give a command to tell someone what to do. It is very polite and you can use **favor de** with a friend, an adult, or any group of people.

> **Favor de venir aquí (acá).**
> **Favor de no hablar.**
> **Favor de volver pronto.**

Favor de
lavarse las manos

2. Whenever a pronoun is used with the infinitive, the pronoun is attached to it.

> **Favor de ayudarme.**
> **Favor de traerme el menú.**
> **Favor de darme el libro.**
> **Favor de levantarte.** *(to a friend)*
> **Favor de levantarse.** *(to an adult or group of friends)*

Práctica

LEER • HABLAR

12 Escoge.

| un amigo | un adulto o un grupo de personas |

1. Favor de sentarte.
2. Favor de sentarse aquí.
3. Favor de quitarte las botas.
4. Favor de ponerte los zapatos.
5. Favor de quedarse aquí.
6. Favor de lavarte las manos.
7. Favor de levantarse.

Comunicación

13 You and a friend are planning to do something, for example, take a trip. There are many things you need to do to get ready and you need help. Make a diagram similar to the one below and tell your partner what to do to help. Take turns.

buscar algo   llamar un taxi

comprar los boletos   hacer un viaje   hacer la maleta

PRONUNCIACIÓN

La h, la y y la ll

H in Spanish is silent. It is never pronounced. Repeat the following.

hijo	helado	higiénico	hola
hace	hermano	huevos	hispano

Y in Spanish can be either a vowel or a consonant. As a vowel, it is pronounced exactly the same as the vowel **i**. Repeat the following.

el hijo y el hermano
el hotel y el hospital

Y is a consonant when it begins a word or a syllable. As a consonant, **y** is pronounced similarly to the **y** in the English word *yo-yo*. This sound has several variations throughout the Spanish-speaking world. Repeat the following.

ya	desayuno	ayuda	playa
yo	oye	leyó	

Ll is pronounced as a single consonant in Spanish. In many areas of the Spanish-speaking world, it is pronounced the same as the **y**. It too has several variations. Repeat the following.

llama	botella	taquilla	toalla	lleva
llega	pastilla	llueve	rollo	cepillo

Dictado

Pronounce the following sentences carefully. Then write them to prepare for a dictation.

La hermana habla hoy con su hermano en el hotel.
Está lloviendo cuando ella llega a la calle Hidalgo.
El hombre lleva una botella de agua a la playa bella.
Él no lo oyó; lo leyó.

Refrán

Can you guess what the following proverb means?

Quien mucho duerme, poco aprende.

¡Bravo!

You have now learned all the vocabulary and grammar in this chapter. Continue to use and practice all that you know while learning more cultural information. **¡Vamos!**

QuickPass

Go to glencoe.com
For: **Conversation practice**
Web code: **ASD4003c11**

De camping

Rafael	A ti te gusta mucho el camping, ¿no?
Pablo	A mí, sí.
Rafael	La verdad es que no me interesa mucho. ¿Dónde duermes? ¿Te acuestas al aire libre?
Pablo	No. Siempre voy con uno o dos amigos y montamos una carpa. Y dormimos en un saco de dormir.
Rafael	¿Qué hacen para comer?
Pablo	Muy fácil. Preparamos hamburguesas y salchichas en una barbacoa.
Rafael	Hay muchos insectos, ¿no?
Pablo	Pues, hay. Pero, ¡qué va! No nos molestan.
Rafael	¿Cómo pasan el día entero? ¿No se aburren?
Pablo	Al contrario, damos caminatas y nadamos en el lago. Nos acostamos temprano porque nos levantamos temprano también.
Rafael	Me parece que tienen que levantarse cuando se levanta el sol.
Pablo	Sí, pero no me molesta porque soy madrugador. Pero hay una cosa que no me gusta.
Rafael	¿Verdad? ¿Qué?
Pablo	Lavarme en agua fría.

¿Comprendes?

A Completa según la información en la conversación.

1. A _____ le gusta el camping.
2. A _____ no le interesa mucho.
3. Cuando Pablo y su(s) amigo(s) van de camping, montan _____.
4. Duermen en _____.
5. Comen _____.
6. Las preparan en _____.
7. _____ no les molestan.
8. Durante el día _____.
9. Se acuestan temprano porque _____.
10. A Pablo no le gusta _____.

B **Resumiendo** Relata la información en la conversación en tus propias palabras.

C **Comparando** Compara y contrasta los gustos de Rafael y Pablo.

D **Dando opiniones** ¿Estás de acuerdo(a) con las opiniones de Rafael o de Pablo sobre el camping?

GeoVistas

To learn more about Chile, take a tour on pages SH58–SH59.

CULTURA
Saltos de Petrohue cerca del lago Llanquihue en Chile

READING STRATEGY
Using prior knowledge Prior knowledge is what you already know. Using what you have read, seen, or experienced will help you understand what you read.

Antes de leer

Have you ever done any backpacking? When and where? If not, do you think you would like to? Think about it. Would you rather go camping or stay in a youth hostel? Explain why.

¿Llevan maletas los jóvenes?

Durante la lectura

How would you like to travel and make new friends from around the world? Would it be fun?

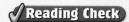

¿Por qué van a albergues juveniles?

✓**Reading Check**

¿Cuáles son unas inconveniencias?

Después de leer

After reading, are your opinions the same about backpacking around the globe?

Los mochileros

Si decides hacer un viaje por España o Latinoamérica con un grupo de amigos, vas a encontrar a muchos jóvenes de muchas nacionalidades haciendo turismo también. Todos tienen el deseo de ver y conocer el mundo. Pero como no tienen mucho dinero, tienen que viajar de una manera económica. ¿Tú no tienes mucho dinero tampoco? Pues, no hay problema. Como los otros aventureros, puedes poner todo lo que necesitas en una mochila grande y salir a ver el mundo.

Vamos a hablar con un mochilero típico. Se llama Antonio. Es de Tejas.

—Me encanta viajar y ver el mundo y lo hago sin mucho dinero. Como en restaurantes económicos y a veces mis compañeros y yo vamos a un mercado donde compramos comida para un picnic. Por lo general pasamos la noche en un albergue juvenil. Son muy económicos pero sus facilidades son limitadas. No tienes baño privado. Te levantas por la mañana y a veces tienes que lavarte en agua fría porque no hay agua caliente. Pero a mí no me importan estas pequeñas inconveniencias. Lo importante es poder hacer nuevos amigos de todas partes del mundo y llegar a apreciar sus costumbres y manera de vivir. ¿Qué te parece? ¿Por qué no nos encontramos un día en México o Chile?

—¡Hola! Me llamo Antonio y soy de Texas. Me encanta viajar con mi mochila y ver el mundo. Soy un verdadero trotamundos.

¿Comprendes?

Más práctica

■ Workbook, p. 11.10
● StudentWorks™ Plus

A Recordando hechos Contesta.

1. ¿De dónde vienen los mochileros que viajan por España o Latinoamérica?
2. ¿Cuál es una cosa que tienen en común?
3. ¿Dónde comen los mochileros?
4. ¿Dónde se quedan los mochileros?

B Describiendo Describe.

1. un albergue juvenil
2. un mochilero
3. a Antonio

C Analizando Contesta.

¿Cuáles son las ventajas, o conveniencias, y desventajas, o inconveniencias, de quedarse en un albergue juvenil?

D Explicando Antonio piensa que los jóvenes se divierten mucho y al mismo tiempo aprenden a apreciar a gente de muchas culturas. Explica el significado de su opinión.

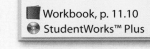

CULTURA

Un hostal o albergue en Punta Arenas en la Patagonia chilena

CULTURA

Los jóvenes están en un camping en Burgos, España.

385

El camping

Antes de leer

¿Fuiste de camping una vez? Si contestas que sí, ¿te gustó o no? Piensa en tu experiencia. Si contestas que no, que nunca fuiste de camping, ¿qué crees? ¿Te interesa el camping o no? A ver si tienes la misma opinión después de leer esta lectura.

Hoy en día muchos turistas, sobre todo los mochileros jóvenes, llevan equipo para hacer camping. En Latinoamérica hay campings en los parques nacionales y reservas naturales. Pasar unas noches en un camping puede ser una experiencia agradable. Tienes la oportunidad de conocer a otros turistas y también a familias locales porque a muchas familias les gusta hacer camping. Es una manera económica de viajar.

Los campers se levantan temprano—cuando se levanta el sol. Pasan el día dando caminatas por unas regiones de una belleza natural increíble.

CULTURA

Campers al pie del Aconcagua en los Andes de Argentina. El Aconcagua es mucho más alto que el monte McKinley en Alaska.

De noche regresan al camping. Se sientan alrededor de una fogata¹ y preparan comida en la fogata o en una barbacoa. Después de un día de mucha actividad física y una buena comida todos están cansados y van a su carpa. Cada uno desenrolla su saco de dormir y enseguida se duerme. Y, ¿mañana? Otro día de experiencias nuevas.

Con solamente mochila, carpa y saco de dormir es posible disfrutar de² unas vacaciones estupendas rodeado de un paisaje espectacular.

¹fogata   *bonfire*   ²disfrutar de   *to enjoy*

¿Comprendes?

Escoge.

1. ¿Quiénes hacen camping?
   a. solo los mochileros
   b. solo los turistas de otros países
   c. los mochileros y otros turistas
   d. nadie

2. Los campings en Latinoamérica se encuentran en _____.
   a. las ciudades
   b. los alrededores de una ciudad
   c. zonas rurales
   d. caminatas

3. ¿Cuándo se levantan los campers?
   a. temprano por la mañana
   b. cuando regresan al camping
   c. cuando toman el sol
   d. de noche

4. Las montañas y los lagos ofrecen _____.
   a. una experiencia cultural
   b. un paisaje espectacular
   c. un viaje económico
   d. una comida estupenda

CULTURA

Los jóvenes dan una caminata en un valle andino en Chile.

Vocabulario

1 **Escoge la palabra apropiada.**

1. Hay cinco (dedos, pies) en cada mano.

2. Escribo con la (mano, pierna) izquierda.

3. Ana se estira (las piernas, los codos) antes de correr.

4. Cuando tengo dolor de (dientes, cabeza) no puedo leer bien.

2 **Completa.**

5. Los amigos van de camping. Arman una _____.

6. Es mi amiga. ¿Quieres saber su nombre? Ella _____ _____ Susana.

7–8. El joven _____ _____ a las diez y media de la noche. Pero no _____ _____ enseguida porque pasa una hora leyendo en la cama.

9. Necesito _____. Voy a lavarme el pelo.

10. No puedo hacerlo. ¿Me puedes _____?

11. Los mochileros dan una _____ por el parque nacional.

Gramática

3 **Contesta.**

12. ¿Cómo te llamas?

13. ¿A qué hora te levantas?

14. ¿A qué hora te acuestas?

4 **Completa.**

15. Yo _____ a la mesa. (sentarse)

16. ¿Tú _____ a qué hora? (acostarse)

17. Ellos _____ Raúl y Magdalena. (llamarse)

18. Nosotros _____ enseguida. (dormirse)

19. Yo _____ las manos. (lavarse)

20. Ustedes _____ en la sala. (sentarse)

21. Ellos _____ mucho. (divertirse)

22. Ella _____ temprano cada día. (despertarse)

To review **Vocabulario 1,** turn to pages 366–367.

To review **Vocabulario 1** and **Vocabulario 2,** turn to pages 366–367 and 370–371.

To review **los verbos reflexivos,** turn to pages 374–375 and 378.

5 **Forma frases.**

23. tú / sentarse / para comer
24. usted / acostarse / a las diez de la noche
25. mis primos / llamarse / Carlos y Felipe
26. yo / cepillarse / los dientes
27. nosotros / divertirse / durante una fiesta
28. ustedes / ponerse / los guantes

6 **Completa con un pronombre si es necesario.**

29. Ella _____ mira en el espejo cuando se peina.
30. Ella _____ mira a la profesora.
31. Yo _____ lavo a mi perro.
32. Yo _____ lavo antes de ir a la escuela.

7 **Escribe un mandato con favor de. Sigue el modelo.**

MODELO **No como.**
        Favor de comer.

33. No salgo.
34. No leo las notas.
35. No escribo la tarea.
36. No paso la sal.

To review **favor de,** turn to page 380.

To review this cultural information, turn to pages 384–385.

Cultura

8 **Contesta.**

37. ¿Cómo viajan muchos jóvenes en España y Latinoamérica?
38. ¿Dónde pasan la noche?
39. ¿Cómo son los albergues?
40. ¿Por qué a los jóvenes les gustan los albergues juveniles?

CULTURA

El camping es muy popular en Asturias, España.

¡UNA RUTINA DIFERENTE!

Prepárate para el examen
Practice for oral proficiency

1 **Mi familia**

✓ *Talk about family routines*

Work with a classmate. Discuss your family routines. What things do you and your family typically do and at what times? Do your families have similar routines or are they quite different?

2 **No es siempre igual.**

✓ *Compare your weekday and weekend routines*

Most people like a change of pace on the weekend. Compare the things you do or do not do during the week with the things you do or do not do during the weekend.

CULTURA

Están tomando una siesta en hamacas en un camping en las afueras de Santa Marta, Colombia.

3 **Una excursión de camping**

✓ *Talk about a camping trip*

Work with a classmate. A friend's family invited you both to join them on a camping trip. Discuss the things you will need to take. Also discuss some of the things you'll probably do during the camping trip.

4 **Un día ideal**

✓ *Talk about your ideal day*

Interview a classmate to find out about his or her ideal day. Take turns. See who can come up with the most original ideas. Share the information with the class.

5 **Favor de...**

✓ *Ask someone to do something*

Work with a classmate and tell each other to do things. Act out what you're told to do.

Prepárate para el examen
Practice for written proficiency

Tarea

For the next week keep **un diario** *(diary)* in Spanish. Write down everything you do in the course of each day.

Writing Strategy

Writing in a journal There are many types of personal writing. One example of personal writing is keeping a journal. One type of journal writing involves writing about what you do each day, along with your thoughts and impressions about these events or activities. It's similar to "thinking out loud."

 **Prewrite**

- Find a notebook or journal in which you will feel comfortable writing.
- Decide what time of day you will write in your journal, preferably before you go to bed.
- Remember that journal writing is informal, but in this case you still want to use correct vocabulary, grammar, and sentence structure. Use as many reflexive verbs as you can. Don't try to write anything you haven't learned yet.

- To help refresh your memory, ask yourself questions such as the following: What did I do when I woke up? Did I go to school? What did I do at school? What did I do after school? Did I eat dinner with my family? What homework did I do? Did I wash my hair? Many activities will be different for the weekend days.
- Read over your diary. Check for correct vocabulary, verb forms, and grammar.

Write

Keeping a diary should be an enjoyable, thoughtful experience.

- Write the date at the top of the page. Write down your activities and thoughts for each day. Remember that your teacher will be reading it!

Evaluate

Don't forget that your teacher will evaluate you on your sequencing of events and activities, use of vocabulary, correctness of grammar and sentence structure, and the completeness of your message.

Repaso del Capítulo (11)

Gramática

- ### Verbos reflexivos *(pages 374–375)*

  Review the forms of the reflexive verbs. These verbs have an extra pronoun that refers back to the subject because the subject is both the performer (doer) and receiver of the action of the verb.

lavarse			
yo	me lavo	nosotros(as)	nos lavamos
tú	te lavas	vosotros(as)	os laváis
Ud., él, ella	se lava	Uds., ellos, ellas	se lavan

- ### Verbos reflexivos de cambio radical *(page 378)*

  Some reflexive verbs have a stem change in the present. Review the following verbs.

acostarse			
yo	me acuesto	nosotros(as)	nos acostamos
tú	te acuestas	vosotros(as)	os acostáis
Ud., él, ella	se acuesta	Uds., ellos, ellas	se acuestan

divertirse			
yo	me divierto	nosotros(as)	nos divertimos
tú	te diviertes	vosotros(as)	os divertís
Ud., él, ella	se divierte	Uds., ellos, ellas	se divierten

- ### Mandatos con **favor de** *(page 380)*

  You can use the expression **favor de** followed by the infinitive to tell someone what to do. Review the following.

  Favor de empezar ahora.
  Favor de no poner la ropa aquí.

  Remember that when a pronoun is used with the infinitive, the pronoun is attached to it.

  Favor de ayudarme.

CULTURA

Los jóvenes se divierten al aire libre en el Parque Nacional de Cazorla en Andalucía, España.

Vocabulario

Stating daily activities

la rutina diaria	quedarse	peinarse	dormirse
despertarse	tomar una ducha	mirarse	ponerse (la ropa)
estirarse	lavarse	sentarse	quitarse (la ropa)
levantarse	cepillarse	acostarse	llamarse

Identifying articles for grooming and hygiene

el espejo	el peine	el tubo de crema	el rollo de papel
el champú	el cepillo de dientes	dental	higiénico
el cepillo		la barra de jabón	

Identifying more parts of the body

el cuerpo humano	la espalda	el dedo	la pierna
la cabeza	el brazo	la rodilla	el pie
los dientes	el codo		

Describing camping

el parque	el saco (la bolsa)	ir de camping	divertirse,
el camping	de dormir	montar, armar	pasarlo bien
la carpa, la tienda	el/la mochilero(a)	dar una caminata	
de campaña			

Other useful words and expressions

derecho(a)	el/la madrugador(a)	tener frío (calor)	acá
izquierdo(a)	el suéter	Favor de (+ *infinitive*)	¡Ya voy!

Repaso cumulativo

Repasa lo que ya has aprendido

These activities will help you review and remember
what you have learned so far in Spanish.

 Escucha las frases. Indica si la frase ocurre en el presente
o en el pasado.

en el presente	en el pasado

 Cambia al presente progresivo.

1. Él compra un juego de computadora.
2. Ellos hacen un álbum de fotografías electrónicas.
3. Compro un regalo para mi papá.
4. ¿Qué lees?
5. No comprendemos nada.
6. Ellos viven en Caracas.
7. ¡Vamos! Sale nuestro vuelo.
8. Hacen cola.

 Completa con una palabra apropiada.

1. Tengo que _____ una composición para mi clase
de inglés.
2. Mañana voy a _____ a la playa donde voy a _____
en el mar.
3. No tengo hambre porque acabo de _____.
4. Mis amigos acaban de _____ de Colombia donde
pasaron sus vacaciones.
5. Yo voy a _____ a la tienda porque tengo que _____
un regalo para el cumpleaños de Teresa.

 Forma frases en el presente.

1. nosotros / poder
2. nosotros / jugar
3. yo / querer
4. ella / pensar que sí
5. ellos / preferir

6. nosotros / querer
7. nosotros / volver
8. ustedes / volver
9. tú / tener que

CULTURA

Una playa en la costa del Caribe
en Colombia

5 **Completa con ser o estar.**

1. Quiero acostarme. _____ cansado(a).
2. José tiene que prepararse para un examen.
   _____ un poco nervioso.
3. Teresa no se siente bien. _____ enferma.
4. La muchacha se baña. El jabón que usa _____
   muy bueno.
5. Los alumnos se duermen porque el profesor _____
   muy aburrido y ellos _____ aburridos.

6 **Escribe el contrario.**

1. El niño tiene algo en la boca.
2. Ellos siempre se acuestan muy temprano.
3. Yo siempre me duermo enseguida.
4. Alguien va a pie y alguien va en bicicleta.
5. Tenemos algo en la mochila.

7 **Mira los dibujos. Describe todo lo que ves.**

Literary Reader

Contenido

The literary selections in the pages
that follow will introduce you to Hispanic
literature while helping you to develop
reading skills and a better understanding
of Hispanic culture. These selections have
been carefully adapted to match your
developing language skills. As you draw
on your knowledge of Spanish grammar
and vocabulary and apply the reading
strategies you have learned, you will
discover that you are able to comprehend
and enjoy the selections. **¡A leer!**

◀ **La biblioteca de El Escorial, un palacio y monasterio cerca de Madrid, construido en el siglo dieciséis**

El Cid

El héroe, el Cid, es famoso en Estados Unidos también. Aquí el Cid está montado a su caballo, Babieca, en una estatua en San Diego, California.

Vocabulario

Estudia las siguientes palabras y sus definiciones.

el rey   monarca

el siglo   un período de cien años

feliz   contento(a), alegre

triste   contrario de «feliz»

un pueblo   una ciudad muy pequeña

enseguida   inmediatamente, ahora mismo

por fin   finalmente

luchar   tener batallas

Práctica

Completa.

1. No vamos en una hora. Vamos _____, ahora mismo.
2. Estamos en el _____ veintiuno.
3. Es una persona _____. Siempre está contenta.
4. No. Él no es una persona alegre. Es una persona _____.
5. Él no tiene muchos amigos porque _____ con sus amigos.
6. Los reyes católicos son Fernando e Isabel. Fernando es el _____. Isabel es la reina.

INTRODUCCIÓN

El poema de mío Cid es el título del famoso poema épico español. Es de un autor anónimo. El poema canta de las acciones o hazañas del gran héroe, el Cid. Pero, ¿quién es el Cid?

El Cid

En el siglo XI nace el señor Rodrigo Díaz de Vivar en un pueblo pequeño cerca de Burgos en Castilla, España. Allí tiene una vida° feliz con su mujer, Jimena, y sus dos hijas.

Rodrigo Díaz de Vivar tiene el título de el Cid. El Cid es una palabra árabe. En aquel entonces° los árabes ocupan una gran parte de España.

Un día el Cid tiene un conflicto con el rey de Castilla, Alfonso. Por eso, tiene que abandonar la ciudad de Burgos. Está muy triste porque tiene que abandonar a su familia también. El Cid sale° de Burgos en su caballo, Babieca. Inmediatamente tiene que luchar contra los árabes. Lucha valientemente y mucha gente ayuda° al Cid en su lucha.

Después de mucho tiempo, llega° a Valencia. Es una ciudad que ocupan los árabes. El Cid tiene unas batallas horribles con los árabes y por fin el Cid y sus hombres conquistan la ciudad. Enseguida el Cid envía por su mujer (esposa) y sus dos hijas. El Cid reina en Valencia hasta su muerte° en mil noventa y nueve (1099).

una vida *life*

En aquel entonces *At that time*

sale *leaves*

ayuda *help*
llega *he arrives*

muerte *death*

CULTURA
Una vista de Burgos

CULTURA

Valencia, España

~2~

saben *learn*

ven *see*

tienen mucho miedo
they are scared

entierra *she buries*

Cuando los árabes saben° de la muerte del Cid, regresan a Valencia y atacan la ciudad. La mujer del Cid es muy astuta y tiene un plan. Ella embalsama a su marido y coloca su cadáver en su caballo Babieca. Cuando los árabes ven° al Cid en su caballo tienen mucho miedo° y escapan. Jimena toma la oportunidad de escapar también. Regresa a Burgos donde entierra° a su esposo en la famosa Catedral de Burgos. Hoy turistas de todas partes del mundo visitan las tumbas del Cid y de su valiente mujer, Jimena.

¿Comprendes?

A Buscando información Identifica.
1. el otro nombre del Cid
2. el nombre de la mujer del Cid
3. el número de hijas que tienen el Cid y su mujer
4. la ciudad de donde es el Cid
5. el nombre del caballo del Cid

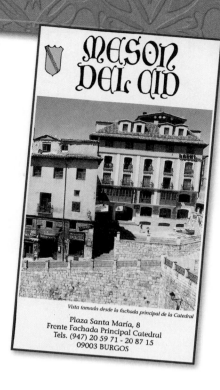

Vista tomada desde la fachada principal de la Catedral

Plaza Santa María, 8
Frente Fachada Principal Catedral
Tels. (947) 20 59 71 - 20 87 15
09003 BURGOS

B Determinando Escoge.
1. El Cid tiene que (abandonar, conquistar) la ciudad de Burgos.
2. El Cid está (feliz, triste) cuando tiene que abandonar a su familia.
3. Los (árabes, romanos) ocupan una gran parte de España durante la época del Cid.
4. El Cid sale de Burgos (a pie, en su caballo).
5. Durante su expedición de conquista el Cid llega a (Burgos, Valencia).

C Confirmando información ¿Sí o no?
1. Los árabes regresan a Valencia después de la muerte del Cid.
2. La mujer del Cid es una señora inteligente.
3. Los árabes toman la ciudad de Valencia cuando saben de la muerte del Cid.
4. La mujer del Cid regresa a Valencia donde entierra a su marido.

D Describiendo Describe.
Describe el plan que tiene la mujer del Cid para engañar (fool, deceive) a los árabes.

E Analizando Contesta.
¿Qué acciones del Cid indican que es una persona buena?

CULTURA

Patio de los leones de La Alhambra, una maravilla arquitectónica de los moros en Granada

Una leyenda mexicana— Iztaccíhuatl y Popocatépetl

CULTURA

Los volcanes Iztaccíhuatl y Popocatépetl

Vocabulario

Estudia las siguientes palabras y sus definiciones.

el cacique   el líder, el jefe
el guerrero   una persona que lucha en una batalla o guerra; un soldado
subir   ir hacia la parte superior
casarse   contraer matrimonio, tomar como esposo(a)
desconsolado(a)   muy triste
la leyenda   un cuento tradicional

Reading Tip

Remember that as you read you should look for cognates—words that look alike in both Spanish and English and have the same meaning. In this selection, you will come across the following cognates. Can you find others?

el volcán	el emperador	la torcha
el origen	la princesa	la montaña
la versión	la batalla	la erupción
el valle	suicidar	omnipotente
severo	posesiones	informar
horrible	flameante	victorioso

Práctica

Expresa de otra manera.

1. ¿Es *el líder* de un grupo indígena?
2. Él está *triste* porque su madre está muy enferma.
3. Ellos tienen que *ir a la parte superior.*
4. Ellos van a *ser esposo y esposa.*
5. *Los soldados* luchan mucho. Toman parte en muchas batallas.

INTRODUCCIÓN

Cerca de la Ciudad de México hay dos volcanes gigantescos—el Iztaccíhuatl y el Popocatépetl. Hay una leyenda sobre el origen de los dos volcanes. Como muchas leyendas, la leyenda sobre Iztaccíhuatl y «Popo» tiene varias versiones. Aquí tenemos una versión popular.

Iztaccíhuatl y Popocatépetl

⪪ 1 ⪫

Antes de la llegada de Cristóbol Colón los aztecas viven en México. El emperador de los aztecas es un señor omnipotente y bastante severo. Hay otros grupos indígenas que viven en el valle de México que no están contentos con él. Están cansados de tener que dar sus posesiones y dinero a un emperador opresivo. Entre los grupos que no están contentos con él son los tlaxcaltecas.

El cacique de los tlaxcaltecas tiene una hija bonita, la princesa Iztaccíhuatl. La princesa está enamorada de° Popocatépetl, uno de los guerreros más valientes de su padre. Su padre envía a «Popo» a una batalla contra los aztecas. El padre promete° a Popocatépetl que puede tener la mano de su hija (tomar como esposa a su hija) si regresa victorioso. Popo está muy contento. Él va a ganar la batalla y la princesa va a ser su esposa.

El calendario azteca

enamorada de *in love with*

promete *promises*

Escenas de la vida en Tenochtitlán, la capital de los aztecas

CULTURA

Plaza de las Tres Culturas,
Ciudad de México

❧ 2 ❧

pretendiente *suitor*
amado *loved one*
muerto *dead*

Mientras Popocatépetl está ausente otro joven pretendiente° informa a Iztaccíhuatl que su amado° está muerto°; que pierde la vida en una batalla horrible. Él convence a Iztaccíhuatl a casarse con él.

Después de poco Popocatépetl regresa victorioso de la batalla. Está muy feliz porque ahora piensa que va a casarse con Iztaccíhuatl. Cuando la princesa aprende del regreso de su amado está desconsolada. Ahora no puede casarse con él porque ya tiene esposo. No quiere vivir sin su «Popo». La desconsolada princesa se suicida.

❧ 3 ❧

brazos *arms*
hombros *shoulders*

enciende *lights*

sigue vigilando *keeps watch over*

El padre de la princesa, el cacique, informa al soldado de la muerte de su hija. Popo toma a Iztaccíhuatl en sus brazos°. Levanta a su amada y con su cuerpo cargado en sus hombros° sube varias montañas. Cuando llega cerca del cielo coloca el cuerpo de Iztaccíhuatl en el pico de una de las montañas y enciende° una torcha. Empieza a nevar y dentro de poco la nieve cubre los dos cuerpos y forma dos volcanes majestuosos—el Iztaccíhuatl y el Popocatépetl. Aún hoy «Popo» sigue vigilando° a su querida (amada) Iztaccíhuatl y a veces vemos su torcha flameante con «Popo» cuando entra en erupción.

¿Comprendes?

A **Recordando hechos** Contesta.

1. ¿Quiénes viven en México antes de la llegada de Cristóbal Colón?
2. ¿Hay otros grupos indígenas también?
3. ¿Todos están contentos con los aztecas?
4. ¿Hay batallas entre los diferentes grupos?

B **Describiendo** Describe.

1. Describe al emperador de los aztecas.
2. Describe a Iztaccíhuatl.
3. Describe a Popocatépetl.
4. Describe la relación entre Iztaccíhuatl y Popocatépetl.

C **Identificando** Contesta.

¿Cuáles son las acciones o hazañas profesionales y personales de Popocatépetl?

D **Explicando** Explica.

1. por qué no puede Iztaccíhuatl ser la esposa de Popocatépetl
2. el origen y formación de los dos volcanes

CULTURA

Bailadores aztecas en el Zócalo, la Ciudad de México

La camisa de Margarita

de Ricardo Palma

Hay mucha influencia colonial en todas las ciudades peruanas como vemos aquí en la Plaza de Armas en Lima.

Nota

In this story you will come across the following words that describe money used in Peru in the eighteenth century. From the context of the reading you will be able to tell which were of little value and which were of great value. It is not necessary for you to learn these words: **un ochavo, un real, un maravedí, un duro, un morlaco.**

Vocabulario

Estudia las siguientes palabras y sus definiciones.

la guerra una seria de luchas o batallas
el galán un señor elegante
la flecha lo que tira Cúpido en el corazón de una persona
el soltero un joven que no está casado; que no tiene esposa
el suegro el padre del marido o de la mujer
el sacerdote un padre (religioso) católico
el pobretón un muchacho pobre que no tiene dinero
el chisme una historieta, un rumor
altivo(a) arrogante
con mucha plata que tiene mucho dinero, rico
gallardo no tiene miedo; valiente

Práctica

A Contesta.

1. ¿Es un galán un tipo elegante o pobre?
2. ¿Tiene esposa un soltero?
3. ¿Tira flechas Cúpido? ¿En dónde entran sus flechas?
4. ¿Tiene un rico mucha o poca plata?
5. ¿Qué tipo de individuo es una persona altiva?

B Expresa de otra manera.

1. Él es un padre religioso.
2. Es el padre de mi mujer.
3. Es un tipo muy arrogante.
4. No es un joven que tiene mucho dinero.
5. No sé si es verdad. Es un rumor.
6. Es una seria de batallas horribles.

INTRODUCCIÓN

Ricardo Palma es uno de los hombres más famosos de letras peruanas de todos los tiempos. Él da origen a un nuevo género literario—la tradición. La tradición es una anécdota histórica.

Ricardo Palma publica sus *Tradiciones peruanas* en diez tomos de 1872 a 1910. Las tradiciones presentan la historia de Perú desde la época precolombina hasta la guerra con Chile (1879–1883). Las tradiciones más interesantes y más famosas son las tradiciones que describen la época colonial. *La camisa de Margarita* es un ejemplo de una tradición de la época colonial.

La camisa de Margarita

Cuando las señoras viejas de Lima quieren describir algo que cuesta mucho, ¿qué dicen°? Dicen:—¡Qué! Si esto es más caro que la camisa de Margarita Pareja.

Margarita Pareja es la hija mimada° de don Raimundo Pareja, un colector importante del Callao. La muchacha es una limeñita que es tan bella que puede cautivar° al mismo diablo°. Tiene unos ojos negros cargados° de dinamita que hacen explosión sobre el alma° de los galanes limeños.

Llega de España un arrogante joven llamado don Luis de Alcázar. Don Luis tiene en Lima un tío aragonés, don Honorato. Don Honorato es solterón y es muy rico. Si el tío es rico, no lo es el joven. No tiene ni un centavo.

⁓2⁓

En la procesión de Santa Rosa, don Luis ve a la linda Margarita. La muchacha le flecha el corazón. El joven le echa flores°. Ella no le contesta ni que sí ni que no. Pero con sonrisas y otras armas del arsenal femenino le da a entender al joven que es plato muy de su gusto.

Los enamorados° olvidan° que existe la aritmética. Don Luis no considera su presente condición económica un obstáculo. Va al padre de Margarita y le pide su mano°. Al padre de Margarita, don Raimundo, no le gusta nada la petición del joven arrogante. Le dice que Margarita es muy joven y no puede tomar marido.

Pero la edad de su hija no es la verdadera razón. Don Raimundo no quiere ser suegro de un pobretón. Les dice la verdad a sus amigos. Uno de ellos va con el chisme al tío aragonés. El tío—un tipo muy altivo, se pone° furioso.

—¡Cómo! ¡Desairar° a mi sobrino! No hay más gallardo en todo Lima. Ese don Raimundo va a ver . . .

---

dicen *do they say*

mimada *spoiled*

cautivar *captivate, charm*
diablo *devil*
cargados *charged*
alma *soul*

le echa flores *compliments her*

enamorados *lovers*
olvidan *forget*

le pide su mano *asks for her hand*

se pone *becomes*
Desairar *To snub*

3

peso *weight*

Y la pobre Margarita se pone muy enferma. Pierde peso° y tiene ataques nerviosos. Sufre mucho. Su padre se alarma y consulta a varios médicos y curanderos. Todos declaran que

salvar *save*

la única medicina que va a salvar° a la joven no está en la farmacia. El padre tiene que permitir a la muchacha casarse con el hombre de su gusto.

Don Raimundo va a la casa de don Honorato. Le dice: —Usted tiene que permitir a su sobrino casarse con mi hija.

morir *to die*

Porque si no, la muchacha va a morir°.

—No puede ser—contesta de la manera más desagradable el tío. —Mi sobrino es un pobretón. Lo que usted debe buscar para su hija es un hombre con mucha plata.

borrascoso *stormy*

El diálogo entre los dos es muy borrascoso°.

matar *to kill*

—Pero, tío, no es cristiano matar° a quien no tiene la

culpa *blame*

culpa°—dice don Luis.

—¿Tú quieres casarte con esa joven?

—Sí, de todo corazón, tío y señor.

—Pues bien, muchacho. Si tú quieres, consiento. Pero con una condición. Don Raimundo me tiene que jurar° que no va

jurar *to swear*

a regalar un ochavo a su hija. Y no le va a dejar° un real en la

dejar *to leave*

herencia—. Aquí empieza otra disputa.

4

dote *dowry*

—Pero, hombre, mi hija tiene veinte mil duros de dote°.

—Renunciamos a la dote. La niña va a venir a casa de su

tiene puesta *has on*

marido con nada más que la ropa que lleva o tiene puesta°.

—Entonces me permite regalar a mi hija los muebles y el

vestido de novia *wedding dress*

vestido de novia°.

—Ni un alfiler°.

alfiler *pin*

—Usted no es razonable, don Honorato. Mi hija necesita llevar una camisa para reemplazar la que lleva.

—Bien, usted le puede regalar la camisa de novia y se acaba, nada más.

Dice el padre de Margarita:—Juro no dar a mi hija más que la camisa de novia.

cumple con *fulfills*

Y don Raimundo cumple con° su promesa. Ni en la vida ni en la muerte le da después a su hija un maravedí.

encajes *lace*

Los encajes° de Flandes que adornan la camisa de la novia cuestan dos mil setecientos duros. Además la camisa tiene muchos diamantes que tienen un valor de treinta mil morlacos.

merecida *deserved*

Ahora sabemos por qué es muy merecida° la fama que tiene la camisa nupcial de Margarita Pareja.

¿Comprendes?

A **Recordando hechos** Contesta.

    1. ¿Quiénes dicen:—¡Qué! Si esto es más caro que la camisa de Margarita Pareja?

    2. ¿Quién es Margarita Pareja?

    3. ¿Cómo es Margarita?

    4. ¿Quién llega a Perú?

    5. ¿De dónde viene?

    6. ¿Quién es?

    7. ¿Cómo es el tío?

    8. ¿Cómo es el sobrino?

B **Buscando información** Completa.

    1. Don Luis conoce a Margarita en _____.

    2. Margarita le _____. Y don Luis le _____.

    3. Don Luis no considera su condición económica _____.

    4. Don Luis va al padre de Margarita y _____.

    5. Al padre no le gusta nada _____.

    6. No le gusta la petición porque _____.

    7. Cuando el tío sabe lo que dice don Raimundo, él se pone _____.

C **Interpretando** In English, give your interpretation of the attitudes and actions of the two uncles.

D **Analizando** Analyze the reasons that people say, **Si esto es más caro que la camisa de Margarita.**

E **Llegando a conclusiones** Tell what you think the consequences would have been if the uncle had not allowed Margarita to marry don Luis.

Una calle colonial en el centro de Lima

F **Describiendo** Completa con las características de cada uno de los siguientes personajes.

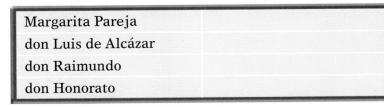

Margarita Pareja	
don Luis de Alcázar	
don Raimundo	
don Honorato	

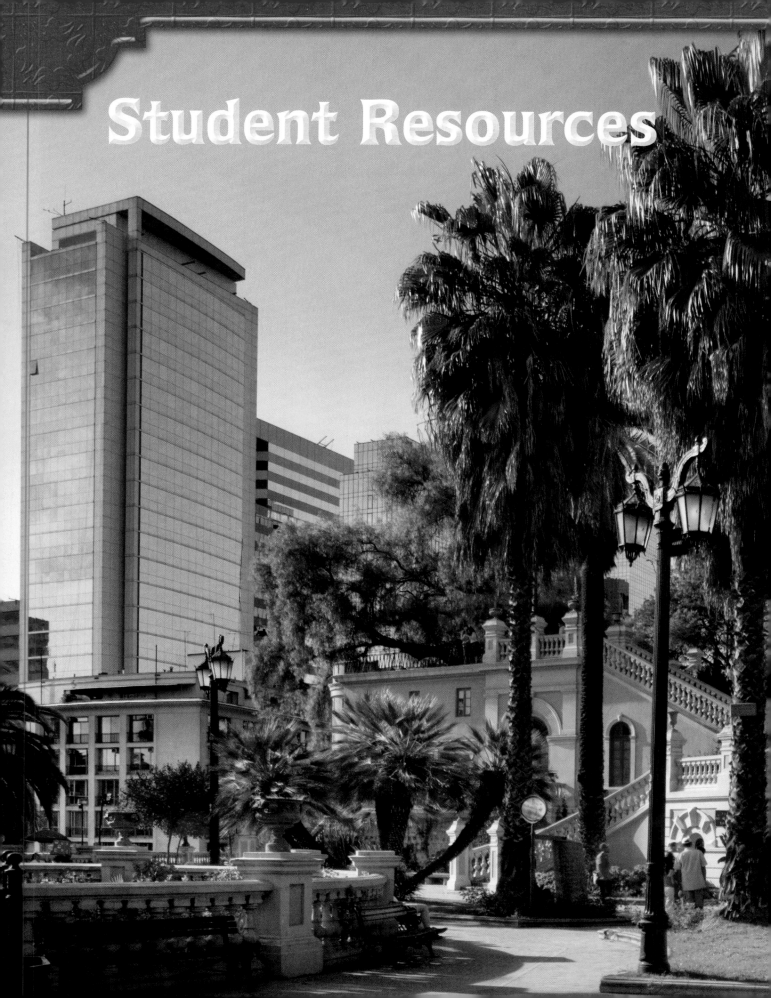
Student Resources

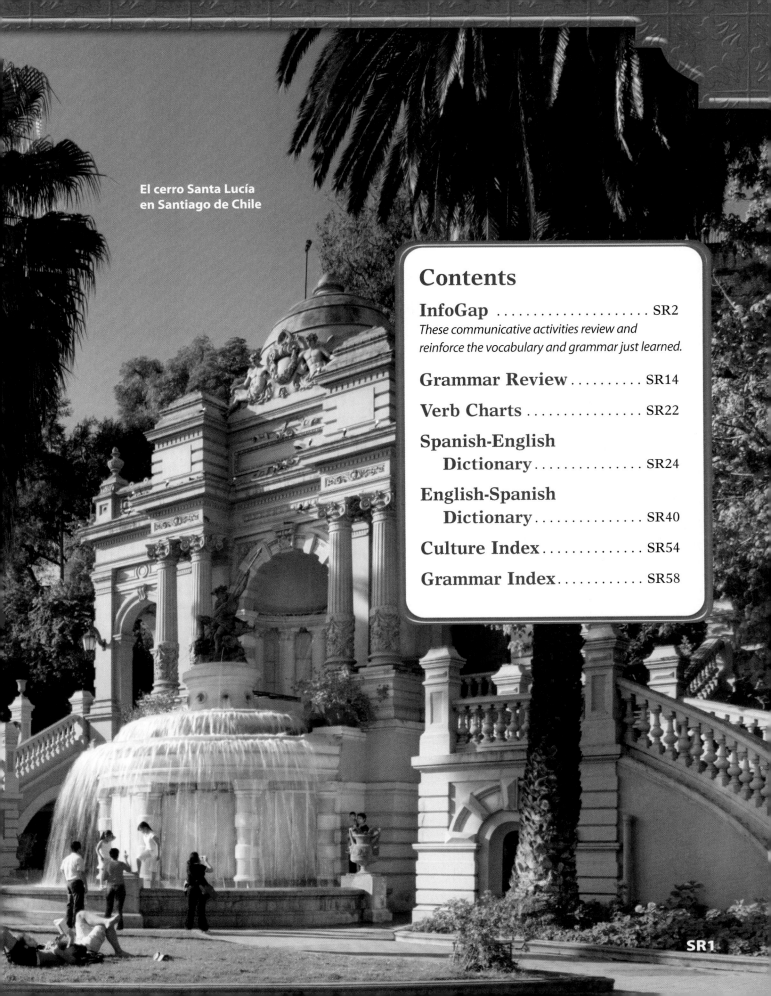

El cerro Santa Lucía en Santiago de Chile

Contents

InfoGap

Activity LP

InfoGap

Alumno A Ask your partner the following questions. Correct answers are in parentheses.

1. ¿Qué día es hoy? *(Hoy es lunes.)*

2. ¿Cuál es la fecha de hoy?
(Hoy es el seis de julio.)

3. ¿Qué hora es? *(Son las nueve y cuarenta y cinco.)*

4. ¿Qué tiempo hace? *(Hace [mucho] calor.)* or *(Hace [mucho] sol.)*

Alumno A Answer your partner's questions based on the pictures below.

1.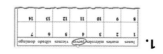

2.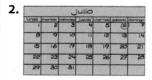

3.

4.

Alumno B Answer your partner's questions based on the pictures below.

1.

2.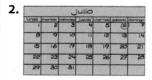

3.

4.

Alumno B Ask your partner the following questions. Correct answers are in parentheses.

1. ¿Qué día es hoy?
(Hoy es jueves.)

2. ¿Cuál es la fecha de hoy?
(Hoy es el diez de enero.)

3. ¿A qué hora es la clase de español? *(La clase de español es a la una y cincuenta.)*

4. ¿Qué estación es? *(Es el otoño.)*

Activity 1

Sara

Cristina

Alumno A Ask your partner the following questions. Correct answers are in parentheses.

1. ¿Cómo es Marta, rubia o morena? *(Marta es morena.)*

2. ¿Cómo es Roberto, simpático o antipático? *(Roberto es simpático.)*

3. ¿Es Julio un amigo de Teresa? *(Sí, Julio es un amigo de Teresa.)*

4. ¿Cómo es Elena, cómica o seria? *(Elena es seria.)*

5. ¿Es Teresa una amiga de Julio? *(Sí, Teresa es una amiga de Julio.)*

Alberto

Diana/Alejandro

Alumno A Answer your partner's questions based on the photos below.

Alumno B Answer your partner's questions based on the photos below.

Teresa/Julio

Elena

Roberto

Marta

Alumno B Ask your partner the following questions. Correct answers are in parentheses.

1. ¿Es Alejandro un amigo de Diana? *(Sí, Alejandro es un amigo de Diana.)*

2. ¿Cómo es Sara, graciosa o seria? *(Sara es graciosa.)*

3. ¿Cómo es Cristina, rubia o morena? *(Cristina es rubia.)*

4. ¿Cómo es Alberto, simpático o antipático? *(Alberto es simpático.)*

5. ¿Es Diana una amiga de Alejandro? *(Sí, Diana es una amiga de Alejandro.)*

InfoGap

Alumno A Ask your partner the following questions. Correct answers are in parentheses.

1. ¿Quién es la hermana de Juan?
   (*Elisa es la hermana de Juan.*)

2. ¿Quién es la madre de Carlos?
   (*Ana es la madre de Carlos.*)

3. ¿Cuántas mascotas tiene Elisa?
   (*Elisa tiene dos mascotas.*)

4. ¿Tiene nietos Antonio?
   (*Sí, Antonio tiene nietos.*)

Alumno A Answer your partner's questions based on the photo below.

(from left to right) Lucas Alba, Lila Alba, Marcos Alba, Jorge Alba, Víctor Alba, Duque

---

Alumno B Answer your partner's questions based on the picture below.

Alumno B Ask your partner the following questions. Correct answers are in parentheses.

1. ¿Quién es el padre de Lucas?
   (*Jorge es el padre de Lucas.*)

2. ¿Tiene Víctor un perro?
   (*Sí, Víctor tiene un perro.*)

3. ¿Cuántos hijos tienen Lila y Jorge? (*Lila y Jorge tienen tres hijos.*)

4. ¿Quiénes son los hermanos de Marcos? (*Lucas y Víctor son los hermanos de Marcos.*)

Alumno A Ask your partner the following questions. Correct answers are in parentheses.

1. ¿Qué das al profesor? *(Doy un libro al profesor.)*

2. ¿Qué escuchas cuando estás en casa? *(Escucho la música cuando estoy en casa.)*

3. ¿Dónde están ustedes y con quiénes hablan? *(Estamos delante de la escuela y hablamos con nuestros amigos.)*

4. ¿Cuándo vas a la tienda? *(Voy a la tienda a las cuatro y veinte.)*

5. ¿Profesores, qué dan ustedes todos los viernes? *(Damos un examen los viernes.)* or *(Damos una prueba todos los viernes.)*

Alumno A Answer your partner's questions based on the photos below.

3.

2.

5.

4.

1.

Alumno B Answer your partner's questions based on the photos below.

1.

2.

3.

4.

5.

Alumno B Ask your partner the following questions. Correct answers are in parentheses.

1. ¿En qué clase estás a las diez? *(Estoy en la clase de ciencia a las diez.)*

2. ¿Con quiénes hablas cuando regresas a casa a pie? *(Hablo con mis amigas cuando regreso a casa a pie.)*

3. ¿A quién das el dinero? *(Doy el dinero a la empleada.)*

4. ¿Qué compras cuando vas a la tienda? *(Compro una carpeta cuando voy a la tienda.)*

5. ¿Dónde están ustedes y su gato? *(Estamos en la sala.)*

InfoGap

Activity 4

CAPÍTULO 4, Vocabulario 2, pages 132–133

Alumno A Ask your partner the following questions. Correct answers are in parentheses.

1. ¿Qué toma Jaime? *(Jaime toma un batido de jugos tropicales.)*

2. ¿Qué lee Marisol? *(Marisol lee el menú.)*

3. ¿Qué va a comer Adriana? *(Adriana va a comer unos tostones.)*

4. ¿Quién habla con los amigos? *(El mesero habla con los amigos.)*

5. ¿Qué van a comer los amigos? *(Los amigos van a comer empanadas.)*

Alumno A Answer your partner's questions based on the photos below.

1.

2.

3.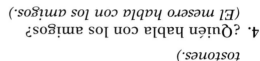

4.

5.

Alumno B Answer your partner's questions based on the photos below.

1.

2.

3.

4.

5.

Alumno B Ask your partner the following questions. Correct answers are in parentheses.

1. ¿Qué va a comer José Luis? *(José Luis va a comer unos pinchitos.)*

2. ¿Qué escribe el mesero? *(El mesero escribe la orden.)*

3. ¿Qué toma Silvia? *(Silvia toma agua mineral con gas.)*

4. ¿Qué desean Ana y Pablo? *(Ana y Pablo desean unas albóndigas.)*

5. ¿Adónde van los amigos? *(Los amigos van al café.)*

InfoGap

Alumno A Ask your partner the following questions. Correct answers are in parentheses.

1. ¿Te interesa el béisbol?
   (No, no me interesa el béisbol. Me interesan el fútbol y el baloncesto.)

2. ¿Te gustan los camarones?
   (No, no me gustan los camarones. Me gusta la carne.)

3. ¿Te gusta la clase de arte?
   (No, no me gusta la clase de arte. Me gustan las ciencias.)

4. ¿Te gusta comer pizza?
   (No, no me gusta comer pizza. Me gusta comer enchiladas.)

Alumno A Answer **no** to your partner's questions and tell what you like or what interests you instead based on the cues below.

1. tu gato

2. los deportes de equipo

3. camarones

4. los estudios sociales

Alumno B Answer **no** to your partner's questions and tell what you like or what interests you instead based on the cues below.

1. el fútbol y el baloncesto

2. la carne

3. las ciencias

4. enchiladas

Alumno B Ask your partner the following questions. Correct answers are in parentheses.

1. ¿Te gustan mis perros? *(No, no me gustan tus perros. Me gusta tu gato.)*

2. ¿Te interesa el tenis?
   (No, no me interesa el tenis. Me interesan los deportes de equipo.)

3. ¿Te gusta comer carne?
   (No, no me gusta comer carne. Me gusta comer camarones.)

4. ¿Te interesa la clase de biología?
   (No, no me interesa la clase de biología. Me interesan los estudios sociales.)

InfoGap

Activity 6

Alumno A Ask your partner the following questions. Correct answers are in parentheses.

1. ¿Cómo es Armando, flexible o terco? *(Armando es terco.)*

2. ¿Cómo está Patricia, contenta o triste? *(Patricia está contenta.)*

3. ¿Está Natalia bien o enferma? *(Natalia está enferma.)*

4. ¿Cómo es Pepe, ambicioso o perezoso? *(Pepe es ambicioso.)*

Alumno A Answer your partner's questions based on the photos below.

el jugador

Beatriz

Sofía

Jorge

Alumno B Answer your partner's questions based on the photos below.

Armando

Patricia

Natalia

Pepe

Alumno B Ask your partner the following questions. Correct answers are in parentheses.

1. ¿Cómo es Sofía, bien educada o mal educada? *(Sofía es bien educada.)*

2. ¿Cómo está Jorge, cansado o lleno de energía? *(Jorge está cansado.)*

3. ¿Está el jugador bien o enfermo? *(El jugador está bien.)*

4. ¿Está Beatriz de buen humor o de mal humor? *(Beatriz está de mal humor.)*

Alumno A Ask your partner who did the following activities. Correct answers are in parentheses.

1. ¿Quién miró el DVD?
   (Marta miró el DVD.)

2. ¿Quién ganó el partido?
   (Nosotros ganamos el partido.)

3. ¿Quién prestó atención en la clase? *(Todos los alumnos prestaron atención en la clase.)*

4. ¿Quién bajó la pista avanzada?
   (Yo bajé la pista avanzada.)

5. ¿Quién tomó el sol?
   (Tú tomaste el sol.)

Alumno A Use the chart below to answer your partner's questions.

¿Quién?	Actividad
Raúl y Reina	sacar
la señora López	enseñar
yo	llevar
mi primo y yo	alquilar
tú	nadar

Alumno B Use the chart below to answer your partner's questions.

¿Quién?	Actividad
Marta	mirar
nosotros	ganar
todos los alumnos	prestar
yo	bajar
tú	tomar

Alumno B Ask your partner who did the following activities. Correct answers are in parentheses.

1. ¿Quién sacó fotos ayer? *(Raúl y Reina sacaron fotos ayer.)*

2. ¿Quién enseñó la clase de español? *(La señora López enseñó la clase de español.)*

3. ¿Quién llevó uniforme a la escuela? *(Yo llevé uniforme a la escuela.)*

4. ¿Quién alquiló los esquís? *(Mi primo y yo alquilamos los esquís.)*

5. ¿Quién nadó en el mar? *(Tú nadaste en el mar.)*

InfoGap

Activity 8 **CAPÍTULO 8, Vocabulario 1, 2, pages 266–267, 270–271**

Alumno A Ask your partner the following questions. Correct answers are in parentheses.

1. ¿Qué visitó Juanita?
   (*Juanita visitó el museo.*)

2. ¿Qué vieron los amigos?
   (*Los amigos vieron una película.*)
   or (*Los amigos vieron un filme.*)

3. ¿Qué tienen los invitados para Ana? (*Los invitados tienen muchos regalos para Ana.*) or (*Los invitados tienen una torta para Ana.*)

4. ¿Quién recibe muchos aplausos?
   (*La cantante recibe muchos aplausos.*)

Alumno A Answer your partner's questions based on the pictures below.

1.

2.

3.

4.

Alumno B Answer your partner's questions based on the pictures below.

1.

2.

3.

4.

Alumno B Ask your partner the following questions. Correct answers are in parentheses.

1. ¿Qué perdió Ernesto?
   (*Ernesto perdió el autobús.*)

2. ¿Fueron al cine las amigas o alquilaron una película? (*Las amigas alquilaron una película.*)

3. ¿Tiene algo en la mano el cantante? (*No, el cantante no tiene nada en la mano.*)

4. ¿Qué comen los invitados?
   (*Los invitados comen vegetales crudos.*)

InfoGap

Alumno A Ask your partner the following questions. Correct answers are in parentheses.

1. ¿Quién es más alto que Luis?
   (Nadie es más alto que Luis.)

2. ¿Cuál es la camisa más cara de todas? *(La camisa azul es la más cara de todas.)*

3. ¿Quién juega mejor que Juan?
   (Alicia juega mejor que Juan.)

4. ¿La chaqueta negra me queda mejor que o peor que la otra? *(La chaqueta negra te queda peor que la otra.)*

Alumno A Answer your partner's questions based on the cues below.

1. Ana

2. más caros

3. mejor que

4. menos grande

Alumno B Answer your partner's questions based on the cues below.

1. nadie

2. la camisa azul

3. Alicia

4. peor que

Alumno B Ask your partner the following questions. Correct answers are in parentheses.

1. ¿Quién es el/la más inteligente de la clase? *(Ana es la más inteligente de la clase.)*

2. ¿Son los precios más bajos o más caros en esta tienda? *(Los precios son más caros en esta tienda.)*

3. ¿Enrique esquió mejor que o peor que Armando? *(Enrique esquió mejor que Armando.)*

4. ¿Es la clase de español más grande o menos grande que la clase de química? *(La clase de español es menos grande que la clase de química.)*

InfoGap

Alumno A Ask your partner the following questions. Correct answers are in parentheses.

1. ¿Es una tarjeta de embarque o un carnet de identidad? *(Es una tarjeta de embarque.)*

2. ¿Qué hace Julia? *(Julia factura su equipaje.)*

3. ¿Quiénes esperan a los pasajeros? *(Los taxistas esperan a los pasajeros.)*

4. ¿Dónde están la madre y su hija? *(La madre y su hija están en el aeropuerto.)*

Alumno A Answer your partner's questions based on the photos below.

1.

2.

3.

4.

Alumno B Answer your partner's questions based on the photos below.

1.

2.

3.

4.

Alumno B Ask your partner the following questions. Correct answers are in parentheses.

1. ¿Dónde pone el padre el equipaje? *(El padre pone el equipaje en la maletera [el baúl].)*

2. ¿Dónde está la pasajera? *(La pasajera está en el mostrador de la línea aérea.)*

3. ¿El avión acaba de despegar o de aterrizar? *(El avión acaba de aterrizar.)*

4. ¿Cuál es el número del asiento del pasajero? *(El número del asiento del pasajero es 8A.)*

los muchachos

Federico

Elisa

Rolando

Alumno A Answer your partner's questions based on the photos below.

Alumno A Ask your partner the following questions. Correct answers are in parentheses.

1. ¿Qué hace Catalina? (*Catalina se cepilla los dientes.*) or (*Catalina se lava los dientes.*)

2. ¿Se acuesta Omar o se estira? (*Omar se acuesta.*)

3. ¿Qué hace Ernesto? (*Ernesto se pone un suéter.*)

4. ¿Se sienta la joven a la mesa o se cepilla el pelo? (*La joven se sienta a la mesa.*)

Alumno B Answer your partner's questions based on the photos below.

Alumno B Ask your partner the following questions. Correct answers are in parentheses.

la joven

Ernesto

Omar

Catalina

1. ¿Qué hace Elisa? (*Elisa se despierta.*) or (*Elisa se estira.*)

2. ¿Qué hace Rolando? (*Rolando se lava la cara.*)

3. ¿Qué hacen los muchachos? (*Los muchachos se peinan.*) or (*Los muchachos se miran en el espejo.*)

4. ¿Se mira en el espejo Federico o se lava el pelo? (*Federico se lava el pelo.*)

Grammar Review

Nouns and articles

Nouns and definite articles

A noun is the name of a person, place, or thing. Unlike English, all nouns in Spanish have a gender—either masculine or feminine. Almost all nouns that end in **-o** are masculine and almost all nouns that end in **-a** are feminine. Note that the definite article **el** is used with masculine nouns. The definite article **la** is used with feminine nouns.

MASCULINE	FEMININE
el muchach**o**	**la** muchach**a**
el libr**o**	**la** escuel**a**

Nouns that end in **-e** can be either masculine or feminine. It is necessary for you to learn the gender.

MASCULINE	FEMININE
el padre	**la madre**
el billete	**la carne**

Many nouns that end in **-e** and refer to a person can be either masculine or feminine.

el cliente	**la cliente**
el paciente	**la paciente**

It is also necessary to learn the gender of nouns that end in a consonant.

el comedor	**la flor**
el jamón	**la capital**

Note, however, that nouns that end in **-ción, -dad, -tad** are always feminine.

la habitación	**la universidad**	**la dificultad**

Irregular nouns

There are not many irregular nouns in Spanish. So far, you have learned **la mano, el problema,** and **la foto** (*from* **la fotografía**).

Plural of nouns

To form the plural of nouns you add **-s** to nouns that end in a vowel. You add **-es** to nouns that end in a consonant. Note, too, that the definite articles **el** and **la** become **los** and **las** in the plural.

MASCULINE PLURAL	FEMININE PLURAL
los libro**s**	**las** novela**s**
los coche**s**	**las** carne**s**
los comedor**es**	**las** flor**es**

Nouns that end in **-ción** drop the accent in the plural.

la estación	**las estaciones**

Indefinite articles

The indefinite articles are *a, an,* and *some* in English. They are **un, una, unos, unas** in Spanish. Note that the indefinite article, like the definite article, must agree with the noun it modifies in both gender (masculine or feminine) and number (singular or plural).

SINGULAR		PLURAL	
un alumno	**una** alumna	**unos** alumnos	**unas** alumnas
un café	**una** clase	**unos** cafés	**unas** clases
un árbol	**una** flor	**unos** árboles	**unas** flores

Contractions

The prepositions **a** *(to, at)* and **de** *(of, from)* contract (combine) with the definite article **el** to form one word, **al** or **del.** There is no contraction with **la, los,** or **las.**

> **Voy al mercado; no vuelvo del mercado.**
> **Es el dinero del empleado, no del cliente.**

A personal

Remember that whenever a person is the direct object of the verb, it must be preceded by **a.** This **a personal** also contracts with **el.**

> **Conozco a Juan.**
> **Pero no conozco al hermano de Juan.**

Nouns and adjectives

Agreement of nouns and adjectives

An adjective is a word that describes a noun. An adjective must agree in gender (masculine or feminine) and number (singular or plural) with the noun it describes or modifies.

Adjectives that end in **-o** have four forms, the same as nouns that end in **-o.**

	SINGULAR	PLURAL
MASCULINE	**el muchacho simpático**	**los muchachos simpáticos**
FEMININE	**la muchacha simpática**	**las muchachas simpáticas**

Adjectives that end in **-e** have only two forms—singular and plural.

	SINGULAR	PLURAL
MASCULINE	**un alumno inteligente**	**los alumnos inteligentes**
FEMININE	**una alumna inteligente**	**las alumnas inteligentes**

Adjectives that end in a consonant have only two forms—singular and plural. Note that the plural ends in **-es.**

	SINGULAR	PLURAL
MASCULINE	**un curso fácil**	**dos cursos fáciles**
FEMININE	**una tarea fácil**	**dos tareas fáciles**

Possessive adjectives

A possessive adjective tells who owns or possesses something—*my* book and *your* pencil. Like other adjectives in Spanish, possessive adjectives agree with the noun they modify. Note that only **nuestro** and *vuestro* have four forms.

MASCULINE SINGULAR	FEMININE SINGULAR	MASCULINE PLURAL	FEMININE PLURAL
mi tío	mi tía	mis tíos	mis tías
tu tío	tu tía	tus tíos	tus tías
su tío	su tía	sus tíos	sus tías
nuestro tío	nuestra tía	nuestros tíos	nuestras tías
vuestro tío	*vuestra tía*	*vuestros tíos*	*vuestras tías*

Note that **su** can refer to many different people, as indicated below.

su familia

la familia de Juan	la familia de él
la familia de María	la familia de ella
la familia de Juan y María	la familia de ellos
la familia de usted	
la familia de ustedes	

Demonstratives

Until recently the demonstrative pronoun had to carry a written accent to differentiate it from a demonstrative adjective. That is no longer the case and the pronouns are the same as the adjectives.

In Spanish there are three demonstrative adjectives: **este** *(this)*, **ese** *(that)*, and **aquel** *(that, farther away)*. Each of the demonstratives has four forms and must agree in gender and number with the noun it modifies.

MASCULINE SINGULAR	FEMININE SINGULAR	MASCULINE PLURAL	FEMININE PLURAL
este libro	esta chaqueta	estos libros	estas chaquetas
ese libro	esa chaqueta	esos libros	esas chaquetas
aquel libro	aquella chaqueta	aquellos libros	aquellas chaquetas

Comparative and superlative

Regular forms

You use the comparative *(more, -er)* and the superlative *(most, -est)* to compare people or things.

To form the comparative in Spanish you use **más** (or **menos**) before the adjective. The comparative is followed by **que: más (menos)… que.**

> **Él es más (menos) inteligente que los otros.**
> **Ella es más ambiciosa que los otros.**

To form the superlative you use the definite article with **más.** Note that **de** follows the superlative: **el (la) más… de.**

> **Él es el más ambicioso de todos.**
> **Ella es la alumna más inteligente de todos.**

Irregular forms

The adjectives **bueno** and **malo** and the adverbs **bien** and **mal** have irregular comparative and superlative forms.

	COMPARATIVE	SUPERLATIVE
bueno	mejor	el/la mejor
malo	peor	el/la peor
bien	mejor	el/la mejor
mal	peor	el/la peor

> **Él es mejor jugador que su hermano.**
> **Pero su hermana Teresa es la mejor jugadora de los tres.**
> **La verdad es que ella juega mejor que nadie.**
> **Ella juega mejor que yo.**

Note that the comparative is followed by the subject pronoun or a negative word.

> **más alto que yo (tú, él, nosotros)**
> **más alto que nadie**

(El) mayor and **(el) menor** are also comparative and superlative forms. They most often refer to age and sometimes size.

> **Mi hermano menor tiene trece años.**
> **Y mi hermana mayor tiene diecisiete.**
> **La Ciudad de México tiene el mayor número de habitantes.**

Pronouns

A pronoun is a word that replaces a noun. Review the forms of the pronouns that you have learned so far.

SUBJECT PRONOUNS	DIRECT OBJECT PRONOUNS	INDIRECT OBJECT PRONOUNS	REFLEXIVE PRONOUNS
yo	me	me	me
tú	te	te	te
Ud., él, ella	lo, la	le	se
nosotros(as)	nos	nos	nos
vosotros(as)	*os*	*os*	*os*
Uds., ellos, ellas	los, las	les	se

Remember that an object pronoun comes right before the verb.

Ella me ve.
Ella nos habla.

The direct object pronoun is the direct receiver of the action of the verb. The indirect object is the indirect receiver of the action of the verb.

The direct object pronouns **lo, la, los, las** can refer to a person or a thing.

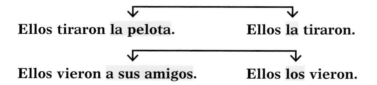

Ellos tiraron la pelota.   **Ellos la tiraron.**

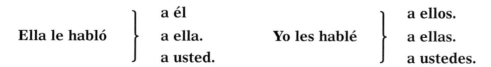

Ellos vieron a sus amigos.   **Ellos los vieron.**

The indirect object pronouns **le, les** refer to people. They are often accompanied by a phrase for clarification.

Ella le habló ⎱ **a él**
⎰ **a ella.**
⎱ **a usted.**

Yo les hablé ⎱ **a ellos.**
⎰ **a ellas.**
⎱ **a ustedes.**

Affirmative and negative expressions

To make a sentence negative, you merely put **no** before the verb or before the object pronoun that precedes the verb.

El gato no está en el jardín.
No lo veo.

Review the following affirmative and negative expressions.

AFFIRMATIVE	NEGATIVE
algo	**nada**
algien	**nadie**
siempre	**nunca**

Nadie está aquí.

Note that in Spanish, unlike in English, more than one negative word can be used in the same sentence.

No ves a nadie.

Ellos nunca hablan a nadie de nada.

The negative of **también** is **tampoco.**

A Juan le gusta. A mí también.

A Juan no le gusta. Ni a mí tampoco.

Verbs such as interesar, aburrir, gustar

In Spanish, the verbs **interesar** and **aburrir** take an indirect object.

La historia me interesa.
Me interesa la historia. } *History interests me.*

Los deportes no les aburren.
No les aburren los deportes. } *Sports don't bore them.*

Gustar functions the same as **interesar** and **aburrir.** It conveys the meaning *to like,* but it literally means *to please.*

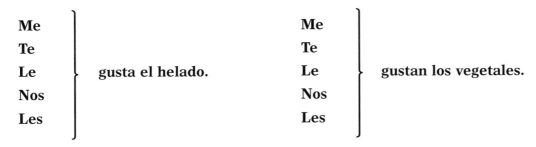

Me		**Me**	
Te		**Te**	
Le	gusta el helado.	**Le**	gustan los vegetales.
Nos		**Nos**	
Les		**Les**	

Ice cream pleases
me, you, him. . . .

Vegetables please
me, you, him. . . .

Expressions with the infinitive

The infinitive is the form of the verb that ends in **-ar, -er,** or **-ir.** The infinitive often follows another verb.

> **Ellos quieren salir.**
> **Yo debo estudiar más.**
> **Me gusta leer.**

Three very common expressions that are followed by the infinitive are:

> **Tener que** *(to have to)*
>> **Tengo que trabajar y estudiar más.**
>
> **Ir a** *(to be going to)*
>> **Y voy a trabajar y estudiar más.**
>
> **Acabar de** *(to have just)*
>> **Acabo de recibir una nota mala.**

You can use the expression **favor de** followed by an infinitive to ask someone in a polite way to do something.

> **Favor de escribir tu nombre.**
> **Favor de ayudarme.**

Note that the object pronoun is added to the end of the infinitive.

Ser and estar

Spanish has two verbs that mean *to be.* They are **ser** and **estar** and each one has distinct uses.

Ser

You use **ser** to express a characteristic, where someone or something is from, or what something is made of.

> **Él es guapo. Es inteligente también.**
> **Ellos son de Nuevo México.**
> **Su casa es de adobe.**

Estar

You use **estar** to express a condition or location.

> **Él está muy cansado y está triste también.**
> **Madrid está en España.**
> **Sus amigos están en Madrid.**

Saber and conocer

Both **saber** and **conocer** mean *to know.*

Saber means to know a fact or to have information about something. With an infinitive it expresses how to do something.

> **Yo sé su número de teléfono.**
> **Sabemos que ella va a viajar.**
> **Todos saben usar el Internet.**

Conocer means *to know* in the sense to be familiar with. It is used with people or complex, abstract concepts.

> **Yo conozco a su amigo, Tadeo.**
> **Ellos conocen bien la historia de España.**

Reflexive verbs

When the subject is both the doer and receiver of the action of the verb, you have to use a reflexive pronoun with the verb. Study the following examples of the reflexive construction.

REFLEXIVE	NONREFLEXIVE
Ella se levanta.	**Ella levanta al niño.**
Él se divierte.	**Él divierte a sus amigos.**
Me cepillo.	**Cepillo a mi perro.**

When the reflexive is followed by an article of clothing or a part of the body, you use a definite article in Spanish. (In English the possessive adjective is used.)

> **Me lavo la cara y las manos.**
> **Ella tiene frío y se pone el suéter.**

Verbs

See the following charts for the verb forms you have learned.

Verb Charts

Regular verbs			
INFINITIVO	hablar *to speak*	comer *to eat*	vivir *to live*
PRESENTE	hablo hablas habla hablamos *habláis* hablan	como comes come comemos *coméis* comen	vivo vives vive vivimos *vivís* viven
PRETÉRITO	hablé hablaste habló hablamos *hablasteis* hablaron	comí comiste comió comimos *comisteis* comieron	viví viviste vivió vivimos *vivisteis* vivieron
PARTICIPIO PRESENTE	hablando	comiendo	viviendo

Stem-changing verbs (-ar and -er verbs)				
INFINITIVO	empezar (e→ie)[1] *to begin*	acostar(se) (o→ue)[2] *to go to bed*	perder (e→ie)[3] *to lose*	volver (o→ue)[4] *to return*
PRESENTE	empiezo empiezas empieza empezamos *empezáis* empiezan	acuesto acuestas acuesta acostamos *acostáis* acuestan	pierdo pierdes pierde perdimos *perdéis* pierden	vuelvo vuelves vuelve volvemos *volvéis* vuelven

Stem-changing verbs (-ir verbs)		
INFINITIVO	preferir (e→ie) *to prefer*	dormir (o→ue)[5] *to sleep*
PRESENTE	prefiero prefieres prefiere preferimos *preferís* prefieren	duermo duermes duerme dormimos *dormís* duermen

[1]**Comenzar, sentar, pensar** are similar. [2]**Costar** and **jugar (u→ue)** are similar. [3]**Querer** and **entender** are similar. [4]**Poder** is similar. [5]**Morir** is similar.

Irregular verbs

The following are the verbs you have already learned that are either irregular or have a spelling change.

	conocer *to know, to be familiar with*					
PRESENTE	conozco	conoces	conoce	conocemos	*conocéis*	conocen

	dar *to give*					
PRESENTE	doy	das	da	damos	*dais*	dan
PRETÉRITO	di	diste	dio	dimos	*disteis*	dieron

	estar *to be*					
PRESENTE	estoy	estás	está	estamos	*estáis*	están

	hacer *to do, to make*					
PRESENTE	hago	haces	hace	hacemos	*hacéis*	hacen

	ir *to go*					
PRESENTE	voy	vas	va	vamos	*vais*	van
PRETÉRITO	fui	fuiste	fue	fuimos	*fuisteis*	fueron

	leer *to read*					
PRETÉRITO	leí	leíste	leyó	leímos	*leísteis*	leyeron

	oír *to hear*					
PRESENTE	oigo	oyes	oye	oímos	*oís*	oyen
PRETÉRITO	oí	oíste	oyó	oímos	*oísteis*	oyeron

	poner *to put*					
PRESENTE	pongo	pones	pone	ponemos	*ponéis*	ponen

	saber *to know (how)*					
PRESENTE	sé	sabes	sabe	sabemos	*sabéis*	saben

	salir *to leave, to go out*					
PRESENTE	salgo	sales	sale	salimos	*salís*	salen

	ser *to be*					
PRESENTE	soy	eres	es	somos	*sois*	son
PRETÉRITO	fui	fuiste	fue	fuimos	*fuisteis*	fueron

	tener *to have*					
PRESENTE	tengo	tienes	tiene	tenemos	*tenéis*	tienen

	traer *to bring*					
PRESENTE	traigo	traes	trae	traemos	*traéis*	traen

	venir *to come*					
PRESENTE	vengo	vienes	viene	venimos	*venís*	vienen

	ver *to see*					
PRESENTE	veo	ves	ve	vemos	*veis*	ven
PRETÉRITO	vi	viste	vio	vimos	*visteis*	vieron

Spanish-English Dictionary

*The Spanish-English Dictionary contains all productive and some receptive vocabulary from the text. The numbers following each productive entry indicate the chapter and vocabulary section in which the word is introduced. For example, **3.2** means that the word was taught in **Capítulo 3, Vocabulario 2**. LP refers to the **Lecciones preliminares**. If there is no number following an entry, this means that the word or expression is there for receptive purposes only.*

A

a at
  a eso de las tres (cuatro, diez, etc.) at around three (four, ten, etc.) o'clock
  a la una (a las dos, a las tres) at one o'clock (two o'clock, three o'clock), **LP**
  ¡A propósito! By the way!, **8.2**
  ¿a qué hora? at what time?, **LP**
  a veces at times, sometimes, **6.1**
  abajo: (ir) para abajo (to go) down
  abordar to board, **10.2**
  abordo aboard, **10.2**
  abreviado(a) abbreviated, shortened
el **abrigo** coat
  abril April, **LP**
  abrir to open, **4.2**
  abrochado(a) fastened, **10.2**
la **abuela** grandmother, **2.1**
el **abuelo** grandfather, **2.1**
los **abuelos** grandparents, **2.1**
  abundoso(a) abundant
  aburrido(a) boring, **1.2**
  aburrir to bore, **5.2**
  acá here
  acabar de to have just (done something), **4.2**
la **academia** school
el **aceite** oil
la **aceituna** olive, **4.2**
el **acento** accent
  acompañado(a) de accompanied by
  acordarse (ue) to remember
  ¿Te acuerdas? Do you remember?
  acostarse (ue) to go to bed, **11.1**
la **actividad** activity

actual present-day, current
actuar to act, take action
acuerdo: estar de acuerdo con to agree with
adelante ahead
  ir hacia adelante to move forward, ahead
además furthermore, what's more; besides
  además de in addition to
¡Adiós! Good-bye., **LP**
adivinar to guess
¿adónde? (to) where?, **3.2**
el **aeropuerto** airport, **10.1**
el/la **aficionado(a)** fan, **5.1**
afine: la palabra afine cognate
las **afueras** suburbs, **2.2**
el/la **agente** agent, **10.1**
agosto August, **LP**
agradable pleasant, friendly, agreeable
agresivo(a) aggressive
el **agua** (*f.*) water, **4.1**
  el agua mineral (con gas) (sparkling) mineral water, **4.2**
ahora now
el **aire** air
  al aire libre open-air, outdoor
aislado(a) isolated
la **alberca** swimming pool, **7.1**
el **albergue juvenil** youth hostel
la **albóndiga** meatball, **4.2**
el **álbum** album
alcanzar to reach
la **alcoba** bedroom, **2.2**
la **aldea** small village
alegre happy, **6.1**
la **alegría** happiness, joy
alemán(ana) German
los **alemanes** Germans
algo something, **4.1**; anything, **9.2**
  ¿Algo más? Anything else?, **9.2**
alguien someone, somebody, **8.2**

algunos(as) some
allá over there, **9.1**
allí there
el **alma** (*f.*) soul
el **almuerzo** lunch, **4.1**
  tomar el almuerzo to have lunch, **4.1**
alpino: el esquí alpino downhill skiing, **7.2**
alquilar to rent, **7.1**
alrededor de around, **2.2**
los **alrededores** surroundings
altivo(a) arrogant
alto(a) tall, **1.1**; high, **3.1**
la **altura** altitude
el/la **alumno(a)** student, **1.2**
amarillo(a) yellow, **5.1**
la **ambición** ambition
ambicioso(a) hard-working, **1.2**
el **ambiente** atmosphere, environment
la **América del Sur** South America
americano(a) American
el/la **amigo(a)** friend, **1.1**
  el amigo falso false cognate, **2.1**
el **amor** love
amurallado(a) walled
anaranjado(a) orange (*color*), **5.1**
ancho(a) wide
andino(a) Andean, of the Andes
la **angustia** distress, anguish
animado(a) lively
el **animal** animal
anoche last night, **7.1**
anónimo(a) anonymous
el **anorak** anorak, ski jacket, **7.2**
los **anteojos de sol** sunglasses, **7.1**
antes de before, **10.1**
los **antibióticos** antibiotics
antiguo(a) ancient, old
antipático(a) unpleasant, not nice **1.1**
los **antojitos** snacks, nibbles, **4.2**

anunciar to announce

el **anuncio** announcement

el **año** year, **LP**

    el año pasado last year, **7.1**

    ¿Cuántos años tiene? How old is he (she)?, **2.1**

    cumplir... años to be (turn) . . . years old

la **apariencia** appearance, looks

    ¿Qué apariencia tiene? What does he (she) look like?

el **apartamento** apartment, **2.2**

el **apartamiento** apartment, **2.2**

apetecer to feel like, to crave

aplaudir to applaud, to clap, **5.1**

el **aplauso** applause, **5.1**

    recibir aplausos to be applauded, **5.1**

apreciado(a) appreciated, liked

aprender to learn, **4.2**

aproximadamente approximately

aquel(la) that, **9.1**

aquí here, **9.1**

aragonés(esa) from Aragon (*Spain*)

el **árbol** tree, **2.2**

la **arena** sand, **7.1**

argentino(a) Argentine

árido(a) dry, arid

la **aritmética** arithmetic

armar to put up (a tent), **11.2**

la **arqueología** archeology

el **arroz** rice, **4.1**

el **arte** art, **1.2**

la **artesanía** crafts, **9.2**

el/la **artista** artist

la **ascendencia** heritage, background

así thus, so

el **asiento** seat, **10.1**

    el número del asiento seat number, **10.1**

el/la **asistente de vuelo** flight attendant, **10.2**

asistir (a) to attend, **8.1**

astuto(a) astute, smart

la **atención** attention

    ¡Atención! Careful!

    prestar atención to pay attention, **3.1**

el **aterrizaje** landing, **10.2**

aterrizar to land, **10.2**

el/la **atleta** athlete

atrapar to catch, **5.2**

el **atributo** attribute, positive feature

el **atún** tuna, **9.2**

aun even

aún still

ausente absent

auténtico(a) authentic, real

automático(a) automatic, **10.2**

    el distribuidor automático boarding pass kiosk, automatic dispenser, **10.2**

el **autobús** bus, **8.1**

    perder el autobús to miss the bus, **8.1**

la **autopista** highway

el/la **autor(a)** author

avanzado(a) difficult, **7.2;** advanced

la **avenida** avenue

la **aventura** adventure

el **avión** plane, **10.1**

la **avioneta** small plane

ayer yesterday, **7.1**

    ayer por la tarde yesterday afternoon, **7.1**

la **ayuda** help, assistance

ayudar to help, **10.1**

azul blue, **2.1**

el **azulejo** glazed tile, floor tile

B

el **bacón** bacon, **4.1**

el/la **bailador(a)** dancer

bailar to dance

bajar to go down, **7.2**

bajo(a) short, **1.1;** low, **3.1**

el **balcón** balcony

el **balneario** seaside resort, beach resort, **7.1**

el **balón** ball, **5.1**

el **baloncesto** basketball, **5.2**

la **banda** band, **8.1**

la **bandera** flag

el **bañador** swimsuit, **7.1**

bañarse to take a bath, to bathe oneself

el **baño** bath

    el cuarto de baño bathroom, **2.2**

barato(a) inexpensive, cheap, **9.1**

    Todo te sale más barato. It's all a lot cheaper (less expensive)., **9.1**

la **barbacoa** barbecue

¡Bárbaro! Great!, Awesome!, **5.2**

el **barquito** small boat, **7.1**

la **barra** bar (of soap), **11.2**

el **barrio** neighborhood, area

la **base** base, **5.2**

el **básquetbol** basketball, **5.2**

la **cancha de básquetbol** basketball court, **5.2**

bastante rather, quite, **1.2**

el **bastón** ski pole, **7.2**

la **batalla** battle

el **bate** bat, **5.2**

el/la **bateador(a)** batter, **5.2**

    batear to hit, to bat, **5.2**

    batear un jonrón to hit a home run

el **batido** shake, smoothie, **4.2**

el **baúl** trunk (*of a car*), **10.1**

beber to drink, **4.1**

la **bebida** beverage, drink, **4.1**

el **béisbol** baseball, **5.2**

    el/la beisbolista baseball player, **5.2**

    el campo de béisbol baseball field, **5.2**

la **belleza** beauty

bello(a) beautiful

la **bicicleta** bicycle, **2.2**

bien well, fine, **LP**

    bien educado(a) polite, well-mannered, **6.1**

    estar bien to be well, fine, **6.1**

    Muy bien. Very well., **LP**

bienvenido(a) welcome

el **bife** beef

el **biftec** steak, **4.1**

el **billete** ticket, **10.1**

    el billete electrónico e-ticket, **10.1**

la **biología** biology

el/la **biólogo(a)** biologist

el **bizcocho** cake

blanco(a) white, **5.1**

bloquear to block, **5.1**

el **blue jean** jeans, **9.1**

la **blusa** blouse, **3.1**

la **boca** mouth, **6.2**

el **bocadillo** sandwich, **4.1**

los **bocaditos** snacks

la **bodega** grocery store

la **boletería** ticket window, **7.2**

el **boleto** ticket, **7.2**

    el boleto electrónico e-ticket, **10.1**

el **bolígrafo** pen, **3.1**

el **bolívar** bolivar (*currency of Venezuela*)

la **bolsa de dormir** sleeping bag, **11.2**

la **bombilla** (*drinking*) container

Spanish-English Dictionary

Spanish-English Dictionary

bonito(a) pretty, **1.1**
el **bosque** woods
la **bota** boot, **7.2**
el **bote** can, **9.2**
la **botella** bottle, **9.2**
bravo(a) rough, stormy
el **brazo** arm, **11.1**
bronce bronze, **8.2**
bucear to go snorkeling, **7.1;** to scuba dive
el **buceo** snorkeling, **7.1;** scuba diving
bueno(a) good, **1.1**
  Buenas noches. Good evening., **LP**
  Buenas tardes. Good afternoon., **LP**
  Buenos días. Good morning., **LP**
  Hace buen tiempo. The weather is nice., **LP**
  sacar notas buenas to get good grades, **3.1**
el **burrito** burrito
el **bus** bus
  el bus escolar school bus, **3.2**
  perder el bus to miss the bus, **8.1**
  tomar el bus to take the bus
buscar to look for, to seek, **3.2**

C

el **caballero** gentleman
  el caballero andante knight errant
el **caballo** horse
la **cabeza** head, **6.2**
  tener dolor de cabeza to have a headache, **6.2**
la **cabina de mando** cockpit *(airplane)*
el **cacahuate** peanut, **8.1**
el **cacahuete** peanut
el **cacique** leader, chief
cada each, every, **2.2**
caer to fall
la **caja** cash register, **3.2**
el **café** café, **3.1;** coffee, **4.1**
la **cafetería** cafeteria, **4.1**
la **caída** drop
los **calcetines** socks, **5.1**
la **calculadora** calculator, **3.1**
caliente hot, **4.1**
  el chocolate caliente hot chocolate, **4.1**

la **calle** street
calmo(a) calm, **6.1**
el **calor** heat
  Hace calor. It's hot., **LP**
  tener calor to be hot, **11.1**
calzar to wear, to take (shoe size), **9.1**
  ¿Qué número calzas? What size shoe do you wear (take)?, **9.1**
la **cama** bed, **2.2**
  guardar cama to stay in bed *(illness)*, **6.2**
  quedarse en la cama to stay in bed, **11.1**
la **cámara digital** digital camera, **7.1**
el/la **camarero(a)** waiter (waitress), server
los **camarones** shrimp, **4.2**
cambiar to change
la **caminata: dar una caminata** to take a hike, **11.2**
el **camino** road
  tomar el camino to set out for
la **camisa** shirt, **3.1**
  la camisa de manga corta (larga) short-sleeved (long-sleeved) shirt, **9.1**
la **camiseta** T-shirt, **5.1**
el/la **campeón(ona)** champion
el/la **campesino(a)** farmer, peasant
el **camping** camping, **11.2;** campsite
  ir de camping to go camping, **11.2**
el **campo** field, **5.1;** country, countryside
  el campo de béisbol baseball field, **5.2**
  el campo de fútbol soccer field, **5.1**
la **canasta** basket, **5.2**
la **cancha** court, **5.2**
  la cancha de básquetbol (tenis) basketball (tennis) court, **5.2**
  la cancha de voleibol volleyball court, **7.2**
la **canción** song
el **cangrejo de río** crayfish
cansado(a) tired, **6.1**
el/la **cantante** singer, **8.1**
cantar to sing, **8.1**
la **cantidad** quantity, amount
la **cantina** cafeteria

la **capital** capital
la **cara** face, **6.1**
la **característica** feature, trait
cargado(a) thrown (over one's shoulders)
caribe Caribbean
  el mar Caribe Caribbean Sea
cariñoso(a) adorable, affectionate, **2.1**
la **carne** meat, **4.1**
el **carnet de identidad** ID card, **10.2**
caro(a) expensive, **9.1**
la **carpa** tent, **11.2**
  armar (montar) una carpa to put up a tent, **11.2**
la **carpeta** folder, **3.1**
la **carrera** career
el **carrito** shopping cart, **9.2**
el **carro** car, **2.2**
la **carta** letter
la **casa** house, **2.2**
  en casa at home
  regresar a casa to go home, **3.2**
  la casa de apartamentos apartment building, **2.2**
casarse to get married
el **casco** helmet, **7.2**
  el casco antiguo old (part of) town
casi almost, practically, **8.2**
el **caso** case
castaño(a) brown, chestnut *(eyes, hair)*, **2.1**
catarro: tener catarro to have a cold, **6.2**
el/la **cátcher** catcher, **5.2**
catorce fourteen, **LP**
cautivar to captivate, to charm
el **CD** CD
la **cebolla** onion, **9.2**
celebrar to celebrate
la **cena** dinner, **4.1**
cenar to have dinner, **4.1**
el **cenote** natural water well
el **centro comercial** shopping center, mall, **9.1**
cepillarse to brush, **11.1**
el **cepillo** brush, **11.2**
  el cepillo de dientes toothbrush, **11.2**
las **cerámicas** ceramics, **9.2**
cerca (de) near, **3.2**
el **cereal** cereal, **4.1**

cero zero, LP

el cesto basket, **5.2**

el champú shampoo, **11.2**

¡Chao! Good-bye!, Bye!, LP

la chaqueta jacket, **9.1**

la chaqueta de esquí ski jacket, anorak, **7.2**

chileno(a) Chilean

el chiringuito refreshment stand

el chisme rumor, gossip

el chocolate chocolate, **4.1**

el chocolate caliente hot chocolate, **4.1**

el churro *(type of)* doughnut

ciego(a) blind

el/la ciego(a) blind man (woman)

el cielo sky

cien(to) one hundred, LP

la ciencia science, **1.2**

cierto(a) true, certain

cinco five, LP

cincuenta fifty, LP

el cine movie theater, movies, **8.2**

ir al cine to go to the movies, **8.2**

el cinturón de seguridad seat belt, **10.2**

la ciudad city, **2.2**

la civilización civilization

claro(a) clear

claro que of course

la clase class, **1.2**

el/la cliente customer, **9.2**

el clima climate

el coche car

la cocina kitchen, **2.2**; cooking, cuisine

el codo elbow, **11.1**

la cola cola (soda), **4.1**; line *(of people)*, **10.2**

hacer cola to wait in line, **10.2**

el colegio secondary school

la colocación placement

colocar to place, to put

colombiano(a) Colombian

colonial colonial

el color color, **5.1**

de color marrón brown, **5.1**

el comedor dining room, **2.2**

comenzar (ie) to begin, **5.2**

comer to eat, **4.1**

dar de comer a to feed

cómico(a) funny, comical, **1.1**

la comida meal, **4.1**; food

como like, as

¿cómo? how?, **1.1**

¿Cómo es él? What's he like? What does he look like?, **1.1**

¡Cómo no! Sure! Of course!

el/la compañero(a) companion

comparar to compare

el compartimiento superior overhead bin, **10.2**

compartir to share

completar to complete, to fill in

el comportamiento behavior, conduct, **6.1**

la composición composition

la compra purchase, **9.2**

el/la comprador(a) shopper, customer

comprar to buy, **3.2**

compras: ir de compras to shop, to go shopping, **9.1**

comprender to understand, **4.2**

la computadora computer, **3.2**

con with

con frecuencia often

el concierto concert, **8.1**

el condominio condominium

la conducta conduct, behavior, **6.1**

tener buena conducta to be well-behaved, **6.1**

conectado(a) on-line, connected

la conexión connection

conforme: estar conforme to agree, be in agreement

confortar to soothe

congelado(a) frozen, **9.2**

el conjunto band, musical group, **8.1**

conocer to know, to be familiar with, **9.1**; to meet

conocido(a) known

consecuencia: por consecuencia as a result, consequently

el/la consejero(a) counselor

considerar to consider

consiguiente: por consiguiente consequently

la consonante consonant

la consulta doctor's office, **6.2**

consultar to consult

el consultorio doctor's office, **6.2**

contagioso(a) contagious

contar (ue) to tell, to count

contemporéneo(a) contemporary

contento(a) happy, **6.1**

contestar to answer, **3.1**

el continente continent

contra against

contrario(a) opposite; opposing

al contrario on the contrary

el equipo contrario opposing team, **7.1**

contrastar to contrast

el control de seguridad security (checkpoint), **10.2**

pasar por el control de seguridad to go through security, **10.2**

la conversación conversation

conversar to converse

la copa: la Copa Mundial World Cup

el corazón heart

la corbata tie, **9.1**

el correo electrónico e-mail, **3.2**

correr to run, **5.2**

la cortesía courtesy

corto(a) short, **5.1**

el pantalón corto shorts, **5.1**

la cosa thing, **3.1**

la costa coast

costar (ue) to cost, **9.1**

¿Cuánto cuesta? How much does it cost?, **3.2**

costarricense Costa Rican

la costumbre custom

crear to create

creer to believe, to think

creo que sí (que no) I (don't) think so, **4.2**

la crema dental toothpaste, **11.2**

la crema solar suntan lotion, **7.1**

el/la criado(a) housekeeper

criticar to criticize

crudo(a) raw, **8.1**

los vegetales crudos raw vegetables, crudités, **8.1**

el cuaderno notebook, **3.1**

el cuadro painting, **8.2**

¿cuál? which? what?

¿Cuál es la fecha de hoy? What is today's date?, LP

cualquier(a) any

cualquier otro(a) any other

cuando when, **3.1**

¿cuándo? when?, **3.2**

¿cuánto? how much?

¿A cuánto está(n)... ? How much is (are) . . . ?, **9.2**

¿Cuánto es? How much is it (does it cost)?, LP

¿cuántos(as)? how much? how many?, **2.1**

Spanish-English Dictionary

¿Cuántos años tiene? How old is he (she)?, **2.1**

cuarenta forty, **LP**

el **cuarto** room, **2.2;** quarter

  el cuarto de baño bathroom, **2.2**

  el cuarto de dormir bedroom, **2.2**

  y cuarto a quarter-past (the hour), **LP**

cuatro four, **LP**

cuatrocientos(as) four hundred, **9.2**

cubano(a) Cuban

cubanoamericano(a) Cuban American

cubierto(a) covered; indoor

la **cuenca** basin *(river)*

la **cuenta** check *(restaurant)*, **4.2;** account

  por su cuenta on its own

  tomar en cuenta to take into account

el **cuerdo** string

el **cuerpo** body, **11.1**

la **culpa** blame, guilt

la **cultura** culture

el **cumpleaños** birthday, **8.1**

cumplir... años to be (turn) . . . years old

cumplir un sueño to fulfill a wish, make a wish come true

el **curso** class, course, **1.2**

D

dar to give, **3.1**

  dar de comer a to feed

  dar un examen (una prueba) to give a test, **3.1**

  dar una caminata to take a hike, **11.2**

  dar una fiesta to throw a party, **8.1**

los **datos** data, facts

de of, from

  ¿de dónde? from where?, **1.1**

  De nada. You're welcome., **LP**

  ¿de qué nacionalidad? what nationality?, **1.1**

  No hay de qué. You're welcome., **LP**

debajo de below, underneath, **10.2**

deber to have to, must, **4.2**

decidir to decide

la **decisión** decision

  tomar una decisión to make a decision

dedicado(a) devoted

el **dedo** finger, **11.1**

  el dedo del pie toe

el **defecto** defect

definido(a) definite

dejar to leave (something)

delante de in front of, **2.2**

demás (the) rest

demasiado too *(adv.)*, too much

la **demora** delay, **10.2**

dental: la crema dental toothpaste, **11.2**

dentífrica: la pasta dentífrica toothpaste

dentro de within

  dentro de poco shortly thereafter, **10.2**

el **departamento** apartment, **2.2**

  el departamento de orientación guidance office

el/la **dependiente** salesperson, employee, **9.1**

el **deporte** sport, **5.1**

  el deporte de equipo team sport

  el deporte individual individual sport

deportivo(a) *(related to)* sports

deprimido(a) sad, depressed, **6.1**

derecho(a) right, **11.1**

desafortunadamente unfortunately

desagradable unpleasant, not nice

el **desastre** disaster

desastroso(a) disastrous, catastrophic

el **desayuno** breakfast, **4.1**

  tomar el desayuno to have breakfast, **4.1**

desconsolado(a) very sad

describir to describe

la **descripción** description

desde since; from

desear to want, to wish, **4.2**

  ¿Qué desean tomar? What would you like (to eat)?, **4.2**

desembarcar to deplane, disembark

el **deseo** wish, desire

desesperado(a) desperate

el **desfile** parade

el **desierto** desert

despegar to take off *(plane)*, **10.2**

el **despegue** takeoff *(plane)*, **10.2**

despertarse (ie) to wake up, **11.1**

después (de) after, **3.1**

destino: con destino a (going) to; for, **10.2**

detrás de in back of, behind, **2.2**

devolver (ue) to return (something), **5.2**

el **día** day

  Buenos días. Good morning., **LP**

  ¿Qué día es hoy? What day is it today?, **LP**

el **diablo** devil

el **diagnóstico** diagnosis

diaria: la rutina diaria daily routine, **11.1**

el **dibujo** drawing, illustration

diciembre December, **LP**

el **dictado** dictation

diecinueve nineteen, **LP**

dieciocho eighteen, **LP**

dieciséis sixteen, **LP**

diecisiete seventeen, **LP**

los **dientes** teeth, **11.1**

  cepillarse (lavarse) los dientes to brush one's teeth, **11.1**

diez ten, **LP**

  de diez en diez by tens

la **diferencia** difference

diferente different

difícil difficult, **1.2**

la **dificultad** difficulty

  sin dificultad easily

dinámico(a) dynamic, **6.1**

el **dinero** money, **3.2**

la **dirección** address; direction

disfrutar (de) to enjoy

disponible available

el **distribuidor automático** boarding pass kiosk, automatic dispenser, **10.1**

el **distrito** district, area, section

divertido(a) fun, amusing

divertir (ie) to amuse, **11.2**

divertirse (ie) to have a good time, to have fun, **11.2**

divino(a) divine, heavenly

dobles doubles *(tennis)*, **5.1**

doce twelve, **LP**

el **dólar** dollar

doler (ue) to ache, hurt, **6.2**
    Me duele(n)... My . . .
      ache(s)., **6.2**

el **dolor** pain, ache, **6.2**
    tener dolor de cabeza to
      have a headache, **6.2**
    tener dolor de estómago
      to have a stomachache, **6.2**
    tener dolor de garganta to
      have a sore throat, **6.2**

domesticado(a) domesticated

el **domingo** Sunday, **LP**

dominicano(a) Dominican
    la República Dominicana
      Dominican Republic

¿dónde? where?, **1.1**
    ¿de dónde? from where?, **1.1**

dormir (ue) to sleep, **5.2**
    el cuarto de dormir
      bedroom, **2.2**
    el saco de dormir sleeping
      bag, **11.2**
    la bolsa de dormir sleeping
      bag, **11.2**

dormirse (ue) to fall asleep,
    11.1

el **dormitorio** bedroom

dos two

doscientos(as) two hundred,
    9.2

driblar to dribble, **5.2**

la **ducha** shower, **11.1**
    tomar una ducha to take a
      shower, **11.1**

la **duda** doubt

el **dulce** sweet

durante during, **3.2**

durar to last

duro(a) hard, difficult, **1.2**

el **DVD** DVD, **3.2**

E

económico(a) inexpensive

ecuatoriano(a) Ecuadoran, **1.1**

la **edad** age

el **edificio** building, **2.2**

la **educación** education
    la educación física physical
      education, **1.2**

educado(a) mannered
    estar bien (mal)
      educado(a) to be polite
      (rude), **6.1**

egoísta selfish, egotistical

el **ejemplo** example
    por ejemplo for example

el **el** the

él he

electrónico electronic, **10.1**
    el boleto (billete)
      electrónico e-ticket, **10.1**
    el correo electrónico e-mail,
      3.2

elemental elementary

ella she

ellos(as) they

el **e-mail** e-mail

el **embarcar** to board, **10.2**

el **embarque** boarding, **10.2**
    la hora de embarque
      boarding time, **10.1**

emocionante moving;
    exciting

la **empanada** meat pie, **4.2**

empezar (ie) to begin, **5.1**

el/la **empleado(a)** salesperson,
    employee, **3.2**

empujar to push

en in
    en casa at home

enamorado(a) de in love with

encantar to love, adore

encerrar (ie) to enclose

la **enchilada** enchilada

encima: por encima de above,
    over, **5.2**

encontrar (ue) to find,
    encounter

encontrarse (ue) to be found

la **encuesta** survey

energético(a) energetic, **6.1**

la **energía** energy, **6.1**

enero January, **LP**
    el primero de enero
      January 1, **LP**

enfadado(a) angry, mad, **6.1**

enfadar to make angry, annoy,
    6.1

el/la **enfermero(a)** nurse, **6.2**

enfermo(a) ill, sick, **6.1**

el/la **enfermo(a)** sick person

enlazar to connect

enojado(a) angry, mad,
    annoyed, **6.1**

enojar to make angry, annoy,
    6.1

enorme enormous

la **ensalada** salad, **4.1**

enseguida right away, **4.2**

enseñar to teach, **3.1**

entender (ie) to understand, **8.2**

entero(a) entire, whole

enterrar (ie) to bury

la **entrada** ticket, **8.1**

entrar to enter, to go into, **5.1**

entre between, among

el/la **entrenador(a)** coach,
    manager

entusiasmado(a)
    enthusiastic

el **entusiasmo** enthusiasm, **6.1**

enviar to send, **3.2**

la **época** times, period

el **equipaje** luggage, baggage, **10.1**
    el equipaje de mano hand
      luggage, carry-on bags, **10.2**

el **equipo** team, **5.1**; equipment
    el deporte de equipo team
      sport

el **escaparate** store window, **9.1**

la **escena** scene

escoger to choose

escolar *(related to)* school
    el bus escolar school bus, **3.2**
    los materiales escolares
      school supplies, **3.1**

escribir to write, **4.2**

escrito(a) written

escuchar to listen (to), **3.2**

la **escuela** school, **1.2**
    la escuela primaria
      elementary school
    la escuela secundaria
      secondary school, high
      school, **1.2**

el/la **escultor(a)** sculptor

ese(a) that, that one

eso: a eso de at about *(time)*
    por eso for this reason,
      that is why

la **espalda** back, **11.1**

España Spain

el/la **español(a)** Spaniard, *adj.*
    Spanish

el **español** Spanish *(language)* **1.2**

la **especia** spice

especialmente especially

el **espectáculo** show, spectacle

el/la **espectador(a)** spectator

el **espejo** mirror, **11.1**

esperar to wait (for) **10.2**

la **esplendidez** splendor

espontáneo(a) spontaneous

la **esposa** wife, **2.1**

el **esposo** husband, **2.1**

el **esquí** ski; skiing, **7.2**
    el esquí acuático
      waterskiing, **7.1**
    el esquí alpino downhill
      skiing
    el esquí nórdico cross-
      country skiing

el/la **esquiador(a)** skier, **7.2**

esquiar to ski, **7.2**
    esquiar en el agua
      to water-ski, **7.1**

Spanish-English Dictionary

establecer to establish

la **estación** season, **LP**

  ¿Qué estación es? What season is it?, **LP**

la **estación de esquí** ski resort, **7.2**

el **estadio** stadium

Estados Unidos United States

estar to be, **3.1**

la **estatua** statue, **8.2**

este(a) this, this one, **9.1**

el **este** east

estereofónico(a) stereo

estirarse to stretch, **11.1**

el **estómago** stomach, **6.2**

  el dolor de estómago stomachache, **6.2**

estrecho(a) narrow

el **estrés** stress, **6.2**

el/la **estudiante** student

estudiar to study, **3.1**

el **estudio** study

  los estudios sociales social studies, **1.2**

estupendo(a) terrific, stupendous

la **etnia** ethnicity, ethnic group

el **euro** euro *(currency of most of the countries of the European Union)*

el **evento** event

el **examen** test, exam, **3.1**

  el examen físico physical, **6.2**

examinar to examine, **6.2**

excelente excellent

la **excepción** exception

la **excursión** excursion, outing

el/la **excursionista** hiker

existir exist

el **éxito** success, **6.1**

  tener éxito to succeed, be successful, **6.1**

exótico(a) exotic

el/la **experto(a)** expert

explicar to explain

el/la **explorador(a)** explorer

la **exposición de arte** art show, exhibition, **8.2**

la **expresión** expression

extranjero(a) foreign

extraordinario(a) extraordinary

fabuloso(a) fabulous

fácil easy, **1.2**

facturar el equipaje to check luggage, **10.1**

la **falda** skirt, **3.1**

falso(a) false

faltar to be lacking, not to have, **6.1**

  Le falta paciencia. He (She) has no patience., **6.1**

la **familia** family, **2.1**

familiar *(related to the)* family

los **familiares** family members

famoso(a) famous

la **fantasía** fantasy

fantástico(a) fantastic

el/la **farmacéutico(a)** pharmacist

la **farmacia** pharmacy, drugstore, **6.2**

el **favor** favor

  Favor de (+ infinitive). Please (do something)., **11.2**

  por favor please, **LP**

favorito(a) favorite

febrero February, **LP**

la **fecha** date, **LP**

  ¿Cuál es la fecha de hoy? What is today's date?, **LP**

feliz happy

feo(a) unattractive, ugly, **1.1**

la **fiebre** fever, **6.2**

  tener fiebre to have a fever, **6.2**

la **fiesta** party, **8.1**; holiday

  dar una fiesta to throw a party, **8.1**

la **fila** line *(of people)*

  estar en fila to wait in line

el **film** film, movie

el **filme** film, movie, **8.2**

el **fin** end

  el fin de semana weekend, **7.1**

  por fin finally

final: al final de at the end of

fingir to pretend

físico(a) physical

  la apariencia física physical appearance, looks

  la educación física physical education, **1.2**

flaco(a) thin

el **flan** flan, custard, **4.1**

la **flauta** flute

la **flecha** arrow

flexible open-minded, flexible, **6.1**

la **flor** flower, **2.2**

la **fogata** bonfire, campfire

la **forma** form, piece, **10.2**

  la forma de identidad piece of ID, **10.2**

formar to form, to put together

la **foto** photo, **7.1**

el **francés** French *(language)*, **1.2**

el **franciscano** Franciscan

el **frasco** jar, **9.2**

la **frase** sentence

frecuencia: con frecuencia often, frequently

fresco(a) cool, **LP**

  Hace fresco. It's cool *(weather).*, **LP**

los **frijoles** beans, **4.1**

frío(a) cold, **4.2**

  Hace frío. It's cold *(weather).*, **LP**

  tener frío to be cold, **11.1**

el **frío** cold

frito(a) fried

  las patatas (papas) fritas french fries, **4.1**

la **frontera** border

la **fruta** fruit, **9.2**

  el puesto de frutas fruit stand, **9.2**

la **frutería** fruit stand, **9.2**

la **fuente** fountain

fuera de outside

fuerte strong; substantial

el **fútbol** soccer, **5.1**

  el campo de fútbol soccer field, **5.1**

  el fútbol americano football

el/la **futbolista** soccer (football) player

las **gafas para el sol** sunglasses, **7.1**

el **galán** elegant man, heartthrob

gallardo(a) brave, dashing

las **galletas** crackers, **8.1**

la **gamba** shrimp, prawn

ganar to win, **5.1**; to earn

el **garaje** garage, **2.2**

la **garganta** throat, **6.2**

  el dolor de garganta sore throat, **6.2**

el **gas: el agua mineral con gas** carbonated (sparkling) mineral water, **4.1** la **gaseosa** soda, carbonated drink, **4.1**

gastar to spend, to waste

el/la **gato(a)** cat, **2.1**

el/la **gemelo(a)** twin, **2.1**

general general

  en general in general

  por lo general generally speaking, as a rule

la **gente** people, **9.1**

la **geografía** geography

el **gimnasio** gym(nasium)

la **gitanilla** little gypsy

el **gobierno** government

el **gol** goal, **5.1**

  meter un gol to score a goal, **5.1**

golpear to hit *(a ball)*, **5.2**

gordo(a) fat

el **gorro** ski hat, **7.2**

gozar de to enjoy

Gracias. Thank you., **LP**

  dar gracias a to thank

gracioso(a) funny, **1.1**

gran, grande big, large, **1.2**

grave serious

gris gray, **5.1**

gritar to yell

el **grupo** group, **8.1**

la **guagua** bus

el **guante** glove, **5.2**

guapo(a) attractive, good-looking, **1.1**

guardar to guard, **5.1**

  guardar cama to stay in bed *(illness)*, **6.2**

la **guardería** shelter

guatemalteco(a) Guatemalan

la **guerra** war

el **guerrero** warrior

el/la **guía** guide

la **guía** guidebook

el **guisante** pea, **9.2**

la **guitarra** guitar

gustar to like, to be pleasing to, **5.1**

el **gusto** pleasure; like; taste

  Mucho gusto. Nice (It's a pleasure) to meet you.

la **habitación** bedroom

el/la **habitante** inhabitant

hablar to speak, to talk, **3.1**

  hablar por teléfono to talk on the phone

  hablar en el móvil to talk on the cell phone

¿Hablas en serio? Are you serious?

hacer to do, to make, **10.2**

  Hace buen tiempo. The weather is nice., **LP**

  Hace (mucho) calor. It's (very) hot *(weather)*., **LP**

  Hace fresco. It's cool *(weather)*., **LP**

  Hace frío. It's cold *(weather)*., **LP**

  Hace mal tiempo. The weather is bad., **LP**

  Hace sol. It's sunny., **LP**

  Hace viento. It's windy., **LP**

  hacer cola to wait in line, **10.2**

  hacer la maleta to pack, **10.1**

  hacer un viaje to take a trip, **10.1**

el **hambre** *(f.)* hunger

  tener hambre to be hungry, **4.1**

la **hamburguesa** hamburger, **4.1**

la **harina** flour

hasta until; up to; as far as

  ¡Hasta luego! See you later!, **LP**

  ¡Hasta mañana! See you tomorrow!, **LP**

  ¡Hasta pronto! See you soon!, **LP**

hay there is, there are, **2.2**

  hay que it's necessary to (do something), one must, **10.2**

  Hay sol. It's sunny., **LP**

  No hay de qué. You're welcome., **LP**

  ¿Qué hay? What's new (up)?

la **hazaña** achievement

el **hecho** fact

el **helado** ice cream, **4.1**

la **hermana** sister, **2.1**

la **hermanastra** stepsister, **2.1**

el **hermanastro** stepbrother, **2.1**

el **hermano** brother, **2.1**

hermoso(a) beautiful

el **héroe** hero

la **heroína** heroine

el **hielo** ice, **7.2**

  el patinaje sobre el hielo ice-skating, **7.2**

las **hierbas** herbs

higiénico: el rollo de papel higiénico roll of toilet paper, **11.2**

la **hija** daughter, **2.1**

el **hijo** son, child, **2.1**

  el hijo único only child, **2.1**

los **hijos** children, **2.1**

hispano(a) Hispanic

hispanohablante Spanish-speaking

el/la **hispanohablante** Spanish speaker

la **historia** history, **1.2**

la **hoja de papel** sheet of paper, **3.1**

¡Hola! Hello!, **LP**

el **hombre** man

el **hombro** shoulder

honesto(a) honest

la **hora** hour; time, **10.1**

  ¿a qué hora? at what time?, **LP**

  la hora de embarque boarding time, **10.1**

  la hora de salida departure time, **10.2**

  ¿Qué hora es? What time is it?, **LP**

hoy today, **LP**

  ¿Cuál es la fecha de hoy? What's today's date?, **LP**

  hoy en día nowadays

  ¿Qué día es hoy? What day is it today?, **LP**

el **huevo** egg, **4.1**

humanitario(a) humanitarian

humano(a) human, **11.1**

humilde humble

el **humor** mood; humor

  estar de buen (mal) humor to be in a good (bad) mood, **6.1**

  tener un buen sentido de humor to have a good sense of humor, **6.1**

el **huso horario** time zone

![I]

la **idea** idea

la **identidad** identification, **10.2**

  el carnet de identidad ID card, **10.2**

identificar to identify

la **iglesia** church

igual que as well as

impaciente impatient, **6.1**

importa: No importa. It doesn't matter.

la **importancia** importance

importante important

imposible impossible

incluir to include

  ¿Está incluido el servicio? Is the tip included?, **4.2**

increíble incredible

Spanish-English Dictionary

indicar to indicate

indígena native, indigenous, **9.2**

el/la **indígena** indigenous person

individual: el deporte individual individual sport

individuales singles *(tennis)*, **5.1**

industrializado(a) industrialized

la **infinidad** infinity

la **influencia** influence

la **información** information, **3.2**

el **inglés** English *(language)*, **1.2**

inhóspito(a) inhospitable

inmenso(a) immense

inteligente intelligent, **1.2**

el **interés** interest

interesante interesting, **1.2**

interesar to interest, **5.1**

internacional international, **10.1**

el **Internet** the Internet, **3.2**

navegar el Internet to surf the Net, **3.2**

intervenir (ie) to intervene

la **introducción** introduction

el **invierno** winter, **LP**

el/la **invitado(a)** guest, **8.1**

invitar to invite

ir to go, **3.2**

ir a to be going to (do something), **4.2**

ir a casa to go home, **3.2**

ir a pie to go on foot, **3.2**

ir al cine to go to the movies, **8.2**

ir de camping to go camping, **11.2**

ir de compras to go shopping, **9.1**

la **isla** island

el **istmo** isthmus

italiano(a) Italian

izquierdo(a) left, **11.1**

el **jabón** soap,

la barra (pastilla) de jabón bar of soap, **11.2**

el **jamón** ham, **4.1**

el sándwich de jamón y queso ham and cheese sandwich, **4.1**

el **jardín** garden, **2.2**

el/la **jardinero(a)** outfielder, **5.2**

el **jonrón** home run

batear un jonrón to hit a home run

joven young, **1.1**

el/la **joven** young person, **1.1**

las **judías verdes** green beans, **9.2**

el **juego** game, **5.1**

el **jueves** Thursday, **LP**

el/la **jugador(a)** player, **5.1**

jugar (ue) to play *(sport)*, **5.1**

el **jugo** juice, **4.1**

el jugo de naranja orange juice, **4.1**

junio June, **LP**

julio July, **LP**

juntos(as) together

el **kilo** kilo(gram) (2.2 lbs.), **10.2**

la **la** the

el **laboratorio** lab(oratory)

laborioso(a) hardworking

el **lado** side

al lado de beside, next to, **2.2**

el **lago** lake

la **lámpara** lamp, **2.2**

el/la **lanzador(a)** pitcher, **5.2**

lanzar to kick, to throw, **5.1**

el **lapicero** ballpoint pen

el **lápiz** pencil, **3.1**

largo(a) long, **5.1**

a lo largo de along

la **lata** can, **9.2**

latino(a) Latino

Latinoamérica Latin America

latinoamericano(a) Latin American

lavar to wash, **11.2**

lavarse to wash oneself, **11.1**

lavarse el pelo (la cara, las manos) to wash one's hair (face, hands), **11.1**

lavarse los dientes to clean (brush) one's teeth, **11.1**

le to him, to her; to you *(formal) (pron.)*

la **lección** lesson

la **leche** milk, **4.1**

la **lechuga** lettuce, **4.1**

la **lectura** reading

leer to read, **4.2**

la **legumbre** vegetable, **4.1**

lejos (de) far (from), **3.2**

la **lengua** language

les to them; to you *(formal) (pron.)*

las **letras** literature

levantar to raise, **3.1**

levantar la mano to raise one's hand, **3.1**

levantarse to get up, **11.1**

la **leyenda** legend

la **libra** pound *(weight)*

libre free, unoccupied, **4.2**

el tiempo libre spare time, **8.1**

el **libro** book, **3.1**

el **líder** leader

la **liga** league

las Grandes Ligas Major Leagues

el **limón** lemon

la **limonada** lemonade

lindo(a) beautiful

la **línea aérea** airline, **10.1**

la **liquidación** sale, **9.1**

la **literatura** literature

la **llama** llama

llamar to call, **11.2**

llamarse to call oneself, to be called, named, **11.1**

Me llamo... My name is . . . , **11.1**

llegar to arrive, **4.1**

llenar to fill

lleno(a) de full of, **6.1**

llevar to carry; to wear, **3.1**; to take; to bear

llover (ue) to rain

Llueve. It's raining., **LP**

lluvioso(a) rainy

lo him; you *(formal) (pron.)*

lo que what

la **loción bronceadora** suntan lotion, sunblock, **7.1**

lógico(a) logical

el **loro** parrot

el **lote** lot

la **lucha** fight

luego later, **LP**; then, **3.2**

¡Hasta luego! See you later!, **LP**

el **lugar** place

el **lunes** Monday, **LP**

M

la **madera** wood
la **madrastra** stepmother, **2.1**
la **madre** mother, **2.1**
el/la **madrugador(a)** early riser, **11.1**
magnífico(a) magnificent, splendid
el **maíz** corn, **9.2**
mal bad
Hace mal tiempo. The weather is bad., **LP**
mal educado(a) ill-mannered, rude, **6.1**
el **malecón** boardwalk (seafront)
la **maleta** suitcase, **10.1**
hacer la maleta to pack, **10.1**
la **maletera** trunk (of a car), **10.1**
malicioso(a) malicious
malo(a) bad, **1.2**
sacar notas malas to get bad grades, **3.1**
mamá mom, mommy
mandar to send
el **mandato** command
la **manera** manner, way
de ninguna manera in no way, by no means
la **manga: de manga corta (larga)** short- (long-) sleeved, **9.1**
el **maní** peanut, **8.1**
la **mano** hand, **3.1**
el equipaje de mano carry-on luggage, **10.2**
manso(a) gentle
la **mantequilla** butter, **4.1**
la **manzana** apple, **9.2**
mañana tomorrow, **LP**
¡Hasta mañana! See you tomorrow!, **LP**
la **mañana** morning
por la mañana in the morning
la **máquina** machine
el **mar** sea, ocean, **7.1**
el mar Caribe Caribbean Sea
marcar to score, **5.1**
marcar un tanto to score a point, **5.1**
la **marcha** march
en marcha working
el **marido** husband, **2.1**
los **mariscos** seafood
marrón: de color marrón brown, **5.1**
el **martes** Tuesday, **LP**

marzo March, **LP**
más more, **9.1**
¡Qué... más... ! What a . . . !
la **máscara de oxígeno** oxygen mask, **10.2**
la **mascota** pet, **2.1**
las **matemáticas** mathematics, math, **1.2**
los **materiales escolares** school supplies, **3.1**
mayo May, **LP**
la **mayonesa** mayonnaise, **9.2**
mayor older
el/la **mayor** the oldest
la **mayoría** majority
mayoritario(a) (related to the) majority
me me (pron.)
medio(a) half
y media half-past (the hour), **LP**
mediano(a) medium, medium-size
el **medicamento** medicine, **6.2**
la **medicina** medicine, **6.2**
el/la **médico(a)** doctor, **6.2**
la **medida** measurement
el **medio de transporte** means of transport
el **mediodía** noon
mejor better
el/la **mejor** best
menor younger
el/la **menor** the youngest
menos less, **9.1**
el **menú** menu, **4.2**
el **mercado** market, **9.2**
la **merienda** snack, **4.2**
la **mermelada** jam, marmalade
el **mes** month, **LP**
la **mesa** table, **2.2**
el/la **mesero(a)** waiter, server, **4.2**
la **mesita** table, **2.2**
meter to put, to place
meter un gol to score a goal, **5.1**
el **metrópoli** metropolis, big city
mexicano(a) Mexican, **1.2**
la **mezcla** mixture
mi my
mí me
el **miedo** fear
tener miedo to be afraid, **7.2**
el/la **miembro(a)** member, **2.1**
mientras while
el **miércoles** Wednesday, **LP**
mil a thousand, **9.2**
el **millón** million, **9.2**
mimado(a) spoiled (person)

la **mina** mine
¡Mira! Look!, **3.1**
mirar to look at, **3.2**
mirarse to look at oneself, **11.1**
mismo(a) same, **1.2**; own
misterioso(a) mysterious
mixto(a) co-ed
la **mochila** backpack, knapsack, **3.1**
el/la **mochilero(a)** backpacker, hiker, **11.2**
viajar de mochilero to go backpacking, hiking
los **modales** manners, **6.1**
tener buenos (malos) modales to have good (bad) manners, to be well- (ill-) behaved, **6.1**
moderno(a) modern
molestar to bother, annoy, **6.1**
el **mono** monkey
la **montaña** mountain, **7.2**
montañoso(a) mountainous
montar to put up (tent), **11.2**
el **montón** bunch, heap
el **monumento** monument
morder (ue) to bite
moreno(a) dark-haired, brunette, **1.1**
morir (ue) to die
el **mostrador** counter, **10.1**
mostrar (ue) to show, **10.2**
el **motivo** theme
el **móvil** cell phone, **3.2**
el **MP3** MP3 player
la **muchacha** girl, **1.1**
el **muchacho** boy, **1.1**
mucho a lot, many, much; **2.2**; very, **LP**
Hace mucho calor (frío). It's very hot (cold)., **LP**
Mucho gusto. Nice to meet you.
los **muebles** furniture, **2.2**
la **muerte** death
muerto(a) dead
la **mujer** wife, **2.1**
la **mula** mule
mundial: la Copa Mundial World Cup
el **mundo** world
el **mural** mural
el/la **muralista** muralist
el **muro** wall
el **museo** museum, **8.2**
la **música** music, **1.2**
el/la **músico(a)** musician, **8.1**
muy very, **LP**
muy bien very well, **LP**

Spanish-English Dictionary

N

nacer to be born
nacional national
la **nacionalidad** nationality, **1.1**
   ¿de qué nacionalidad?
     what nationality?, **1.1**
nada nothing, not anything, **8.2**
   De nada. You're welcome., **LP**
   Nada más. Nothing else., **9.2**
   Por nada. You're welcome., **LP**; for no reason
nadar to swim, **7.1**
nadie nobody, not anybody, **8.2**
la **naranja** orange (fruit), **4.1**
natal pertaining to where someone was born
la **naturaleza** nature
navegar la red (el Internet) to surf the Web (the Internet), **3.2**
necesitar to need, **3.2**
negativo(a) negative
negro(a) black, **2.1**
nervioso(a) nervous, **6.1**
nevado(a) snowy, snow-covered
nevar (ie) to snow
   Nieva. It's snowing., **LP**
ni neither, nor
   Ni idea. No idea.
nicaragüense Nicaraguan
la **nieta** granddaughter, **2.1**
el **nieto** grandson, **2.1**
la **nieve** snow, **7.2**
ninguno(a) none
   de ninguna manera in no way, by no means
el/la **niño(a)** boy, girl, child, **6.2**
el **nivel** level
no no
   No hay de qué. You're welcome., **LP**
la **noche** night, evening
   Buenas noches. Good evening., **LP**
   esta noche tonight, **4.1**
   por la noche in the evening
nombrar to name
el **nombre** name, **2.1**
normal normal, **6.2**
el **norte** north

norteamericano(a) American, North American
nos us (pron.)
nosotros(as) we
la **nota** grade, mark, **3.1**
   sacar notas buenas (malas) to get good (bad) grades, **3.1**
las **noticias** news
novecientos(as) nine hundred, **9.2**
la **novela** novel
noventa ninety, **LP**
noviembre November, **LP**
la **nube** cloud, **7.1**
nublado(a) cloudy, **7.1**
nuestro(a) our
nueve nine, **LP**
nuevo(a) new, **1.1**
el **número** shoe size, **9.1**; number, **10.1**
   el número del asiento seat number, **10.1**
   el número del vuelo flight number, **10.1**
   ¿Qué número calzas? What size shoe do you wear (take)?, **9.1**
nunca never, not ever, **8.2**

O

o or
objetivo objective
obligatorio(a) required, obligatory
la **obra** work; work of art
observar to observe, notice
el **obstáculo** obstacle
obstinado(a) obstinate, stubborn, **6.1**
occidental western
ochenta eighty, **LP**
ocho eight, **LP**
ochocientos(as) eight hundred, **9.2**
octubre October, **LP**
ocupado(a) occupied, **4.2**
el **oeste** west
ofrecer to offer
oír to hear, **8.1**
¡Ojo! Watch out! Be careful!
el **ojo** eye, **2.1**
   tener ojos azules (castaños, verdes) to have blue (brown, green) eyes, **2.1**

la **ola** wave, **7.1**
olvidar to forget
once eleven, **LP**
la **opinión** opinion
el/la **opresor(a)** oppressor
opuesto(a) opposite
la **oración** sentence
la **orden** order (restaurant), **4.2**
el **ordenador** computer, **3.2**
la **orfebrería** craftmanship in precious metals
organizar to organize, set up
el **órgano** organ
oriental eastern
el **origen** origin, background
las **orillas** banks, shores
   a orillas de on the shores of
el **oro** gold
la **orquesta** orchestra, band
la **orquídea** orchid
el **otoño** autumn, fall, **LP**
otro(a) other, another
otros(as) others
¡Oye! Listen!, **1.2**

P

la **paciencia** patience
paciente patient (adj.), **6.1**
el/la **paciente** patient, **6.2**
el **padrastro** stepfather, **2.1**
el **padre** father, **2.1**
los **padres** parents, **2.1**
pagar to pay, **3.2**
el **país** country
el **paisaje** landscape
la **paja** straw, thatch
el **pájaro** bird
la **palabra** word
   la palabra afine cognate
   la palabra relacionada related word
el **palacio** palace
la **paloma** pigeon
el **pan** bread
   el pan tostado toast, **4.1**
el **panecillo** roll, **4.1**
la **pantalla** screen
el **pantalón** pants, **3.1**
   el pantalón corto shorts, **5.1**
   el pantalón largo long pants, **9.1**
la **papa** potato, **4.1**
   las papas fritas french fries, **4.1**

el **papel** paper, **3.1**; role

el rollo de papel higiénico roll of toilet paper, **11.2**

la hoja de papel sheet of paper, **3.1**

el **paquete** package, **9.2**

el **par** pair, **9.1**

para for; in order to

el **paraíso** paradise

parear to match

parecer to seem (like)

a mi (tu, su, etc.) parecer in my (your, his, etc.) opinion

¿Qué te parece? What do you think?

el/la **pariente** relative, **2.1**

el **parque** park, **11.2**

el **párrafo** paragraph

la **parte** part

participar to participate, take part in

el **partido** game, **5.1**

el **pasabordo** boarding pass

pasado(a) last, **7.1**

el año pasado last year, **7.1**

la semana pasada last week, **7.1**

el/la **pasajero(a)** passenger, **10.1**

el **pasaporte** passport, **10.2**

pasar to pass, to go, **5.2**; to spend (time), **7.1**

pasarlo bien to have a good time, **11.2**

¿Qué pasa? What's going on? What's happening?

el **paseo: dar un paseo** to take a walk

el **pasillo** aisle, **10.2**

la **pasta dentífrica** toothpaste

el **pastel** cake

la **pastilla** bar (of soap)

los **patacones** slices of fried plantain

la **patata** potato, **4.1**

las patatas fritas french fries, **4.1**

el **patín** ice skate, **7.2**

el/la **patinador(a)** ice-skater, **7.2**

el **patinaje sobre hielo** ice-skating, **7.2**

patinar to skate, **7.2**

patinar sobre el hielo to ice-skate, **7.2**

pausado(a) slow, deliberate

peinarse to comb one's hair, **11.1**

el **peine** comb, **11.2**

la **película** movie, film, **8.2**

peligroso(a) dangerous

pelirrojo(a) redheaded, **1.1**

el **pelo** hair, **2.1**

tener el pelo rubio (castaño, negro) to have blond (brown, black) hair, **2.1**

la **pelota** ball (baseball, tennis), **5.2**

la pelota vasca jai alai

la **pena** pain, sorrow

¡Qué pena! What a shame!, **5.1**

pensar (ie) to think, **5.1**

pensar en to think about

¿Qué piensas? What do you think?, **5.1**

el **peón** peasant, farm laborer

peor worse, **9.2**

el/la **peor** worst, **9.2**

pequeño(a) small, little, **1.2**

perder (ie) to lose, **5.1**; to miss, **8.1**

perdón pardon me, excuse me

perezoso(a) lazy, **1.2**

el **periódico** newspaper

permiso: Con permiso. Excuse me., **10.1**

pero but

el/la **perro(a)** dog, **2.1**

la **persona** person

el **personaje** character (in a novel, play, etc.)

la **personalidad** personality, **6.1**

peruano(a) Peruvian

pesar: a pesar de in spite of

el **pescado** fish, **4.1**

el **peso** peso; weight

picar to nibble on, **8.1**

picaresco(a) picaresque

el/la **pícher** pitcher (baseball), **5.2**

el **pico** mountain top, **7.2**

el **pie** foot, **5.1**

a pie on foot, **3.2**

la **pierna** leg, **11.1**

la **pieza** bedroom; piece

la **pila** swimming pool

el **pimiento** (green) pepper, **9.2**

los **pinchitos** kebabs, **4.2**

pintar to paint

el/la **pintor(a)** painter, artist, **8.2**

pintoresco(a) picturesque

la **piña** pineapple, **9.2**

el **piso** floor, **2.2**; apartment

la **pista** ski slope, **7.2**; runway, **10.2**

la pista de patinaje ice-skating rink, **7.2**

la **pizza** pizza, **4.1**

placentero(a) pleasant

la **plancha de vela** windsurfing; windsurfboard, **7.1**

practicar la plancha de vela to windsurf, to go windsurfing, **7.1**

la **plata** silver

el **plátano** banana, **9.2**

el **platillo** home plate, **5.2**

el **plato** dish (of food); plate

la **playa** beach, **7.1**

la **plaza** square

la **pluma** (fountain) pen

la **población** population

pobre poor

poco(a) a little; few, **2.2**

un poco más a little more

poder (ue) to be able, **5.1**

el **pollo** chicken, **4.1**

poner to put, to place, to set, **10.2**

ponerse to put on (clothes), **11.1**; to become

popular popular

por for, by

por ejemplo for example

por encima de over, **5.2**

por eso that's why, for this reason

por favor please, **LP**

por fin finally

por la mañana in the morning

por la tarde in the afternoon

Por nada. You're welcome., **LP**; for no reason

¿por qué? why?, **3.2**

porque because, **3.2**

el/la **porrista** cheerleader

el/la **porteño(a)** person from Buenos Aires

la **portería** goal, **5.1**

el/la **portero(a)** goalie, **5.1**

poseer to possess

posible possible

positivo(a) positive

el **postre** dessert, **4.1**

practicar to practice (a sport)

practicar la plancha de vela (la tabla hawaiana, etc.) to go windsurfing (surfing, etc.), **7.1**

el **precio** price, **9.1**

preferir (ie) to prefer, **5.2**

la **pregunta** question, **3.1**

preguntar to ask, to ask a question

el **premio** prize, award

preparar to prepare, get ready

la **prepa(ratoria)** high school

Spanish-English Dictionary

presentar to introduce
prestar: prestar atención to pay attention, **3.1**
el **pretendiente** suitor
primario(a) primary, elementary
    la escuela primaria elementary school
la **primavera** spring, **LP**
primero(a) first, **LP**
    el primero de enero (febrero, etc.) January (February, etc.) 1, **LP**
el/la **primo(a)** cousin, **2.1**
principal main
el/la **principiante** beginner, **7.2**
privado(a) private, **2.2**
el **problema** problem
    No hay problema. No problem.
procedente de coming, arriving from, **10.2**
producir to produce
el **producto** product, **9.2**
la **profesión** profession, occupation
profesional professional
el/la **profesor(a)** teacher, **1.2**
prometer to promise
pronto soon
    ¡Hasta pronto! See you soon!, **LP**
la **propina** tip *(restaurant)*
propio(a) own, **5.1**
propósito: ¡A propósito! By the way, **8.2**
la **prueba** test, exam, **3.1**
el **pueblo** town
la **puerta de salida** gate *(airport)*, **10.2**
el **puerto** port
puertorriqueño(a) Puerto Rican
pues well
el **puesto** market stall, **9.2**
el **pulso** pulse, **6.2**
el **punto** point
el **pupitre** desk, **3.1**

Q

que that
¿qué? what? how?
    ¿A qué hora? At what time?, **LP**

¿de qué nacionalidad? what nationality?, **1.1**
No hay de qué. You're welcome., **LP**
¿Qué desea Ud.? May I help you? *(in a store)*
¿Qué día es hoy? What day is it today?
¿Qué hay? What's new (up)?
¿Qué hora es? What time is it?, **LP**
¡Qué... más... ! What a . . . !
¿Qué pasa? What's going on? What's happening?
¡Qué pena! What a shame!, **5.1**
¿Qué tal? How are things? How are you?, **LP**
¿Qué tal le gustó? How did you like it? *(formal)*
¿Qué tiempo hace? What's the weather like?, **LP**
quedar bien to suit, to fit, to look good on, **9.1**
quedar(se) to remain, to stay, **11.1**
querer (ie) to want, to wish, **5.1**
querido(a) dear, beloved
el **queso** cheese, **4.1**
    el sándwich de jamón y queso ham and cheese sandwich, **4.1**
el **quetzal** quetzal *(currency of Guatemala)*
¿quién? who?, **1.1**
¿quiénes? who?, **1.2**
quince fifteen, **LP**
la **quinceañera** fifteen-year-old girl
quinientos(as) five hundred, **9.2**
quitarse to take off *(clothes)*, **11.1**
quizá(s) maybe, perhaps, **7.2**

R

la **raqueta** tennis racket, **5.2**
raro(a) rare
el **ratón** mouse
la **raza** breed
la **razón** reason
rebajar to lower *(prices)*, **9.1**

la **recámara** bedroom, **2.2**
el/la **receptor(a)** catcher, **5.2**
la **receta** prescription, **6.2**
recetar to prescribe, **6.2**
recibir to receive, **4.2;** to catch
    recibir aplausos to be applauded, **8.1**
reclamar to claim
reconocer to recognize
recordar (ue) to remember
recuperar to claim, to get back
la **red** the Web, **3.2;** net, **5.2**
    navegar la red to surf the Web, **3.2**
    pasar por encima de la red to go over the net, **5.2**
el **refresco** soft drink, **4.2**
refrito(a) refried
el **regalo** gift, present, **8.1**
regatear to bargain, **9.2**
la **región** region
la **regla** rule
regresar to go back, to return, **3.2**
    regresar a casa to go home, **3.2**
reinar to rule, reign
renombrado(a) famous
rentar to rent, **7.1**
repasar to review
el **repaso** review
la **república** republic
    la República Dominicana Dominican Republic
respetado(a) respected
respetar to respect
responsable responsible
la **respuesta** answer
el **restaurante** restaurant
resultar to turn out to be, to wind up being
el **retraso** delay, **10.2**
el **retrato** portrait
la **reunión** meeting, get-together
la **revista** magazine
revueltos: huevos revueltos scrambled eggs
el **rey** king
rico(a) rich; delicious
    ¡Qué rico! How delicious!
el **río** river
el **ritmo** rhythm
robar to steal
la **roca** rock, stone
rodeado(a) surrounded

la **rodilla** knee, **11.1**
rojo(a) red, **5.1**
el **rol** role
el **rollo de papel higiénico** roll of toilet paper, **11.2**
el **rompecabezas** puzzle
romper to break
la **ropa** clothing, **9.1**
rosado(a) pink, **5.1**
rubio(a) blond, **1.1**
las **ruinas** ruins
la **rutina diaria** daily routine, **11.1**

S

el **sábado** Saturday, **LP**
saber to know, **9.1**
sacar to get; to take
sacar fotos to take pictures, **7.1**
sacar notas buenas (malas) to get good (bad) grades, **3.1**
el **saco de dormir** sleeping bag, **11.2**
la **sal** salt
la **sala** living room, **2.2**
la sala de clase classroom, **3.1**
la **salchicha** sausage
el **saldo** sale, **9.1**
la **salida** departure, **10.1**
la hora de salida time of departure, **10.1**
la puerta de salida gate (airport), **10.2**
salir to leave; to go out, **8.1**
Todo te sale más barato. It's all a lot cheaper (less expensive)., **9.1**
la **salud** health, **6.1**
saludar to greet
salvar to save
la **sandalia** sandal
el **sándwich** sandwich, **4.1**
el sándwich de jamón y queso ham and cheese sandwich, **4.1**
el **sarape** blanket
el **sato** a type of dog from Puerto Rico
secundario(a) secondary, **1.2**
la escuela secundaria high school, **1.2**
la **sed** thirst, **4.1**
tener sed to be thirsty, **4.1**
seguir to follow
según according to

segundo(a) second
seguramente surely, certainly
la **seguridad: el control de seguridad** security (airport), **10.2**
seguro(a) sure; safe
seguro que certainly
seis six, **LP**
seiscientos(as) six hundred, **9.2**
la **selva** jungle, forest
la **semana** week, **LP**
la semana pasada last week, **7.1**
sencillo(a) single, simple
sentarse (ie) to sit down, **11.1**
el **sentido de humor** sense of humor, **6.1**
la **señal** sign, **10.2**
la señal de no fumar no-smoking sign
el **señor** sir, Mr., gentleman, **LP**
la **señora** Ms., Mrs., madam, **LP**
los **señores** Mr. and Mrs.
la **señorita** Miss, Ms., **LP**
septiembre September, **LP**
ser to be
¿Cuánto es? How much does it cost (is it)?, **LP**
serio(a) serious, **1.1**
¿Hablas en serio? Are you serious?
el **servicio** tip, **4.2**; restroom, **10.2**
¿Está incluido el servicio? Is the tip included?, **4.2**
servir to serve
sesenta sixty, **LP**
setecientos(as) seven hundred, **9.2**
setenta seventy, **LP**
severo(a) harsh, strict
si if
sí yes, **LP**
siempre always, **8.2**
siento: Lo siento mucho. I'm sorry. (That's too bad.), **5.1**
la **siesta** nap
siete seven, **LP**
el **siglo** century
significar to mean
la **silla** chair, **2.2**
similar similar
simpático(a) nice, **1.1**
sin without
sincero(a) sincere
el **síntoma** symptom
el/la **snowboarder** snowboarder, **7.2**

sobre on, on top of; about
sobre todo above all, especially
sobrevolar (ue) to fly over
la **sobrina** niece, **2.1**
el **sobrino** nephew, **2.1**
social social
los estudios sociales social studies, **1.2**
el **sofá** sofa, **2.2**
el **sol** sun
Hace (Hay) sol. It's sunny., **LP**
tomar el sol to sunbathe, **7.1**
solamente only
solar: la crema solar suntan lotion, **7.1**
solas: a solas alone
el **soldado** soldier
soler (ue) to be used to, to do something usually
solo(a) single; alone
solo only
el/la **soltero(a)** single, unmarried person
el **sombrero** hat
el **sonido** sound
la **sonrisa** smile, **6.1**
la **sopa** soup
la **sorpresa** surprise, **4.1**
su his, her, their, your (formal)
subir to go up, **7.2**
los **suburbios** suburbs, **2.2**
Sudamérica South America
sudamericano(a) South American
el/la **suegro(a)** father-in-law, mother-in-law
el **suelo** ground, floor
el **sueño** dream
la **suerte** luck
¡Buena suerte! Good luck!
¡Qué suerte tengo! How lucky I am!, **9.1**
el **suéter** sweater, **11.1**
sufrir to suffer
superior upper, top
el compartimiento superior overhead bin (airplane), **10.2**
el **supermercado** supermarket, **9.2**
el **sur** south
la América del Sur South America
el **surtido** assortment
sus their, your (pl.)

Spanish-English Dictionary

T

la **tabla hawaiana** surfboard, **7.1**
   practicar la tabla hawaiana to surf, to go surfing, **7.1**
el **taco** taco
la **tajada** slice, **9.2**
 tal such *(a thing)*
   ¿Qué tal? How are things? How are you?, **LP**
   ¿Qué tal tu clase de español? How's your Spanish class?
   tal vez maybe, perhaps, **7.2**
la **talla** size, **9.1**
   ¿Qué talla usas? What size do you take?, **9.1**
el **tamaño** size
 también also, too, **1.2**
el **tambor** drum
 tampoco either, neither
 tan so
el **tanto** score, point, **5.1**
   marcar un tanto to score a point, **5.1**
las **tapas** snacks, nibbles, **4.2**
la **taquilla** box office, ticket window, **8.2**
 tarde late, **10.2**
la **tarde** afternoon
   ayer por la tarde yesterday afternoon, **7.1**
   Buenas tardes. Good afternoon., **LP**
la **tarea** homework
la **tarjeta** card; pass
   la tarjeta de abordar boarding pass
   la tarjeta de embarque boarding pass, **10.1**
la **tarta** cake, **8.1**
el **taxi** taxi, **10.1**
el/la **taxista** taxi driver, **10.1**
la **taza** cup, **4.1**
 te you *(fam. pron.)*
el **té** tea
el **teclado** keyboard
 tejano(a) Texan
los **tejidos** fabrics, **9.2**
la **tele** TV
el **teléfono** telephone
   el teléfono celular cell phone
   hablar por teléfono to speak on the phone
la **telenovela** serial, soap opera

el **telesilla** chairlift, ski lift, **7.2**
el **telesquí** ski lift, **7.2**
la **televisión** television
el **tema** theme
la **temperatura** temperature, **7.2**
 temprano(a) early, **11.1**
el **tenderete** market stall, **9.2**
 tener (ie) to have, **2.1**
   tener... años to be . . . years old, **2.1**
   tener calor (frío) to be hot (cold), **11.1**
   tener catarro to have a cold, **6.2**
   tener dolor de... to have a(n) . . . -ache, **6.2**
   tener el pelo rubio (castaño, negro) to have blond (brown, black) hair, **2.1**
   tener éxito to be successful, **6.1**
   tener fiebre to have a fever, **6.2**
   tener hambre to be hungry, **4.1**
   tener miedo to be afraid, **7.2**
   tener ojos azules (castaños, verdes) to have blue (brown, green) eyes, **2.1**
   tener que to have to (do something), **4.2**
   tener sed to be thirsty, **4.1**
el **tenis** tennis
   la cancha de tenis tennis court, **5.2**
   jugar (al) tenis to play tennis, **5.2**
los **tenis** sneakers, **9.1**
el/la **tenista** tennis player
la **tensión: la tensión arterial** blood pressure, **6.2**
 tercer(o)(a) third
 terco(a) stubborn, **6.1**
 terminar to end, finish
la **terraza** terrace, balcony
el **terremoto** earthquake
el **tesoro** treasure
 ti you *(pron.)*
la **tía** aunt, **2.1**
el **ticket** ticket, **7.2**
el **tiempo** weather, **LP**; half *(soccer)*, **5.1**
   a tiempo on time, **10.2**
   a tiempo completo (parcial) full- (part-) time

   Hace buen tiempo. The weather is nice., **LP**
   Hace mal tiempo. The weather is bad., **LP**
   ¿Qué tiempo hace? What's the weather like?, **LP**
la **tienda** store, **3.2**
la **tienda de campaña** tent, **11.2**
el **tiquet(e)** ticket
los **timbales** small drums, kettledrums
 tímido(a) shy
el **tío** uncle, **2.1**
 típico(a) typical
el **tipo** guy, type, **6.1**
 tirar to throw, **5.2**
el **título** title
la **toalla** towel, **7.1**
 tocar to touch, **5.1**; to play *(a musical instrument)*, **8.1**
   ¡Te toca a ti! It's your turn!
el **tocino** bacon, **4.1**
 todo everything
   sobre todo above all, especially
 todo(a) all, **6.2**
 todos(as) everyone, **8.1**; everything; all
   en todas partes everywhere
 tomar to take, **3.1**; to have (a meal), **4.1**
   tomar el almuerzo (el desayuno) to have lunch (breakfast), **4.1**
   tomar el bus to take the bus
   tomar el sol to sunbathe, **7.1**
   tomar el pulso to take someone's pulse, **6.2**
   tomar fotos to take pictures, **7.1**
   tomar la tensión arterial to take someone's blood pressure, **6.2**
   tomar un examen to take a test, **3.1**
el **tomate** tomato, **4.1**
 tonto(a) foolish, crazy
la **torta** cake, **4.1**; sandwich
la **tortilla** tortilla
la **tos** cough, **6.2**
   tener tos to have a cough, **6.2**
 toser to cough, **6.2**
la **tostada** tostada
las **tostadas** toast, **4.1**

tostado(a) toasted
   el pan tostado toast, **4.1**
los **tostones** slices of fried plantain, **4.2**
   trabajar to work, **3.2**
el **trabajo** work
   tradicional traditional
   traer to carry, to bring, to take, **10.2**
el **traje** suit
el **traje de baño** swimsuit, **7.1**
   tranquilo(a) calm, **6.1**
el **tratamiento** treatment
   tratar to treat
   trece thirteen, **LP**
   treinta thirty, **LP**
   trienta y cinco thirty-five, **LP**
   treinta y cuatro thirty-four, **LP**
   treinta y dos thirty-two, **LP**
   treinta y nueve thirty-nine, **LP**
   treinta y ocho thirty-eight, **LP**
   treinta y seis thirty-six, **LP**
   treinta y siete thirty-seven, **LP**
   treinte y tres thirty-three, **LP**
   treinta y uno thirty-one, **LP**
   tres three, **LP**
   trescientos(as) three hundred, **9.2**
   triste sad, **6.1**
la **trompeta** trumpet
las **tropas** troops
   tropical tropical
el **trotamundos** globe-trotter
el **T-shirt** T-shirt
   tu your
   tú you *(fam.)*
el **tubo** tube, **11.2**
el **turismo** tourism

   Ud., usted you *(sing.)* *(formal)*
   Uds., ustedes you *(pl.)* *(formal)*
   último(a) last; final
   un(a) a, an, **1.1**
   único(a) only, **2.1**
   el/la hijo(a) único(a) only child, **2.1**
el **uniforme** uniform, **3.1**
la **universidad** university
   uno(a) one, **LP**
   unos(as) some
   urbano(a) urban
   usar to use, **3.2;** to wear *(size)*, **9.2**

¿Qué talla usas? What size do you wear (take)?, **9.1**
el/la **usuario(a)** user
la **uva** grape, **9.2**

las **vacaciones** vacation, **7.1**
   estar de vacaciones to be on vacation
   vacante vacant
la **vainilla** vanilla
   vale: No vale. It's not worth it., **7.1**
el **valle** valley
   varios(as) several
el **varón** man, boy
   vasco(a) Basque
   la pelota vasca jai alai
el **vaso** glass, **4.1**
   veces: a veces at times, sometimes, **6.1**
el/la **vecino(a)** neighbor
el **vegetal** vegetable, **4.1**
   los vegetales crudos raw vegetables, crudités, **8.1**
   vegetariano(a) vegetarian, **4.1**
   veinte twenty, **LP**
   veinticinco twenty-five, **LP**
   veinticuatro twenty-four, **LP**
   veintidós twenty-two, **LP**
   veintinueve twenty-nine, **LP**
   veintiocho twenty-eight, **LP**
   veintiséis twenty-six, **LP**
   veintisiete twenty-seven, **LP**
   veintitrés twenty-three, **LP**
   veintiuno twenty-one, **LP**
la **vela** candle, **8.1**
el/la **vendedor(a)** merchant, **9.2**
   vender to sell, **6.2**
   venezolano(a) Venezuelan
   venir (ie) to come, **10.2**
la **venta** small hotel
la **ventanilla** ticket window, **7.2;** window *(plane)*, **10.2**
   ver to see, **4.2**
el **verano** summer, **LP**
la **verdad** truth
   Es verdad. That's true (right)., **9.1**
   ¿verdad? right?
   verdadero(a) real, true
   verde green, **2.1**
la **verdulería** vegetable store, **9.2**
el **vestido** dress, **9.1**
   el vestido de novia wedding dress

la **vez** time
   a veces at times, sometimes, **6.1**
   cada vez each time, every time
   de vez en cuando from time to time, occasionally
   una vez más once again, one more time
   viajar to travel
el **viaje** trip, voyage **10.1**
   hacer un viaje to take a trip, **10.1**
la **vida** life
el **video** video
   viejo(a) old, **2.2**
el **viento** wind, **LP**
   Hace viento. It's windy., **LP**
el **viernes** Friday, **LP**
el **vino** wine
el **violín** violin
   visitar to visit, **8.2**
la **vista** view
la **viuda** widow
   vivir to live, **4.2**
   vivo(a) lively
la **vocal** vowel
   volar (ue) to fly
el **volcán** volcano
el **voleibol** volleyball, **7.1**
   la cancha de voleibol volleyball court, **7.1**
   volver (ue) to return, **5.1**
   volver a casa to go back (return) home, **8.1**
   vosotros(as) you
el **vuelo** flight, **10.1**

   y and
   ya already
   ¡Ya voy! I'm coming!, **11.2**
   yo I

Z

la **zanahoria** carrot, **9.2**
las **zapatillas** (sports) shoes, sneakers, **5.1**
los **zapatos** shoes, **9.1**
la **zona** area, zone
el **zumo** juice

English-Spanish Dictionary

This English-Spanish Dictionary contains all productive and some receptive vocabulary from the text. The numbers following each productive entry indicate the chapter and vocabulary section in which the word is introduced. For example, **3.2** means that the word was taught in **Capítulo 3, Vocabulario 2. LP** refers to the **Lecciones preliminares**. If there is no number following an entry, this means that the word or expression is included for receptive purposes only.

A

a un(a)
able: to be able poder (ue), **5.1**
aboard abordo (de), **10.2**
about *(time)* a eso de
above por encima de, **5.2**
  above all sobre todo
absent ausente
according to según
ache el dolor, **6.2**
  My . . . ache(s). Me duele(n)... , **6.2**
  to have a(n) . . . ache tener dolor de... , **6.2**
activity la actividad
address la dirección
adorable cariñoso(a), **2.1**; adorable
advanced avanzado(a), **7.2**
affectionate cariñoso(a), **2.1**
afraid: to be afraid tener miedo, **7.2**
after después (de), **3.1**; *(time)* y
  It's ten after one. Es la una y diez., **LP**
afternoon la tarde
  Good afternoon. Buenas tardes., **LP**
  this afternoon esta tarde, **7.1**
  yesterday afternoon ayer por la tarde, **7.1**
against contra
agent el/la agente
to **agree (with)** estar de acuerdo (con)
air el aire
  open-air (outdoor) café (market) el café (mercado) al aire libre
airline la línea aérea, **10.1**
airplane el avión, **10.1**
airport el aeropuerto, **10.1**
aisle el pasillo, **10.2**

album el álbum
all todo(a), **6.2**; todos(as), **8.1**
  above all sobre todo
almost casi, **8.2**
already ya
also también, **1.2**
always siempre, **8.2**
A.M. de la mañana
American americano(a)
among entre
to **amuse** divertir (ie), **10.2**
amusing divertido(a)
ancient antiguo(a)
and y, **LP**
Andean andino(a)
angry enojado(a), enfadado(a), **6.1**
animal el animal
to **annoy** molestar, enfadar, enojar, **6.1**
another otro(a)
answer la respuesta
to **answer** contestar, **3.1**
any cualquier(a)
any other cualquier otro(a)
anybody alguien, nadie, **8.2**
anything algo, nada, **8.2**
  Anything else? ¿Algo más?, **9.2**
apartment el apartamento, el apartamiento, el departamento, **2.2**; el piso
  apartment building el edificio, la casa de apartamentos, **2.2**
to **applaud** aplaudir, **5.1**
  to be applauded recibir aplausos, **8.1**
apple la manzana, **9.2**
appreciated apreciado(a)
April abril, **LP**
area la zona
Argentine argentino(a)
arithmetic la aritmética
arm el brazo, **11.1**
around *(time)* a eso de
around *(space)* alrededor de, **2.2**

to **arrive** llegar, **4.1**
arriving from procedente de, **10.2**
arrogant altivo(a)
arrow la flecha
art el arte, **1.2**
  art show (exhibition) la exposición de arte, **8.2**
artist el/la artista; el/la pintor(a), **8.2**
as como
to **ask (a question)** preguntar
at a, en
  at around *(time)* a eso de
  at home en casa, **2.2**
  at night por la noche; de noche
  at one o'clock (two o'clock, three o'clock . . .) a la una (a las dos, a las tres...), **LP**
  at times a veces, **6.1**
  at what time? ¿a qué hora?, **LP**
to **attend** asistir (a), **8.1**
attention: to pay attention prestar atención, **3.1**
attractive guapo(a), **1.1**
August agosto, **LP**
aunt la tía, **2.1**
author el/la autor(a)
autumn el otoño, **LP**
avenue la avenida
Awesome! ¡Bárbaro!, **5.2**

B

back: in back of detrás de, **2.2**
background la ascendencia
backpack la mochila, **3.1**
backpacker el/la mochilero(a), **11.2**
bacon el tocino, el bacón, **4.1**
bad malo(a), **1.2**; mal, **LP**
  The weather is bad. Hace mal tiempo., **LP**

to be in a bad mood estar de mal humor, **6.1**

to get bad grades sacar notas malas, **3.1**

baggage el equipaje, **10.1**

  carry-on baggage el equipaje de mano, **10.1**

balcony el balcón

ball (soccer, basketball) el balón, **5.1**; (volleyball), el balón, **7.1**; (baseball, tennis) la pelota, **5.2**

  to kick (throw) the ball lanzar el balón, **5.1**

  to hit the ball batear, golpear, **5.2**

ballpoint pen el bolígrafo, **3.1**; el lapicero, la pluma

banana el plátano, **9.2**

band la banda, **8.1**

bar (soap) la barra de jabón, **11.2**; la pastilla de jabón

to **bargain** regatear, **9.2**

base *(baseball)* la base, **5.2**

baseball el béisbol, **5.2**

  baseball field el campo de béisbol, **5.2**

  baseball player el/la jugador(a) de béisbol, el/la beisbolista, **5.2**

basket *(basketball)* el cesto, la canasta, **5.2**

  to make a basket encestar, meter el balón en la cesta, **5.2**

basketball el básquetbol, el baloncesto, **5.2**

  basketball court la cancha de básquetbol, **5.2**

bat el bate, **5.2**

to **bat** batear, **5.2**

bathing suit el bañador, el traje de baño, **7.1**

bathroom el cuarto de baño, **2.2**; el servicio, **10.2**

batter el/la bateador(a), **5.2**

to **be** ser, **1.1**; estar, **3.1**

  to be able (to) poder (ue), **5.1**

  to be afraid tener miedo, **7.2**

  to be applauded recibir aplausos, **5.1**

  to be born nacer

  to be called (named) llamarse, **11.1**

  to be cold (hot) tener frío (calor), **11.1**

  to be fine (well) estar bien, **6.2**

  to be going to (do something) ir a, **4.2**

to be hungry tener hambre, **4.1**

to be pleasing (to someone) gustar, **5.1**

to be sick estar enfermo(a), **6.2**

to be successful tener éxito, **6.1**

to be thirsty tener sed, **4.1**

to be . . . years old tener... años, **2.1**

beach la playa, **7.1**

  beach resort el balneario, **7.1**

  beach towel la toalla, **7.1**

beans los frijoles, **4.1**

  green beans las judías verdes, **9.2**

beautiful bello(a), hermoso(a)

because porque, **3.2**

bed la cama, **2.2**

  to go to bed acostarse (ue), **11.1**

  to stay in bed guardar cama, **6.2**; quedarse en la cama, **11.1**

bedroom el cuarto de dormir, la recámara, **2.2**; el dormitorio, la habitación, la alcoba, la pieza

beef el bife

before antes de, **10.1**

to **begin** empezar (ie), comenzar (ie), **5.1**

beginner el/la principiante

behaved: to be well-behaved tener buena conducta, **6.1**

behavior la conducta, el comportamiento, **6.1**

behind detrás de, **2.2**

to **believe** creer

below por debajo de, **7.1**

beside al lado de, **2.2**

between entre

beverage la bebida, el refresco, **4.1**

bicycle la bicicleta, **2.2**

big gran, grande, **1.2**

biologist el/la biólogo(a)

biology la biología

bird el pájaro

birthday el cumpleaños, **8.1**

black negro(a), **2.1**

blind ciego(a)

to **block** bloquear, **5.1**

blond rubio(a), **1.1**

  to have blond hair tener el pelo rubio, **2.1**

blood pressure la tensión arterial, **6.2**

blouse la blusa, **3.1**

blue azul, **2.1**

blue jeans el blue jean, **9.1**

board: on board abordo (de), **10.2**

to **board** embarcar, abordar, **10.2**

boarding el embarque, **10.1**

boarding pass la tarjeta de embarque, **10.1**; la tarjeta de abordar, el pasabordo

boarding time la hora de embarque, **10.1**

boat el barquito, **7.1**

body (human) el cuerpo (humano), **11.1**

book el libro, **3.1**

boot la bota, **7.2**

to **bore** aburrir

boring aburrido(a), **1.2**

born: to be born nacer

to **bother** molestar, enfadar, enojar, **6.1**

bottle la botella, **9.2**

box office la taquilla, **8.2**

boy el muchacho, **1.1**; el niño, **6.2**

brave gallardo(a), valiente, no tener miedo

bread el pan

to **break** romper

breakfast el desayuno, **4.1**

  to have breakfast tomar el desayuno, **4.1**; desayunarse

breed la raza

to **bring** traer, **10.1**

bronze *(adj.)* de bronce, **8.2**

brother el hermano, **2.1**

brown castaño(a), **2.1**; de color marrón, **5.1**

  to have brown eyes tener ojos castaños, **2.1**

  to have brown hair tener el pelo castaño, **2.1**

brunette moreno(a), **1.1**

brush el cepillo, **11.2**

  toothbrush el cepillo de dientes, **11.2**

to **brush** cepillar, **11.1**

  to brush one's hair cepillarse, **11.1**

  to brush one's teeth cepillarse (lavarse) los dientes, **11.1**

building el edificio, **2.2**

burrito el burrito

to **bury** enterrar (ie)

bus el autobús, el bus

  school bus el bus escolar, **3.2**

  to miss the bus perder el autobús, **8.1**

English-Spanish Dictionary

but pero

butter la mantequilla, **4.1**

to **buy** comprar, **3.2**

by por; en

by plane (car, bus, etc.) en
avión (carro, autobús, etc.)

by tens de diez en diez

By the way! ¡A propósito!,
8.2

Bye! ¡Chao!, **LP**

café el café, **3.1**

cafeteria la cafetería, **4.1**

cake la torta, **4.1**; el pastel,
la tarta **8.1**; el bizcocho

calculator la calculadora, **3.1**

to **call** llamar, **11.2**

calm calmo(a), tranquilo(a),
6.1

camera la cámara, **7.1**

digital camera la cámara
digital, **7.1**

campfire la fogata

camping el camping, **11.2**

to go camping ir de
camping, **11.2**

can el bote, la lata, **9.2**

candle la vela, **8.1**

capital la capital

car el carro, **2.2**; el coche

carbonated drink la gaseosa,
4.1

Caribbean Sea el mar Caribe

carrot la zanahoria, **9.2**

to **carry** llevar, **3.1**; traer, **10.1**

carry-on bags el equipaje
de mano, **10.2**

cart el carrito, **9.2**

cash register la caja, **3.2**

cashier el/la cajero(a)

cat el/la gato(a), **2.1**

to **catch** atrapar, **5.2**

catcher el/la cátcher, el/la
receptor(a), **5.2**

to **celebrate** celebrar

celebration la celebración

cell phone el móvil, **3.2**;
el teléfono celular

center el centro

century el siglo

ceramics las cerámicas, **9.2**

cereal el cereal, **4.1**

chair la silla, **2.2**

chairlift el telesilla,
el telesquí, **7.2**

character el personaje

cheap barato(a), **9.1**

It's all a lot cheaper. Todo
te sale más barato., **9.1**

check *(restaurant)* la cuenta,
4.2

to **check luggage** facturar
el equipaje, **10.1**

cheerleader el/la porrista

cheese el queso, **4.1**

ham and cheese sandwich
el sándwich de jamón y
queso, **4.1**

chemistry la química

chicken el pollo, **4.1**

child el/la niño(a), **6.2**

children los hijos, **2.1**

Chilean chileno(a)

chocolate el chocolate

hot chocolate el chocolate
caliente, **4.1**

to **choose** escoger

city la ciudad, **2.2**

civilization la civilización

to **clap** aplaudir, **5.1**

class la clase; el curso, **1.2**

classroom la sala de clase, **3.1**

clothing la ropa, **9.1**

clothing store la tienda
de ropa, **9.1**

cloud la nube, **7.1**

cloudy nublado(a), **7.1**

coach el/la entrenador(a)

co-ed mixto(a)

coffee el café, **4.1**

cognate la palabra afine

false cognate el amigo falso,
2.1

cola la cola, **4.1**

cold el frío; frío(a), **4.2**;
(illness) el catarro, **6.2**

It's cold *(weather)*. Hace
frío., **LP**

to be cold tener frío, **11.1**

to have a cold tener catarro,
6.2

color el color, **5.1**

Colombian colombiano(a)

comb el peine, **11.2**

to **comb one's hair** peinarse, **11.1**

to **come** venir (ie), **10.2**

coming from procedente de,
10.2

I'm coming! ¡Ya voy!, **11.2**

comical cómico(a),
gracioso(a), **1.1**

companion
el/la compañero(a)

to **complete** completar

composition la composición

computer la computadora,
el ordenador, **3.2**

concert el concierto, **8.1**

condo(minium) el
condominio

conduct la conducta, **6.1**

connected conectado(a)

connection la conexión

consonant la consonante

continent el continente

conversation la conversación

cool fresco(a), **LP**

It's cool *(weather)*.
Hace fresco., **LP**

corn el maíz, **9.2**

to **cost** costar (ue), **3.2**

How much does it cost?
¿Cuánto cuesta?, **3.2**

Costa Rican costarricense

cough la tos, **6.2**

to have a cough tener tos,
6.2

to **cough** toser, **6.2**

counter *(airline)* el mostrador,
10.1

country el país; el campo

**Spanish-speaking
countries** los países
hispanohablantes

course el curso, **1.2**

court la cancha, **5.2**

basketball (tennis) court
la cancha de básquetbol
(tenis), **5.2**

volleyball court la cancha
de voleibol, **7.1**

courtesy la cortesía

cousin el/la primo(a), **2.1**

crackers las galletas, **8.1**

crafts la artesanía, **9.2**

cross-country skiing el esquí
nórdico

Cuban cubano(a)

Cuban American
cubanoamericano(a)

culture la cultura

cup la taza, **4.1**

custard el flan, **4.1**

customer el/la cliente, **9.2**

D

to **dance** bailar
dangerous peligroso(a)
dark-haired moreno(a), **1.1**
data los datos
date la fecha, **LP**
 What's today's date? ¿Cuál es la fecha de hoy?, **LP**
daughter la hija, **2.1**
day el día, **LP**
 What day is it (today)? ¿Qué día es hoy?, **LP**
dead muerto(a)
dear querido(a)
death la muerte
December diciembre, **LP**
to **decide** decidir
delay el retraso, la demora, **10.2**
delicious delicioso(a); rico(a)
departure la salida, **10.1**
 departure gate la puerta de salida, **10.2**
 departure time la hora de salida, **10.1**
to **deplane** desembarcar, **10.2**
to **describe** describir
description la descripción
desert el desierto
desk el pupitre, **3.1**
dessert el postre, **4.1**; la sobremesa
dictation el dictado
to **die** morir (ue)
difference la diferencia
different diferente, **9.2**
difficult difícil, duro(a), **1.2**; avanzado(a), **7.2**
difficulty la dificultad
digital camera la cámara digital, **7.1**
dining room el comedor, **2.2**
dinner la cena, **4.1**
 to have dinner cenar, **4.1**
direction la dirección
disagreeable desagradable
to **disembark** desembarcar
dish el plato
dispenser: automatic boarding pass dispenser el distribuidor automático, **10.1**
to **dive** bucear, **7.1**
divine divino(a)
to **do** hacer, **10.2**

doctor el/la médico(a), **6.2**
 doctor's office el consultorio, la consulta, **6.2**
dog el/la perro(a), **2.1**
Dominican dominicano(a)
 Dominican Republic la República Dominicana
doubles *(tennis)* dobles, **5.2**
doughnut (type of) el churro
down: to go down bajar, **7.2**
downhill skiing el esquí alpino
dozen la docena
drawing el dibujo
dress el vestido, **9.1**
to **dribble** driblar (con el balón), **5.2**
drink (beverage) el refresco, la bebida, **4.2**
to **drink** beber, **4.1**
drugstore la farmacia, **6.2**
during durante, **3.2**
DVD el DVD, **3.1**
dynamic dinámico(a), **6.1**

E

each cada, **2.2**
early temprano, **10.2**
early riser el/la madrugador(a), **11.1**
to **earn** ganar
earthquake el terremoto
easily sin dificultad, **7.2**
easy fácil, **1.2**
to **eat** comer, **4.1**
 to eat breakfast (lunch) tomar el desayuno (el almuerzo), **4.1**
 to eat dinner cenar, **4.1**
Ecuadoran ecuatoriano(a), **1.1**
education la educación
 physical education la educación física, **1.2**
egg el huevo, **4.1**
eight ocho, **LP**
eight hundred ochocientos(as), **9.2**
eighteen dieciocho, **LP**
eighty ochenta, **LP**
either tampoco
elbow el codo, **11.1**
electronic electrónico(a)
elementary: elementary school la escuela primaria
eleven once, **LP**
else: Anything else? ¿Algo más?, **9.2**
 Nothing else. Nada más., **9.2**

e-mail el correo electrónico, **3.2**; el e-mail
to **e-mail** enviar un correo electrónico, **3.2**
employee el/la empleado(a), **3.2**; el/la dependiente, **9.1**
enchilada la enchilada
end el fin
energetic energético(a), **6.1**
energy la energía, **6.1**
English el inglés, **1.2**
to **enjoy** disfrutar de, gozar de
enough bastante
to **enter** entrar, **5.1**
enthusiasm el entusiasmo, **6.1**
enthusiastic lleno(a) de entusiasmo, **6.1**; entusiasmado(a)
especially especialmente, sobre todo
e-ticket el boleto (billete) electrónico, **10.1**
euro el euro
even aun
evening la noche
 Good evening. Buenas noches., **LP**
 in the evening por la noche
 yesterday evening anoche, **7.1**
everyone todos(as), **8.1**
everything todo(a), **6.2**; todos(as)
everywhere en todas partes
exam el examen, la prueba, **3.1**
 physical exam el examen físico, **6.2**
 to take an exam tomar un examen, **3.1**
to **examine** examinar, **6.2**
example: for example por ejemplo
excellent excelente
exception la excepción
Excuse me. Con permiso., **10.1**
exhibition la exposición (de arte), **8.2**
exotic exótico(a)
expensive caro(a), **9.1**
expert el/la experto(a), **7.2**
to **explain** explicar
extraordinary extraodinario(a)
eye el ojo, **2.1**
 to have blue (green, brown) eyes tener ojos azules (verdes, castaños), **2.1**

English-Spanish Dictionary

English-Spanish Dictionary

F

fabrics los tejidos, **9.2**
fabulous fabuloso(a)
face la cara, **6.1**
fact el hecho
fall *(season)* el otoño, **LP**
to **fall** caer
to **fall asleep** dormirse (ue), **11.1**
false falso(a)
family la familia, **2.1**
famous famoso(a)
fan el/la aficionado(a), **5.1**
fantastic fantástico(a)
far lejos (de), **3.2**
fast rápido(a)
fastened abrochado(a), **10.2**
fat gordo(a)
father el padre, **2.1**
favor el favor
favorite favorito(a)
feature la característica
February febrero, **LP**
fever la fiebre, **6.2**
  to have a fever tener fiebre, **6.2**
few poco(a), pocos(as), **2.2**
  a few unos(as)
field el campo, **5.1**
  baseball field el campo de béisbol, **5.2**
  soccer field el campo de fútbol, **5.1**
fifteen quince, LP
  fifteen-year-old girl la quinceañera
fifty cincuenta, **LP**
fight la lucha
film el filme, la película, **8.2**; el film
fine bien, **LP**
  to be fine estar bien, **6.2**
finger el dedo, **11.1**
to **finish** terminar
first primero(a), **LP**
fish el pescado, **4.1**
five cinco, **LP**
five hundred quinientos(as), **9.2**
flag la bandera
flan el flan, **4.1**

flight el vuelo, **10.1**
  flight number el número del vuelo, **10.1**
floor el piso, **2.2**
flower la flor, **2.2**
to **fly** volar (ue)
folder la carpeta, **3.1**
to **follow** seguir
food la comida, **4.1**; el comestible
foolish tonto(a)
foot el pie, **5.1**
  on foot a pie, **3.2**
football el fútbol americano
for por, para; con destino a, **10.2**
  for example por ejemplo
foreign extranjero(a)
to **forget** olvidar
forty cuarenta, **LP**
four cuatro, **LP**
four hundred cuatrocientos(as), **9.2**
fourteen catorce, **LP**
free libre, **4.2**
French *(language)* el francés, **1.2**
french fries las papas (patatas) fritas, **4.1**
frequently con frecuencia, frecuentemente
Friday el viernes, **LP**
fried frito(a)
friend el/la amigo(a), **1.1**; el/la compañero(a)
friendly agradable
from de, **LP**
  from where? ¿de dónde?, **1.1**
front: in front of delante de, **2.2**
frozen congelado(a), **9.2**
fruit la fruta, **9.2**
fruit stand la frutería, **9.2**
full of lleno(a) de, **6.1**
fun: to have fun divertirse (ie), **11.2**
funny cómico(a); gracioso(a), **1.1**; divertido(a)
furniture los muebles, **2.2**
future el futuro

G

game el juego, el partido, **5.1**
garage el garaje, **2.2**

garden el jardín, **2.2**
gate (airport) la puerta de salida, **10.2**
general general
  generally, in general en general, por lo general
generous generoso(a)
gentle manso(a)
gentleman el señor, **LP**
geography la geografía
geometry la geometría
to **get** sacar, **3.1**
  to get good (bad) grades sacar notas buenas (malas), **3.1**
  to get dressed ponerse la ropa, **11.1**
  to get up levantarse, **11.1**
gift el regalo, **8.1**
girl la muchacha, **1.1**; la niña, **6.2**
to **give** dar, **3.1**
  to give an exam dar un examen (una prueba), **3.1**
  to give (throw) a party dar una fiesta, **8.1**
glass *(drinking)* el vaso, **4.1**
glove el guante, **5.2**
to **go** ir, **3.2**; pasar, **5.2**
  to be going (to do something) ir a, **4.2**
  to go back regresar, **3.2**; volver (ue), **5.1**
  to go camping ir de camping, **11.2**
  to go down bajar, **7.2**
  to go for a hike dar una caminata, **11.2**
  to go home regresar a casa, **3.2**; volver (ue) a casa
  to go ice-skating patinar sobre el hielo, **7.2**
  to go out salir, **8.1**
  to go over the net pasar por encima de la red, **5.2**
  to go snorkeling bucear, **7.1**
  to go shopping ir de compras, **9.1**
  to go skiing esquiar, **7.2**
  to go surfing practicar la tabla hawaiana, **7.1**
  to go through pasar por, **10.2**
  to go to bed acostarse (ue), **11.1**
  to go to the movies ir al cine, **8.2**

to go up subir, **7.2**

to go waterskiing esquiar en el agua, **7.1**

to go windsurfing practicar la plancha de vela, **7.1**

goal el gol, **5.1**

goal *(box)* la portería, **5.1**

to score a goal meter un gol, **5.1**

goalie el/la portero(a), **5.1**

going to con destino a, **10.2**

good bueno(a), **1.1**

to get good grades sacar notas buenas, **3.1**

Good afternoon. Buenas tardes., **LP**

Good evening. Buenas noches., **LP**

Good morning. Buenos días., **LP**

Good-bye. ¡Adiós!, ¡Chao!, **LP**

good-looking guapo(a), bonito(a), **1.1**

grade la nota, **3.1**

to get good (bad) grades sacar notas buenas (malas), **3.1**

grandchildren los nietos, **2.1**

granddaughter la nieta, **2.1**

grandfather el abuelo, **2.1**

grandmother la abuela, **2.1**

grandparents los abuelos, **2.1**

grandson el nieto, **2.1**

grape la uva, **9.2**

gray gris, **5.1**

great gran, grande

Great! ¡Bárbaro!, **5.2**

green verde, **2.1**

green beans las judías verdes, **9.2**

green pepper el pimiento, **9.2**

greeting el saludo, **LP**

group *(musical)* el grupo, el conjunto, **8.1**

to **guard** guardar, **5.1**

Guatemalan guatemalteco(a)

guest el/la invitado(a), **8.1**

guitar la guitarra

gym(nasium) el gimnasio

hair el pelo, **2.1**

to brush one's hair cepillarse, **11.1**

to comb one's hair peinarse, **11.1**

to have blond (brown, black) hair tener el pelo rubio (castaño, negro), **2.1**

half *(soccer)* el tiempo, **5.1**

second half *(soccer)* el segundo tiempo, **5.1**

half-past *(hour)* y media, **LP**

ham el jamón, **4.1**

ham and cheese sandwich el sándwich de jamón y queso, **4.1**

hamburger la hamburguesa, **4.1**

hand la mano, **3.1**

to raise one's hand levantar la mano, **3.1**

hand baggage el equipaje de mano, **10.1**

handsome guapo(a), **1.1**

happy alegre, contento(a), **6.1**; feliz

hard *(adj.)* difícil, duro(a), **1.2**

hardworking ambicioso(a), **1.2**; trabajador(a)

to **have** tener (ie), **2.1**

to have a cold tener catarro, **6.2**

to have a fever tener fiebre, **6.2**

to have a good time pasarlo bien, divertirse (ie), **11.2**

to have a headache tener dolor de cabeza, **6.2**

to have a party dar una fiesta, **8.1**

to have a snack tomar una merienda, **4.2**

to have a sore throat tener dolor de garganta, **6.2**

to have a stomachache tener dolor de estómago, **6.2**

to have blond (brown, black) hair tener el pelo rubio (castaño, negro), **2.1**

to have blue (brown, green) eyes tener ojos azules (castaños, verdes), **2.1**

to have breakfast tomar el desayuno, **4.1**; desayunarse

to have dinner cenar, **4.1**

to have fun pasarlo bien, divertirse (ie), **11.2**

to have lunch tomar el almuerzo, **4.1**

to have to (do something) tener que, **4.2**

he él, **1.1**

head la cabeza, **6.2**

headache: to have a headache tener dolor de cabeza, **6.2**

health la salud, **6.1**

to **hear** oír, **8.1**

heart el corazón

heat el calor

Hello! ¡Hola!, **LP**

helmet el casco, **7.2**

to **help** ayudar, **10.1**

her su(s); la *(pron.)*

here aquí, acá

hero el héroe

heroine la heroína

Hi! ¡Hola!, **LP**

high alto(a), **3.1**

high school la escuela secundaria, **1.2**; el colegio

hike: to take (go for) a hike dar una caminata, **11.2**

hiker el/la mochilero(a), **11.2**

him lo; le

his su(s)

Hispanic hispano(a)

history la historia, **1.2**

to **hit** *(baseball)* batear, *(tennis)* golpear, **5.2**

to hit a home run batear un jonrón

holiday la fiesta

home la casa, **2.2**; a casa, **3.2**

at home en casa

to go home regresar a casa, **3.2**; volver a casa, **8.1**

home plate el platillo, **5.2**

home run el jonrón

to hit a home run batear un jonrón

homework la tarea

honest honesto(a)

hot: to be hot tener calor, **11.1**

It's (very) hot (weather). Hace (mucho) calor., **LP**

hot caliente, **4.1**

hour la hora

house la casa, **2.2**

apartment house el edificio, **2.2**; la casa de apartamentos

how? ¿cómo?, **1.1**; ¿qué?, **LP**

How are you? ¿Cómo estás?

How are things going? ¿Qué tal?, **LP**

how many? ¿cuántos(as)?, **2.1**

How much does it cost? ¿Cuánto cuesta?, **3.2**

How much is (are) . . . ? ¿A cuánto está(n)... ?, **9.2**

How much is it? ¿Cuánto es?, **LP**

How old is he (she)? ¿Cuántos años tiene?, **2.1**

English-Spanish Dictionary

humor: to have a good sense of humor tener un buen sentido de humor, **6.1**
hundred cien(to), **LP**
hunger el hambre (f.)
hungry: to be hungry tener hambre, **4.1**
to **hurt** doler (ue), **6.2**
    Me duele la cabeza (el estómago, etc.). My head (stomach, etc.) hurts.
husband el esposo, el marido, **2.1**

I yo
ice el hielo, **7.2**
ice cream el helado, **4.1**
ice skate el patín, **7.2**
to **ice-skate** patinar sobre el hielo, **7.2**
ice-skater el/la patinador(a), **7.2**
ice-skating el patinaje sobre el hielo, **7.2**
    ice-skating rink la pista de patinaje, **7.2**
ID card el carnet de identidad, **10.2**
idea la idea
identification la identidad, **10.2**
to **identify** identificar
if si
ill-mannered mal educado(a), **6.1**
immediately enseguida, **4.2**
impatient impaciente, **6.1**
important importante
impossible imposible
in en
    in back of detrás de, **2.2**
    in front of delante de, **2.2**
to **include** incluir
    Is the tip included? ¿Está incluido el servicio?, **4.2**
incredible increíble
indicate indicar
indigenous indígena, **9.2**
individual: individual sport el deporte individual
indoor cubierto(a)
inexpensive barato(a), **9.1**
influence la influencia
information la información, **3.2**

inhabitant el/la habitante
intelligent inteligente, **1.2**
Internet el Internet, **3.2**
    to surf the Net navegar el Internet, **3.2**
interest el interés
to **interest** interesar, **5.1**
interesting interesante, **1.2**
international internacional, **10.1**
to **invite** invitar
island la isla
it lo, la
Italian italiano(a)

jacket la chaqueta, **9.1**
    ski jacket la chaqueta de esquí, el anorak, **7.2**
January enero, **LP**
jar el frasco, **9.2**
jeans el blue jean, **9.1**
juice el jugo, el zumo, **4.1**
    orange juice el jugo de naranja, **4.1**
July julio, **LP**
June junio, **LP**
just: to have just (done something) acabar de, **4.2**

kebabs los pinchitos, **4.2**
to **kick** lanzar, **5.1**
kilo(gram) el kilo, **9.2**
king el rey
kitchen la cocina, **2.2**
knapsack la mochila, **3.1**
knee la rodilla, **11.1**
to **know** saber; conocer, **9.1**
    to know how (to do something) saber, **9.1**

to **lack** faltar, **6.1**
    He/She lacks . . . Le falta... , **6.1**
lake el lago
lamp la lámpara, **2.2**
to **land** aterrizar, **10.2**
landing el aterrizaje, **10.2**
language la lengua

large gran, grande, **1.2**
last pasado(a), **7.1**; último(a)
    last night anoche, **7.1**
    last week la semana pasada, **7.1**
    last year el año pasado, **7.1**
late tarde, con un retraso (una demora), **10.2**
later luego, **LP**
    See you later! ¡Hasta luego!, **LP**
Latin America Latinoamérica
Latin American latinoamericano(a)
Latino latino(a)
lazy perezoso(a), **1.2**
league la liga
to **learn** aprender, **4.2**
to **leave** salir, **8.1**; dejar
left izquierdo(a), **11.1**
leg la pierna, **11.1**
legend la leyenda
lemonade la limonada
less menos, **9.1**
lesson la lección
to **let** dejar; permitir
lettuce la lechuga, **4.1**
life la vida
like como
to **like** gustar, **5.1**
    What would you like (to eat)? ¿Qué desean tomar?, **4.2**
line (of people) la cola, **10.2**; la fila
    to wait in line hacer cola, **10.2**; estar en fila
to **listen to** escuchar, **3.2**
    Listen! ¡Oye!
literature la literatura
little pequeño(a), **1.2**
    a little poco(a), **2.2**
to **live** vivir, **4.2**
living room la sala, **2.2**
long largo(a), **5.1**
to **look at** mirar, **3.2**
    Look! ¡Mira!, **3.1**
to **look at oneself** mirarse, **11.1**
to **look for** buscar, **3.2**
to **lose** perder (ie), **5.1**
lot: a lot mucho(a), **LP**; muchos(as), **2.1**
lotion: suntan lotion la crema solar, la loción bronceadora, **7.1**

low bajo(a), **3.1**

to **lower (prices)** rebajar, **9.1**

love el amor

  in love enamorado(a)

  loved one el/la amado(a)

luggage el equipaje, **10.1**

  hand luggage el equipaje de mano, **10.1**

lunch el almuerzo, **4.1**

  to have lunch tomar el almuerzo, **4.1**

mad enojado(a), enfadado(a), **6.1**

Madam la señora, **LP**

magazine la revista

main principal

majority la mayoría; mayoritario(a) *(adj.)*

to **make** hacer, **10.2**

  to make a basket encestar, meter el balón en la cesta, **5.2**

mall el centro comercial, **9.1**

man el hombre

manager el/la entrenador(a)

manners los modales, **6.1**

  to have good (bad) manners tener buenos (malos) modales, **6.1**

many muchos(as), **2.2**

  how many? ¿cuántos(as)?, **2.1**

March marzo, **LP**

mark la nota, **3.1**

  bad (low) mark la nota mala (baja), **3.1**

  good (high) mark la nota buena (alta), **3.1**

  to get good (bad) marks sacar notas buenas (malas), **3.1**

market el mercado, **9.2**

  native market el mercado indígena, **9.2**

  market stall el puesto, el tenderete, **9.2**

to **marry: to get married** casarse

to **match** parear

mathematics las matemáticas, **1.2**

May mayo, **LP**

maybe quizá, quizás, tal vez, **7.2**

mayonnaise la mayonesa, **9.2**

me mí; me

meal la comida, **4.1**

to **mean** significar

meat la carne, **4.1**

meatball la albóndiga, **4.2**

meat pie la empanada, **4.2**

medicine el medicamento, la medicina, **6.2**

medium-sized mediano(a)

member el/la miembro(a), **2.1**

menu el menú, **4.2**

merchant el/la vendedor(a), **9.2**

Mexican mexicano(a), **1.2**

Mexican American mexicanoamericano(a)

milk la leche, **4.1**

million el millón, **9.2**

  a million dollars un millón de dólares, **9.2**

mineral water el agua mineral, **4.2**

mirror el espejo, **11.1**

Miss señorita, **LP**

to **miss (the bus)** perder (ie) (el autobús)

modern moderno(a)

mom mamá

Monday el lunes, **LP**

money el dinero, **3.2**

month el mes, **LP**

mood el humor, **6.1**

  to be in a good (bad) mood estar de buen (mal) humor, **6.1**

more más, **9.1**

morning la mañana

  Good morning. Buenos días., **LP**

  in the morning por la mañana

mother la madre, **2.1**

mountain la montaña, **7.2**

mountain top el pico, **7.2**

mouth la boca, **6.2**

movie la película, el filme, **8.2**; el film

movie theater el cine, **8.2**

movies: to go to the movies ir al cine, **8.2**

MP3 player el MP3

Mr. (el) señor, **LP**

Mr. and Mrs. los señores

Mrs. (la) señora, **LP**

Ms. (la) señorita, (la) señora, **LP**

much mucho(a), **LP**

  how much? ¿cuánto?

  How much does it cost (is it)? ¿Cuánto es?, **LP**; ¿Cuánto cuesta?, **3.2**

museum el museo, **8.2**

music la música, **1.2**

musician el/la músico(a), **8.1**

my mi, mis

name el nombre, **2.1**

  My name is . . . Me llamo... , **11.1**

  What is your name? ¿Cómo te llamas?, **11.1**; ¿Cuál es su nombre? *(formal)*

national nacional

nationality la nacionalidad, **1.1**

  what nationality? ¿de qué nacionalidad?, **1.1**

native indígena, **9.2**

  native person el/la indígena

near cerca de, **3.2**

to **need** necesitar, **3.2**

necktie la corbata, **9.1**

neighbor el/la vecino(a)

neighborhood el barrio

neither tampoco

nephew el sobrino, **2.1**

nervous nervioso(a), **6.1**

net (World Wide Web) la red, **3.2**; (tennis), **5.2**

  to surf the Net navegar el Internet, **3.2**

never nunca, **8.2**

new nuevo(a), **1.1**

newspaper el periódico

next to al lado de, **2.2**

nice simpático(a), **1.1**; (weather) buen (tiempo)

  Nice to meet you. Mucho gusto.

  The weather is nice. Hace buen tiempo., **LP**

niece la sobrina, **2.1**

night la noche

  at night por la noche

  Good night. Buenas noches., **LP**

  last night anoche, **7.1**

nine nueve, **LP**

nine hundred novecientos(as), **9.2**

nineteen diecinueve, **LP**

ninety noventa, **LP**

no no, **LP**; ninguno(a)

  by no means de ninguna manera

nobody nadie, **8.2**

none ninguno(a)

English-Spanish Dictionary

noon el mediodía

no one nadie, **8.2**

normal normal, **6.2**

north el norte

North American norteamericano(a)

no-smoking sign la señal de no fumar, **10.2**

not no, **1.2**

notebook el cuaderno, **3.1**

nothing nada, **8.2**

  Nothing else. Nada más., **9.2**

novel la novela

November noviembre, **LP**

now ahora

number el número, **10.1**

  flight number el número del vuelo, **10.1**

  seat number el número del asiento, **10.1**

nurse el/la enfermero(a), **6.2**

objective el objetivo

obligatory obligatorio(a)

to **observe** observar

obstinate obstinado(a), **6.1**

occupied ocupado(a)

ocean el océano

o'clock: It's two o'clock. Son las dos., **LP**

October octubre, **LP**

of de

of course claro que... , ¡cómo no!

office: doctor's office la consulta del médico, **6.2**

old viejo(a), **2.2**

  How old is he (she)? ¿Cuántos años tiene?, **2.1**

older mayor

oldest el/la mayor

on sobre, en

  on board abordo (de), **10.2**

  on foot a pie

  on time a tiempo, **10.2**

  on top of sobre

one uno; uno(a), **LP**

one hundred cien(to), **LP**

one thousand mil, **9.2**

onion la cebolla, **9.2**

only único(a), **2.1**; solo; solamente

to **open** abrir, **4.2**

open-air al aire libre

open-minded flexible, **6.1**

opinion la opinión

opponents el equipo contrario, **5.2**

opposing: opposing team el equipo contrario, **5.2**

opposite el contrario

or o

orange (color) anaranjado(a), naranja, **5.1**

orange (fruit) la naranja, **4.1**

  orange juice el jugo (zumo) de naranja, **4.1**

order (restaurant) la orden, **4.2**

other otro(a)

  any other cualquier otro(a)

our nuestro(a), nuestros(as)

outdoor al aire libre

outfielder el/la jardinero(a), **5.2**

over por encima de, **5.2**

overhead bin el compartimiento superior, **10.2**

oxygen mask la máscara de oxígeno, **10.2**

to **pack** hacer la maleta, **10.1**

package el paquete, **9.2**

pain el dolor, **6.2**

painter el/la pintor(a), **8.2**

painting el cuadro, **8.2**; la pintura

pair el par, **9.1**

pants el pantalón, **3.1**

  long pants el pantalón largo, **9.1**

paper: sheet of paper la hoja de papel, **3.1**

parents los padres, **2.1**

park el parque, **11.2**

parrot el loro

part la parte

party la fiesta, **8.1**

  to (have) throw a party dar una fiesta, **8.1**

to **pass** pasar, **5.2**

passenger el/la pasajero(a), **10.1**

passport el pasaporte, **10.2**

patience la paciencia, **6.1**

patient (adj.) paciente, **6.1**

patient (n.) el/la enfermo(a), **6.2**

to **pay** pagar, **3.2**

  to pay attention prestar atención, **3.1**

pea el guisante, **9.2**

peanut el cacahuate, el maní, **8.1**; el cacahuete

pen el bolígrafo, **3.1**; el lapicero, la pluma

pencil el lápiz, **3.1**; lápices (pl.)

people la gente, **9.1**

perhaps quizá, quizás, tal vez, **7.2**

person la persona

personality la personalidad, **6.1**

Peruvian peruano(a)

pet la mascota, **2.1**

pharmacist el/la farmacéutico(a)

pharmacy la farmacia, **6.2**

photo(graph) la foto(grafía)

  to take photos sacar (tomar) fotos, **7.1**

physical (exam) el examen físico, **6.2**

physical education la educación física, **1.2**

piano el piano

picture la foto(grafía)

  to take pictures sacar (tomar) fotos, **7.1**

picturesque pintoresco(a)

pineapple la piña, **9.2**

pink rosado(a), **5.1**

pitcher (baseball) el/la pícher, el/la lanzador(a), **5.2**

pizza la pizza, **4.1**

place el lugar

plane el avión, **10.1**

plantain: slices of fried plantain los tostones, **4.2**; los patacones

to **play (sport)** jugar, **5.1**; (musical instrument) tocar, **8.1**

player el/la jugador(a), **5.1**

  baseball player el/la jugador(a) de béisbol, el/la beisbolista, **5.2**

pleasant agradable

please por favor, **LP**; favor de (+ infinitive), **11.2**

pleasure: It's a pleasure to meet you. Mucho gusto.

P.M. de la tarde, de la noche

point el tanto, **5.1**

    to score a point marcar un tanto, **5.1**

polite bien educado(a), **6.1**

pool la piscina, la alberca, **7.1**

poor pobre

population la población

portrait el retrato

possible posible

potato la papa, la patata, **4.1**

    french fried potatoes las papas (patatas) fritas, **4.1**

pound *(weight)* la libra

practically casi, **8.2**

to **practice** practicar

to **prefer** preferir (ie)

to **prepare** preparar

to **prescribe** recetar, **6.2**

prescription la receta, **6.2**

present el regalo, **8.1**

to **present** presentar

pretty bonito(a), **1.1**

price el precio, **9.1**

primary primario(a)

private privado(a), **2.2**

prize (award) el premio

problem el problema

product el producto, **9.2**

to **promise** prometer

Puerto Rican puertorriqueño(a)

pulse el pulso, **6.2**

purchase la compra, **9.2**

to **push** empujar

to **put** poner, **10.2**

to **put on** *(clothes)* ponerse, **11.1**

to **put up** *(tent)* armar, montar, **11.2**

quarter: a quarter past (the hour) y cuarto, **LP**

question la pregunta, **3.1**

    to ask a question preguntar

quite bastante, **1.2**

racket la raqueta, **5.2**

to **rain** llover (ue)

    It's raining. Llueve., **LP**

to **raise** levantar, **3.1**

    to raise one's hand levantar la mano, **3.1**

rather bastante, **1.2**

raw crudo(a), **8.1**

    raw vegetables los vegetales crudos, **8.1**

to **read** leer, **4.2**

reading la lectura

to **receive** recibir, **4.2**

red rojo(a), **5.1**

redheaded pelirrojo(a), **1.1**

to **reduce** rebajar, **9.1**

relative el/la pariente

to **remain** quedarse, **11.1**

to **remember** recordar (ue)

to **rent** alquilar, rentar, **7.1**

to **repeat** repetir

republic la república

    Dominican Republic la República Dominicana

required obligatorio(a)

resort: seaside resort el balneario, **7.1**

rest lo demás

restaurant el restaurante

restroom el servicio, **10.2**

to **return** regresar, **3.2**; volver (ue), **5.1**; (something) devolver (ue), **5.2**

review el repaso

rice el arroz, **4.1**

right derecho(a), **11.1**

right away enseguida, **4.2**

rink (ice-skating) la pista de patinaje, **7.2**

river el río

roll *(bread)* el panecillo, **4.1**

roll of toilet paper el rollo de papel higiénico, **11.2**

room el cuarto, **2.2**

    bathroom el cuarto de baño, **2.2**

    classroom la sala de clase

    dining room el comedor, **2.2**

    living room la sala, **2.2**

routine la rutina, **11.1**

    daily routine la rutina diaria, **11.1**

rude mal educado(a), **6.1**

ruins las ruinas

rumor el chisme

to **run** correr, **5.2**

runway la pista, **10.2**

rural rural

sad triste, deprimido(a), **6.1**

salad la ensalada, **4.1**

sale el saldo, la liquidación, **9.1**

salesperson el/la empleado(a), **3.2**; el/la dependiente, **9.1**

salt la sal

same mismo(a), **1.2**

sand la arena, **7.1**

sandal la sandalia, **9.2**

sandwich el sándwich, el bocadillo, **4.1**; la torta

    ham and cheese sandwich el sándwich de jamón y queso, **4.1**

Saturday el sábado, **LP**

to **save** salvar

to **say** decir

scared: to be scared tener miedo, **7.2**

school la escuela, **1.2**; el colegio; la academia

    elementary school la escuela primaria

    high school la escuela secundaria, **1.2**; el colegio

school (related to) escolar

    school bus el bus escolar, **3.2**

    school supplies los materiales escolares, **3.1**

science la ciencia, **1.2**

score el tanto, **5.1**

    to score a goal meter un gol, **5.1**

    to score a point marcar un tanto, **5.1**

screen la pantalla

sculptor el/la escultor(a)

sculpture la escultura, **8.2**

sea el mar, **7.1**

    Caribbean Sea el mar Caribe

seaside resort el balneario, **7.1**

season la estación, **LP**

    ¿Qué estación es? What season is it?, **LP**

seat el asiento, **10.1**

    seat number el número del asiento, **10.2**

    seat belt el cinturón de seguridad, **10.2**

second segundo(a)

    second half *(soccer)* el segundo tiempo, **5.1**

secondary secundario(a), **1.2**

English-Spanish Dictionary

security (checkpoint) el control de seguridad, **10.2**

  to go through security pasar por el control de seguridad, **10.2**

to **see** ver, **4.2**

  See you later! ¡Hasta luego!, **LP**

  See you soon! ¡Hasta pronto!, **LP**

  See you tomorrow! ¡Hasta mañana!, **LP**

to **seem** parecer

  It seems to me . . . Me parece...

to **sell** vender, **6.2**

to **send** enviar, **3.2**

sense: sense of humor el sentido de humor, **6.1**

  to have a good sense of humor tener un buen sentido de humor, **6.1**

sentence la frase, la oración

September septiembre, **LP**

serious serio(a), **1.1**

server el/la mesero(a), **4.2**; el/la camarero(a)

seven siete, **LP**

seven hundred setecientos(as), **9.2**

seventeen diecisiete, **LP**

seventy setenta, **LP**

several varios(as)

shake (drink) el batido, **4.2**

shame: What a shame! ¡Qué pena!, **5.1**

shampoo el champú, **11.2**

she ella, **1.1**

sheet: sheet of paper la hoja de papel, **3.1**

shirt la camisa, **3.1**

shoe size el número, **9.1**

shoes las zapatillas, **5.1**; los zapatos, **9.1**

to **shop** ir de compras, **9.1**

shopping cart el carrito, **9.2**

shopping center el centro comercial, **9.1**

short (person) bajo(a), **1.1**; (length) corto(a), **9.1**

shorts el pantalón corto, **5.1**

shoulder el hombro

to **show** mostrar (ue), **10.2**

shower la ducha, **11.1**

  to take a shower tomar una ducha, **11.1**

shrimp los camarones, **4.2**; las gambas

shy tímido(a)

sick enfermo(a), **6.2**

sign la señal

  no-smoking sign la señal de no fumar, **10.2**

silver la plata

similar similar

since desde; como

sincere sincero(a)

to **sing** cantar, **8.1**

singer el/la cantante, **8.1**

single solo(a)

singles (tennis) individuales, **5.2**

sir señor, **LP**

sister la hermana, **2.1**

to **sit down** sentarse (ie), **11.1**

six seis, **LP**

six hundred seiscientos(as), **9.2**

sixteen dieciséis, **LP**

sixty sesenta, **LP**

size (clothing) la talla; (shoes) el número, **9.1**

  What size do you take? ¿Qué talla usas?, **9.1**

  What size shoe do you wear? ¿Qué número calzas?, **9.1**

to **skate** patinar, **7.2**

ski el esquí, **7.2**

  ski hat el gorro, **7.2**

  ski jacket la chaqueta de esquí, el anorak, **7.2**

  ski lift el telesilla, el telesquí, **7.2**

  ski pole el bastón, **7.2**

  ski resort la estación de esquí, **7.2**

  ski slope la pista, **7.2**

to **ski** esquiar, **7.2**

  to water-ski esquiar en el agua, **7.1**

skier el/la esquiador(a), **7.2**

skiing el esquí, **7.2**

  cross-country skiing el esquí nórdico

  downhill skiing el esquí alpino

  waterskiing el esquí acuático (náutico), **7.1**

skinny flaco(a)

skirt la falda, **3.2**

to **sleep** dormir (ue), **5.2**

sleeping bag el saco (la bolsa) de dormir, **11.2**

sleeved: short- (long-) sleeved de manga corta (larga), **9.1**

slice la tajada, **9.2**

slope la pista, **7.2**

small pequeño(a), **1.2**

smile la sonrisa, **6.1**

smoking: no-smoking sign la señal de no fumar, **10.2**

snack la merienda; las tapas, los antojitos, **4.2;** los bocaditos

sneakers las zapatillas, **5.1;** los tenis, **5.2**

snow la nieve, **7.2**

to **snow** nevar (ie), **7.2**

  It's snowing. Nieva., **LP**

snowboarder el/la snowboarder, **7.2**

so tan

soap el jabón, **11.2**

  bar of soap la barra de jabón, **11.2;** la pastilla de jabón

soap opera la telenovela

soccer el fútbol, **5.1**

social studies los estudios sociales, **1.2**

socks los calcetines, **5.1**

soda la cola, la gaseosa, **4.1;** el refresco, **4.2**

sofa el sofá, **2.2**

soft drink el refresco, **4.2**

some unos(as); algunos(as)

someone alguien, **8.2**

something algo, **4.1**

sometimes a veces, **6.1**

son el hijo, **2.1**

soon pronto, **LP**

  See you soon! ¡Hasta pronto!, **LP**

sore throat: to have a sore throat tener dolor de garganta, **6.1**

sorry: I'm sorry. Lo siento mucho., **5.1**

soup la sopa

south el sur

South America la América del Sur, la Sudamérica

Spain España

Spanish (language) el español, **1.2**

  Spanish speaker el/la hispanohablante

  Spanish-speaking hispanohablante

spare: spare time el tiempo libre, **8.1**

to **speak** hablar, **3.1**

spectator el/la espectador(a)

to **spend (time)** pasar, **7.1**

sport el deporte, **5.1**

  individual sport el deporte individual

  team sport el deporte de equipo

sports *(related to)* deportivo(a)

spring la primavera, **LP**

stadium el estadio

to **stand in line** hacer cola, estar en fila, **10.2**

statue la estatua, **8.2**

to **stay** quedarse, **11.1**

  to stay in bed *(illness)* guardar cama, **6.2;** *(idleness)* quedarse en la cama, **11.1**

steak el biftec

stepbrother el hermanastro, **2.1**

stepfather el padrastro, **2.1**

stepmother la madrastra, **2.1**

stepsister la hermanastra, **2.1**

stomach el estómago, **6.2**

  to have a stomachache tener dolor de estómago, **6.2**

store tienda, **3.2**

street la calle

stress el estrés, **6.2**

to **stretch** estirarse, **11.1**

stubborn obstinado(a), terco(a), **6.1**

student el/la alumno(a), **1.1;** el/la estudiante

study el estudio

  social studies los estudios sociales, **1.2**

to **study** estudiar, **3.1**

stupendous estupendo(a)

suburbs las afueras, los suburbios, **2.2**

to **succeed** tener éxito, **6.1**

successful: to be successful tener éxito, **6.1**

such tal

to **suit (fit)** quedar, **9.1**

  Esta chaqueta no te queda bien. This jacket doesn't suit you., **9.1**

suitcase la maleta, **10.1**

  to pack one's suitcase hacer la maleta, **10.1**

summer el verano, **LP**

sun el sol

to **sunbathe** tomar el sol, **7.1**

Sunday el domingo, **LP**

sunglasses los anteojos de sol, las gafas para el sol, **7.1**

sunny: It's sunny. Hace (Hay) sol., **LP**

suntan lotion la crema solar, la loción bronceadora, **7.1**

supermarket el supermercado, **9.2**

supplies: school supplies los materiales escolares, **3.1**

to **surf** practicar la tabla hawaiana, **7.1**

  to surf the Web (the Net) navegar la red (el Internet), **3.2**

surfboard la tabla hawaiana, **7.1**

surfing la tabla hawaiana, el surfing, **7.1**

surprise la sorpresa, **4.1**

sweater el suéter, **11.1**

to **swim** nadar, **7.1**

swimming pool la piscina, la alberca, **7.1;** la pila

swimsuit el bañador, el traje de baño, **7.1**

table la mesa, la mesita, **2.2**

to **take** tomar, **3.1;** traer, **10.1**

  to take *(size)* usar, calzar, **9.1**

  to take a bath bañarse

  to take a flight tomar un vuelo

  to take a hike dar una caminata, **11.2**

  to take a shower tomar una ducha, **11.1**

  to take a test tomar un examen, **3.1**

  to take a trip hacer un viaje, **10.1**

  to take off *(airplane)* despegar, **10.2;** *(clothes)* quitarse, **11.1**

  to take pictures (photos) sacar (tomar) fotos, **7.1**

  to take someone's blood pressure tomar la tensión arterial, **6.2**

  to take someone's pulse tomar el pulso, **6.2**

  to take the (school) bus tomar el bus (escolar), **3.2**

taken ocupado(a), **4.2**

takeoff el despegue, **10.2**

to **talk** hablar, **3.1**

  to talk on the phone hablar por teléfono

  to talk on a cell phone hablar en el móvil, **3.2**

tall alto(a), **1.1**

taste el gusto

taxi el taxi, **10.1**

taxi driver el/la taxista, **10.1**

tea el té

to **teach** enseñar, **3.1**

teacher el/la profesor(a), **1.2**

team el equipo, **5.1**

  opposing team el equipo contrario, **7.1**

  team sport el deporte de equipo, **5.1**

teeth los dientes, **11.1**

  to brush one's teeth cepillarse (lavarse) los dientes, **11.1**

telephone el teléfono

  to talk on the phone hablar por teléfono

television la televisión, la tele

temperature la temperatura, **7.2**

ten diez, **LP**

  by tens de diez en diez

tennis el tenis

  tennis court la cancha de tenis, **5.2**

  tennis player el/la tenista

  tennis racket la raqueta, **5.2**

  tennis shoes los tenis, **9.1**

  to play tennis jugar (al) tenis, **5.2**

tent la carpa, la tienda de campaña, **11.2**

  to put up a tent armar, montar la carpa (la tienda de campaña), **11.2**

terrace la terraza

test el examen, la prueba, **3.1**

  to give a test dar un examen (una prueba), **3.1**

  to take a test tomar un examen, **3.1**

Texan tejano(a)

Thank you. Gracias., **LP**

that (one) aquel(la), ese(a), **9.2**

the el, la, los, las, **1.1**

English-Spanish Dictionary

their su(s)

them las, los

then luego, **3.2**

there allí, allá

there is, there are hay, **2.2**

they ellos(as), **1.1**

thin flaco(a)

thing la cosa

to **think** pensar (ie), **5.1**

   What do you think? ¿Qué piensas?, **5.1**

thirsty: to be thirsty tener sed, **4.1**

thirteen trece, **LP**

thirty treinta, **LP**

thirty-eight treinta y ocho, **LP**

thirty-five treinta y cinco, **LP**

thirty-four treinta y cuatro, **LP**

thirty-nine treinta y nueve, **LP**

thirty-one treinta y uno, **LP**

thirty-seven treinta y siete, **LP**

thirty-six treinta y seis, **LP**

thirty-three treinta y tres, **LP**

thirty-two treinta y dos, **LP**

this (one) este(a)

thousand mil, **9.2**

three tres, **LP**

three hundred trescientos(as), **9.2**

throat la garganta, **6.2**

   to have a sore throat tener dolor de garganta, **6.2**

to **throw** tirar, **5.2**

   to throw (give) a party dar una fiesta, **8.1**

Thursday el jueves, **LP**

ticket el boleto, el ticket, **7.2**; la entrada, **8.1**; el billete, **10.1**; el tiquet(e)

   e-ticket el boleto (billete) electrónico, **10.1**

ticket counter *(airport)* el mostrador, **10.1**

ticket window la boletería, la ventanilla, **7.2**; la taquilla, **8.2**

tie la corbata, **9.1**

time la hora, **LP**; la vez

   at times (sometimes) a veces, **6.1**

   at what time? ¿a qué hora?, **LP**

boarding time la hora de embarque, **10.1**

departure time la hora de salida, **10.1**

full-time a tiempo completo

on time a tiempo, **10.2**

part-time a tiempo parcial

spare time el tiempo libre, **8.1**

   What time is it? ¿Qué hora es?, **LP**

timid tímido(a)

tip el servicio, **4.2**

   Is the tip included? ¿Está incluido el servicio?, **4.2**

tired cansado(a), **6.1**

toast las tostadas, el pan tostado, **4.1**

today hoy, **LP**

   What day is it today? ¿Qué día es hoy?, **LP**

   What is today's date? ¿Cuál es la fecha de hoy?, **LP**

toe el dedo del pie

together juntos(as)

toilet paper el papel higiénico, **11.2**

   roll of toilet paper el rollo de papel higiénico, **11.2**

tomato el tomate, **4.1**

tomorrow mañana, **LP**

   See you tomorrow! ¡Hasta mañana!, **LP**

tonight esta noche, **4.1**

too también, **1.2**

toothbrush el cepillo de dientes, **11.2**

toothpaste la crema dental, **11.2**; la pasta dentífrica

   tube of toothpaste el tubo de crema dental, **11.2**

to **touch** tocar, **5.1**

towel la toalla, **7.1**

town el pueblo

to **travel** viajar

tree el árbol, **2.2**

trip el viaje, **10.1**

   to take a trip hacer un viaje, **10.1**

true: That's true. Es verdad., **9.1**

trunk *(car)* el baúl, la maletera, **10.1**

truth la verdad

T-shirt la camiseta, **5.1**; el T-shirt

tube el tubo, **11.2**

Tuesday el martes, **LP**

tuna el atún, **9.2**

   can of tuna un bote (una lata) de atún, **9.2**

TV la tele

twelve doce, **LP**

twenty veinte, **LP**

twenty-eight veintiocho, **LP**

twenty-five veinticinco, **LP**

twenty-four veinticuatro, **LP**

twenty-nine veintinueve, **LP**

twenty-one veintiuno, **LP**

twenty-seven veintisiete, **LP**

twenty-six veintiséis, **LP**

twenty-three veintitrés, **LP**

twenty-two veintidós, **LP**

twin el/la gemelo(a), **2.1**

two dos, **LP**

two hundred doscientos(as), **9.2**

type el tipo

typical típico(a)

ugly feo(a), **1.1**

unattractive feo(a), **1.1**

uncle el tío, **2.1**

under debajo de, **10.2**

underneath debajo de, **10.2**

to **understand** comprender, **4.2**; entender (ie), **8.2**

uniform el uniforme, **3.2**

United States Estados Unidos

university la universidad

unoccupied libre, **4.2**

unpleasant antipático(a), **1.1**

until hasta, **LP**

up: to go up subir, **7.2**

upper superior

urban urbano(a)

us nos

to **use** usar, **3.2**

vacation las vacaciones

vanilla vainilla

English-Spanish Dictionary

various varios(as)
vegetable la legumbre, la verdura, el vegetal, **4.1**
vegetable store, stall la verdulería, **9.2**
vegetarian vegetariano(a), **4.1**
Venezuelan venezolano(a)
very muy, **LP**; mucho, **LP**
   It's very hot (cold). Hace mucho calor (frío)., **LP**
   Very well. Muy bien., **LP**
view la vista
to visit visitar
volcano el volcán
volleyball el voleibol, **7.1**
   volleyball court la cancha de voleibol, **7.1**
vowel la vocal

to wait esperar, **10.2**
   to wait in line hacer cola, **10.2**; estar en fila
waiter (waitress) el/la mesero(a), **4.2**; el/la camarero(a)
to wake up despertarse (ie), **11.1**
wall el muro
to want querer (ie), **5.1**; desear
war la guerra
to wash lavar, **11.2**
to wash oneself lavarse, **11.1**
   to wash one's hair (face, hands) lavarse el pelo (la cara, las manos), **11.1**
to watch mirar, **3.2**; ver, **4.2**
water el agua, **4.1**
   (sparkling) mineral water el agua mineral (con gas), **4.2**
to water-ski esquiar en el agua, **7.1**
waterskiing el esquí acuático (náutico), **7.1**
wave la ola, **7.1**
we nosotros(as)
to wear llevar, **3.1**; *(shoe size)* calzar, **9.1**; *(clothing size)* usar, **9.1**
weather el tiempo, **LP**
   It's cold (weather). Hace frío., **LP**
   It's cool (weather). Hace fresco., **LP**
   The weather is bad. Hace mal tiempo., **LP**

The weather is nice. Hace buen tiempo., **LP**
   What's the weather like? ¿Qué tiempo hace?, **LP**
Web la red, **3.2**
   to surf the Web navegar la red, **3.2**
Wednesday el miércoles, **LP**
week la semana, **LP**
   last week la semana pasada, **7.1**
weekend el fin de semana, **7.1**
weight el peso
welcome: You're welcome. De nada., Por nada., No hay de qué., **LP**
well bien, **LP**; pues
   Very well. Muy bien., **LP**
well-mannered bien educado(a), **6.1**
west el oeste
what? ¿qué?; ¿cuál?; ¿cuáles?; ¿cómo?
   at what time? ¿a qué hora?, **LP**
   What a shame! ¡Qué pena!, **5.1**
   What day is it (today)? ¿Qué día es hoy?, **LP**
   What does he (she, it) look like? ¿Cómo es?, **1.1**
   What is he (she, it) like? ¿Cómo es?, **1.1**
   What is today's date? ¿Cuál es la fecha de hoy?, **LP**
   what nationality? ¿de qué nacionalidad?, **1.1**
   What's happening? What's going on? ¿Qué pasa?, **3.1**
   What's new (up)? ¿Qué hay?
   What time is it? ¿Qué hora es?, **LP**
when cuando, **3.1**
when? ¿cuándo?, **3.2**
where donde
where? ¿dónde?, **1.1**; ¿adónde?, **3.2**
   from where? ¿de dónde?, **1.1**
which? ¿cuál?; ¿cuáles?
while mientras
white blanco(a), **5.1**
who? ¿quién?, **1.1**; ¿quienes?, **1.2**
why? ¿por qué?, **3.2**
wide ancho(a)
wife la esposa, la mujer, **2.1**
to win ganar, **5.1**

wind el viento, **LP**
window *(store)* el escaparate, **9.1**; *(plane)* la ventanilla, **10.2**
windsurfing la plancha de vela, **7.1**
   to go windsurfing practicar la plancha de vela, **7.1**
windy: It's windy. Hace viento., **LP**
winter el invierno, **LP**
with con
without sin, **7.2**
word la palabra
work la obra, el trabajo
to work trabajar, **3.2**
world el mundo
   World Cup la Copa Mundial
worse peor
to be worth: It's not worth it. No vale., **7.1**
to write escribir, **4.2**
written escrito(a)

year el año, **LP**
   last year el año pasado, **7.1**
   to be turning . . . years old cumplir... años
   to be . . . years old tener... años, **2.1**
yellow amarillo(a), **5.1**
yes sí, **LP**
yesterday ayer, **7.1**
   yesterday afternoon ayer por la tarde, **7.1**
   yesterday evening anoche, **7.1**
you tú *(sing. fam.)*, usted *(sing. form.)*, ustedes *(pl. form.)*, vosotros(as) *(pl. fam.)*; ti, te *(fam. pron.)*, le *(pron.)*
   You're welcome. De (Por) nada., No hay de qué., **LP**
young joven, **1.1**
young person el/la joven, **1.1**
younger menor
youngest el/la menor
your tu(s), su(s)
   It's your turn! ¡Te toca a ti!
youth hostel el albergue juvenil

zero cero, **LP**
zone la zona

Culture Index

Culture Index

Culture Index

Grammar Index

a personal 107 (3); 244 (7)

acabar de 136 (4)

adjectives to describe looks and personalities, 22 (1); to describe nationality, 23 (1); agreement in gender and number with nouns, 32 (1); ending in -**e**, 32 (1); ending in a consonant, 32 (1); with a group of both boys and girls, 32 (1); possessive adjectives, 70 (2); demonstrative adjectives, 312 (9)

affirmative and negative expressions **algo, alguien, nada, nadie, nunca, siempre,** 278 (8)

agreement (in gender and number) of articles and nouns, 30 (1); of nouns and adjectives, 30 (1)

al contraction of **a + el,** 107 (3)

-ar verbs present tense, 100 (3); preterite tense, 238 (7)

articles definite and indefinite, 30 (1)

commands with **favor de** + *infinitive,* 380 (11)

comparatives 311 (9)

conocer present tense, 308 (9)

conocer vs. saber 308 (9)

dar present tense, 105 (3); preterite tense, 274 (8)

deber with infinitive, 136 (4)

del contraction of **de + el,** 107 (3)

demonstratives adjectives and pronouns, 312 (9)

direct object pronouns **me, te, nos,** 209 (6); **lo, la, los, las,** 244 (7)

-er verbs present tense, 136 (4); preterite tense, 274 (8)

estar present tense, 105 (3); to tell how you feel, 105 (3); to tell where you are, 105 (3); to express a temporary state, emotion, or condition, 204 (6); to express where something or someone is located, 206 (6)

estar vs. ser temporary states or conditions vs. inherent characteristics, 204 (6); location vs. origin, 206 (6)

gustar to express likes and dislikes, 175 (5); verbs similar to **gustar: aburrir, interesar,** 175 (5)

hacer present tense, 340 (10)

hay 63 (2)

indirect object pronouns **me, te, nos,** 209 (6); **le, les,** 210 (6)

infinitive 100 (3); expressions with **acabar de, ir a, tener que,** 140 (4); commands with **favor de,** 380 (11)

ir present tense, 105 (3); **ir a** + *infinitive,* 140 (4); preterite tense, 242 (7)

-ir verbs present tense, 136 (4); preterite tense, 274 (8)

irregular verbs present tense: **conocer,** 308 (9); **dar,** 105 (3); **estar,** 105 (3); **hacer,** 340 (10); **ir,** 105 (3); **poner,** 340 (10); **saber,** 308 (9); **salir,** 340 (10); **ser,** 34 (1); **tener,** 66 (2), 340 (10); **traer,** 340 (10); **venir,** 340 (10); **ver,** 136 (4); preterite tense: **dar,** 274 (8); **ir,** 277 (8); **leer,** 277 (8); **oír,** 277 (8); **ser,** 242 (7); **ver,** 274 (8)

leer preterite tense, 277 (8)

negative and affirmative expressions **algo, alguien, nada, nadie, nunca, siempre,** 278 (8)

nouns masculine and feminine, 30 (1); singular and plural, 30 (1)

numbers 306 (9)

oír present tense, 277 (8); preterite tense, 277 (8)

poder present tense, 172 (5)

poner present tense, 340 (10)

possessive adjectives forms and agreement with nouns, 70 (2)

present participle 343 (10)

Grammar Index

Credits

The McGraw-Hill Companies, Inc. would like to acknowledge the artists and agencies who participated in illustrating this program: Michael Arnold; Bill Dickson represented by Contact Jupiter; Glencoe/McGraw-Hill; Pat Lewis; Cedric Hohnstadt; Geo Parkin represented by American Artists Rep., Inc.

Photo Credits

Cover Jon Hicks/CORBIS; **iv** Andrew Payti; **v** Anthony West/CORBIS; **vi** (l)Xavier Florensa/age fotostock, (r)David H. Brennan; **vii** BananaStock/PictureQuest; **viii** (l)graficart.net/Alamy Images, (r)Brand X Pictures/Alamy Images; **ix** Larry Hamill; **x** (l)Steve Weinstein, (r)The McGraw-Hill Companies; **xi** (r)AP Images, (l)imagebroker/Alamy Images; **xii** Dynamic Graphics Group/Creatas/Alamy Images; **xiii** (l)COMSTOCK Images/age fotostock, (r)Kerri Galloway; **xiv** David H. Brennan; **xv** Andrew Payti; **xvi** David H. Brennan; **xvii** (l)CORBIS/age fotostock, (r)Index Stock Imagery; **xviii** (t)Andrew Payti, (b)Renaud Visage/Getty Images; **xx** (tl)Andrew Payti, (tr)Yvonne Cadiz, (b)Scott Gries/Getty Images; **SH1** (tl)Fotosearch, (tr)Rebecca Smith, (b)Clasos Agencia International/CORBIS SYGMA; **SH2** Getty Images; **SH2–SH3** BananaStock/Jupiter Images; **SH3** Andersen Ross/age fotostock; **SH4** Siede Preis/Getty Images **SH5** Brand X Pictures/age fotostock; **SH6** Bananastock/PictureQuest/Jupiter Images; **SH20** File Photo; **SH35** (t)Andrew Payti, (c)Gabriela Zamudio, (bl)Rebecca Smith, (br)Matthew Johnston/Alamy Images; **SH42–SH43** Anthony West/CORBIS; **SH44** (tl)Fernando Fernández/age fotostock, (tr)Juan Manuel Silva/age fotostock, (bl)CORBIS, (br)Randa Bishop/Imagestate; **SH44–SH45** (c)Alan Copson/JAI/CORBIS; **SH45** (tl)Jose Fuste Raga/CORBIS, (tc)Hans Georg Roth/CORBIS, (tr)Kirk Weddle/Getty Images, (c)Alex Segre/Alamy Images, (b)Pablo Galán Cela/age fotostock; **SH46** (tl)CORBIS, (tr)Fritz Poelking/age fotostock, (c)Radius Images/Alamy Images, (bl)Andrew Payti, (br)Brian Stablyk/Getty Images; **SH46–SH47** Andrew Payti; **SH47** (t)Greg Vaughn/Alamy Images, (cl)Maria Lourdes Alonso/age fotostock, (cr b)Andrew Payti; **SH48** (tl)Andrew Payti, (tr)Jordi Cami/age fotostock, (cl)Keren Su/China Span/Alamy Images, (cr)Michele Molinari/Alamy Images, (bl)Frank Lukasseck/age fotostock, (br)Lori Ernfridsson; **SH49** (t)Kevin Schafer/age fotostock, (cl)Reuters/CORBIS, (cr)Panoramic Images/Getty Images, (b)Oswaldo Rivas/Reuters/CORBIS; **SH50** (tl)nik wheeler/Alamy Images, (tr)Andrew Payti, (c)Torino/age fotostock, (bl)Kevin Schafer/age fotostock, (br)Roberto Escobar/epa/CORBIS; **SH51** (tl)Torino/age fotostock, (tr)José Enrique Molina/age fotostock, (c)Philip Scalia/Alamy Images, (b)Andrew Payti; **SH52** (tl)Woodfall Wild Images/Alamy Images, (tr)Jose Fuste Raga/age fotostock, (c)Gail Shumway/Getty Images, (bl)age fotostock, (br)Keren Su/China Span/Alamy Images; **SH53** (t)Andrew Payti, (bl)fstop2/Alamy Images, (br)Humberto Olarte Cupas/Alamy Images; **SH54** (tl)Danita Delimont/Alamy Images, (tr)James Marshall/CORBIS, (c)Gianni Dagli Orti/CORBIS, (b)Morales/age fotostock; **SH55** (tl)age fotostock/SuperStock, (tr)Stock Connection/Alamy Images, (cr)Reuters/CORBIS, (bl)Krzysztof Dydynski/Getty Images, (br)David Uribe Photography/eStock Photo;

SH56 (tl)Bill Bachmann/eStock Photo, (tr)CORBIS, (c)Gavin Hellier/Getty Images, (b)Andrew Payti; **SH56–SH57** SuperStock/age fotostock; **SH57** (t)John Arnold Images/age fotostock, (c)Klaus Lang/age fotostock, (bl)JTB Photo Communications, Inc./Alamy Images, (br)P. Narayan/age fotostock; **SH58** (tl)Anthony Cassidy/JAI/CORBIS, (tc)Robert Frerck/Getty Images, (tr)Michael Lewis/CORBIS, (bl)IML Image Group Ltd/Alamy Images, (br)David R. Frazier Photolibrary, Inc./Alamy Images; **SH59** (tl c)Andrew Payti, (tr)imagebroker/Alamy Images, (bl)M&M Valledor/age fotostock, (br)Abacana/age fotostock; **SH60** (tl)Brian Atkinson/Alamy Images, (tr)Scenics & Science/Alamy Images, (cl)Dorling Kindersley/Getty Images, (cr)John Hicks/CORBIS, (b)imagestate; **SH61** (tl)Neil Setchfield/Alamy Images, (tr)James Balog/age fotostock, (bl)David Lyons/Alamy Images, (br)Ramond Forbes/age fotostock; **SH62** (tl)WaterFrame/Alamy Images, (tr)M. Timothy O'Keefe/Alamy Images, (cl)Jose Fuste Raga/CORBIS, (cr)Hola Images/Getty Images, (b)Robert Harding Picture Library, Ltd/Alamy Images; **SH63** (t)Envision/CORBIS, (c)Danny Lehman/CORBIS, (bl)Raymond Mendez/Animals Animals—Earth Scenes, (br)Richard Brommer; **SH64** (tl)Frances M. Roberts/Alamy Images, (tr)Danita Delimont/Alamy Images, (cl)Blend Images/Alamy Images, (cr)Ron & Patty Thomas/Getty Images, (b)Jon Arnold Images/Alamy Images, (inset)David R. Frazier Photolibrary, Inc./Alamy Images; **SH65** (t)AP Images, (c)Ian Dagnall/Alamy Images, (bl)Jeff Greenberg/Alamy Images, (bc)Robert Fried/Alamy Images, (br)Sylvain Grandadam/age fotostock; **1** Larry Hamill; **2** David H. Brennan; **3** (t)Bill Bachmann/Alamy Images, (bl br)Frederico Gil; **4** Frederico Gil; **6** (t)Frederico Gil, (b)Rebecca Smith; **7** (t)Andrew Payti, (c)Laura Sifferlin, (b)Danita Delimont/Alamy Images; **9** (l to r, t to b)Frederico Gil, (2–4)Larry Hamill, (5 6) The McGraw-Hill Companies; **10 11** The McGraw-Hill Companies; **12** The Studio Dog/Getty Images; **13** (l to r, t to b) (1 8)CORBIS (2 12)The McGraw-Hill Companies, (3)Brand X Pictures/PunchStock, (4 7)Getty Images, (5)Brand X Pictures/PunchStock, (6)C Squared Studios/Getty Images, (9 11)Brand X Pictures/PunchStock, (10)C Squared Studios/Getty Images, (13)Xavier Florensa/age fotostock, (14)David H. Brennan; **14** (tl)Gonzalo Azumendi/age fotostock, (tr)Thomas Dressler/age fotostock, (bl)Hidalgo and Lopesino/age fotostock, (br)Santiago Fdez Fuentes/age fotostock; **16** (l)Rebecca Smith, (r)Michele Molinari/Alamy Images; **18–19** David H. Brennan; **20** (t)David Dudenhoefer/Odyssey Productions, Inc., (b)Monica Jimenez; **21** (tl c)Kelli Drummer-Avendaño, (tr)Larry Hamill, (bl)Andrew Payti, (br)Robert Frerck/Odyssey Productions, Inc.; **22** David H. Brennan; **24** (t)Getty Images, (b)Lori Ernfridsson; **25** (t)Monica Jimenez, (b)Brand X Pictures/PunchStock; **26** (t c)Frederico Gil, (b)David H. Brennan; **27** David H. Brennan; **28** (tl)Larry Hamill, (tr)Mitch Diamond/Alamy Images, (cl)Kelli Drummer-Avendaño, (cr)Jeff Greenberg/Alamy Images, (b)mylife photos/Alamy Images; **29** Keith Dannemiller/CORBIS; **30** Creatas/PunchStock; **31** (t)Lori Ernfridsson, (b)Tom & Dee Ann McCarthy/CORBIS; **32** (b)Bill Bachmann/Alamy Images, (t)The McGraw-Hill Companies; **33** (t)Lori Ernfridsson, (b)Andrew Payti; **34** (t)Keith

Credits

208 Andrew Payti; 209 The McGraw-Hill Companies; 210 (t)Richard Hutchings, (b)Lori Ernfridsson; 213 Neil Beer/Getty Images; 215 Jose Joaquin Fernandez de Lizardi (1776–1827) (litho), Spanish School, (19th century)/Private Collection, Index/The Bridgeman Art Library 216 (l)Pixtal/age fotostock, (r)The McGraw-Hill Companies; 217 age fotostock/Superstock; 218 Lori Ernfridsson; 219 The McGraw-Hill Companies; 220 Getty Images; 221 Image Source/PunchStock; 222 Andrew Payti; 224 Lori Ernfridsson; 226–227 Galen Rowell/CORBIS; 228 (t)David Hiser/Getty Images, (c)Andrew Payti, (b)Kerri Galloway; 229 (tl)Bill Harrigan/Stephen Frink Collection/Alamy Images, (tr)Terry Harris/Alamy Images, (cl)David Lyons/Alamy Images, (cr)Paco Ayala/age fotostock, (b)Gonzalo Azumendi/age fotostock; 230 (t)David H. Brennan, (bl)Andrew Payti, (b)Getty Images; 231 (t)David H. Brennan, (c)GOwst/Alamy Images, (b)Alissa Everette/Alamy Images; 232 (tl)Gabriela Zamudio, (tr br)Andrew Payti, (bl)Getty Images; 233 (t)Getty Images, (b)Andrew Resek/The McGraw-Hill Companies, (l to r, t to b)C Squared Studios/Photodisc, (2)Comstock Images/Alamy Images, (3)Andrew Payti, (4)Jennifer Doyle; 234 (t)Gareth Roberts/StockShot/Alamy Images, (b)blickwinkel/Alamy Images; 235 (tl)Suzy Bennett/Alamy Images, (tr)The McGraw-Hill Companies, (c)Paco Ayala/age fotostock, (b)Jack Cox/Alamy Images; 236 Christian Kober/Alamy Images; 237 (l)Michele Molinari/Alamy Images, (r)Kerri Galloway; 238 Andrew Payti; 239 Asia Images Group/Getty Images; 240 (l)The McGraw-Hill Companies, (r)Kerri Galloway, (inset)Jack Hollingsworth/Getty Images; 241 Andrew Payti; 242 (t)Andrew Payti, (b)Alan Dawson Photography/Alamy Images; 243 Robert Frerck and Odyssey Productions; 244 Andrew Payti; 245 COMSTOCK Images/age fotostock; 246 Andrew Payti; 248 Steve Mason/age fotostock; 249 Tony Arruza/CORBIS; 250 Andrew Payti; 251 (t)Travelshots.com/Alamy Images, (b)Nicholas Stubbs/Alamy Images; 252 253 SuperStock/age fotostock; 254 (tl)Brand X Pictures/Punchstock, (tr)Getty Images, (cl)Getty Images, (cr)Karl Weatherly/Getty Images, (b)Getty Images; 256 (l)Andrew Payti, (r)Nicholas Stubbs/Alamy Images; 257 258 Andrew Payti; 260 Kerri Galloway; 261 Andrew Payti; 262–263 Jon Arnold Images/Alamy Images; 264 (tl)Robert Frerck/Getty Images, (tr)Jeremy Horner/CORBIS, (c)Andrew Payti, (b)The McGraw-Hill Companies, (br)MJ Photography/Alamy Images; 265 (tl br)Andrew Payti, (tr c)Lori Ernfridsson, (bl)Anders Ryman/CORBIS; 266 (t)David H. Brennan, (c bl br)The McGraw-Hill Companies; 267 (t b)David H. Brennan, (c)STR/AFP/Getty Images; 268 (tl)Keith Bedford/Reuters/Landov, (tr)Mark Leibowitz/Masterfile, (bl)Brand X Pictures, (bc)Spike Mafford/Getty Images, (br)Getty Images; 269 (t c)Getty Images, (tr b)Andrew Payti; 270 David H. Brennan; 271 (l)David H. Brennan, (r)Javier Larrea/age fotostock; 272 (t)Photo by Tanya Ahmed © Courtesy of El Museo del Barrio, NY, (b)Javier Larrea/age fotostock; 273 Andrew Payti; 274 Kim Karpeles/Alamy Images; 275 Getty Images; 276 Dynamic Graphics Group/Creatas/Alamy Images; 277 Scott Gries/Getty Images; 278 BananaStock/PictureQuest; 279 Jack Hollingsworth/Getty Images; 280 The McGraw-Hill Companies; 281 (l)Andrew Payti, (r)The McGraw-Hill Companies; 282 (l)Sue Cunningham Photographic/Alamy Images, (r)Alison Jones/Danita Delimont/Alamy Images; 283 The Museum of Modern Art/Licensed by SCALA/Art Resource, NY; 284 (l)CORBIS, (r)David R. Frazier/Alamy Images; 285 Andrew Payti; 286 (tl)Yvonne Cadiz, (cl)Jules Frazier/Getty Images, (cr)Andrew Payti, (b)Andrew Resek/The McGraw-Hill Companies, (tr)Lori Ernfridsson; 287 SuperStock/age fotostock; 289 The McGraw-Hill Companies; 290 AP Images; 292 ImageSource/age fotostock; 294–295 Robert Frerck/Odyssey Productions, Inc.; 296 (t)Andrew Payti, (tr)Super Stock/age fotostock, (cl)Sue Cunningham Photographic/Alamy Images, (cr)Lynsey Addario/CORBIS, (bl)Kord.com/age fotostock, (br)Richard Brommer; 297 (tl bl br)Andrew Payti, (tr)SuperStock/age fotostock, (cl bc)Javier Larrea/age fotostock, (c)Mooch Images/Alamy Images; 298 (t c)Kerri Galloway, (b)The McGraw-Hill Companies, (bc)Jill Braaten/The McGraw-Hill Companies; 299 (l)Paco Ayala/age fotostock, (r)The McGraw-Hill Companies; 300 Oscar Garcia Bayerri/age fotostock; 301 Teresa Ponseti/age fotostock; 302 (t)Rafael Campillo/age fotostock, (c)The McGraw-Hill Companies, (b)Andrew Payti; 303 (t)The McGraw-Hill Companies, (b)Frederico Gil; 304 (t)Andrew Payti, (c)Kelli Drummer-Avendaño, (b)Lori Ernfridsson; 306 The McGraw-Hill Companies; 307 Kerri Galloway; 308 DAJ/Getty Images; 309 310 Andrew Payti; 311 (t)Kerri Galloway, (b)Andrew Payti; 312 Andrew Payti; 314 315 Frederico Gil; 316 (l)Lori Ernfridsson, (r)Andrew Payti; 317 Andrew Payti; 318 (t)Andrew Payti, (b)Kelli Drummer-Avendaño; 319 Keith Dannemiller/Alamy Images; 321 Kelli Drummer-Avendaño; 322 (t)John Powell/Alamy Images, (b)Andrew Payti; 323 Andrew Payti; 324 David Young-Wolff/Alamy Images; 326 (t)Kelli Drummer-Avendaño, (b)David Frazier/The Image Works; 327 The McGraw-Hill Companies; 328 329 Melba Photo Agency/Alamy Images; 330 (l)Kelli Drummer-Avendaño, (t)Stuart Pearce/age fotostock, (b)CORBIS; 331 (cw from top)Andrew Payti, David R. Frazier Photolibrary, Inc., Getty Images, Larry Hamill, SuperStock/age fotostock, The McGraw-Hill Companies; 332 David H. Brennan; 333 (l)Javier Larrea/age fotostock, (r)The McGraw-Hill Companies, (bkgd)David H. Brennan; 334 (t)Creatas/age fotostock, (b)Richard Brommer; 335 (t)Yvonne Cadiz, (b)The McGraw-Hill Companies; 336 David H. Brennan; 337 (t)David H. Brennan, (cr)The McGraw-Hill Companies, (bl)Schwabe, G./Arco Di/age fotostock, (br)Bartomeu Amengual/age fotostock; 338 Jennifer Doyle; 339 (t)Lori Ernfridsson, (bl)Andrew Payti, (br) The McGraw-Hill Companies; 340 Rebecca Smith; 341 (t)Richard Brommer, (b)Yvonne Cadiz; 342 Andrew Payti; 343 Lori Ernfridsson; 344 David H. Brennan; 345 Richard Brommer; 347 Andrew Payti; 348 David H. Brennan; 349 Glowimages/age fotostock; 350 Kelli Drummer-Avendaño; 351 Gardel Bertrand/age fotostock; 352 Dan Bannister/Alamy Images; 353 (t)Roman Soumar/CORBIS, (b)Andrew Payti, (br)C Squared Studios/Getty Images; 354 (tl)Jack Hollingsworth/Getty Images, (tr)Siede Preis/Getty Images, (bl)CORBIS, (bc)PhotoLink/Getty Images; 355 Andoni Canela/age fotostock; 356 David H. Brennan; 357 SW Productions/Getty Images; 358 John Flournoy/The McGraw-Hill Companies; 360 Rebecca Smith; 361 David R.